Capital Letters

FLASHPOINTS

The FlashPoints series is devoted to books that consider literature beyond strictly national and disciplinary frameworks, and that are distinguished both by their historical grounding and by their theoretical and conceptual strength. Our books engage theory without losing touch with history and work historically without falling into uncritical positivism. FlashPoints aims for a broad audience within the humanities and the social sciences concerned with moments of cultural emergence and transformation. In a Benjaminian mode, FlashPoints is interested in how literature contributes to forming new constellations of culture and history and in how such formations function critically and politically in the present. Series titles are available online at http://escholarship.org/uc/flashpoints.

SERIES EDITORS: Ali Behdad (Comparative Literature and English, UCLA), Editor Emeritus; Judith Butler (Rhetoric and Comparative Literature, UC Berkeley), Editor Emerita; Michelle Clayton (Hispanic Studies and Comparative Literature, Brown University); Edward Dimendberg (Film and Media Studies, Visual Studies, and European Languages and Studies, UC Irvine), Founding Editor; Catherine Gallagher (English, UC Berkeley), Editor Emerita; Nouri Gana (Comparative Literature and Near Eastern Languages and Cultures, UCLA); Susan Gillman (Literature, UC Santa Cruz), Coordinator; Jody Greene (Literature, UC Santa Cruz); Richard Terdiman (Literature, UC Santa Cruz), Founding Editor

A complete list of titles begins on p. 267.

Capital Letters
Hugo, Baudelaire, Camus, and the Death Penalty

Ève Morisi

NORTHWESTERN UNIVERSITY PRESS | EVANSTON, ILLINOIS

Northwestern University Press
www.nupress.northwestern.edu

Copyright © 2020 by Northwestern University Press.
Published 2020. All rights reserved.

10 9 8 7 6 5 4 3 2 1

Library of Congress Cataloging-in-Publication Data

Names: Morisi, Ève, author.
Title: Capital letters : Hugo, Baudelaire, Camus, and the death penalty / Ève Morisi.
  Other titles: FlashPoints (Evanston, Ill.)
Description: Evanston, Illinois : Northwestern University Press, 2020. | Series: Flashpoints |
Identifiers: LCCN 2019018289 | ISBN 9780810141513 (paper text : alk. paper) | ISBN 9780810141520 (cloth text : alk. paper) | ISBN 9780810141537 (e-book)
Subjects: LCSH: Capital punishment in literature. | French literature—19th century—History and criticism. | French literature—20th century—History and criticism. | Hugo, Victor, 1802–1885—Criticism and interpretation. | Baudelaire, Charles, 1821–1867—Criticism and interpretation. | Camus, Albert, 1913–1960—Criticism and interpretation.
Classification: LCC PQ295.C35 M67 2020 | DDC 840.9/3556—dc23
LC record available at https://lccn.loc.gov/2019018289

To my mother

Elle pouvait rester à la hauteur de n'importe quelle lumière.
—Albert Camus, *La Peste*

Contents

Acknowledgments ix

Abbreviations and Translations xiii

Introduction: Three Writers and a Punishment 3

PART I. NEW ABOLITIONIST POETICS:
HUGO'S *LE DERNIER JOUR D'UN CONDAMNÉ* 15

Chapter 1. The Death Penalty, from Representation to Expression 21

Chapter 2. Pain and Punishment: The Guillotine's Torture 45

PART II. WORDS THAT KILL IN BAUDELAIRE 67

Chapter 3. Prose Praising Sacrifice: Hugo, Maistre, and Beyond 73

Chapter 4. Poeticized Slaughter? Execution in *Les Fleurs du mal* 103

PART III. CAMUS'S CAPITAL FICTION AND LITERARY RESPONSIBILITY 129

Chapter 5. *Ad nauseam*: Camus's Narrative Roads to Abolitionism 135

Chapter 6. Poetic Accountability: Critical Language and Its Limits	165
Conclusion	207
Notes	215
Works Cited	239
Index	253

Acknowledgments

Writing a book on a grim subject in a foreign language makes unoriginal yet true statements all the more necessary: this monograph, which was several years in the making, could not have been completed without the help of colleagues, friends, and family members.

Thanks are first due to Göran Blix and Bertrand Marchal, two supervisors who were academic models throughout my graduate years, and to two exceptional mentors, Suzanne Nash and Sarah Kay. Together, they shaped my work and experience as a doctoral student for the better.

Until 2011, the Department of French and Italian at Princeton University, Princeton's University Center for Human Values and Graduate School, the Phi Beta Kappa Society, the Université Paris IV–Sorbonne, the Cité du Livre and Fonds Albert Camus in Aix-en-Provence, the Camus family, and Robert Badinter provided various forms of support for which I am grateful. My appreciation also goes to my former peers at Princeton for their friendship during these formative years, and in particular to Katherine Brown, Sandra Field, Brian Jacobs, Yann Robert, Milla Vidina, and Eliza Zingesser.

I am deeply thankful to Susan Gillman, Gianna Mosser, and Richard Terdiman for showing interest in this project and for bearing with me with exemplary patience, helpfulness, and professionalism.

A small number of people read this manuscript in its entirety. Eliza Zingesser went over the very first versions of these chapters and has been a most faithful partner in crime since 2006. With salutary honesty,

David Carroll provided detailed feedback and identified key ways in which the book should be amended. Dick Terdiman also made instrumental suggestions and provided encouragement as I attempted to edit the manuscript. At a critical time, Roger Pearson advised me with the thoughtfulness of a true gentleman. To these giving readers, who offered guidance when it was most needed, I owe a substantial debt.

My appreciation also goes to the two anonymous reviewers appointed by Northwestern University Press for their judicious and benevolent advice; to Haun Saussy, for his astute comments on the book proposal; and to Jean-Paul Avice, *baudelairien hors pair*, who always answered my questions with precision and generosity—as well as delicious lasagna.

Both in the Department of French at the University of St Andrews and in the Department of European Languages and Studies at the University of California, Irvine, I was fortunate to work alongside inspiring, intellectually challenging, and big-hearted colleagues—also true friends. I owe them my understanding of what the academic profession should be: Anke Biendarra, Suzanne Bolding, Daniel Brunstetter, Ellen Burt, David Carroll, Birte Christ, David Evans, Kai Evers, Herschel Farbman, Franca Hamber, Gail Hart, Odile Heberlé, Élise Hugueny-Léger, Margaret-Ann Hutton, Élodie Laügt, Glenn Levine, Robin MacKenzie, Maryse Mijalski, Jane Newman, Carrie Noland, David Pan, Julia Prest, John Smith, and †Oliver Smith.

More recently, my colleagues at St Hugh's College and the French Sub-faculty at Oxford have offered a welcoming community in which to work. In and outside of this new home institution, special thanks are due to the whole team of modernists at Oxford and to my friends Geneviève Adams, Annette Becker, Brigitte Burel, Naomi Davidson, Margit Dirscherl, Jean Giraud, Sébastien Greppo, Mike Holland, Ann Jefferson, Antoine Jérusalem, Chantal Marazia, Maria Pavlova, Xavier Rousseaux, Tom Sanders, Erin Saupe—without whose generous help the book cover that I had in mind would never have come to life—and Seth Whidden for their warmth and good humor over the past few years.

I also thank the Paris Institute for Advanced Study for allowing me to work at the Hôtel de Lauzun for part of the summer of 2016, the Humanities Division of the University of Oxford for an award from the REF Strategic Research Assistance Fund that enabled me to benefit from editorial assistance to complete the monograph, Charlotte Wathey for her editorial work, and Simon Wedge and Paul Wakeling for the critical help they provided at the end of this journey.

Acknowledgments | xi

Parts of this book have previously appeared in journals and edited volumes. I am grateful to the relevant publishers for permission to reuse this material. Chapter 1 appeared in *Death Sentences: Literature and State Killing*, edited with Birte Christ (Oxford: Legenda, 2019). Earlier versions of chapters 4 and 5 respectively appeared as "'Poésie-boucherie': Baudelaire's Aesthetics and Ethics of Execution," in *Thinking Poetry: Philosophical Approaches to Nineteenth-Century French Poetry*, edited by Joseph Acquisto (London: Palgrave Macmillan, 2013), and "La Peine de mort dans les romans de Camus: Motif, mythe, éthique," in *Albert Camus contre la peine de mort* (Paris: Gallimard, 2011).

Parts of chapter 6 elaborate on ideas presented during conferences on Camus's theater (Lourmarin, October 2012), on "Unity and Division" in Europe (UCI, March 2013), and in an essay I was invited to write for *La Revue des Lettres Modernes. Série Albert Camus* in 2014 ("Baudelaire et Camus: Penser la peine de mort"). Thanks are due to the relevant organizers and editors for giving me the opportunity to develop my thoughts on Camus and the death penalty.

* *
*

Before I even knew of literary criticism, there are those who made me love school, and in particular languages and literature, who didn't object to my urge to ask questions, and who provided moral and intellectual support: my elementary school teacher †Mademoiselle Papin, to whom I wish I could show this book today; my first and finest English teacher, Mrs. Königsecker; my rigorous and sensitive literature teacher, Mrs. Bridger; my sarcastic and sympathetic philosophy teacher, Mr. Flament; Bénédicte Deschamps and Michel Imbert, who both nourished my love for American studies at Paris VII; Lucie Laurian, who made it possible for me to apply to graduate school, showed me what writing articles was about, and had enough confidence for two in 2004 and 2005; and my dear Marlène, whose friendship has been unconditional since our undergraduate years.

My thoughts go to another teacher and ally, my maternal grandmother, †Marcelle Jeanne Graulier Dubois, who I know would find a way to read this book in English today if she could. And to her own mother, †Mémé, who, without realizing it, had the work ethic and humility of those she reverently called "les savants."

Despite the intermittence of contact that distance brings, the love of my bright and bubbly nieces Nina, Ava, and Adèle, as well as the many coffee-table Japanese dinners their parents, Elsa and Alban, have invited me to share with them when I have returned home, have provided a support system that reminded me of what life was about as I was trying to think through what sentencing men to death, and representing such justice, could mean.

Finally, words can express only inadequately my indebtedness to three unassuming loved ones. Davide was my anchor for many important years past and will remain my moral and intellectual compass for life. I silently carry his company and standards with me.

Jim made it possible for me to give the long final push to this book by cheering me on, answering numerous questions with care, and proofreading extensive sections of the manuscript. I am grateful for his love, bottomless kindness, wisdom, and shared interest in politics, ethics, and chocolate.

My mother, Anne Morisi, has, at all times, been and done every possible thing one can be and do for a daughter. To this indefatigable interlocutor and supporter, I owe everything that matters, including the love of meaningful texts. In spite of all its flaws, for which I am solely responsible, this book comes from the heart, and therefore belongs with her.

Abbreviations and Translations

The following abbreviations, with their relevant volume and page numbers, are used in the text to refer to the critical editions of Hugo, Baudelaire, and Camus.

CB   Charles Baudelaire. *Correspondance*. Edited by Claude Pichois and Jean Ziegler. 2 vols. Paris: Gallimard, 1973.
CC   Albert Camus. *Camus à Combat*. Edited by Jacqueline Lévi-Valensi. Paris: Gallimard, 2002.
JIB   Charles Baudelaire. *Journaux intimes. Fusées. Mon cœur mis à nu. Carnet*. Edited by Jacques Crépet and Georges Blin. Paris: José Corti, 1949.
OCB   Charles Baudelaire. *Œuvres complètes*. Edited by Claude Pichois. 2 vols. Paris: Gallimard, 1975.
OCC   Albert Camus. *Œuvres complètes*. Edited by by Jacqueline Lévi-Valensi, André Abbou, Zedjiga Abdelkrim, Marie-Louise Audin, Raymond Gay-Crosier, Samantha Novello, Pierre-Louis Rey, Philippe Vanney, David H. Walker, and Maurice Weyembergh. 4 vols. Paris: Gallimard, 2006–8.
OCH   Victor Hugo. *Œuvres complètes: Édition chronologique*. 18 vols. Edited by Jean Massin. Paris: Le Club Français du Livre, 1967–70.

Note: *Le Dernier Jour d'un condamné* is included in the third volume of Massin's edition, preface of 1832 excluded. For references to this novel and its paratext, only the necessary chapter and page numbers are mentioned in parentheses.

The following translations are used for Baudelaire's poetry. Other translations are my own, unless otherwise noted. I thank Eliza Zingesser, Jim House, and Seth Whidden for their assistance.

Charles Baudelaire. *The Flowers of Evil*. Translated with notes by James McGowan. Oxford: Oxford University Press, 1993.
———. *Selected Poems*. Translated by Carol Clark. London: Penguin, 1995.

Note: Carol Clark's translation is in prose. It was chosen for its proximity to Baudelaire's poems. I have inserted line breaks and restored Baudelaire's original punctuation to make it easier to read the translation alongside the original. For the poems that are not included in Clark's selection, I have used James McGowan's translation.

Capital Letters

Introduction

Three Writers and a Punishment

Être un reste, ceci échappe à la langue humaine. Ne plus exister, et persister, être dans le gouffre et dehors, reparaître au-dessus de la mort, comme insubmersible, il y a une certaine quantité d'impossible mêlée à de telles réalités. De là l'indicible. Cet être,—était-ce un être?—ce témoin noir, était un reste, et un reste terrible. Reste de quoi? De la nature, d'abord, de la société ensuite. Zéro et total.

To be a remnant, such a thing escapes human language. To no longer exist and yet persist, to be in the abyss and outside, to reappear beyond death, as if unsinkable, there is a certain amount of impossibility mixed with such realities. Hence the inexpressible. This being,—was it a being?—this dark witness, was a remnant, and a terrible remnant. A remnant of what? Of nature first, and then of society. Nothing and everything.

—Victor Hugo, *L'Homme qui rit,* book 1, chapter 5, in *Œuvres complètes,* on the remains of a hanged man

"The death penalty is the special and eternal sign of barbarity," Victor Hugo declared in 1848.[1] His contemporary, the poet Charles Baudelaire, vigorously begged to differ. Lethal justice, he argued, was sacred and venerable: "It aims to *save* (spiritually) society and the culprit" (*OCB* 1:683). Albert Camus reversed this claim a century later. After relating the nausea his father experienced upon his return from an execution, the Nobel laureate affirmed: "[The ultimate penalty] is no less repulsive than the crime, and . . . this new murder, far from atoning for the offense committed against society, adds a new stain to the first one" (*OCC* 4:128).

Three major authors from the country of the guillotine thus expressed strong and disparate views about a single institution, capital punishment, across the post-Revolutionary period.[2] Hugo, the portraitist of crime and injustice, Baudelaire, the poet of evil, and Camus, the writer of the Absurd and Revolt, did not just probe the nature and function of the death penalty. All three figures also wondered what literary representations could and should cast light on them. Hugo warned against returning to Renaissance poetry after Robespierre's guillotines (OCH 2:460). Baudelaire vowed that he would someday write a counterpoint to Hugo's own *Claude Gueux*, an edifying narrative whose likeable protagonist is eventually beheaded (OCB 1:598). Camus, for his part, worried that writings about the death penalty only, and wrongly, adopted hushed tones (OCC 4:128).

Capital Letters examines both the poetic choices these famous authors made in their literary works that feature lethal justice and the critical ramifications that ensue. It explores their contribution to the representation and understanding of absolute punishment in the modern and contemporary eras. It is my contention that their writings establish an ongoing dialogue about the status and experience of those condemned to death, the violence of the killing state and its imaginary, and literature itself.[3] Beyond post-Revolutionary France, this dialogue provides a critique that retains considerable contemporary relevance: as a punishment that suspends society's prescription not to kill, the death penalty is among the most pressing ethical issues faced by the state and the individual today, with about a third of countries around the world still maintaining the right to kill, including twenty-nine states in the largest Western democracy, the United States.

France did not abolish the death penalty until 1981, the last decapitation having occurred in 1977. The prohibition of capital punishment itself appeared in the Constitution only in 2007.[4] This right to kill was—and still is, in the nations where lethal justice remains—inseparable from, and hinged upon, the way in which it was performed and perceived.[5] In the nineteenth century, France first spectacularly exhibited its scaffolds on public squares to edify the people before these contraptions were removed from the city center by the state authorities in 1832; the scaffold then disappeared altogether following the Crémieux decree (1870), and the death penalty ultimately metamorphosed into a concealed ritual in 1939. From then on, executions took place in the courtyards of prisons following a politics and aesthetics of secrecy established for the sake of public order. Hugo, Baudelaire, and Camus share an acute awareness not only of the exceptional power that underlies state killing and the significance of this punishment—moral, sociopolitical, and symbolic—but also of this central role played by staging and public perception. Through the language they forge to give lethal justice a face and an imaginary, all three authors illuminate its operation, claims, and reliance on the effect produced. They also put themselves in a position to inflect the conception of state killing through their representations.[6]

Numerous nineteenth- and twentieth-century French literary works feature the death penalty beyond those of the three writers examined in this study.[7] In particular, Romanticism and, to a lesser extent, Realism and *fantastique* literature have frequently portrayed state killing. These "capital" publications include abolitionist poetry and drama from the first third of the nineteenth century, such as Lamartine's ode "Contre la peine de mort" (1830) and Vigny's play *La Maréchale d'Ancre* (1831); prose fiction, such as Stendhal's *Le Rouge et le noir* (1830), which famously gives Julien Sorel his theatrical moment on the scaffold, exalted by a satirized Mathilde de La Mole, and Balzac's apology of the executioner (*El Verdugo*); historiography and nonfiction, as exemplified by Michelet's and Chateaubriand's contrasting accounts of executions during the French Revolution in *Histoire de la révolution française* (1847–53) and *Mémoires d'outre-tombe* (posth. 1849–50); and short stories, as illustrated by the fantasized figuration of capital punishment found in Villier de l'Isle-Adam's fin-de-siècle *Contes cruels* (1883). Critics have mainly focused their attention on this rich nineteenth-century corpus.[8] They have shown that these works largely process and tap into an imaginary of the French Revolution and the contemporary *fait divers* (sensational news item), sometimes, but not always, for political ends. In addition, and importantly, the existing scholarship has established that, together, these publications allow for the emergence of a modern, transgressive aesthetics replete with dramatic scenes and figures.[9] Works of reference have also placed a heavy emphasis on the Revolutionary icon, the guillotine,[10] whether through the prism of literary, historical, or cultural studies.[11]

Of interest to me, in the wake of these analyses of the death penalty in the French context, is to investigate the particular and reciprocal relationship between poetics and ethics in a more diversified and *longue durée* corpus. This material reveals an unsuspected conversation between three major writers across texts and centuries, and, while the crossroads of poetics and ethics is vast and long standing, the representations of capital punishment examined here arguably probe it anew.

Hugo's, Baudelaire's, and Camus's literary works make poetic expression shed light on institutionalized lethal violence in unique and nondiscursive ways. Instead of controlling or neutralizing this violence, their writing alternately takes it on, absorbs it, and is subjected to it. The antithetical models commonly used to account for the intersection of poetics and ethics, namely their association through politics in *littérature engagée* or, conversely, their radical separation in a literary "art for art's sake," are equally incapable of accounting for what these works achieve. Transgressing a number of literary and aesthetic standards, clear-cut affects, and argumentative strategies, the corpus under consideration articulates a complex critique of both capital punishment and literature that complements the abundant legal, historical, philosophical, moral, and political discourses that have supported or disqualified the death penalty throughout the modern and contemporary periods.

Time is one of the obvious differences that set Hugo, Baudelaire, and Camus apart. Between the publication of the first work on capital punishment considered here, *Le Dernier Jour d'un condamné* (The Last Day of a Condemned Man; 1829) and 1960, the year Camus's accidental death interrupted his writing of *Le Premier Homme* (The First Man; published posthumously in 1994), more than a century elapsed, and that century saw a number of decisive sociopolitical shifts. France went from a restored monarchy to the Fifth Republic, between which the July Monarchy, the Second Republic, Napoleon's second imperial regime, and the Third and Fourth Republics unfolded. In addition, the country experienced the major upheavals of the July Revolution, the 1848 Revolution, the 1851 coup d'état, and the Paris Commune, as well as the two world wars that marked the twentieth century. Equally important over this long century, from the 1950s onward, was the process of decolonization ending the colonial domination that had culminated under the Third Republic. At the time *Le Premier Homme* was being written, the Algerian War of Independence (1954–62) was raging.

Nevertheless, from the early nineteenth century to the second half of the twentieth, the definition of capital punishment as "the mere deprivation of life" (Article 2 of the Penal Code of 1791) remained unchanged in France. For almost two centuries, this ultimate penalty was obtained in the same way: through head severance and, in Dr. Joseph-Ignace Guillotin's words, "by means of a simple mechanism" (Article 6), that of the guillotine promoted by Dr. Antoine Louis, permanent secretary of the Académie de chirurgie (Academy of Surgeons).[12] This institutional heritage, informed by ideology, science, and technology, unifies the substantial period spanning 1791 to 1981, from the time the *Louisette*—as the guillotine was nicknamed, after its promoter's last name—was adopted, up until the year of abolition.

The enduring use of the guillotine can be explained in part by the perceived virtues with which it was originally associated. During the French Revolution, a humanitarian and progressive spirit motivated penal reform, in particular the abolition of cruel modes of killing, *supplices* (brutal corporal punishment usually leading to death) such as the wheel, quartering, and burning at the stake. This reform had its roots in the European Enlightenment, and more specifically in the thought of the Italian philosopher and jurist Cesare Beccaria (1738–1794), an avid reader of Montesquieu, Rousseau, and the French Encyclopedists. In 1764, Beccaria published an anonymous, groundbreaking treatise entitled *Dei delitti e delle pene* (On Crimes and Punishments). It defended a secular and liberal definition of penalty, provocatively stating in its twenty-eighth chapter that "the death penalty is not a matter of *right* . . . but is an act of war on the part of society against the citizen that comes about when it is deemed necessary or useful to destroy his existence." He then solemnly stated, "But if I can go on to prove that such a death is neither necessary nor useful, I shall have won the cause of humanity."[13]

Abbé Morellet translated *Dei delitti e delle pene* into French at the end of 1765, and such major figures as d'Alembert, Grimm, and Voltaire warmly welcomed it.[14] In 1766, Voltaire also published a *Commentaire* on the treatise and sent Beccaria his *Relation de la mort du Chevalier de la Barre* (Account of the Death of the Chevalier de la Barre). This "enlightened" movement peaked in 1795 with the *décret du 4 Brumaire de l'an IV*, whose first article ensured that the death penalty would be abolished "as of the date of publication [of the declaration] of general peace."[15] While this prospect proved vain, the guillotine's inauguration in 1792 gave shape to the egalitarian and liberal aspirations of the era's law makers. The machine guaranteed the same, supposedly painless and immediate execution for all men convicted of a capital crime regardless of the specifics of what had been committed and the condemned man's social status.[16] Although the *Code pénal* of 1810 abandoned the conditional abolitionist provision of 1795, it upheld the stipulation that "Every individual condemned to death will be beheaded" (Article 12, formerly Article 3). Notwithstanding the fact that its thirteenth article arguably restored cruelty by requesting the severance of the hand for parricides, it thereby sustained most of the reformist principles that motivated the *Louisette*'s adoption and legitimation.[17]

In addition, one founding event turned capital punishment by guillotine into a historical emblem: the Reign of Terror. In 1793 and 1794, the recourse to death sentences was systematized with the paradoxical aim of "building a new world in which capital punishment would no longer have reason to exist," as the historian Jean-Claude Farcy has noted.[18] The Terror marked the climax of a sanctified bloody justice.[19] Seventeen thousand individuals were executed on order of Revolutionary tribunals and about the same number died in prison as "suspects."[20] Decades—indeed centuries—after it ended, the French and European cultural imagination, and particularly literary works, still bear the imprint of this judicial terror. Post-Revolutionary literature in French also frequently features the death penalty because, despite a marked overall decline in death sentences as one moves toward the twentieth century, sporadic increases in condemnations and executions, as well as debates about the legitimacy of lethal justice, recur at key junctures of the nineteenth and twentieth centuries: the First Empire, the Second Restoration, the Revolutions of 1830 and 1848, the 1850s, the Belle Époque, the two world wars, and the Algerian War of Independence.[21]

Hugo, Baudelaire, and Camus are united not just by this dense political and cultural heritage of the Revolution and by the largely unchanged definition and practice of capital justice that spanned the nineteenth and twentieth centuries. Their works also epitomize what is fundamentally at stake in this lengthy period, namely mankind's new sense of responsibility. The 1790s and the guillotine marked the advent of secularization, a process that radically altered French society's understanding of the world. Most obviously, the fall of the absolute monarchy supported by divine right put an end to the idea that society depended exclusively on a transcendent divine authority. Louis XVI's decapitation and the weakening of the Catholic Church, confiscation of its assets, and the civil constitution of the clergy established in 1790 formed part of this major political and religious shift that enacted a distancing from the sacred. These events conjured up the possibility of numerous absences: the absence of a postmortem salvation, about which Hugo's condemned man wonders; the absence of a divine justice capable of compensating for man's flawed judgment; the absence of a superior causality that may supersede human intelligence.

A reconsideration of man's position and powers on earth thus occurred in the post-Revolutionary period. The resistance it produced in the form of counter-Revolutionary movements, restorations, or the preservation of faith could not erase these events and the dramatic symbolic upheaval they caused: society had now caught sight of a new configuration of the world in which human agency prevailed. This secularized consciousness permeated the legal and judicial institutions. Their representatives and, more broadly, society could no longer rely on God so fully to guide their judgment or correct their errors when they carried out justice. Capital punishment therefore became a more human matter at the turn of the nineteenth century and in the decades that followed.[22] Nineteenth-century literature was impelled to reflect this anthropocentric revolution, and twentieth-century history only made more acute this question of the weighty burden of human responsibility in the administering of killing.

There remain, of course, acute literary and ideological differences between Hugo, Baudelaire, and Camus. The first has come to embody French Romanticism and the belief in the progressive function of art. His works have been reputed to show an increasing commitment to humanitarianism.[23] In contrast, the second marked the advent of a modern French poetry that dismantled the traditional association of beauty with goodness. Baudelaire praised dandyism and amoral, if not immoral, aesthetics over the reformist political, social, and moral ideals of his predecessor.[24] As opposed to Hugo, who was prolific in all literary genres, Baudelaire's œuvre is essentially composed of poetry. Conversely, Camus favored the novel and drama. He rejected the supposed gratuitous aestheticism of Baudelaire, who claimed to be "depoliticized" after the Revolution of 1848. Camus stubbornly refused to detach literature from the realities of its time. Yet despite a brief early affiliation with the Communist Party and a clear left-wing sensibility, he also resisted any binding party-based ideological and political allegiance. Likewise, he opposed the mature Hugo's desire to have literary works serve a prescribed sociopolitical and moral agenda. Furthermore, unlike Hugo, the Nobel laureate never represented a particular literary school, although he is often mistakenly presented as an existentialist. Lastly, it seems that Hugo's and Camus's styles could not be more at odds, if one thinks of the former's ample and emphatic prose and of the latter's often "blank writing" (*écriture blanche*), in the words of Roland Barthes.[25]

Examining the three writers' treatment of the death penalty helps us to comprehend some of these remarkable divergences and allows us to qualify others. It reveals biographical, but also, more importantly, literary and philosophical points of contact. In his youth, Baudelaire read Hugo's most important work of fiction on the death penalty, *Le Dernier Jour d'un condamné*. Later, he wished to rebut not just *Claude*

Gueux (1834), as mentioned previously, but also Jean Valjean, the protagonist of *Les Misérables*.[26] The young Camus too knew *Le Dernier Jour*: the first prose piece he ever published, in the inaugural issue of the high school publication *Sud*, was entitled "Le Dernier Jour d'un mort-né" (The Last Day of a Still-Born; 1931). Later on, in such works as *L'Étranger* (1942) and "Réflexions sur la guillotine" (1957), Camus would appropriate some of the issues, central images, and enunciative and narrative devices foregrounded in *Le Dernier Jour d'un condamné*, all the while criticizing what he called Hugo's "good convicts" (*OCC* 4:159). *L'Homme révolté* (The Rebel; 1951) would also examine both Baudelaire's status as a "poet of crime" and a dandy relishing terror, and Joseph de Maistre, the poet's supposed favorite reactionary thinker.

Beyond these sporadic literary encounters, all three authors interrogate the human condition, and the ways literature may portray it. Killing, both legal and illegal, feeds into these interrogations and often sheds light on the crossroads of the historical and the metaphysical. Hugo reflected on killing through direct and indirect evocations of the French Revolution and its legacy in narratives such as *Han d'Islande* (Hans of Iceland), *Le Dernier Jour d'un condamné*, and *Quatrevingt-Treize* (Ninety-Three). Albeit less extensively, Baudelaire and Camus followed suit in *Mon cœur mis à nu* (My Heart Laid Bare) and *L'Homme révolté* respectively. All three writers' texts also carried the imprint of the capital crimes that seemed to characterize post-Revolutionary France, whether owing to the brutal political ruptures, exponential growth of cities and rampant pauperization that marked the nineteenth century (Hugo and Baudelaire) or due to the climax of mass murder reached with the Second World War and twentieth-century totalitarianisms (Camus). Bloody crimes, political crimes, crimes of passion, gloomy *faits divers*, gratuitous crimes, or what we now call crimes against humanity, all punishable by death, occupy a privileged place in the poetic and fictional writings considered here.

Both a substantial corpus and an original triangular reflection on paroxysmal violence, and more particularly on lethal crime and state killing, can therefore be found in Hugo, Baudelaire, and Camus. The chapters that follow focus on works of particular literary richness in these authors' extensive œuvres: Hugo's early novel *Le Dernier Jour d'un condamné*, Baudelaire's celebrated collection *Les Fleurs du mal* (The Flowers of Evil), as well as what is commonly called his *Journaux intimes*, and Camus's novels *L'Étranger*, *La Peste* (The Plague), and *Le Premier Homme*. These writings present individuals in contexts that challenge their humanity and humaneness. They portray characters and personae who experience forms of exclusion, imminent destruction, as well as self-questioning and tentative resilience in the face of the death penalty understood literally, figuratively, or both. Hugo features an anonymous criminal awaiting his execution; Baudelaire conjoins the condemned man and the poet as actors of a society, if not of a human race, marked by devastation and corruption; Camus produces other scenarios and protagonists exploring lethal justice: the innocent criminal convicted because he "does not play the game" and "wanders, on the sideline, at the outer edge of private, solitary, sensual life" (*OCC* 1:215), the humble people resisting all forms of death, and the simple man discovering his solidarity with even the most brutal murderer.

Above all, what connects these writings is the sophisticated poetic work undertaken to bring to life the *cas limite* of a unique institution and its imaginary. It gives the condemned man, the executioner, the victim, and the spectator greater visibility, or a new ability to see. Hugo, Baudelaire, and Camus present the reader with what could be called "capital literature": not only does it feature capital punishment and its imaginary, but such literature also deals with matters of life and death that challenge both conscience and representability, and it undertakes crucial work in sharpening our critical understanding of justice at the extremes. The death penalty is extreme in that it delineates multiple, stratified limits: between life and death, of course, but also between illegal and legal murder, between criminal and victim, since one may be transformed into the other when death looms, and between various mental states. And, in the case of decapitation, limits between head and body, between the visible and the invisible—for the moment of beheading is so swift witnesses have sometimes deemed it imperceptible[27]—between understandable penalty and unintelligible, unbearable violence, or between intense suffering and insensibility. The three authors share a quest for words and images that address these limits and the zone between them.

A word on method is in order. Encompassing works in prose and verse from the Romantic, post-Romantic, and contemporary periods, this book emphasizes the close reading of major texts. It aims to dissect the linguistic and imagistic devices the authors use to represent capital punishment, but also to reflect on the impact that the institution of capital punishment may have on literature. It is my contention that state killing and its imaginary lead Hugo, Baudelaire, and Camus to interrogate the function, tools, and limits of their art. While foregrounding textual analysis, this study also aims to remain attentive to the specific sociopolitical, judicial, and literary contexts in which the narratives and poems appeared. This careful contextualization accounts for the outline chosen and its chronological basis. The monograph begins with a detailed examination of Hugo's most significant narrative on the death penalty and goes on to examine Baudelaire's and Camus's works taken both individually and comparatively.

Where this proves fruitful, the close readings proposed in this book are informed by the reflections of Giorgio Agamben, Michel Foucault, René Girard, and Jacques Rancière on actual or symbolic violence, discourse, and state power. Ultimately, my readings attempt to cast light on encounters between poetics and ethics. I take "poetics" to refer to "everything that concerns the creation or the composition of works for which language (le langage) is at once the substance and the means," in accordance with Paul Valéry's etymologically inflected definition of the term.[28] "Ethics" is understood, with Paul Ricœur, as meaning "to live well, with and for the other, in fair institutions."[29]

Part I analyzes the groundbreaking abolitionist poetics deployed in Hugo's *Le Dernier Jour d'un condamné*. This text, which takes the form of a condemned man's diary, specifically stages the intersection of capital punishment and writing. Chapter 1 shows how, and with what effect, the novel turns on its head conventional modes of representation and replaces them with a regime of expression that transforms the reader's usual perception of the death penalty. Chapter 2 examines one of the results of this poetics, namely Hugo's critique of a penal modernity assumed to move away from pain and toward Enlightenment values such as human rights.

Part II considers Baudelaire's pro–death penalty statements and projects on the death penalty as well as his verse foregrounding capital violence and bloodshed. Chapter 3 contextualizes Baudelaire's trenchant defense of capital punishment in several prose pieces and interrogates his redefinition of this institution as a kind of sacrifice in relation to Hugo's and Joseph de Maistre's work. Chapter 4 turns to Baudelaire's 1855 essay "De l'essence du rire et généralement du comique dans les arts plastiques" (On the Essence of Laughter and Generally on the Comic in the Plastic Arts) and to the most graphic poems of *Les Fleurs du mal* in order to determine how their imaginary of execution problematizes the poet's praise of sacrifice.

Part III further probes the relationship between lethal punishment, poetic craft, and ethical reflection, with a focus on Camus's novels featuring the death penalty and, peripherally, his plays and the essay "Réflexions sur la guillotine." It studies both the idiosyncrasies of these works and their relation to Hugo's and Baudelaire's critique of state killing. Chapter 5 explores the figuration of the death penalty in *L'Étranger*, *La Peste*, and *Le Premier Homme* and the decisive role it comes to play in their storylines and characterizations. Chapter 6 addresses the question of language as it preoccupies not just Camus but also Hugo and Baudelaire, when they represent lethal justice and its imaginary. It investigates how their works engage with the writer's responsibility as he portrays the death penalty. Together, I argue, the three writers establish both a transhistorical dialogue on the status of modern lethal law and a profound critical reflection on modern literary modes of engagement.

PART I

New Abolitionist Poetics

Hugo's Le Dernier Jour d'un condamné

Dans le jury, il suffisait parfois d'une voix pour sauver la tête d'un homme. Combien ont été sauvés parce que les jurés avaient lu *Le Dernier Jour d'un condamné*?

In the jury, one vote was sometimes enough to save a man's life. How many were saved because the jurors had read *The Last Day of a Condemned Man*?

—Robert Badinter, preface to *Choses vues à travers Hugo: Hommage à Guy Rosa* (2007)

HUGO'S SCAFFOLDS

The death penalty was both familiar and repulsive to Victor Hugo (1802–1885) from a very young age. He reportedly caught sight of the remains of hanged men suspended from trees in Italy in 1807 and saw a terrified Spanish man who had been condemned to death walking to the scaffold in 1812, the year his own godfather, General Lahorie, was executed.[1] In 1820, Louis Pierre Louvel, the murderer of the duc de Berry, was also led to the scaffold before Hugo's eyes. This, and the greasing of the guillotine he witnessed before the execution of a young man guilty of a crime of passion in September 1827, allegedly led Hugo to write his work of fiction that focuses exclusively on capital punishment: *Le Dernier Jour d'un condamné* (1829).[2]

Hugo arguably developed the most extensive portrayal of and ethical reflection on state killing of the nineteenth century. In myriad other texts, he created a gallery of memorable visions and brought forward moral, sociopolitical, and religious arguments in favor of abolition. Not only did the issue of capital punishment permeate many of his novels, from *Bug-Jargal* (1820, 1826) to *Han d'Islande* (1823), *Notre-Dame de Paris* (1831), *Claude Gueux* (1834), *Les Misérables* (1862), *L'Homme qui rit* (The Man Who Laughs; 1869) or *Quatrevingt-Treize* (1874), but it also punctuated his dramatic, poetic, and visual works.[3]

As he became a figure increasingly committed to social progress and the defense of all *misérables*, the death penalty also found itself at the center of his most forceful political speeches.[4] The one he delivered before the Assemblée constituante on September 15, 1848, famously called for "l'abolition pure, simple et définitive de la peine de mort" (the pure, simple, and definitive abolition of the death penalty), as opposed to the abolition of the death penalty for political crimes only. In 1851, he spoke against capital punishment at the Cour d'assises de la Seine when his own son Charles was put on trial and sentenced to six months in prison for criticizing an execution. In addition, he supported the abolitionist cause abroad, acting as a tireless rhetorician and a sort of moral guarantor for a number of foreign authorities seeking to question lethal justice. Most important, perhaps, the author intervened publicly and in private in favor of men condemned to death. Among them were such individuals as John Charles Tapner, the English criminal he defended in vain before his botched hanging in 1854; the American abolitionist John Brown, executed in 1859; and the condemned men of the Paris Commune.

CONTEXTUALIZING "LE LIVRE DE LA TÊTE COUPÉE"

The two chapters that follow limit themselves to the investigation of *Le Dernier Jour d'un condamné*, both because of space constraints and because the text's literary richness and emphasis on the death penalty are unequaled. It laid the groundwork for major reflections on and representations of the death penalty by such prominent figures as Fyodor Dostoevsky, Albert Camus, and Robert Badinter. Written for the most part in December 1828, Hugo's novel was first published in early February 1829. It relates, in the form of a first-person account, the experience of a man condemned to death, from his sentencing to the day of his decapitation. Hence the telling nickname that the author gave to his creation: "le livre de la tête coupée" (the book of the severed head; *OCH* 9:1275).

Le Dernier Jour d'un condamné came out at a time of economic hardship and strict penal measures. A dramatic increase in poverty marked the end of the 1820s in France. The price of bread, which went up by 65 percent between 1826 and 1828, made the lower classes extremely vulnerable.[5] Fearful of the misdeeds that might tempt such *misérables*, the wealthier workers and owners pushed for harsher penalties. Extreme penal severity characterized the reign of Charles X (1824–1830), and the *Code pénal* of 1810 did not do away with capital punishment despite the 1795 decree according to which the death sentence was to be abolished as of the date of publication of the declaration of general peace. It found over thirty-five crimes punishable by death, established that parricides would have their hand cut off, reinstated branding, and made aiding and abetting a capital crime in certain cases.[6] Attempted capital crimes were also subject to the death penalty.[7] An additional drastic measure was adopted in 1825, making the death penalty applicable to acts of sacrilege.

Against this exacting justice, an abolitionist campaign was launched. In 1826, the Société de la morale chrétienne in Paris and the comte de Sellon in Geneva organized two *concours* (essay competitions) on capital punishment and abolition. Newspapers such as *Le Globe* and *La Gazette des Tribunaux* published articles on the subject, and politico-penal essays by Benjamin Constant, François Guizot, Charles Lucas (winner of the two 1826 *concours*), and Pierre-Simon Ballanche, among others, argued to varying degrees for the inappropriateness, the uselessness, or the illegitimacy of lethal justice.[8]

This activism failed to affect the law.[9] Yet the liberals had a strong voice in the Chambre des députés, and 114 people were sentenced to death in 1828, compared to over 500 in 1816 and 1817, and 304 in 1820.[10] Historians have argued that, because of the severity of the 1810 penal code, which led to more capital sentencing than in the last decades of the Ancien Régime, juries began to circumvent the death penalty, either through acquittals or through petitions in favor of more tailored and humane treatments of individual cases.[11] Hugo's fiction relies on a potent investigative and literary protocol that appears to echo this concern with the inhuman nature of capital justice: a protagonist's close observation and writing of distress in a situation of radical exclusion and imminent death that the reader perceives through imposed voyeurism.

"FANTAISIE" VS. POLITICS?

A number of reviewers have expressed a particular reservation about *Le Dernier Jour d'un condamné*, however. Addressing this hesitation before turning to the novel's substance is useful in that it calls for a closer examination of its production and specificities. The reservation in question concerns the nature of Hugo's enterprise and authorial intention. Some critics have asked: Is his book an opportunistic "fantaisie" (preface of 1829, 641)—a figment of the imagination at the basis of a formally free work in keeping with the trend of the day—or a true abolitionist plea?[12]

Hugo was not the first French writer to address the death penalty in the 1820s. A friend of his, the Romantic author Jules Lefèvre-Deumier, had written several poems on the issue by 1825.[13] In 1828, Vidocq, a former criminal turned director of the Brigade de sûreté, published the first two volumes of his famous memoirs, and in 1829, a melodrama about the beheaded Revolutionary heroine Charlotte Corday, proud murderer of the Jacobin Jean-Paul Marat, came out.[14] In addition, in or shortly after 1830, such renowned Romantic writers as Alphonse de Lamartine, Alfred de Vigny, and Charles Nodier denounced lethal justice.[15] Lesser-known writers also dealt with the subject.[16] Thus one might have reason to believe that Hugo's work essentially is a literary exercise designed to emulate his era's many publications on a popular and sensationalistic question. Proponents of this view have argued that Hugo's text was defined as a defense of the abolition of capital punishment only a posteriori. They have noted that he used neither the term "plea" (*plaidoyer*) nor an explicit and fully developed abolitionist argument until 1832, when he grafted onto his novel an extensive and emphatic preface explicitly condemning capital punishment.

Notwithstanding the fact that authorial intention may not be as important as artistic content and form, and besides the possibility that several motivations may underlie a single work of art, one should not, however, neglect meaningful data. First, evidence reveals that Hugo wished to take part in the impassioned campaign against lethal justice previously mentioned. The postscriptum that closes his letter of January 3, 1829, to his editor Gosselin indicates that he aimed for *Le Dernier Jour* to influence this public ethical and political debate: "It is important to send *The Condemned Man* to press quickly, if you want it to be published before the Chamber [convenes], which is of the utmost importance [*sic*]" (1243). Hugo here refers to the debate that was to occur on February 28, 1829, at the Chambre des députés about the possible reconsideration of counterfeiting as a capital crime.[17]

Second, as early as February 28, 1829, "A Comedy about a Tragedy," the play-preface that was inserted in the book just three weeks after its first publication and that set out to mock its detractors, mentions Hugo's abolitionist intent most explicitly and suggests that it was well understood by readers:

> QUELQU'UN: Mais, ce roman, dans quel but l'a-t-il fait? . . .
>
> UN PHILOSOPHE: À ce qu'il paraît, dans le but de concourir à l'abolition de la peine de mort. (65)
>
> SOMEONE: But, this novel, for what purpose did he write it? . . .
>
> A PHILOSOPHER: Rumor has it it was to contribute to the abolition of the death penalty.

At the end of this satirical addendum, a "thin Monsieur" laments, "Maintenant on veut abolir la peine de mort, et pour cela on fait des romans cruels, immoraux et de mauvais goût, le Dernier Jour d'un Condamné, que sais-je?" (Now people want to abolish the death penalty, and to that end, cruel, immoral, and inappropriate novels are written, *The Last Day of a Condemned Man*, or what have you?; 654). A note added to the edition of 1832 also highlights the avalanche of hostile political, moral, and literary criticism that *Le Dernier Jour* elicited as a participant in the public debate on abolitionism in the late 1820s (643).

Le Dernier Jour was intended as an abolitionist plea from the start, then, and well before Hugo wrote a substantial second preface to his book in 1832.[18] That the novel itself is abolitionist in nature does not prevent it from also functioning as a "fantaisie" in the sense of an imaginative work. Quite the contrary: part I investigates the particulars of this very interface between politics and creation. It shows that the novel's compelling efficacy as a "plea" is lodged in the poetic modalities of Hugo's narrative.[19]

CHAPTER I

The Death Penalty, from Representation to Expression

> On louait des tables, des chaises, des échafaudages, des charrettes. Tout pliait de spectateurs. Des marchands de sang humain criaient à tue-tête:
> —Qui veut des places?
> Une rage m'a pris contre ce peuple. J'ai eu envie de leur crier:
> —Qui veut la mienne?
>
> People were renting tables, chairs, scaffolding. The whole place was bursting with spectators. Dealers in human blood were shouting their heads off:
> "Who would like seats?"
> A rage against this people came over me. I felt like shouting at them:
> "Who would like mine?"
>
> —Victor Hugo, *Le Dernier Jour d'un condamné*, chapter XLVIII

When, in 1829, *Le Dernier Jour d'un condamné* first came out, Victor Hugo did not oppose the death penalty in his own name: this publication was initially anonymous. Nor did he seek to articulate religious or utilitarian abolitionist arguments.[1] Before him, Chateaubriand, the Catholic writer he so revered, and, at greater length, Pierre-Simon Ballanche had asserted that the crucifixion of Christ constituted an exceptional and sufficiently bloody expiation of man's sins, which terrestrial justice was therefore not to replicate. The eighteenth-century jurist Cesare Beccaria, and the French and European philosophers who followed his lead, had tended to insist on the useless, if not counterproductive, character of the death penalty by focusing on a cost-benefit calculation that pointed to the negative political consequences of capital justice.² As if anticipating Robert Badinter's claim that "one does not overthrow scaffolds with arguments but with words, images, and emotions to which they give birth," Hugo instead forged a new kind of writing to reach the affectivity of his audience, in addition to using reason.³ In 1825, he had indirectly set a challenge for himself:

> Tu veux être poète—
> —Sais-tu quelle pensée agite
> Une tête qui va tomber? (*OCH* 2:961)

> You want to be a poet—
> —Do you know what thought agitates
> A head about to be cut off?

Four years later, the form of *Le Dernier Jour* arguably answered this question thanks to formal reinvention.

UNDOING CLASSICAL REPRESENTATION

Once an ultraconservative whose political sensibility became increasingly progressive, Hugo sided with the literary Moderns in 1823, when he gushingly praised the anti–death penalty poetry of Jules Lefèvre-Deumier, author of *Le Parricide, poëme suivi d'autres poésies*.⁴ He commended its "strong and daring imagination . . . often rough and reckless in its conceptions," its "expression, new and picturesque . . . frequently bizarre," and the "torture" it sometimes imposed on poetic language (*OCH* 2:51). The proponents of Classicism deemed both the topic chosen and the manner used to be iconoclastic and undesirable (50).⁵ Hugo, who attended the execution of the parricide Pierre-Louis Martin with Lefèvre-Deumier in 1820,⁶ had in fact already featured the death penalty in his own first two novels, *Bug-Jargal* (1820, 1826) and *Han d'Islande* (1823). They bore the imprint of the Gothic and of what Charles Nodier named the "Frenetic School," which challenged the topical and poetic standards imposed by Classicism.⁷ But *Le Dernier Jour* set out to move beyond both these early narratives and the originality that Hugo hailed in Lefèvre-Deumier.⁸ It displayed even more radically revolutionary features to decry capital punishment, including the unpicking of time, space, events, and character.

Dead time prevails in *Le Dernier Jour*. Forty-nine concise chapters providing glimpses into the condemned man's consciousness are bracketed between the pronouncement of a death to come (the exclamation "Condamné à mort!" [Condemned to death!] inaugurates and punctuates the novel) and death itself: an interrupted ending and the capitalization of the final words "QUATRE HEURES" (FOUR O'CLOCK) point to the imminent moment of the legal killing. Spatially, the novel is also locked in: enclosure reigns in the courtroom, the cell, and, above all, the mind. The condemned man is "en prison dans une idée" (imprisoned in an idea), that of the death sentence, "courbé sous son poids" (bent over under the weight of it; I, 657). An embedded incarceration, judicial and mental, therefore frames the narrative and has it function as a peculiar tragedy in which little room is left for action.

Except for writing, no significant deed marks the condemned man's experience. Rather, he inhabits a world of fearful thoughts and micro-events, and, even when it comes to these modest happenings, he is unable to partake in them fully or actively. In his recollection of his trial, he remains inert despite his desire to speak; during most of his captivity, he finds himself reduced to watching the walls of his cell and interacting superficially with the prison guards and his fellow convicts. This inactivity clearly distinguishes the protagonist from Hugo's other famous, and always dynamic, convicts, from Claude Gueux, to the man in the iron mask, to Jean Valjean. The knowledge that all the other characters (his peers, the judicial and state authorities, and the people) are shown to have of the condemned man's status and the repeated reminders of his impending execution bring home his inescapable passivity.

Instead of relating a dynamic sequence of events, the novel foregrounds the protagonist's moral and emotional wandering through internal focalization. This results in a relative diegetic discontinuity within the narrative's dead time: analepses, prolepses, and digressions alternate in the condemned man's prose as his mind races to come to terms with his sentence. The narrative breaks with the conventions of early nineteenth-century French fiction, which did explore the interior life and subjectivity of characters in depth but was still concerned with the unfolding of a plot or a particular destiny—from Chateaubriand to Constant, de Staël, Stendhal, or the early Balzac. In contrast, Hugo stages a nameless and, even more strikingly, story-less protagonist.

Indeed, the chapter meant to reveal the condemned man's life and misdeed (XLVII) is left blank. Contrary to what some critics have asserted, his identity and history are not erased entirely, however.[9] Several cues suggest that he is educated (III, 662) and belongs to a relatively privileged social sphere: his knowledge of Latin, his manners, his disgust when he wakes up on a pallet bed in the prison infirmary (XIV, 674), and his clothing, elegant and unworn (XXIII, 689), for instance. The condemned man's portrayal therefore constitutes what might be called a countersketch: it is minimalistic, but provides enough information for him to emerge as the counterpoint to the stereotypical nineteenth-century criminal. Hugo thereby reverses the figure of the irredeemable proletarian gangster found in contemporary medical and criminological discourses.[10] And while the narrative is structured as a tragedy, the represented subject is not an aristocratic or heroic figure. Hugo replaces these forms of characterization imposed by deterministic sociology and rigid literary genres with a suffering silhouette into which the bourgeois reader is absorbed.

The overlap created between character and reader is furthered by the occasional confusion of voices and other modes of conflation between character, author, and audience. The injunctive formula "Condemned to death!" that inaugurates the text and recurs throughout cannot be assigned to a single voice, for instance, although that of the condemned man otherwise predominates. Rather, this exclamation leads the reader to wonder whether it constitutes a performative utterance emanating from the judicial institution; the whisper of the alienated condemned man's interior voice—he does claim, after all, that "une voix a murmuré à [son] oreille" (a voice has whispered in [his] ear; I, 658); or a collective hateful shout (661). With this opening phrase, whose source remains unclear and whose repetition in the first chapters gives it a chorus-like quality, Hugo raises the question of who is responsible for the death sentence, as an utterance and a reality. Such enunciative instability disorients the reader, all the more so as we quickly become the possible doppelgänger of each of the actors liable to utter these ominous few words: the judge, hearing and assessing the protagonist's case; the stunned protagonist himself, into whose shoes we are put; and the people, reacting with emotion and voyeurism to a criminal's condemnation.

Symmetrically, doubts arise regarding the text's recipient. For if, in theory, the condemned man's writing in the first person comes across as self-addressed and diaristic, several moments of interpellation trouble this logic. He repeatedly hints at the presence of some possible readership or witness. First, he envisages the future publication of his story and, later, considers its reception by "ceux qui condamnent" (those who pass judgment; VI, 664) and by a wider, indefinite audience: an all-embracing "on" (they; 698).¹¹ Second, the frequent use of exclamations and rhetorical questions calls for outside sympathy or indignation in the present time of his writing:

> Depuis l'heure où mon arrêt a été prononcé, combien sont morts qui s'arrangeaient pour une longue vie! Combien m'ont devancé qui, jeunes, libres et sains, comptaient bien aller voir tel jour tomber ma tête en place de Grève! Combien d'ici là peut-être qui marchent et respirent au grand air, entrent et sortent à leur gré, et qui me devanceront encore!
> Et puis, qu'est-ce que la vie a donc de si regrettable pour moi? (III, 662)

> Since the hour when my sentence was pronounced, think how many have died who were all set for a long life! How many have preceded me, young, free, and healthy, who were fully expecting to go and see me lose my head this or that day on the Place de Grève! Before that time comes, how many are there walking and breathing in the open air, coming and going as they please, who might yet still die before I do!
> And besides, what is there about my life that I will regret so much?

Such apostrophic rhetoric de facto forces us into the fictional space of the novel.

Likewise, the author occasionally brings himself into the diary. He is the implicit figure who proves the condemned man wrong when the protagonist declares himself unable to "voir un être humain qui [le] croie digne d'une parole et à qui [il] le rende" (see any human being who believes [him] worthy of being either spoken to or about; III, 662). Hugo also injects an italicized citation from his own *Han d'Islande* into the condemned man's prose in chapter III and, throughout, distills analogies between himself and his protagonist. While the first edition of *Le Dernier Jour* was anonymous, subsequent editions were not and capitalized on Hugo's name, which was hardly unknown after the publication of his *Préface de Cromwell* of 1827, the manifesto of French Romantic drama.¹² More important, a passage superimposes writer and character independently of Hugo's particular identity: chapter VI thematizes the question of writing and conjoins the condemned man penning his ordeal and, at the metafictional level, the author crafting his novel. After the condemned man questions the point of transcribing his thoughts and feelings onto paper, he concludes that his enterprise is legitimate and ends up justifying the very form and agenda Hugo adopted for his book:

> Ce journal de mes souffrances, heure par heure, minute par minute, supplice par supplice, si j'ai la force de le mener jusqu'au moment où il me sera physiquement impossible de continuer, cette histoire, nécessairement inachevée, mais aussi complète que possible, de mes sensations, ne portera-t-elle point avec elle un grand et profond enseignement? N'y aura-t-il pas dans ce procès-verbal de la pensée agonisante, dans cette progression toujours croissante de douleurs, dans cette espèce d'autopsie intellectuelle d'un condamné, plus d'une leçon pour ceux qui condamnent? Peut-être cette lecture leur rendra-t-elle la main moins légère, quand il s'agira quelquefois de jeter une tête qui pense, une tête d'homme, dans ce qu'ils appellent la balance de la justice? Peut-être n'ont-ils jamais réfléchi, les malheureux, à cette lente succession de tortures que renferme la formule expéditive d'un arrêt de mort? Se sont-ils jamais arrêtés à cette idée poignante que dans l'homme qu'ils retranchent il y a une intelligence; une intelligence qui avait compté sur la vie, une âme qui ne s'est point disposée pour la mort? Non. (VI, 664)

> This daily record of my sufferings, hour by hour, minute by minute, ordeal by ordeal, if I have the strength to carry on with it until the moment when it will be physically impossible for me to continue, this story of my sensations, necessarily unfinished, but as complete as possible, won't it contain a great and profound teaching? Won't there be, in these minutes of agonizing thought, in this increasing progression of pain, in this sort of intellectual autopsy of a condemned man, many a lesson for those who condemn? Maybe this reading will make them less heavy-handed in the future, when it comes to throwing a thinking head, a man's head, into what they call the scales of justice? Maybe, poor them, they have never thought about this slow succession of ordeals contained in the expeditious formula of a death sentence? Have they ever paused to consider this poignant idea

that, in the man they are removing, there is a mind; a mind that had counted on life, a soul that did not prepare itself for death? No, they haven't.

Some of the terms used here possess a manifesto-like quality and anticipate those Hugo will choose for his preface of 1832. They thus challenge the text's internal focalization. As if by means of ventriloquism, the character accounts for the author's didactic enterprise of laying bare the psychic reality behind capital punishment.

Le Dernier Jour therefore destabilizes spatiotemporal coordinates, atomizes plot and action under the pressure of the obsession of death, empties out character, represents an unexpected subject, intermittently conflates protagonist, author, and audience, and blocks off the possibility of a dénouement by making the spectacle and narrative of (his own) decapitation inaccessible to the protagonist. In so doing, it resolutely undoes key tenets of classical representation. Instead, what prevails is a discourse disorganized by fear.

FURTHER DISORDER: NARRATIVE INCONSISTENCY AND DEFICTIONALIZATION

There is more to the literary disorder orchestrated by Hugo. The book's very title, when confronted with its actual content, creates an aporia. Several time markers point to a duration that far exceeds the twenty-four hours it promises to the reader (I, 657; II, 661). We in fact witness the last week of the condemned man's existence, and the month and a half subsequent to his condemnation is also narrated. The text oscillates between retrospection and contemporaneity, and the latter does not take over until the chilling wake-up call of chapter XIX: "C'est pour aujourd'hui!" (Today's the day!; 679). In addition to these narrative inconsistencies, the condemned man, against all verisimilitude, seems to have the strength, time and ability to put pen to paper continuously until his very last hour.[13]

Contrary to what one might expect, however, these breaches of the narrative ethos do not generate mistrust in the speaker or an estrangement effect that points to the illusory nature of the condemned man's story. While they do fulfill the Brechtian agenda of making the audience a "consciously critical observer" led to ponder sociopolitical matters, the opposite of a distancing occurs: the discontinuities and incoherence of *Le Dernier Jour* lead to the reader's full adhesion to the protagonist's experience, as they appear to both reveal and be produced by the irresistible violence and inner turmoil triggered by the sentence pronouncement that launches the book's inexorable race to the scaffold. The condemned man's prose implements a peculiar realism anchored in the immediate life of a threatened psyche and thereby creates a literature that refuses to regulate anguish.

The genre of *Le Dernier Jour* partakes in this removal from the realm and rules of fiction. Jean Rousset has argued that the text marked the invention of the "roman-journal" (novel-diary).[14] Combining a single protagonist, a single locus (the prison), and a single, autocentric discourse allowed Hugo to deepen the sense of intimacy characteristic of writings based on self-expression, such as first-person narratives, autobiographies, and epistolary novels, which, from Rousseau to Laclos, had flourished during the French eighteenth century. The faux diary also suppresses the minimal distancing found in the published poems, novels in the third person, short stories, and memoirs that addressed the issue of capital punishment in the 1820s. Instead, it exposes a speaker's experience and subjectivity as unaffected by the social codes and intersubjective dynamics present in some of these other highly popular genres, pushing to its limits the sense of veracity and privacy they strove to achieve.

What further defictionalizes the novel-diary is the context in which it was produced and the paratext with which Hugo envelops the condemned man's account. As an early reviewer did not fail to notice, the book came out after periodicals published first-person narratives relating the in extremis experience of actual men condemned to death.[15] One such publication was the diary of a Corsican convict who starved himself to death, all the while reporting on his slow and painful demise.[16] Another was the testimony of an Englishman who miraculously survived his hanging. Published in *Le Globe* on January 3, 1828, the latter piece is strikingly similar to the novel in several respects. Not only does the title of the article in which it is inserted, "Dernières sensations d'un homme condamné à mort" (Last Sensations of a Man Condemned to Death), bear an obvious likeness to the title of Hugo's novel; the framing, descriptions, and analytical quality of the Englishman's diary, which *Le Globe* summarizes as "everything he felt from the verdict until his execution," including "the gradual extinction of all moral thought, sensory perceptions becoming clearer and more distinct as the faculties of the soul grow weaker, the almost-absolute impossibility of turning to religious ideas," are also the same as those of *Le Dernier Jour*.[17] The repeated anticipation of the execution, visions, hallucinations, and alterations of the condemned man's consciousness that pervade *Le Dernier Jour* structure this British source text as well. Hugo complemented these testimonies, presented as genuine, with accurate or colorful depictions of the realities of carceral life with which he sought to become familiar through direct and indirect examination, including visits to the Bicêtre prison.[18]

Le Dernier Jour reinforces such a reality effect through an efficient paratext. The book's first edition of 1829, as well as the following one, comprised two elements: a preface suggesting that the condemned man's story may (or may not) have been transcribed from a "liasse de papiers jaunes et inégaux" (bundle of discolored papers of various sizes; 641) and, more remarkably, a foldout facsimile of the argot song heard by the condemned man from within his cell, reportedly annotated by him, and found in his papers following his death (712; see also Figure 1).

The process that underlies these multiple defictionalizing devices is one of recording: the novel stages the exhaustive logging of the condemned man's mental, physical and social experience. It was Dostoevsky, such an avid reader of *Le Dernier Jour* that he referred to it when he himself faced a mock execution, who perhaps best pinpointed the psychological dimension of this quest for exhaustiveness. He argued that Hugo's fiction, just like his own short story "A Gentle Creature" (1876), has a "fantastic element" to it that paradoxically makes it "one of the most realistic and most truthful [novels the Frenchman] ever wrote." In the Russian writer's opinion, the novel functions as if the transcription of a "psychological sequence" in its totality could be carried out by a "stenographer" while a character would tell "a story, interrupted by all sorts of digressions and interludes ... in a rather rambling way ... sometimes ... speaking to himself, sometimes ... addressing an invisible listener, a sort of judge."[19]

The fact that *Le Dernier Jour d'un condamné* stages diaristic writing, inserts itself into a paratext and lineage of documents presented as genuine, and resorts to a hybrid scientific-administrative procedure of comprehensive recording that brings realism to border on the unreal may account for the label that Hugo's own satirical play-preface, "Une comédie à propos d'une tragédie," attributes to his fiction: that of "nouveau roman" (647). He coined this now-familiar phrase long before Émile Henriot proposed it in 1957 and before Alain Robbe-Grillet subsequently adopted it to describe the enterprise of twentieth-century writers themselves eager to break away

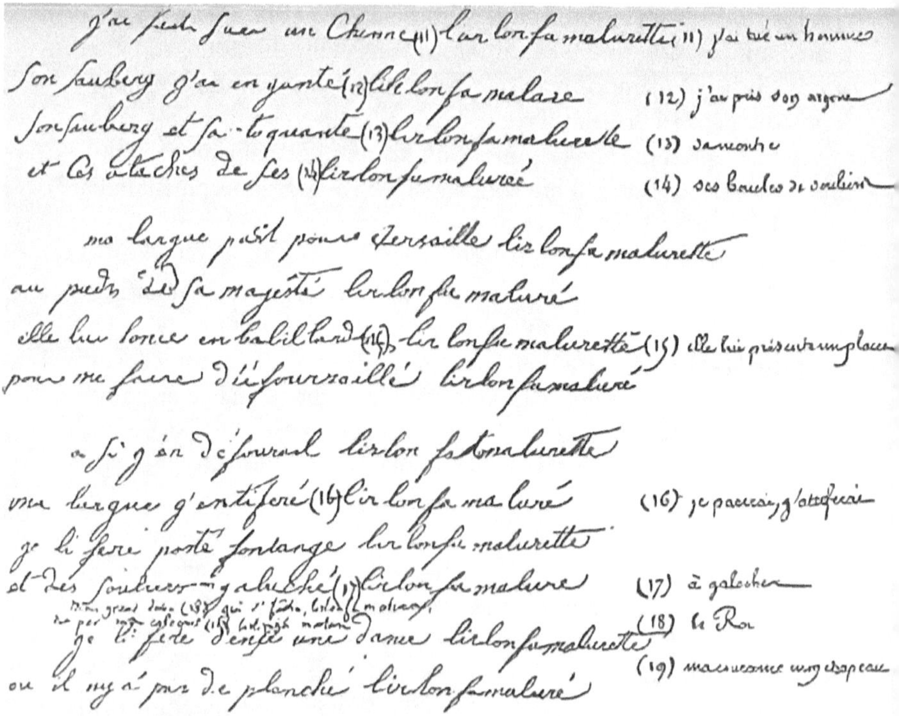
J'ai fait suer un chêne (11) lirlonfa malurette (11) j'ai tué un homme
Son sauberg j'ai engrante (12) lirlonfa malurée (12) j'ai pris son argent
Son sauberg et sa toquante (13) lirlonfa malurette (13) sa montre
et ses attaches de ses (14) lirlonfa malurée (14) ses boucles de souliers

ma largue part pour Versailles lirlonfa malurette
aux pieds de sa majesté lirlonfa malurée
elle lui lance un babillard (15) lirlonfa malurette (15) elle lui présente un placet
pour me faire défourailler lirlonfa malurée

ah si j'en défouraille lirlonfa malurette
ma largue j'entiferai (16) lirlonfa malurée (16) je passerai j'épouserai
je li ferai porter fontange lirlonfa malurette
et des souliers galuchés (17) lirlonfa malurée (17) à galoches
je li ferai danser une danse lirlonfa malurette (18) le Roi
où il n'y a pas de planche lirlonfa malurée (19) [illegible]

Figure 1. Victor Hugo. Foldout facsimile insert included in the first edition of *Le Dernier Jour d'un condamné*. 1829. Maison de Victor Hugo, Paris / Guernesey.

from the consecrated genre of the novel.[20] Negative critiques published shortly after *Le Dernier Jour* first came out emphasize the unacceptability of its new generic and poetic features—which have also puzzled twentieth-century critics.[21] Hugo's own sales-oriented publisher, Charles Gosselin, shared this concern and also expressed reservations about the unique genre of *Le Dernier Jour*. But Hugo responded that he wished to publish an "analytical" novel devoid of antecedents (1242–43).[22]

The "drame intérieur" of *Le Dernier Jour* thus appears to actualize deliberately, in the realm of prose fiction, what Hugo's radical *Préface de Cromwell* of 1827 prescribed for the theater: a liberated form, a drama redefined as a kind of complete and modern poetry that renders reality in all its variety and starkest tensions. The narrative inconsistencies, hyperrealism, and defictionalization used to shed crude light on an "agonizing thought" reinforce the novel's break away from what Jacques Rancière has called "representative poetry": "Representative poetry was composed of stories submitted to principles of concatenation, characters submitted to principles of verisimilitude, and discourses submitted to principles of decorum."[23] By contrast, Hugo crafts a transgressive poetics that problematizes any palatable representation of the capital experience and abolishes the protective distance usually enjoyed by the reader of fiction, showing the inability of both to do justice to a story of life and (state-imposed) death.

CRISIS OF COMMUNICATION

The question of speech and communication prolongs that of a deliberately troubled representation in *Le Dernier Jour d'un condamné*. A profound crisis of linguistic exchanges pervades the novel. It problematizes the very articulation of language and key functions of verbal communication: expressive, conative, phatic, and referential.

Upon the pronouncement of his sentence and as the president of the court consults his lawyer concerning how the punishment should be applied, the condemned man's phonation apparatus partly fails. His tongue is petrified, his breath short, and his bodily and verbal expression is reduced to a single motion and a sole monosyllable:

> J'aurais eu, moi, tout à dire, mais rien ne me vint. Ma langue resta collée à mon palais.
> ... Mille émotions ... se disputaient ma pensée. Je voulus répéter à haute voix ce que je lui avais déjà dit: Plutôt cent fois la mort! Mais l'haleine me manqua, et je ne pus que l'arrêter [mon avocat] rudement par le bras, en criant avec une force convulsive: Non!

> I myself would have had so much to say, but nothing came to me. My tongue remained stuck to the roof of my mouth.
> ... A thousand emotions ... were competing for my thoughts. I wanted to repeat out loud what I had already told him [my lawyer]: I'd rather die a hundred times! But I didn't have enough breath left, and all I could do was stop him briskly with my arm, shouting with convulsive force: No! (II, 661)

This semiparalysis symbolizes the weight of a disproportionate institutional violence that crushes the accused (whose past bravado vis-à-vis his lawyer becomes ironic) and shows this violence to block off complex dialogue and efficient refutation.

The metaphorical deafness of the protagonist's interlocutors mirrors this dictional difficulty. Immediately after he leaves the courtroom, we are told that two young women show their excitement in anticipation of the day of the execution. Their exclamation "Ce sera dans six semaines!" (It will take place in six weeks! II, 661) and, even more patently, the body language one of them displays, clapping her hands out of impatient enthusiasm, indicate that the phrase "Condamné à mort!" can take on a jubilatory quality for some auditors. On several occasions, the text emphasizes this process of loss or perversion of meaning, following a gradation that culminates in the description of a voluble crowd whose voice becomes "plus vaste, plus glapissante, plus joyeuse encore" (even more vast, more yelping, more joyful) once the execution is imminent (XLVIII, 711).

The priest, the very actor whose task is to comfort the condemned man, prepares the ground for such uninhibited *contre-sens*. His logorrheic speech has

> rien de senti, rien d'attendri, rien de pleuré, rien d'arraché à l'âme, rien qui vînt de son cœur pour aller au mien, rien qui fût de lui à moi. Au contraire, je ne sais quoi de vague, d'inaccentué, d'applicable à tout et à tous; emphatique où il eût été besoin de profondeur, plat où il eût fallu être simple; une espèce de sermon sentimental et d'élégie théologique.... Et puis, il avait l'air de réciter une leçon déjà vingt fois récitée, de repasser un thème, oblitéré dans sa mémoire à force d'être su. Pas un regard dans l'œil, pas un accent dans la voix, pas un geste dans les mains. (XXX, 693)

> nothing heartfelt about it, nothing tender, nothing tearful, nothing torn from the soul, nothing coming from his heart to mine, nothing from him to me. Quite the opposite, something vague, flat, applicable to everything and everyone; emphatic when he should have needed to be deep, plain when he should have been simple; a sort of sentimental sermon and theological elegy.... Besides, he seemed to be going over a lesson that he had already recited twenty times, to rehearse a theme, obliterated in his memory because he knew it like the back of his hand. Not a look in his eye, not a stress in his voice, not a gesture with his hands.

The mechanical rhetoric described here jeopardizes the expressive function of language.[24] It is no surprise that, correspondingly, the reception of such messages should be hindered, if not nullified. The condemned man cannot establish true contact with or hear the words of his interlocutors from the religious and judiciary orders without some reticence: "Mais ce bon vieillard, qu'est-il pour moi? que suis-je pour lui? un individu de l'espèce malheureuse, une ombre comme il en a déjà tant vu, une unité ajoutée au chiffre des exécutions" (But this good old man, what is he to me? What am I to him? An individual of the desperate kind, a shadow like the many he has already seen, a simple unit added to the number of executions; XXX, 694). One also thinks of the "paroles caressantes" (caressing words) of the jailer, "prison incarnée" (prison incarnate), whose "œil . . . flatte et . . . espionne" (eye . . . flatters and . . . spies; XX, 680), or of the cynicism that lies behind judicial transcription as it appears in chapter XXIII: "Nous ferons les deux procès-verbaux à la fois, cela s'arrange bien" (We will complete the two certificates at the same time, that's quite convenient; 686). While the mechanical, duplicitous, or cynical use of language may be a common trait of human communication, the condemned man's critical situation appears to systematize it and to associate it closely with cruelty, intentional or otherwise. It morphs into a marker through which his interlocutors disavow his individuality, minimize the value of his existence, and contribute actively but inconspicuously to his fate.

What about the condemned man's language itself, then? It has difficulty being in touch with the outside world. On the one hand, this struggle manifests itself in a disconnect from factual reality: the protagonist's writing alternates between segments that refer to and then shut out actual events. His alienated consciousness, shocked upon hearing the death sentence, pays attention to his objective environment only in a discontinuous manner before returning to the obsession of his execution. So much so that actuality repeatedly takes him by surprise, such as when he gets off his cart and seems to catch sight of the guillotine:

> Entre les deux lanternes du quai, j'avais vu une chose sinistre.
> Oh! c'était la réalité! (XLVIII, 711)[25]

> Between the two lanterns on the quay, I had seen a sinister thing.
> Oh! T'was reality!

On the other hand, the words of the man condemned to death sometimes come across as inoperative. He is unable to make the bailiff and the priest realize that the bad news of the day is his beheading (chapter XXII), does not manage to talk an old gendarme into exchanging clothes with him (XXIII), and, even in the course of a most elementary conversation with the prison's clerk, he is unsuccessful at making himself truly heard:

> —Il fait beau, dis-je au guichetier.
> Il resta un moment sans me répondre, comme ne sachant si cela valait la peine de dépenser une parole; puis avec quelque effort il murmura brusquement:
> —C'est possible. . . .
> —Voilà une belle journée, répétai-je.
> —Oui, me répondit l'homme, on vous attend. (II, 659)

> "Lovely weather," I said to the desk clerk.
> A moment went by without him responding to me, as if he didn't know if it was worth his wasting a word; then, with some effort, he muttered abruptly, "Could be." . . .
> "Today's a fine day," I repeated.
> "Yes," the man answered, "they are waiting for you."

In this instance, the mere attempt at bringing the other closer by way of a phatic, innocuous chat fails. Beyond the fact that scathing irony colors the protagonist's tentative small talk about the nice weather on the very day he is sentenced to death, a dismissive reply is obtained at the cost of self-repetition. The state employee is also quick to send the protagonist back to the cold institutional reality that awaits him and to signal that he can no longer enjoy the status of legitimate interlocutor even before the condemnation has been pronounced. He has already become a paradoxical figure, both invisible and overexposed, undeserving of the most trivial words and acting as society's absolute center of attention. All surround and watch him, the "juges chargés de haillons ensanglantés . . . trois rangs de témoins aux faces stupides . . . deux gendarmes aux deux bouts de mon banc . . . les têtes de la foule . . . les douze jurés' (judges in bloodied rags . . . three rows of witnesses with stupid faces . . . two gendarmes at either end of my bench . . . the heads of the crowd . . . the twelve jurors; II, 659). His hybrid position, at once subaltern and "royal"—"vous serez seul dans votre loge comme le roi" (you will be alone in your own box like the king; XIII, 670)—largely compromises the possibility of standard social contact through language.

Communication is thus aborted in many ways in *Le Dernier Jour*. This breakdown goes as far as to affect the heart of human linguistic exchanges, namely the message itself. While there are moments of relative linguistic transparency in the novel-diary, as when the condemned man clinically recounts his premortem grooming (chapter XLVIII) and other dehumanizing processes, Hugo intermittently inflects or suspends the immediate intelligibility of such prose. As if corroborating the impossible elementary linguistic interactions noted earlier, the idioms of the speaker and the judicial institution at times reject literal meaning, highlight paradoxes, and point to the duplicity of the sign. The protagonist wields dark humor when he leaves the sick room, for example: "Malheureusement, je n'étais pas malade" (Unfortunately, I wasn't unwell; XV, 676). Later, he underlines the linguistic hypocrisy of the prison director, who, careful to show concern for the condemned man, emphatically calls him *monsieur* and, against all expectations, asks, on the day of the execution, whether he slept well with the most courteous turns of phrase (XIX, 679–80). Here, as in the scene where the condemned man officially finds out about the rejection of his appeal, the satire of the paternalistic and falsely gracious masquerade that drapes the death penalty is denounced through the exhibition of a language centered on form and devoid of much content. The elaborate and dignified rhetoric with which the protagonist mockingly mimics the bailiff's wooden speech underscores this critique:

> —Monsieur, m'a-t-il dit avec un sourire de courtoisie, je suis huissier près de la cour royale de Paris. J'ai l'honneur de vous apporter un message de la part de monsieur le procureur général. . . .
> —C'est monsieur le procureur général, lui ai-je répondu, qui a demandé si instamment ma tête? Bien de l'honneur pour moi qu'il m'écrive. J'espère que ma mort lui va faire grand plaisir? car il me serait dur de penser qu'il l'a sollicitée avec tant d'ardeur et qu'elle lui était indifférente. . . .
> —L'arrêt sera exécuté aujourd'hui en place de Grève. . . . Nous partons à sept heures et demie précises pour la Conciergerie. Mon cher monsieur, aurez-vous l'extrême bonté de me suivre? (XXI, 681)

"Sir," he said to me with a courteous smile, "I am a bailiff for the Royal Court of Paris. I am honored to deliver a message to you on behalf of his honor the Attorney General." . . .

"Is his honor the Attorney General," I answered, "the one who requested so insistently that I be decapitated? Honored indeed that he should write to me. I hope that my death will greatly please him? For it would pain me to think that he requested it with such ardor and that it left him indifferent." . . .

"The decision will be carried out today on the place de Grève. . . . We are leaving for the Conciergerie at seven and a half sharp. My dear Sir, will you be so very kind as to follow me?"

Civility here paradoxically reveals barbarity. The 'message' presented on behalf of the attorney general is a pure formality denying the condemned man's status as an interlocutor. As the "arrêt" then confirms, both as a thing (an irrevocable judicial decision signifying his death) and as a telling noun (evocative of termination), what is presented as a "message" masks pure violence and may indeed constitute such violence itself.

Irony, grating overtones, deceptive ornamentation: the signified is subject to caution in the condemned man's account. So is the signifier, whose gratuitous nature is underscored by the text. The protagonist twice evokes the mysterious combinations of letters that could be fatal or providential to him: "guillotine" (XXVII, 691), with its ten graphemes portrayed as repulsive and "Charles" (XL, 701), the name of the king who can grant pardon, with its seven letters. The two signs have the formidable power to make fundamental and contrasting realities exist: death and life. "Il suffirait qu'il écrivît avec cette plume les sept lettres de son nom au bas d'un morceau de papier, ou même que son carrosse rencontrât ta charrette!" (It would suffice for him to write with this quill the seven letters of his name at the bottom of a piece of paper, or even for his carriage to come across your cart!; 701). This insistence on the arbitrariness inherent in the signifier and in the occurrence of the king's name or appearance points to another arbitrary reality: that of the death penalty.

By thus staging the vanity, fraudulence, and randomness of the sign along with failing intersubjective relationships, Hugo designs a poetics of dysfunctional, if not impossible, communication. In this light, the conspicuous blank space in which the speaker's "story" is engulfed (chapter XLVII) seems as much caused by the lack of time before his execution (as indicated by a "note de l'éditeur") as it symbolizes communicational failure. Another suspension of speech adds to this silence: that of all the executed men unable to testify about the experience of beheading. The "rusted" and "fragment[ed]" written traces they are reduced to leaving on the walls of the protagonist's cell materialize their muteness. His own diary ends abruptly. After writing down the time of the day at which he is taken from his cell for the last time, "QUATRE HEURES" (FOUR O'CLOCK; XLIX, 711), he seems noiselessly driven to death. This forced quietness marks a final climax in the indistinction and unverifiability of language that several episodes had announced. It also underlines the limits of literature which the text seeks to resist actively by giving a voice to the soon-to-be-executed prisoner.

If language and its uses undergo various processes of suspension, what *Le Dernier Jour* ultimately reveals is the possibility of absolute inaudibility, be it that of the loudest cries. "Je ne distinguais plus les cris de pitié des cris de joie, les rires des plaintes, les voix du bruit; tout cela était une rumeur qui résonnait dans ma tête comme dans un écho de cuivre" (I could no longer tell the cries of pity from the cries of joy, the laughter from the wailing, the voices from the noise; all that was a rumor resounding in my head as in a brass echo; XLVIII, 710), says the condemned man on his way to the execution. *His* ultimate cry, the one likely to be uttered out of fear on the scaffold, is also obliterated from the narrative. Nevertheless, the cry as a sound does occupy a prominent place in Hugo's text, from the vociferation that opens and traverses it, to the impatient clamor of the crowd (chapters II, XXII, XXVI, XLVIII), the shouts of the convicts (XIII), and, more centrally, the condemned man's own screaming against his condemnation (II) and the ghastly visions that form in his imagination (XIII).[26] While the latter occurrences seem absorbed by the text's overarching narrative—the reduction of man to silence by lethal justice—the novel-diary preserves the properties of the *condamné*'s cry: its violence, power of interpellation, and immediate intelligibility. Indeed, it exacerbates them by forging an expressive poetry.

TOWARD EXPRESSIVE POETRY

The contraventions of conventional dramatic and novelistic representation and of human communication that Hugo stages find a periodic point of contact and contrast in a language able to realize immediate and potent expression; "expressive poetry," as Rancière defines it, in opposition to representational poetry:

> The new poetry—expressive poetry—is made of sentences and images, sentence-images that have inherent value as manifestations of poeticity, that claim a relation immediately expressive of poetry.... In opposition to the primacy of fiction, we find the primacy of language. In opposition to its distribution into genres, the anti-generic principle of the equality of all represented subjects. In opposition to the principle of decorum, the indifference of style with respect to the subject represented. In opposition to the ideal of speech in action, the model of writing.[27]

Following in Gustave Planche's footsteps, Rancière identifies *Notre-Dame de Paris* (1831) as the work that, "much more than *Hernani*, symbolizes the scandal of the new school."[28] *Le Dernier Jour* is already exemplary of this shift, in fact. Not only does it ignore the rules of Aristotelian representation, as shown earlier, but it also establishes the primacy of language and produces meaningful "sentence-images" as described by Rancière. They enable the telling of the unique realities and sensations experienced by the condemned man as his horizon narrows and his decapitation draws closer.[29]

The primacy of language constitutive of expressive poetry may emerge surreptitiously, through the combination of the literal and the figurative, via word plays, or prosodic modulations. These devices allow a number of sentences to conjure up the existential questioning and exceptional violence set off by capital punishment. Marie, the condemned man's daughter, describes the death of her father as follows: "Il est dans la terre et dans le ciel" (He is in the ground and in heaven; XLIII, 705). Imbricating the prosaic and the poetic, the material and the spiritual, her observation captures the totality of his fate and interrogations (chapter XLI). Other passages likewise bring together the metaphorical and the literal. The condemned man calls the thought of his death "l'horrible idée à se briser la tête au mur de son cachot!" (this idea so awful as to make you want to smash your head against your own cell wall!; VII, 665), using a predicate that points to the actual beheading that awaits him. Later on, he also employs a telling adverbial phrase to underline the popular excitement, and the commercialization, that surround his imminent execution: "Des marchands de sang humain criaient à tue-tête" (Dealers in human blood were shouting their heads off), he notes, about those who hire places from which to see the scaffold (XLVIII, 709). Read literally, "à tue-tête" suggests that those participating in the spectacularity of the punishment are co-responsible for the beheading.[30]

In the same chapter, as the condemned man's cart passes by them on its way to the scaffold, the people shout "Chapeaux bas! Chapeaux bas!" (Hats off! Hats off!) and ask that he be greeted like the king. "Eux les chapeaux, moi la tête!" (Off with their hats and off with my head!), he replies (709). The appropriation of the idiom "Chapeau bas!" through this added image of head severance juxtaposes a symbol of deference—not devoid of irony—and one of butchery, an idea soon highlighted by the name of a tower about which the condemned man inquires while his cart is passing by it: "Saint-Jacques-la-Boucherie." In these instances, the poetic properties of language, including the ability to move from one level of meaning to another and to multiply and inflect images, make them the guarantor and reminder of a most brutal reality.

Repeatedly in the novel, prosody and rhythm alone also convey meaning with immediacy. The dilation or interruption of a syntagm, the repetition of a term or phoneme make sense by virtue of the sounds produced:

> Hé bien! avant même que mes yeux lourds aient eu le temps de s'entr'ouvrir pour voir cette fatale pensée écrite dans l'horrible réalité qui m'entoure, sur la dalle mouillée et suante de ma cellule, dans les rayons pâles de ma lampe de nuit, dans la trame grossière de la toile de mes vêtements, sur la sombre figure du soldat de garde dont la giberne reluit à travers le cachot, il me semble que déjà une voix a murmuré à mon oreille:—Condamné à mort! (I, 658)

> Well then! before my heavy eyes even had the time to half open to see this fatal thought written into the horrible reality around me, on the wet and oozing paving stone of my cell, in the pale rays of light of my night lamp, in the coarse weft of the cloth of my garments, on the sombre face of the watchman whose cartridge pouch gleams through the dungeon, it seems to me that a voice has already whispered in my ear:—Condemned to death!

In this sentence-stanza, rugged ([r]), liquid ([l]), and whistling ([s]) sounds partake in the deliquescence that the condemned man describes in his environment. His distorted perception, which affects the surface, texture, chromaticism, grain, and light of the setting, also shows through a stretched, hypotactic construction. Hugo's prose is poetic in its musicality in addition to its images.[31] The signifier sporadically shortcuts the signified and the incommunicability that prevails in the condemned man's world. In fact, the signifier may become a self-sufficient signified—the protagonist's inner state. This use of language helps fulfill the agenda he sets out for his text: to allow his daughter and, implicitly, the reader to "sa[voir] par [lui] [s]on histoire" (know [his] story through [him]; XLVI, 706).

Hugo's expressive poetry may take on a more overt and spectacular form: that of the *argot* used by the convicts (chapters V, XVI and XXIII), for example.[32] This idiom radically counters the disembodied speech of the judicial, penitentiary, and religious authorities that encircle the condemned man.[33] It shows itself to be fully aware of the duplicity of conventional language previously mentioned: the condemned man reports that, in slang, "la langue" (both language and tongue) is called "la menteuse" (the liar). While its traits are coarse, vaudevillian, or grotesque—"c'est toute une langue entée sur la langue générale comme une espèce d'excroissance hideuse, comme une verrue" (it is a whole language grafted onto general language, like some kind of hideous excrescence, like a wart; V, 663)—and while its words sound "difformes et mal faits, chantés, cadencés, perlés" (misshapen and badly formed, sung, rhythmic, pearl-like), as in the young woman's song (XVI, 678), this *argot* allows for a newfound dynamic orality thanks to its "énergie singulière" (V, 663), phonic and metaphorical. For the first time, it ruptures the competing monologic dynamics of lethal justice and of the condemned man's stream of consciousness: the sociolect is taught by the convicts and learned by the speaker, who then rephrases it, so that the reader, the other learner of this language, can assimilate it.

A certain roughness accompanies this regained life and transitivity of language. Discordant and sordid, the convicts' dizzying lexicon about capital punishment entertains a mimetic relationship with its referent and an environment marked by social misery. It feels "sale et ... poudreux" (dirty and ... dusty) like a "liasse de haillons qu'on secouerait devant vous" (bundle of rags being shaken in front of you; V, 663). The aural and imagistic harshness of the *argot* appears to be necessary, nevertheless: it exposes the reality of state killing in contrast to the various *langues de bois* (double talk, literally "wooden speech") that conceal it.[34] It makes palpable for the reader and the condemned man the fact that the death penalty is about leaving traces of blood behind oneself (*"du raisiné sur le trimar"* [claret on the path]; 663), about an eerie intimate union with the noose (*"épouser la veuve"* [marrying the widow]), and about turning a rational mind, *"la sorbonne,"* into a severed head, *"la tronche."*

As rare as it is in the novel-diary, a positive intersubjective relationship emerges from this ruthless and dissonant renaming of the world. Although the condemned man does not feel like he belongs to the community of convicts, he receives a message of sympathy from them. "Ces hommes-là me plaignent, ils sont les seuls. Les geôliers, les guichetiers, les porte-clefs,—je ne leur en veux pas,—causent et rient, et parlent de moi, devant moi, comme d'une chose" (Those men feel sorry for me, and they're the only ones. The jailers, the counter clerks, the guards with the keys—I am not cross with them—chat and laugh, and talk about me, in front of me, as they would of a thing; 663). Overturning the linguistic concealment of lethal justice by making its violence perceptible to the mind's eye and ear, *l'argot* thus sometimes displays the capacity to perceive and, for a moment, preserve the condemned man's human status.

A second kind of manifest poetic expressiveness complements the imagistic and aural freedom of *l'argot*. It is born from the numerous hallucinations that pervade the novel-diary. Within the metaphor of mental incarceration that frames *Le Dernier Jour* and the condemned man's tentatively lucid account of his wait for and obsession with his execution, one repeatedly finds fantastic "sentence-images" through which these visions come into being.[35] They include the "pensée infernale" (infernal thought) of the death sentence, "comme un spectre de plomb à mes côtés, seule et jalouse ... dans mes rêves sous la forme d'un couteau" (like a specter of lead next to me, alone and jealous ... in my dreams in the shape of a knife; I, 658); the "fantasmagorie des juges, des témoins, des avocats, des procureurs du roi" (phantasmagoria of the judges, witnesses, lawyers, king's prosecutors) in addition to the "deux masses de peuple murées de soldats" (two masses of people walled in by soldiers) and their "faces béantes et penchées" (gaping and tilted faces) that seem moved by threads converging toward the condemned man (II, 658, 659); the mental picture of a severed head spinning around in a limbo-like landscape after the execution (chapter XLI); and the ghastly dream of a witch-like incarnation of death, "petite vieille, les mains pendantes, les yeux fermés ... sans voix, sans mouvement, sans regard" (little old lady, with lolling hands, her eyes closed ... voiceless, motionless, with no gaze; XLII, 703). These nightmarish apparitions depend on a performative power of language that conjures them up, makes them as real to the reader's mind as they are to the speaker's, and dissolves them.

A dramatic phantasmagoria illustrates both this process and its figuration. It turns the wall of the protagonist's cell into a palimpsest. After he has symbolically torn off the spider's web that covers their names, anonymous and well-known beheaded criminals ("Jacques," "Papavoine," "Bories," and the rhyming "DAUTUN," "POULAIN," "MARTIN," "CASTAING") come to converse in a free cacophony that culminates in an apocalyptic vision: the severed bodies of these murderers are brought back to life:[36]

> Il m'a semblé tout à coup que ces noms fatals étaient écrits avec du feu sur le mur noir; un tintement de plus en plus précipité a éclaté dans mes oreilles; une lueur rousse a rempli mes yeux; et puis il m'a paru que ce cachot était plein d'hommes, d'hommes étranges qui portaient leur tête dans leur main gauche, et la portaient par la bouche, parce qu'il n'y avait pas de chevelure. Tous me montraient le poing, excepté le parricide.
>
> J'ai fermé les yeux avec horreur, alors j'ai tout vu plus distinctement. (XII, 669)

> It seemed to me all of a sudden that these fatal names were written with fire on the black wall; an ever-hurried chiming burst out in my ears; a reddish glow filled up my eyes; and then it became apparent to me that this dungeon was full of men, strange men who carried their heads in their left hands, and carried them by the mouth, because there was no hair. All of them showed me their fists, except for the parricide.
>
> I closed my eyes with horror, then saw everything more distinctly.

The views of the imagination become visible here only through a language that cultivates spectacularity, hyperbolism, and supernaturalism. As though through a self-reflexive movement, the names of fire on the prison cell point to the ability of a violent distortion of imagery to advance the reader's understanding of the condemned men's distress and fate.

If these "sentence-images" (Rancière) emerging from an internal perspective may give a vivacious life to the impalpable, they may, conversely, erase reality. Following the pronouncement of his sentence, the *condamné* envisions the world with new eyes. By way of a metaphor, his surroundings undergo a sudden metamorphosis. While a warm chromaticism and luminosity initially characterize the scene, this landscape is abruptly obscured once the clerk of the court utters the death sentence. "Ces larges fenêtres lumineuses, ce beau soleil, ce ciel pur, cette jolie fleur, *tout cela était blanc et pâle, de la couleur d'un linceul*" (These large, luminous windows, this beautiful sun, this pure sky, this pretty flower, *all of that was white and pale, the color of a shroud*; II, 661; my emphasis). Reality is anaesthetized, the world discolored and made uniform in a hallucinatory vision. Meschonnic has also noted such radical transformations as men ceasing to be fully animate and the jail ceasing to be inanimate to become an all-encompassing, vigorous, smothering hybrid in the novel.[37]

These many metamorphoses largely rely on metaphors that present the unimaginable as real—through the strong, stative verb "to be" and the presentative turn of phrase "c'est" (this/it is), in particular: "Ces guichetiers, c'est de la prison en chair et en os. La prison est une espèce d'être horrible, complet, indivisible, moitié maison, moitié homme. Je suis sa proie, elle me couve, elle m'enlace de tous ses replis" (These counter clerks, 'tis prison made flesh and blood. The prison building is a sort of horrible being, complete, indivisible, half-house, half-man. I am its prey, it envelops me, it wraps its folds around me; XX, 680). As the text progresses, the condemned man's prose crafts, revisits, or annihilates the same object through figuration, be it the yellow hue of light, the jail, or the thought of death. Reality comes to be annexed or subverted by poetic language just as it is appropriated by his anguished subjectivity. Through this expressive poetry, language no longer seems in charge of conveying his perception in the diary; rather, it becomes live perception itself.

Directly accessing the intimate obsession with, and fear of, a programmed death through language: such is Hugo's tour de force in *Le Dernier Jour d'un condamné*. The novel serves the abolitionist cause through a poetic revolution that infiltrates and makes permanent the condemned man's absolute distress in the face of execution. Literary creation, as if pushed by the gravity of its subject matter, goes against the grain of established codes to create a new voice that sounds eminently real in the alternately shocked and lucid perception of its environment and its desperate attempts to cling to life. Hugo creates a strange, indefectible solidarity between his desperate condemned man and the reader through the cultivation of a representational disorder that explodes classical representation and the rules of fiction. *Le Dernier Jour* refuses, as Flaubert noted, "to offer reflections ... on the death penalty."[38] Indeed, its power stems from the way its unique narrative and dramatic tactics instead force the reader into the inescapable grip of capital punishment so that voyeurism morphs into our living the sentence ourselves. The novel thereby turns around the popular spectacle of the execution, during which the condemned man is typically keenly watched from the outside. The understanding, or rather the shared experience of his ordeal is doubled by another rupture staged in the novel-diary: verbal communication and intersubjectivity are shown to fail in numerous ways once death has been decreed. Hugo sporadically overturns this incommunicability: a regime of expression through which the fixed idea of death, the execution, and the attempts at escaping them are conjured up with immediacy and violence through imagistic and phonic plays. It is also through this episodic liberation of language that *Le Dernier Jour* satisfies the demand implicit in the challenge laid down for the aspiring poet and cited in the introduction to this chapter: to earn his title as poet, Hugo finds a form to both penetrate and formulate the innermost thoughts of a dead man walking, at the border of humanity.

CHAPTER 2

Pain and Punishment

The Guillotine's Torture

> It is easy enough to have such an unfailing machine built; decapitation will be completed in an instant according to the spirit and intention of the new law.... Such a device, if it were necessary, would cause no sensation and would be scarcely noticed.
>
> —Antoine Louis, permanent secretary of the Académie royale de chirurgie, "Avis motivé sur le mode de la décollation," March 14, 1792

Hugo's poetic revolution, which shatters the representation of the capital spectacle, goes hand in hand with a reconsideration of the progressive aspirations that underlay France's penal evolution after the Revolution. At first sight, *Le Dernier Jour d'un condamné* echoes the penal mutations that Michel Foucault summarizes in "Le Corps des condamnés" (The Body of the Condemned), the first section of *Surveiller et punir: Naissance de la prison* (Discipline and Punish: The Birth of the Prison). Foucault argues that, from the second half of the eighteenth century onward, the soul replaced the body as the target of punishment in France:

> It was an important moment. The old partners of the spectacle of punishment, the body and the blood, gave way. A new character came on the scene, masked. It was the end of a certain kind of tragedy; comedy began, with shadow play, faceless voices, impalpable entities. The apparatus of punitive justice must now bite into this bodiless reality.[1]

46 | New Abolitionist Poetics

Hugo's fiction may seem to reflect this evolution in two respects, examined earlier. First, its plot visibly centers on the condemned man's mind. Second, it deprives the reader of the spectacle of the execution: while the narrative foregrounds the death sentence, the protagonist's beheading constitutes a blind spot. Yet the temporal and psychological window Hugo carves out, as well as his figuration of the condemned man's physical and political trajectory, in fact question the gradual disincarnation and detheatricalization of judicial penalties that Foucault identifies with profoundly incisive effect.

UNEXPECTED ERASURES: BODY, MONSTROSITY, HIERARCHY

Few main characters in literature remain as mysterious as Victor Hugo's condemned man. His "faceless[ness]" and "impalpab[ility]," to take up Foucault's terms, are literal. As noted in chapter 1, his portrayal might better be described as a (counter)sketch, insofar as the author skillfully avoids portraying his criminal exhaustively, providing just enough information to contradict an expected lower-class stereotype. However, this erasure has little to do with the trend toward penal disembodiment mentioned by Foucault—and by Hugo himself in his preface of 1832 about the increasing discretion of executions. Instead, the writer subverts this trend.[2] His protagonist's minimal visibility does not serve to give the impression that punishment has been humanized and that its barbarity has disappeared after the suppression of lengthy and vicious penal spectacles. Rather, it highlights his captivity and frailness. The first thing we learn about the condemned man's body is that it is in chains in a cell. The evocations of his physiognomy that follow are limited to his joints (wrists, neck, elbows, armpits, knees) and bodily extremities (hands, foot, chin, and ears; chapters XII, XLVIII), which emphasize the natural boundaries of his physical being, in contrast to their imminent transformation through the slash of the guillotine. By highlighting these articulations and contours, Hugo exposes an anatomy that is generic, helpless, and easily objectified. It suspends the sense of an individual humanity. Hugo's paintings and drawings representing executed bodies in the 1850s and 1860s would take up this very technique (see Figures 2 to 4).

Erasure occurs at the level of moral characterization as well. Hugo invalidates not just the stereotype of the proletarian criminal but also that of the criminal-as-moral-monster that legitimized capital punishment in the eyes of its supporters. As Foucault noted in his *Histoire de*

Figure 2. Victor Hugo. "*Ecce lex*" (*Le Pendu*). 1854. Maison de Victor Hugo, Paris / Guernesey.

la sexualité, "Capital punishment could not be maintained except by invoking less the enormity of the crime itself than the monstrosity of the criminal, his incorrigibility, and the safeguard of society. One had the right to kill those who represent a biological danger to others."[3] While the novel reveals that the condemned man caused blood to be shed before his condemnation (chapter XI), it does not specify whether this led to the victim's death and suggests that the crime for which he is to be beheaded is not due to any perverse essence: "Si on lit un jour mon histoire, après tant d'années d'innocence et de bonheur, on ne voudra pas croire à cette année exécrable, qui s'ouvre par un crime et se clôt par un supplice; elle aura l'air dépareillé" (If people read my story some day, they won't believe that this atrocious year, which begins with a crime

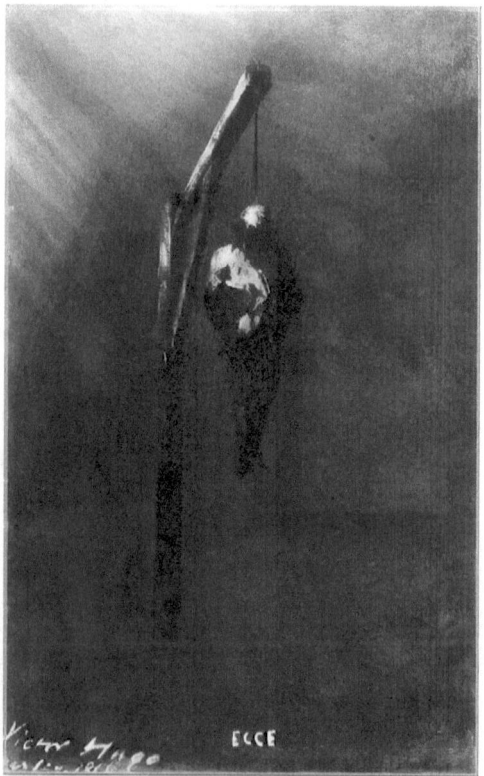

Figure 3. Victor Hugo. *Ecce*. 1854. Maison de Victor Hugo, Paris / Guernesey.

and ends with agony, followed so many years of innocence and happiness; it will seem out of place; XXXIV, 698). The protagonist, whose exact crime remains the text's fundamental ellipsis, can therefore hardly be considered monstrous.⁴

Le Dernier Jour d'un condamné in fact displaces monstrosity. It finds its embodiment, first, in the guillotine, an awe-inspiring and personified, murderous figure. "Quand j'ai vu au-dessus des têtes ces deux bras rouges, avec leur triangle noir au bout, dressés entre deux lanternes du quai, le cœur m'a failli" (My heart skipped a beat when I saw, above the heads, these two red arms with their black triangle at the end, standing between the two lanterns on the quay; XLVIII, 707); second, in a social body that is homogenized by its direct or indirect endorsement of the death penalty. Through their resolution, resignation, indifference, or, conversely, their excitement, as well as through the satirical portrayals

Pain and Punishment | 49

Figure 4. Victor Hugo. *Gibet de prison*. Ca. 1867–69. Maison Vacquerie–Musée Victor Hugo, Villequier—Dept. 76.

to which they are often subject, the representatives of the judicial and legal system, the simple state employees, the members of the clergy, the convicts, and a restless "populace" (709) appear to aggregate around this legal practice as one gargantuan character. Nonetheless, Hugo does single out the people as the most frighteningly buoyant—and the largest—incarnation of this giant execution-condoning social body. "Tout ce peuple rira, battra des mains, applaudira" (The whole crowd will laugh, clap their hands, applaud; 706), the speaker bitterly remarks in chapter XLV. And later: "l'horrible peuple qui aboie, et m'attend, et rit" (the horrible throng barking and awaiting me, and laughing; XLVIII, 707).

The process of penal effacement that Hugo distorts by having erasure affect the condemned man's physical and moral portrayal is extended to his individuality. The protagonist is but *"un* condamné."

His name never appears in the diary, and, as noted previously, the chapter that should relate his story (XLVII) is left blank. The journal also comes to an end without any signature. These multiple lacunae render impossible the new investigative and analytical processes that Foucault identifies as participating in "the knowledge of the criminal, one's estimation of him, what is known about the relations between him, his past and his crime, and what might be expected of him in the future"; these processes, "behind the pretext of explaining an action, are ways of defining an individual."[5] Hugo precludes a multifaceted examination based not only on this knowledge of the criminal's personality and personal history, but also on his physiognomy and cranial structure, at a time when the ideas of Johann Kaspar Lavater and phrenologist Franz Joseph Gall were popular.[6] He replaces this scientific and institutional passion for qualification—a passion that also affects the curious reader—with an aesthetics of indefiniteness that deliberately opposes it, as the preface of 1832 underlines: "Et pour que le plaidoyer soit aussi vaste que la cause, il a dû, et c'est pour cela que *Le Dernier Jour d'un condamné* est ainsi fait, élaguer de toutes parts de son sujet le contingent, l'accident, le particulier, le spécial, le relatif, le modifiable, l'épisode, l'anecdote, l'événement, le nom propre, et se borner (si c'est là se borner) à plaider la cause d'un condamné quelconque, exécuté un jour quelconque, pour un crime quelconque" (And to make the defense speech as vast as the cause, he had to trim—and this is the reason why *Le Dernier Jour d'un condamné* is the way it is—the contingent, the accidental, the particular, the special, the relative, the modifiable, the episodic, the anecdotal, the event, the proper name throughout and to limit himself [if indeed it be a limitation] to defending a random condemned man, executed on a random day, for a random crime; *OCH* 4:480).

Such blurring of identity, which simultaneously bars the protagonist's demonization and resists a criminologico-penal diagnosis, is pushed further by the conflation of the figure of the condemned man with that of the king.[7] Bicêtre has "un air de château de roi" (something of a royal castle about it; IV, 662); when the convicts are chained in the prison, the condemned man sits overlooking the spectacle, "seul dans [sa] loge comme le roi" (alone in [his] own private box, like the king; XIII, 670), and almost enjoys a monopoly on speech; while expecting the ultimate moment of decapitation and facing the clamoring crowd, he also remarks, "Si fort qu'on aime un roi, ce serait moins de fête" (Much as a king might be loved, there could not be more of a greeting for him;

XLVIII, 708). But the longest and most explicit parallel is drawn when the condemned man asserts:

> Il est singulier que je pense sans cesse au roi. J'ai beau faire, beau secouer la tête, j'ai une voix dans l'oreille qui me dit toujours:
> —Il y a dans cette même ville, à cette même heure, et pas bien loin d'ici, dans un autre palais, un homme qui a aussi des gardes à toutes ses portes, un homme unique comme toi dans le peuple, avec cette différence qu'il est aussi haut que tu es bas. (XL, 700)

> Remarkably, I can't stop thinking about the king. However much I try and shake my head, a voice in my ear keeps telling me: "In this very city, at this very hour, and not very far from here, in another palace, there is a man, who also has guards at all of his doors, a man as exceptional in society as you, the only difference being that he is as high above as you are down low."

Here, the king is the inverted figure of the condemned man; in all the other instances, he is a comparable one. This repeated superimposition of the two figures, which covertly recalls the Revolutionary regicide, further invalidates the condemned man's expected monstrosity and sheds light on the possible subjection of every member of society to the guillotine. In other words, the king–condemned man analogy stresses the unconditional power of the modern judicial institution to reduce any life, regardless of its sociopolitical status, to death.

In *Homo Sacer: Sovereign Power and Bare Life* (1995), Giorgio Agamben has theorized the resemblance between the sovereign and a particular lawbreaker condemned to death, namely the *homo sacer*, an outcast characterized by "the unpunishability of his killing and the ban on his sacrifice" in Ancient Rome.[8] The Italian philosopher argues that both are at once inside and outside of the law: the rule "suspend[s] itself" for the sovereign, and thereby produces an exception that still exists in relation the rule; as for the sacred man, his inclusion in the juridical order takes the form of exclusion (he may be killed by anyone in almost any way).[9] The *homo sacer* is comparable to Hugo's condemned man in that, from the perspective of human experience, both await certain death. From a legal standpoint, both are also defined by their capacity to be killed in a way that is not considered homicidal after the pronouncement of their sentence—even if, contrary to the sacred man, the condemned man cannot be eliminated by anyone in almost any way but must be decapitated by the executioner following a precise protocol.[10]

The *homo sacer* and the condemned man also fall prey to the same paradox of a legal exclusion from within, for the social and legal contract that binds the modern man to society—a contract to which he subscribes—is ruptured by the application of the lethal law: once he has been sentenced to death, the protection of his life is short-lived. He becomes analogous to an enemy in time of war, as Rousseau puts it in *Du contrat social* so as to be able to legitimize his defense of the death penalty.[11] The philosopher must transform the citizen into a sort of *hostis humani generis* to condone lethal justice. Although he was an admiring reader of Rousseau, Beccaria did not support this view and underlined the high improbability that a man be willing to surrender his life as one of the fragments of liberty he must cede to benefit from protection and a number of rights:

> By what right can men presume to slaughter their fellows? Certainly not that right which is the foundation of sovereignty and the laws. For these are nothing but the sum of the smallest portions of each man's own freedom; they represent the general will which is the aggregate of the individual wills. Who has ever willingly given up to others the authority to kill him? How on earth can the minimum sacrifice of each individual's freedom involve handing over the greatest of all goods, life itself?[12]

Similarly, participants in the 1791 debate on capital punishment at the Assemblée constituante, such as Pétion, remarked that what drives men to gather together is a search for protection at odds with anyone's consent to punishment by death.[13]

Le Dernier Jour makes visible a double change, of both state and status, that accompanies the condemned man's exclusion from within and his redefinition by the law as a being whose prominent property is his "capacity to be killed" (Agamben) following a specific procedure after he has been sentenced—a sentencing that Hugo places at the very beginning of his work to better shed light on its causal relationship to these two changes. As far as the protagonist's change of state is concerned, a revealing passage reveals the numbness and feeling of radical alienation that affect him, early on, "Une révolution venait de se faire en moi. Jusqu'à l'arrêt de mort, je m'étais senti respirer, palpiter, vivre dans le même milieu que les autres hommes; maintenant, je distinguais clairement comme une clôture entre le monde et moi" (A revolution had just occurred within me. Before my death sentence, I could feel myself breathing, my heart throbbing, and my whole life in the same environment as other men; now, I clearly saw a barrier between the world and me; II, 661). Later, when the condemned man's young daughter visits him in his cell and fails to recognize him, she exclaims, after being asked about her father, "Ah! vous ne savez donc pas? il est mort" (Why, so you don't know? He is dead; XLIII, 705).[14] Soon, the condemned man abandons all hope with these words: "La dernière fibre de mon cœur est brisée. Je suis bon pour ce qu'ils vont faire" (The last piece of my heart is broken. I am ready for what they are going to do; 706). Repeatedly, the protagonist's capital condemnation is represented as triggering forms of *premature* death before the guillotine's activation.

This physical and moral decline sparked by the application of the death sentence runs parallel to a change of status. While the judicial death sentence retains the sociopolitical status of the *condamné* in order to punish him legally, this status seems simultaneously abrogated, as we just saw with Rousseau. Here, Hugo does converge with Foucault in shedding light on "an economy of suspended rights."[15] His novel shows how, after the pronouncement of the sentence, the condemned man becomes the object of rituals and events that the legal and judicial powers initiate or monitor and through which they deprive him of agency. Under their pressure, he metamorphoses into a helpless, empty subject. The novel highlights the cruel contradiction between his new, void status and the extreme care with which he is kept alive as a vacant subject until, or rather *for*, the moment of decapitation. His diary relates the meticulous organization-ritualization that precedes the execution: the hopeless visits paid, his shortened interview with the priest, his final "toilette" consisting of a haircut, the trimming of his shirt, the binding of his hands and feet so that his movements are limited when he is led to the scaffold, his final ride in the condemned man's cart escorted by a "cortège" (XLVIII, 709).

The condemned man has no say in the mechanics of execution. He constitutes a mere, and increasingly faint, physical presence. He is shown to morph into a "bare life," in the words of Walter Benjamin appropriated by Agamben, that is to say a being stripped of all its attributes other than biological, a *zoē*.[16] Many passages indicate that the death-bound prisoner loses his sociopolitical existence. As early as chapter III, he notes that there is not much that the executioner can take away from him, for he has already been reduced to a caged creature who is hardly spoken to (662). "Les geôliers, les guichetiers, les porte-clefs,—je ne leur en veux pas,—causent et rient, et parlent de moi, devant moi, comme d'une chose" (The jailers, the warders, the key keepers—I don't hold a grudge against them—chat and laugh and talk about me, in front of me, as they would do if I were a thing; V, 663). Reification even looms behind this extreme metamorphosis into bare life: "C'était une machine sur une machine" (It was adding a machine to a machine; II, 659), says the condemned man about the handcuffs that are placed on him, with a tautology suggesting that the atomization of his being infects language, which also finds itself impoverished. He also remarks, on his way to the Conciergerie, "J'étais devenu machine comme la voiture" (I had become as mechanical as the vehicle; XXII, 683). And when an architect hired to modernize the jail measures his cell, his physical presence is compared to that of a mineral: "Moi, j'étais là, comme une des pierres qu'il mesurait" (As for me, I stood there, like one of the stones he had been measuring; XXXI, 695).

By effacing the criminal's anticipated monstrosity, his exact physical identity, the hierarchy at the bottom of which this outcast usually stands, and his human integrity, Hugo counters several stereotypes and readerly expectations. These strategic erasures go hand in hand with the scrutiny of the condemned man's sociopolitical demotion and the exposure of his premature and polymorphous annihilation. Together, these devices enforce a significant role reversal: he no longer appears to be a culprit as much as the victim of a crushing lethal justice.

NEW SPECTACLES

Let us return to the diagnosis established in *Surveiller et punir*: from the second half of the eighteenth century onward, Foucault traces the emergence of a penal "comedy," with "impalpable entities," in lieu of "a certain kind of tragedy" centered on "the body and the blood." Hugo proposes an alternative to these two genres. As chapter 1 demonstrated, *Le Dernier Jour* does away with the classical representation that characterized tragedy and largely focuses on the protagonist's mental ordeal—rather than corporeal punishment. But this does not result in the comedic "shadow play" Foucault describes. Instead, Hugo's innovations identified earlier result in a new tragedy: one that is catharsis-free.[17] The readers who feel pity and fear in the face of the condemned man's torment and fate, or the excited witnesses to whom the narrative refers for that matter, cannot have access to any Aristotelian purgation. Catharsis is blocked both by the exclusion of the climactic act of violence—the execution—from the plot, and perhaps more importantly by the fact that, instead of being aware of the nonreality of what is before their eyes, the reader is under the impression that mimesis has been replaced by actual life. The novel eradicates the possibility of leaving behind the condemned man's experience and the pleasure and liberation that ensue. This device is precisely what some contemporaries described, and reproved:

> I do not know whether reading this book had made me tired or lightheaded; but while leaving the hero on the place de Grève, when this living being is already climbing up the scaffold, when this human thought is about to end, under the blade that falls, I was hardly able to judge or remember anything. This narrative of the moral torture that kills the condemned man gradually and prematurely; this strange language of pain, made exclusively of dark and funereal words, was buzzing in my ears like a warning bell; this story of a poor wretch with only twenty-four hours to live, and whose every thought is a thought of death, all this had somehow left me broken and exhausted; and, when I closed the book, I was like a man who has been spinning around and who could no longer feel the earth beneath his feet.[18]

Assailed and exhausted, the reader is subjected to what Jules Janin, who parodied *Le Dernier Jour* with *L'Âne mort et la femme guillotinée* (The Dead Donkey and the Guillotined Woman; 1829), named "a three-hundred-page agony."[19] Interestingly, *Le Dernier Jour* employs the same substantive as Janin—"une agonie de six semaines" (a six-week agony; XXXIX, 700)—but in order to qualify the modern death penalty. While the new, early nineteenth-century, punitive "tragedy" relied on inflicting pain in a much less visible and lengthy way, Hugo's catharsis-free tragedy reverses this objective and seeks to have the character's suffering contaminate the reader.

The novel revisits the spectacle of punishment in parallel to this implosion of catharsis. It emphasizes the crowd's taste for bloody spectacles decades after the Reign of Terror. Hugo's earlier narrative *Han d'Islande* had already warned readers that "a strange feeling within the human heart urges men to behold the spectacle of torture ... to seize the thought of destruction on the distorted features of the man who is going to die" (*OCH* 2:395). *Le Dernier Jour* shows that, while the swift guillotine has replaced extended *supplices*, man's thirst for the display of a fellow human being's final despondency and death is intact. It stresses the persistence of a penal ritual of humiliation rather than any progressive evolution:

> Vis-à-vis ... il y a des cabarets, dont les entresols étaient pleins de spectateurs heureux de leurs belles places. Surtout les femmes. La journée doit être bonne pour les cabaretiers.
> On louait des tables, des chaises, des échafaudages, des charrettes. Tout pliait de spectateurs. Des marchands de sang humain criaient à tue-tête:
> —Qui veut des places? (XLVIII, 709)

> Opposite ... there are cabarets whose mezzanines were packed with spectators delighted to have such a good view. Especially women. Today must be a good day for innkeepers.
> People were renting out tables, chairs, scaffolding, carts. The whole place was brimming with spectators. Dealers in human blood were shouting their heads off: "Who wants a seat?"

Moral regression is at work here, for the audience's impatience is now accompanied by the cynical commercial interests generated by the show. All are condemned by seething sarcasm, and, outside of the fictional space, we the readers, the mirror image of this public, also fall prey to the protagonist's caustic examination of man's malevolent curiosity. The crowd craves the severance of his fully fledged head, and the omission of the moment of the decollation can only amplify the sense of unlawfulness and folly that saturates this depiction of "spectateurs avides et cruels" (XLVIII, 710).

Throughout, the novel problematizes this ocular voracity. Numerous scenes bar visibility or force the gaze to be oblique. They symbolically invalidate both man's basest interest taken in the degradation of others and the punishment itself, while at the same time highlighting how difficult it is to grasp another man's suffering. Hugo prevents the condemned man himself from seeing fully, from within his cell, the chaining of convicts in the prison's courtyard. While his observation tower enables him to overlook the scene, he is trapped behind "une fenêtre grillée" (a barred window) like the "prisonniers, spectateurs de la cérémonie," whose "visages maigres et blêmes" (gaunt and pale faces) are "encadrés dans les entre-croisements des barreaux de fer" (framed within the crisscrossed iron bars; XIII, 670). And he eventually becomes the object of the spectacle, as they suddenly see him watching and turn toward his window. In other words, the spectators themselves become the spectacle at key junctures of *Le Dernier Jour*. Penal spectacularity thereby finds itself repeatedly subverted, and at times even turned on its head, so to speak.

A double visibility, that of the condemned man's mind and that of popular reaction, counters the "instant of invisibility" with which the guillotine was supposed to be synonymous.[20] Yet Hugo's strategy is not devoid of ambiguity: while it proves necessary to expose the invisible (the condemned man's psychic agony), it also relies on the very sensationalist penchant that the narrative and its preface identify in the collective behavior elicited by executions. As the writer unveils the capital trial and the premortem carceral experience, scrutinizing precisely what *Han d'Islande* calls "the thought of destruction on the distorted features of the man who is going to die," he exploits our voyeurism even as he turns it into a painful and critical experience.

Although the new spectacle—and intrusion—Hugo proposes center on a man's anguish, on his reduction to bare life, and on the eager observers of punishment, it does not altogether do away with the old penal spectacle, namely the destruction of the condemned body. In the novel, this body returns through the profound destabilization of the traditional Christian and Cartesian divides between body and soul, and body and mind. The psyche and the body are presented as inseparable after the pronouncement of the sentence. "Ne sont-ce pas les mêmes convulsions, que le sang s'épuise goutte à goutte, ou que l'intelligence s'éteigne pensée à pensée?" (Whether blood runs out drop by drop, or intelligence dies out thought by thought, are they not the same spasms?; XXXIX, 700), the protagonist asks.[21] Corporeality characterizes the soul and mind. The condemned man imagines that, following his decapitation, he might find himself "sur quelque surface plane et humide, rampant dans l'obscurité et tournant sur [lui]-même comme une tête qui roule" (on some flat and humid surface, crawling in the darkness and turning round and round like a head as it rolls; XLI, 701). The text hypothesizes a postmortem visual and tactile sensibility that allows for a precise perception of space—its shape, temperature, and luminosity. The simile of the spinning head, which verges on the grotesque, furthers the "capital hypertrophy" and the materiality that pervade *Le Dernier Jour*.

Indeed, the protagonist's discourse often favors the head over the soul and tends to transform the conventional Christian body/soul dyad into an anatomical body/head dyad—even if Christianity underlies Hugo's abolitionism.[22] "Que gardent-ils de leur corps incomplet et mutilé? Que choisissent-ils? Est-ce la tête ou le tronc qui est spectre?" (What do they keep of their incomplete and mutilated body? What do they choose? Does the head or the body turn into a specter?; XLI, 702). The condemned man's reflections on the spirit as surviving the body are highly incredulous and his ensuing encounter with a priest whom he summons to elucidate his metaphysical interrogations is another remarkable ellipsis in the narrative (chapters XLI–XLII).[23] "Hélas! qu'est-ce que la mort fait avec notre âme? quelle nature lui laisse-t-elle? qu'a-t-elle à lui prendre ou à lui donner? où la met-elle? lui prête-elle quelquefois des yeux de chair pour regarder sur la terre et pleurer?" (Alas! What does death do with our souls? What form does it leave them? What does it have to take from them or leave them? Where does it put them? Does it ever offer them eyes of flesh so they can look down on earth and weep?; XLI, 702). Here again, the condemned man refers to the flesh when evoking the soul. He imagines it as endowed with body parts and as functioning organically. Over and over, the novel represents a body of the mind. The very phrase that defines the narrative, "autopsie intellectuelle," encapsulates this materialism.

Such materialism, questioning of an immaterial soul, and emphasis on sensation have far-reaching critical implications. First, they refute those who support capital punishment because of religious beliefs that focus on man's afterlife: by intimating that human beings know little about life postmortem, Hugo's protagonist counters the reassuring retentionist argument according to which divine justice will correct an imperfect human justice—one that may execute innocent individuals, for instance.[24] Second, the novel's uninterrupted stress on embodied experience directly contradicts the theory of painlessness that legitimated the adoption of the guillotine from 1791 onward.[25] Antoine Louis famously declared, "It is easy enough to have such an unfailing machine built; decapitation will be completed in an instant according to the spirit and intention of the new law. Such a device, if it were necessary, would cause *no sensation* and would be scarcely noticed."²⁶ Two years earlier, on December 1, 1789, Dr. Joseph Ignace Guillotin had evoked the machine's quasi-magical quality: "Gentlemen, with my machine, I can slash off your head in the blink of an eye and you will not suffer.... The device strikes like thunder, the head flies off, blood spurts out, the man is no more!"²⁷ *Le Dernier Jour* begs to differ, and does so cumulatively, foregrounding sensations to relate the capital experience. "Il y a à peine deux pages sur ce texte de la peine de mort [*sic*]. Tout le reste, ce sont des sensations" (Barely two pages of the text are on the death penalty. The rest is all about sensations; "Une comédie à propos d'une tragédie," 650), quips Hugo as he parodies the critics of his novel.²⁸ His condemned man himself explicitly questions the progressive claims of modern capital punishment: "On ne souffre pas, en sont-ils sûrs? Qui le leur a dit? Conte-t-on que jamais une tête coupée se soit dressée sanglante au bord du panier, et qu'elle ait crié au peuple: Cela ne fait pas de mal!" (How can they be sure that it's painless? Who told them? Have you ever heard of a severed head standing on the rim of the basket and shouting to the people: It doesn't hurt!; XXXIX, 700).

A symbolic manipulation of language foregrounding the act of cutting shows painlessness and the absence of sensation to be fictional. This is the other way in which the novel reminds the reader of the physicality of capital punishment. The book as a whole is broken up into a considerable number of compact chapters given its limited length. These forty-nine sections themselves are marked by paragraph fragmentation, the use of strong punctuation markers, aposiopeses (XXXIX, 700; XLVIII, 707; XLIX, 711), and the alternation of specialized discourses—penal and *argotique*, for example—that all produce rhythmic or semantic ruptures.²⁹ Beyond this structural level, severance appears both conspicuously, in the form of a vast lexical field throughout the diary, and more covertly: Hugo often relies on synecdoche, a device that requires incision, to refer to the guillotine, the condemned man, and the crowd;³⁰ he also stages slashing at the lexical level, as when the condemned man declares to the priest, "Je ne suis pas préparé, mais je suis prêt" (I am not prepared, but I am ready; XXI, 680). The syntactic parallelism contained in this statement, as well as the quasi-homophony between the initial syllable of the first epithet and the second epithet, make "paré" stand out in the opening negative clause ("je ne suis pas pré/paré, mais je suis prêt"). With this adjective born out of truncation, another sentence reads, between the lines: "[Je ne suis pas] paré" (I am devoid of protection).

Figure 5. Victor Hugo. *Justitia*. 1857. Maison de Victor Hugo, Paris / Guernesey.

This linguistic emphasis on cutting is particularly visible in the novel's references to the sentence and decapitation. The protagonist's young daughter struggles to decipher the "–A, R, ar R, E, T, rêt" (XLIII, 705) that officializes his sentencing, for instance. And in the following string of self-interrogations about the protagonist's antemortem writing project, form and content merge as plosive consonants, multiple monosyllables, and a remarkable polyptoton ("coupe"/"coupée") symbolically highlight the act of beheading: "Pourquoi? à quoi bon? qu'importe? Quand ma tête aura été coupée, qu'est-ce que cela me fait qu'on en coupe d'autres?" (So what? Why bother? What for? What's the use? When my head has been cut off, what difference does it make to me if they cut off others?; VII, 665). I noted earlier that the protagonist cuts up the word "guillotine" by merely evoking its ten letters. Strikingly, he comments, "Chaque syllabe est comme une pièce de la machine. J'en construis et j'en démolis sans cesse dans mon esprit la monstrueuse charpente" (Each syllable is like a part of the machine. I keep building and dismantling its monstrous frame in my mind; XXVII, 691).[31] Language witnesses the process of dismemberment, in sum. In this instance, it concerns the machine, but in all the other cases, language operates as an anatomical substitute that participates in a veritable demonstrative tactic. Not unlike some of Hugo's drawings, it showcases the physical violence of the death penalty that late eighteenth- and early nineteenth-century reforms sought to mitigate through both technique and representation (Figure 5).[32]

TORTURED AND BARE LIFE

Foucault's inaugural lecture at the Collège de France, *L'Ordre du discours* (1970), underlines society's "anxiety about what discourse is in its material reality as a thing pronounced or written; anxiety about this transitory existence which admittedly is destined to be effaced, but according to a time-scale which isn't ours."[33] Using precisely this "ponderous, formidable materiality" of discourse, Hugo shortcuts what Foucault identifies as procedures designed to limit possible discursive eruptions and to implement exclusion. Although the philosopher's lecture calls for the questioning of the "sovereignty of the signifier," Hugo engages with the latter to resist at least two negating procedures: that which excludes the condemned man from society and that which denies the physical painfulness of modern capital punishment.[34] The language deployed in *Le Dernier Jour* is endowed with efficient performativity—a quality that Foucault does not mention in his reflections, either in *L'Ordre du discours* or in his brief commentary on Hugo's novel in *Surveiller et punir*. It incarnates the condemned man's future severed silhouette and bars its forgetting or erasure by making it perennial on paper. An *en-abyme* analogue to the wall of the prison cell, this language exhibits "inscriptions mutilées ... phrases démembrées ... mots tronqués, corps sans tête comme ceux qui les ont écrits" (mutilated inscriptions ... dismembered sentences ... truncated words, headless bodies like those who wrote them; XI, 667).

The critique built into Hugo's fragmentation of the signifier does not only pertain to the physical pain that persists in the modern implementation of the death penalty. The 1791 *Code pénal* that led to the adoption of the guillotine stipulated that capital punishment was to correspond to "the simple deprivation of life, without the possibility that the condemned ever be subjected to any torture."[35] Hugo's torsion of language may be so extreme as to verge on verbal destruction: the diary occasionally regresses into a prelanguage made of short exclamations, monosyllabic calls, "rugissement[s] étouffé[s]" (muffled howls; XLVIII, 708). "Les mots manquent aux émotions" (Words fail to capture these feelings; 710), the condemned man admits as he takes in every detail of his final ride to the Hôtel de ville. These uses of and reflections on language highlight how unbearable, and inconceivable, the protagonist's punishment is *before* the extreme physical violence that awaits him.

The denunciation of some sort of torture at work in modern capital punishment also occurs in an explicit fashion. The "chevalier," a satirized character in Hugo's play-preface, implies that the death penalty is to post-Revolutionary France what torture was to the Ancien Régime: "Dans l'ancien régime, quelqu'un qui se serait permis de publier un roman contre la *torture!*" (It's as though under the Ancien Régime, someone had dared to publish a novel against *torture!*; OCH 3:653; my emphasis). The condemned man himself refers to this concept in the main body of the text by way of a metaphor that highlights the mental ordeal he endures:

> Eh! Qu'est-ce donc que cette agonie de six semaines et ce râle de tout un jour? Qu'est-ce que les angoisses de cette journée irreparable, qui s'écoule si lentement et si vite? Qu'est-ce que cette échelle de *tortures* qui aboutit à l'échafaud?
>
> Hey! What about this six-week agony and this day-long rattle, then? What about the anguish endured through this fateful day, which passes so slowly and yet so quickly? What about this rising scale of *torture* that ends on the scaffold? (XXXIX, 700; my emphasis)

Later, concerning the ritual leading up to the scaffold, he repeats, "Chacun de ces détails m'apportait sa *torture*" (Each of these details brought me its own *torture*; XLVIII, 710; my emphasis). This figurative torture seems to lie in the acute awareness of his imminent decapitation and in

Pain and Punishment | 63

his scrutiny of the slow and often paradoxically protective procedures that precede it. But the term's metaphorical status finds itself undone by a number of physiological reactions that bring back the literality of torture: the condemned man comes close to "défaillir" (fainting; 710) and sways. "Ma vue s'est troublée, une sueur glacée est sortie à la fois de tous mes membres, j'ai senti mes tempes se gonfler, et j'avais les oreilles pleines de bourdonnements" (Everything became a blur, icy sweat suddenly covered my every limb, I felt my temples throb, and my ears were filled with a buzzing noise). "Ivre, stupide, insensé" (confounded, stupefied, senseless; 710), he feels both paralyzed and "chancelant... du coup" (staggering... from the blow; 711).[36] Oscillating between acute sensations and "diminished sensitivity," his bipolar body language is typical of the experience of torture, even if the physical pain that is central to this experience is not inflicted at any point before the execution.[37]

This may precisely be the point: *Le Dernier Jour* shows modern lethal justice to reinvent torture. Not only does the condemned man display the stigmata of this practice without having been subject to brutalization (yet). The very structure of torture, which, as Elaine Scarry has shown, "consists of a primary physical act, the infliction of pain, and a primary verbal act, the interrogation," is also shown to be modulated.[38] The condemned man internalizes this interrogation: his agony largely stems from the many self-addressed questions that his death sentence triggers: When will they come? How does decapitation feel? Will I be pardoned? Am I really going to die before sunset? etc. (XXVI, 691). The conflation of "the modes of the interrogatory, the declarative, the imperative, as well as the... exclamatory" that Scarry says is specific to the torturer's speech constitutes a prominent trait of the condemned man's prose.[39] Torture is shown to recenter on a single agent, and physical pain is also produced by a psychological ordeal that the sentence pronouncement has sufficed to launch. A new form of torture emerges, subtle and insidious. It is initiated by a law that *denies* the possibility that pain be experienced and is subsequently sustained within and intensified by the condemned man himself. Hugo thereby intimates that modernity's lethal justice has reached a perverse degree of sophistication.

I referred earlier to Agamben's work on the *homo sacer* and to the reduction of his status to "bare life" in antiquity. It is worth adding that the Italian philosopher demonstrates that France's post-Revolutionary era marked the advent of a fusion and a confusion between *zoē* (biological life) and *bios* (political life) in discarding the divine and promoting *The Declaration of the Rights of Man and of the Citizen.*[40] For Agamben, this (con)fusion founds modern biopolitics: "The fact that . . . the 'subject' is, as has been noted, transformed into a 'citizen' means that birth—which is to say, bare natural life as such—here for the first time becomes (thanks to a transformation whose biopolitical consequences we are only beginning to discern today) the immediate bearer of sovereignty."[41] Conjuring up the question of the body in an original language, Hugo's fiction insists that the distinction between *zoē* and *bios* cannot be eclipsed. It denounces the modern French state's deceptive ideology according to which the body is endowed with political rights from birth—so that this body is not, at first, "bare life."

This does not mean that Hugo sheds light on *zoē* exclusively at the expense of *bios*. He does not cease to complicate and look beyond the merely corporeal existence of his condemned man–*homo sacer*. Agamben highlights a crucial aspect of the *homo sacer*'s life that Hugo puts at the heart of his novel: "He [the *homo sacer*] is pure *zoē*, but his *zoē* is as such caught in the sovereign ban *and must reckon with it at every moment, finding the best way to elude or to deceive it. In this sense, no life, as exiles and bandits know well, is more 'political' than his.*"[42] I would argue that the power to act that Hugo places in his language provides a way for the condemned man to "elude" his condition and to reassert the political status that both his sentencing and his ensuing bodily and mental incarceration take away from him. This power to act located in language, the depository of a biological and a political life, is made visible in a perennial way. It reminds the reader of the existence of two inhumane pains: one that appears to last interminably, as the condemned man awaits his execution, and one that occurs in "half a second" but whose intensity is ineffable:

> Se sont-ils jamais mis, seulement en pensée, à la place de celui qui est là, au moment où le lourd tranchant qui tombe mord la chair, rompt les nerfs, brise les vertèbres. . . . Mais quoi! une demi-seconde! la douleur est escamotée. . . .
> Horreur! (XXXIX, 700)

> Have they ever placed themselves, only mentally, in the position of the one lying there, at the instant when the heavy, falling blade bites into the flesh, severs the nerves, breaks the vertebrae. . . . Come on! Half a second! The pain is eclipsed. . . .
> Horror!

Le Dernier Jour d'un condamné subverts the practical and ethical shift toward relative discreetness and progressivism that characterized the modern death penalty in France. While Hugo eclipses the moment of decapitation from his novel and reduces *a minima* the visibility of the condemned man's body proper, he avoids illustrating the slow move away from the body as a focal point of punishment that Foucault highlights, with an emphasis on the beginning of the nineteenth century.[43] Instead, the novel suggests that, *before* justice even lays a hand on the condemned body by decapitating it, it "no longer takes public responsibility for the violence that is bound up with its practice," a violence that nevertheless affects both body and psyche.[44] Through a destabilizing mise-en-scène and by means of a process of delocalization that transposes the biological into the poetic, Hugo applies to his text's body the severance that awaits the condemned man. He contests, and even abolishes, the body/soul dichotomy on which, Foucault argues, modernity's penal system increasingly relied. The interdependence of man's anatomy and man's interiority finds itself affirmed and actualized, as language acts as the symbol, the prolepsis, the written trace—and, consequently, as the future memory—of a "tortured, dismembered, amputated body ... exposed alive or dead to public view."[45] *In fine*, Hugo's verbal manipulations allow him to turn the thesis of "one death per condemned man, obtained by a single blow, without recourse to those 'long and consequently cruel' methods of execution," into a farce.[46] They shed light on the way state power may demote a full human life to mere physical life, on the emergence of a new form of torture, and on society's attempt to suspend a political existence.

* *
*

The representational and poetic devices cultivated in Hugo's fictional diary have an argumentative power of their own.[47] Avoiding analysis, didacticism, and polemic, they differ from the tools used in the novel's overtly militant preface of 1832. Paradoxically, this may account for the effectiveness of *Le Dernier Jour d'un condamné*. The hostile reactions that the book elicited, as well as the parodies it inspired, including Janin's *L'Âne mort et la femme guillotinée* (1829) and the vaudeville *Le Doge et le dernier jour d'un condamné* (The Doge and the Last Day of a Condemned Man, 1829), testify to the powerful effect this strategy had on Hugo's contemporaries, as well as to how seditious it appeared to some of them. *La Gazette de France* deemed the book nightmarish and "extremely dangerous . . . for the minds already predisposed to rebel against the laws," while Deputy Salverte viewed it as "execrable" and responsible for the instauration of extenuating circumstances in 1832.[48]

Hugo never repeated quite a comparable tour de force in his other works of fiction, which, according to *Victor Hugo raconté par un témoin de sa vie* (Victor Hugo by a Witness of His Life) "continued *Le Dernier jour d'un condamné*" (chapter LI).[49] By zooming in on the increasingly bare life of a nameless human being, and by giving him a voice in a highly heterodox narrative, Hugo created an unprecedented proximity to and revulsion for the agony that human justice may cause. *Le Dernier Jour* could thus be said to attack both literature, in its conventions, and the law, in its humanitarian ambition. "Nous l'avons déjà dit ailleurs, et plus d'une fois, le corollaire rigoureux d'une révolution politique, c'est une révolution littéraire. Que voulez-vous que nous y fassions? Il y a quelque chose de fatal dans ce perpétuel parallélisme de la littérature et de la société" (We have already said it elsewhere, and more than once, the direct corollary of a political revolution is a literary revolution. What do you want us to do about it? There is something fatal in this perpetual parallelism between literature and society; *OCH* 5:29), the poet insisted in the preface to *Littérature et philosophie mêlées* (Medley of Philosophy and Literature; 1834).[50] Through its poetics, *Le Dernier Jour* has literary revolution serve a political revolution: it deconstructs the philanthropic premises underlying the reform of justice that occurred during the French Revolution, led to the perennial adoption of its icon, the guillotine, and failed to deliver the abolition promised by the decree of 1795.

PART II

Words That Kill in Baudelaire

Savoir, tuer et créer.

To know, to kill, and to create.

—Charles Baudelaire, *Mon cœur mis à nu*

BAUDELAIRE/*BADELAIRE*

Unlike Hugo, Charles Baudelaire is not usually considered an author of "capital literature." Yet he is, to a significant extent, a poet of violence, if not *the* poet of modern violence: physical, moral, socioeconomic, aesthetic, and symbolic. The death penalty inscribes itself in these multilayered reflections on, and representations of, violence.[1] Upon close examination, it constitutes a persistent component of the imaginary deployed in his works.[2]

Superficially, capital punishment is found in a host of discreet yet recurring references in Baudelaire. This scattered corpus includes odd anecdotes about or by the poet, aborted projects, and an overarching narrative through which he stages himself and his publications. He insistently likened both his patronym and his facial profile to the *badelaire*, a weapon of execution;[3] his conduct and sartorial appearance led some contemporaries, such as Jules Barbey d'Aurevilly (*OCB* 1:1196) and the Goncourt brothers, to name him "le guillotiné" and to view him as a martyr-executioner;[4] he apparently planned to compose an oneiric prose poem on "his" death sentence and another on the last words of Jan Hus, a reformist Czech priest condemned to death for heresy in the fifteenth century (1:367, 369, 371); and he also intended to write a novel or short story on a "parricidal love" that ended with an execution (1:588, 597).

After 1857 in particular, Baudelaire also worked the death penalty into the imagery relating his personal itinerary and that of his verse.

He used the tropes of the capital sentence and severance to dramatize the various rejections he had experienced, and their consequences. Among them were the "conseil judiciaire" that granted a notary control over his inheritance and expenditure in his youth, the trial during which he was accused of offending public morality, as well as the suppression of poems from *Les Fleurs du mal* that ensued, his late aesthetics of the fragmentary, his poverty, and public disgrace.[5] The death penalty thereby serves as an efficient running analogy in the story that Baudelaire forged to portray himself and his poetry, both for himself and for posterity.

DEFENDING THE DEATH PENALTY

There is more. Other planned narratives, *Mon cœur mis à nu* (My Heart Laid Bare) and, to a lesser extent, "Notes nouvelles sur Edgar Poe," the unfinished pamphlet *Pauvre Belgique!* (Poor Belgium!), and key poems explore the anthropological and symbolic ramifications of the death penalty. Both Baudelaire's projects of novels and short stories and *Mon cœur mis à nu* take on a rather truculent form. They claim to legitimize capital punishment, attributing a sacrificial function to it in the polis. The second section of folio 24 in "Liste de titres et canevas de romans et nouvelles" (List of Titles and Sketches of Novels and Short Stories), which revolves around the process of "conver[ting]" reprehensible actions and drives into rightful ones, reads:

> L'envers de Claude Gueux. Théorie du sacrifice.
> Légitimation de la peine de mort. Le sacrifice n'est complet que par le *sponte sua* de la victime. (*OCB* 1:598)

> The opposite of Claude Gueux. Theory of sacrifice.
> Legitimation of the death penalty. Sacrifice is only complete with the victim's *sponte sua*.

Folio 25 proposes a spectacular embodiment of this sacrificial "theory" according to which a man condemned to death should embrace his execution actively. It imagines a peripety during which the convict would oppose his own liberation by the crowd:

Un condamné à mort qui, raté par le bourreau, délivré par le peuple, retournerait au bourreau.—Nouvelle justification de la peine de Mort.

A man condemned to death who, having been missed by the executioner's hand, and then been freed by the crowd, would go back to the executioner.—New justification for the death penalty. (*OCB* 1:598)

These two key passages find an echo in other writings, including the central section of folio 12 of *Mon cœur mis à nu*:

La peine de Mort est le résultat d'une idée mystique, totalement incomprise aujourd'hui. La peine de Mort n'a pas pour but de *sauver* la société, matériellement du moins. Elle a pour but de *sauver* (spirituellement) la société et le coupable. Pour que le sacrifice soit parfait, il faut qu'il y ait assentiment et joie de la part de la victime. Donner du chloroforme à un condamné à mort serait une impiété, car ce serait lui enlever la conscience de sa grandeur comme victime et lui supprimer les chances de gagner le Paradis. (*OCB* 1:683)

The death penalty results from a mystical idea, which is entirely misunderstood nowadays. The death penalty does not aim to *save* society, at least not in a material sense. It aims to *save* (in the spiritual sense) society and the culprit. For the sacrifice to be perfect, there must be consent and joy on the victim's part. Administering chloroform to a man condemned to death would be impious, for it would take from him the consciousness of his grandeur as a victim and would deprive him of the chance to reach Paradise.[6]

Such considerations on the function and logistics of the death penalty complement Baudelaire's singular view on the condemned man's volition. The poet reclaims lethal justice as a transcendent enterprise benefiting all of society, a martyrdom of sorts functioning through the protagonist's full awareness and accepted suffering. Baudelaire thereby elevates the condemned man to new—or perhaps age-old—heights.

Conversely, he castigates those who oppose capital punishment. Folio 14 pursues this criticism openly:

> Observons que les abolisseurs de la peine de mort doivent être plus ou moins *intéressés* à l'abolir.
> Souvent ce sont des guillotineurs. Cela peut se résumer ainsi: "Je veux pouvoir couper ta tête; mais tu ne toucheras pas à la mienne."
> Les abolisseurs d'âme (*matérialistes*) sont nécessairement des abolisseurs d'*enfer*; ils y sont à coup sûr *intéressés*.
> Tout au moins ce sont des gens qui ont *peur de revivre*,— des paresseux. (*OCB* 1:684–85)

> Let us note that those for the abolition of the death penalty must have a *vested interest* in its abolition, to a greater or lesser extent.
> Often they are guillotiners. It could be summed up like this: "I want to be able to cut your head off; but you shall not touch mine."
> Abolitionists of the soul (the *materialists*) are by necessity abolitionists of *Hell*; to be sure, they have an *interest* in the matter.
> At best they are people who are *afraid to live again*—lazy people.

As the author of the above-mentioned *Claude Gueux* and as an "abolisseur de la peine de mort" par excellence, Hugo plays a prominent role in these reflections. Chapter 3 examines this as well as Baudelaire's pro-death penalty corpus.

POETRY ON AND FOR THE "PENDABLES"

At a more figurative level, the death penalty also has its place in Baudelaire's poetry. He considered prefacing *Les Fleurs du mal* with an axiom proclaiming the universality of capital punishment: "Nous sommes tous pendus ou pendables" (We are all hanged or hangable; *OCB* 1:183). A profound sense of man's condemnation—to boredom, sin, crime, pain, and death—traverses the collection. So do motifs, themes, and actors emblematic of lethal justice.

Scaffolds surface in the allegory that concludes the inaugural poem "Au lecteur" (To the Reader), in "Chant d'automne" (Autumn Song) as the speaker's anxiety grows at the end of the summer months, and in "Les Litanies de Satan," where the proud man condemned to death, supported by the devil, looks down upon the beholders of his beheading. The victim-executioner duo is another prominent component of Baudelaire's imagistic appropriation of the death penalty in *Les Fleurs du mal*. It frequently appears in his love poems to revisit the overlap, or the tension, between Eros and Thanatos. *Les Fleurs* arguably enlarges the particular figure of the executioner by foregrounding a range of avatars, namely the butcher, the torturer, and the vampire (in "Le Vampire," "Les Métamorphoses du Vampire," "L'Héautontimorouménos" [The Self-Tormenter], "À une Madone" [To a Madonna], for instance). Along with, or beyond, this vision of love as an often fatal and always unstable affective duel—a vision confirmed in *Fusées* (*OCB* 1:651)—the victim-executioner duo allows the poet to probe a single tormented human being, or even the tormented human race as a whole, as we will see in chapter 4.

Completing this death-penalty overview is the presence of severed and aching heads throughout *Les Fleurs du mal*, from the *caput mortuum* that rests on a bedside table in "Une martyre" to the numerous damaged heads—suffering or broken skulls, minds, "cerveaux" and "cervelles"—found in "Au lecteur," "Spleen" (76), "Spleen" (78), "Le Cygne" (The Swan), "Danse Macabre," "Brumes et pluies" (Mists and Rains), "La Béatrice," "L'Amour et le crâne" (Love and the Skull), "Le Reniement de Saint Pierre" (St. Peter's Denial), "La Fin de la journée" (Day's End), and "Le Voyage." The motif of the severed head in other art forms also fascinates Baudelaire, particularly in his 1855 essay on laughter. In his poems, it is accompanied, if not valorized, by instruments of dismemberment, torture, and execution, such as the guillotine, whose presence is implied in that of the scaffold but also the wheel, the gibbet, and the noose.

In some poems, Baudelaire presents more comprehensive capital scenes. "Un Voyage à Cythère" and "Le Voyage" respectively portray animals attacking the decaying corpse of a hanged man and allude to the sadism of the executioner and to the popularity of bloody spectacles. Albeit in a more enigmatic way, the prose poem "Une mort héroïque" (A Heroic Death) also examines the transgression and process that lead to an execution: an artist is denounced for trying to overthrow his sovereign before performing a stupendous pantomime that fails to stop him from being put to death.[7]

Capital punishment thus permeates both Baudelaire's prose and poetry in distinct ways. The former appears to adopt a retentionist position on unexpected grounds, while the latter cultivates a colorful and highly symbolic "capital aesthetic." Part II attempts to examine the contextual and poetic specificities of these two faces of capital punishment in Baudelaire's writings as well as the the interaction between them.

CHAPTER 3

Prose Praising Sacrifice

Hugo, Maistre, and Beyond

"Sache qu'il faut aimer, sans faire la grimace,
Le pauvre, le méchant, le tortu, l'hébété,
Pour que tu puisses faire, à Jésus, quand il passe,
Un tapis triomphal avec ta charité."
. . . .
Et l'Ange, châtiant autant, ma foi! qu'il aime,
De ses poings de géant torture l'anathème;
Mais le damné répond toujours: "Je ne veux pas!"

"I order you to love without a sneer
The mad, the wretched, those in poverty,
To make for Jesus, when he passes here,
A regal carpet, of your charity."
. . . .
Good God! the Angel, who corrects and loves,
Twists in his fist the sinner from above;
Answers the damned soul, "I will not obey!"

—Charles Baudelaire, "Le Rebelle"

Baudelaire articulated his defense of the death penalty at a time when state killing underwent a paradoxical evolution. With the decrease in capital cases, the reduced number of executioners,[1] the introduction of extenuating circumstances for capital crimes (1832), relocation of the scaffold by the barrière Saint-Jacques (1832), and short-lived abolition of the death penalty for capital crimes in 1848, France adopted measures that weakened lethal justice in the second third of the nineteenth century.[2] In some respects, the country was gradually coming closer to undermining what Hugo had identified as the three pillars on which the social edifice of the past had rested: the priest, the king, and the executioner (OCH 4:495). But in the late 1840s and early 1850s, France also maintained the guillotine and rejected bills in favor of the general and definitive abolition of capital punishment. Baudelaire's writings seem to align themselves with this "retentionist" politics. If anything, they radicalize it. Understanding this stance calls for contextualization. In particular, two of the poet's tutelary figures, Hugo and Joseph de Maistre, play a crucial role in illuminating Baudelaire's prose texts that claim to legitimize the death penalty. A complex and evolving relationship united him to Hugo.[3] Léon Cellier has noted that Baudelaire had two kinds of model: some seemed constant, while others elicited more volatile appreciation. Hugo fell into the latter category, for Cellier.[4] Baudelaire's "raison d'État," in Paul Valéry's words, allegedly was to exist as a poet despite and next to the overwhelming presence and poetic production of the Romantics, chief among them "l'homme-siècle."[5] Admiration, competition, and contempt certainly alternate in Baudelaire's attitude to Hugo. Conversely, Cellier classified Joseph de Maistre as one of Baudelaire's unvarying models, just like Poe. Whether and how Baudelaire's fervent praise of lethal justice confirms this rapport to Hugo and Maistre remains to be seen.

BAUDELAIRE'S "LÉGITIMATION DE LA PEINE DE MORT" IN PERSPECTIVE

In October 1848, a relatively young Baudelaire reportedly scared the readers of a conservative periodical in Châteauroux by praising the proponents of the Reign of Terror for their coherence: "His first article began thus: 'When Marat, this gentle man, and Robespierre, this decent man, respectively asked for three hundred thousand heads and the permanence of the guillotine, they abided by their system's inescapable logic.' Although the conclusion recalled an authoritarianism à la Joseph de Maistre, everybody acted outraged—and poor Baudelaire did not last long in Châteauroux."[6]

Other sources suggest that, with or without Maistre, Baudelaire relished the shock value of killing, the guillotine, and the criminal imaginary. In notes on novelistic projects, he reminds himself that he should write to his publisher Malassis to ask him for books on bandits and sorcerers from the post-Revolutionary era. Among other embryonic ideas, he mentions the figure of Germany's most famous criminal, Schinderhannes—who died by the guillotine—and lists a variety of places and practices liable to elicit horror: "Witchcraft/Kidnappings/Palaces and prisons (underground)." He then concludes, with some amusement, "And torments [*supplices*] and horrors!" (*OCB* 1:593). Perhaps these notes figured among the "pile of sketches and accumulated projects" the poet claimed to have reviewed before writing to François Buloz, the director of the *Revue des Deux Mondes* who received complaints from his subscribers after publishing eighteen "flowers of evil" in early June 1855: "Alas! Sir, I must confess—to my embarrassment? to my advantage?—that I did not find many humane feelings, or feelings that may come across as such. All I saw in them, isn't it ludicrous to admit it, was an attempt to cause surprise or horror" (*CB* 1:314).

Two motivations partly account for this continuous desire to astonish and offend that resurfaces in Baudelaire's exalted declarations on capital punishment: literary ambition and a political posture that finds itself exacerbated at a particular moment in his career. Like Valéry, albeit less severely, a number of critics, such as Pierre Pachet, have underscored Baudelaire's anxiety to make a place for himself on a crowded literary scene.[7] A letter to his mother confirms that Baudelaire's interest in the spiritual valorization of capital punishment was closely connected to a search for literary originality: "I forgot to tell you that I will join the *Revue des Deux Mondes*, with something very sophisticated and very bizarre:—either a novel on *the ideal of conjugal love*,—or a novel that legitimizes and explains the *holiness* of the death penalty" (*CB* 1:354). Both "the ideal of conjugal love" and "the holiness of the death penalty" had the potential to surprise the reader by virtue of their ironic quality. The bourgeois "ideal of conjugal love" travesties Western literature's model of unattainable, courtly love and that of the impossible passions staged in early modern drama. Baudelaire's century was also concerned with another dimension of conjugal love, namely adultery. As for "the holiness of the death penalty," it clearly opposed a number of popular nineteenth-century narratives pleading for progressive reforms.[8] Thus the valorization of capital punishment first seems to have imposed itself as a means rather than an end for Baudelaire: an atypical theme and thesis, it had the potential to make him elicit a vivid reaction in his reader, following in the footsteps of his master Poe who, in "The Philosophy of Composition" (1846), argued that the prime imperative of a literary work was to make an impression on its audience.[9]

Precisely dating all the "retentionist" passages from Baudelaire's novelistic projects and from *Mon cœur mis à nu* sometimes proves difficult.¹⁰ But the above-cited letter, whose content on the death penalty mirrors these passages, was written on July 22, 1856. By that time, although the first edition of *Les Fleurs du mal* had not yet come out, a number of Baudelairean poems dissecting human sins had already been composed, with about thirty of them published in periodicals. Nevertheless, as Claude Pichois has noted, until 1855, Baudelaire's compositions were essentially recited within the "cénacles de la bohème" (*OCB* 2:1294). Publishing a novel praising decapitation after authoring a number of vice-centered compositions would have afforded the poet an opportunity to consolidate and further publicize his heterodox persona.

That some sources testify to Baudelaire's will to portray himself as an unconventional man of letters from—at least—the late 1840s onward does not mean that he instrumentalized the celebration of the death penalty to this exclusive end. An ideological posture and political critique appear to merge with his professional ambition. The presidential and legislative elections that followed Baudelaire's revolutionary aspirations in 1848 significantly dampened his enthusiasm and faith in the people. Likewise, he claimed a posteriori that his "fury" following the coup d'état of 1851 had given way to a form of acceptance of the Second Empire (*OCB* 1:679). At the very end of the 1850s and in the 1860s in particular, Baudelaire increasingly seemed to embrace reaction and to associate the various avatars of his era's progressivism—egalitarianism, humanitarianism, pacifism, and abolitionism—with a dread that social, political, and, above all, moral hierarchies be annihilated.¹¹ The poet lamented the decline of the aristocracy, derided the supporters of democracy, and rejected all that which, in his view, formed part of a collective inclination toward the principle of least effort. "La croyance au progrès est une doctrine de paresseux, une doctrine de *Belges*. C'est l'individu qui compte sur ses voisins pour faire sa besogne" (Belief in progress is a doctrine for lazy people, a doctrine characteristic of the *Belgians*. It is the individual who relies on his neighbors to do his work for him), *Mon cœur mis à nu* eventually claimed (681; folio 9).

Other statements from this period repeatedly associate militant progressivism with intellectual laziness, subjection, and conformism: "Les poètes de combat. Les littérateurs d'avant-garde. Ces habitudes de métaphores militaires dénotent . . . des esprits nés domestiques, des esprits belges, qui ne peuvent penser qu'en société" (The militant poets. The literary avant-garde. This penchant for military metaphors is the sign of . . . minds born servile, Belgian minds, which can only think as part of a group; *OCB* 1:691).¹² Ultimately, Baudelaire accused optimistic and reformist sociopolitical thought of delusively considering all people as equal, masking man's corrupt nature whereas "*nature* in its entirety is part of the original sin" (*CB* 1:337), and precipitating the decadence of nineteenth-century Western society.

Beyond political change, his main concern seems to have been the loss of embodiments of moral superiority. *Fusées* makes this point clear: "L'imagination humaine peut concevoir, sans trop de peine, des républiques ou autres états communautaires, dignes de quelque gloire, s'ils sont dirigés par des hommes sacrés, par de certains aristocrates. Mais ce n'est pas particulièrement par des institutions politiques que se manifestera la ruine universelle, ou le progrès universel; car peu m'importe le nom. Ce sera par l'avilissement des cœurs" (Without too much difficulty, the human imagination can conceive of republics or other community-based states worthy of some glory, if they are led by sacred men, by certain types of aristocrats. But universal ruin, or universal progress, will not manifest itself through political institutions in particular; for the name given to these forms of government matters little to me. Debasement of the heart is what will cause this ruin; *OCB* 1:666). A fantasy, a fear of moral degeneracy increasingly haunted Baudelaire's writings.

Such decadence allegedly showed itself in an excessive attachment to life. Resisting death instead of being stoic in the face of it is degrading, Baudelaire argued, and so is abolitionism, for analogous reasons. *Pauvre Belgique!* reads:

> Ils [les Révolutionnaires] croient à toutes les sottises lancées par les libéraux français.
> (Abolition de la peine de mort. Victor Hugo domine comme Courbet. On me dit qu'à Paris 30 000 pétitionnent pour l'abolition de la peine de mort. 30 000 personnes qui la méritent. Vous tremblez, donc vous êtes déjà coupables. Du moins, vous êtes intéressés dans la question. L'amour excessif de la vie est une descente vers l'animalité.) (*OCB* 2:899; folio 196)

> They [the Revolutionaries] believe in all the idiotic ideas of the French liberals.
> (Abolition of the death penalty. Victor Hugo is a dominant figure like Courbet. I am told that in Paris 30,000 are petitioning for the abolition of the death penalty. 30,000 people

who deserve it. You tremble, so you are already guilty. You have some interest in the matter, at least. Excessive love of life is a descent into an animal-like state.)

By connecting the progressive abolitionist stance with a cowardly, interested, and animalistic attachment to life, Baudelaire mobilized a core argument used by prominent retentionist philosophies of law whose genealogy Jacques Derrida has traced: from Kant to Hegel, Bataille, and aspects of Blanchot's thought.[13] Following this logic, Derrida remarks, life can and should be sacrificed so human dignity, sovereignty, and universal law occur beyond and above biological existence. *Literary* conservatives, such as Balzac, had also rejected abolitionism as a symptom of generalized amorphousness, if not of anarchy, decades before Baudelaire.[14] In a humorous zeugma combining this moral-penal reactionary anxiety with a linguistic one, *Edgar Poe, sa vie et ses œuvres* (1856) lamented the possible "abolition de la peine de mort et de l'orthographe, ces deux folies corrélatives" (abolition of the death penalty and of spelling, these two correlated follies; *OCB* 2:300).

Baudelaire's figure of the *sponte sua* can be better understood in this politico-ideological context revealing of a moral angst. Although not without a biting irony that turns the criminal into a victim, the willing condemned man arguably incarnates regained moral distinction and sacredness as he embraces death and pain with a view to redeeming a corrupt human race. Through his abnegation, he is taken to reestablish a moral order and a spiritual aristocracy of sorts. Hence the insistence on his unadulterated experience of suffering in *Mon cœur* and in one of the narrative projects mentioned earlier: "Donner du chloroforme à un condamné à mort serait une impiété, car ce serait lui enlever la conscience de sa *grandeur* comme victime et lui supprimer les chances de gagner le Paradis" (*OCB* 1:683; my emphasis); "raté par le bourreau, délivré par le peuple, [il] retournerait au bourreau" (598). Pachet has argued that the Baudelairean dandy "looks for distinction, singularization, in a world in which no procedure can guarantee it for him."[15] The figure of the *sponte sua* who calls for his own execution exemplifies this quest for singularization, but he does in fact actualize a selective process, namely election, in the religious sense of the term. As a Christ-like savior, he symbolizes an antimodern heroism of modern life.

With "'Le Sublime B. . . . . !'" which Baudelaire mentions as an underestimated heroic subject of modern life (*OCB* 2:495), the *Salon de 1846* arguably features an avatar of the *sponte sua*. Dolf Oehler has shown that "B." is Pierre-Joseph Poulmann, a murderer sentenced to death on January 27, 1844. For Baudelaire, the fact that Poulmann declined the support of the priest Jean-François Montès on his way to the scaffold made him "sublime." Instead of seeking comfort, the criminal reportedly "couru[t] sus à la guillotine" (threw himself at the guillotine) with "courage" (495)—an anecdote confirmed, indeed magnified by Henri Sanson's *Memoirs*, which relate the condemned man's last words, a witty blend of irony and charity worthy of Baudelaire.[16] Poulmann's remarkable attitude conveniently exemplified the poet's theory that some "happy few" enjoy a redeeming superiority in modern society. *Mon cœur mis à nu* would later contend that these elected figures typically fall into three categories: "le prêtre, le guerrier, le poète" (the priest, the warrior, the poet; OCB 1:684; folio 13), while "le reste est fait pour le fouet" (all other men are made to be slaves; 693; folio 16). The *sponte sua* synthesizes these first two models as he assumes both spirituality and temerity. As for the poet, a closer look at the very project of *Mon cœur mis à nu* suggests that, to some extent, he was ready to sacrifice *himself* in public.

But Baudelaire also elaborates on the positive nature of capital punishment *after* the emergence of this discourse in relatively early writings that bring together a thirst for literary recognition, the search for modern forms of distinction harking back to premodernity, and a certain irony (namely the *Salon de 1846* referring to Poulmann, his article published in Châteauroux, the letters to his mother and other interlocutors in the mid-1850s). Some of his above-mentioned reflections on the death penalty that expand on a reactionary ideology most aggressively date from a later period. *Mon cœur mis à nu* is considered to have been written from 1859 to 1865, with a particular dedication to the project in 1861, 1863, and 1865-66 (OCB 1:1468), and *Pauvre Belgique!* from 1864 to 1866; Baudelaire wanted Arsène Houssaye to publish *Fusées* in 1862.

These works belong to a challenging time in the poet's life. In addition to such serious personal difficulties as Jeanne Duval's hemiplegia and his suicidal thoughts and cerebral crises, he fought with a number of publishers, failed to be elected to the Académie française, saw Poulet-Malassis imprisoned for his debts, dealt with increasing financial difficulties to the point of fearing homelessness, and sold the copyright of his translations of Poe to Michel Lévy because he was in such dire straits. This led to a failed attempt to find success in Belgium. To underscore these particular circumstances is not to say that the personal explains the political altogether, or that Baudelaire's trying material and professional life thoroughly accounts for an intensified resurgence of his praise for the death penalty. Nevertheless, his mounting resentment toward a society he deemed debased and hostile helps shed light on his increasingly incendiary formulation of the rehabilitation of state killing.

Mon cœur mis à nu, for one, distorts its source of inspiration, namely Poe's idea that man's most profound literary ambition and will to attain fame can be fulfilled through the completion of a tell-all book of sorts:

> If any ambitious man have a fancy to revolutionize, at one effort, the universal world of human thought, human opinion, and human sentiment, the opportunity is his own—the road to immortal renown lies straight, open, and unencumbered before him. All that he has to do is to write and publish a very little book. Its title should be simple—a few plain words—"My Heart Laid Bare." But—this little book must be true to its title.
>
> Now, is it not very singular that, with the rabid thirst for notoriety which distinguishes so many of mankind—so many, too, who care not a fig what is thought of them after death, there should not be found one man having sufficient hardihood to write this little book? To *write*, I say. There are ten thousand men who, if the book were once written, would laugh at the notion of being disturbed by its publication during their life, and who could not even conceive *why* they should object to its being published after their death. But to write it—*there* is the rub. No man dare write it. No man ever will dare write it. No man *could* write it, even if he dared. The paper would shrivel and blaze at every touch of the fiery pen.[17]

Baudelaire openly rose to the challenge that Poe deemed both destructive and liable to secure the visibility and originality to which the poet's correspondence had repeatedly referred. At the same time, however, he replaced his American peer's rather open-ended, exploratory ambition of truthfulness with the display of his psyche's darkest corners. "A great book I've been meditating over the last two years: *My Heart Laid Bare*, in which I will accumulate all my rage. Ah! If it ever sees the light of day, *J[ean]-J[acques]'s Confessions* will pale in comparison. You can see that I am dreaming again" (*CB* 2:141; letter to Madame Aupick, April 1, 1861).[18]

Later correspondence from 1861 and 1863 stresses Baudelaire's profound ambition for his anger-filled project and plan to publish it only after having secured a more comfortable position for himself.[19] It also confirms the replacement of Poe by Rousseau, and the use of the latter both as the ultimate reference for confessional writing and as a countermodel whose self-serving autobiography was to be overturned (182, 302). On June 5, 1863, he plainly informed a skeptical Madame Aupick of his project's vengeful nature:

> Well, yes! The book of which I dreamt for so long will be a book of rancours. Of course, my mother, and even my step-father, will be respected. Yet while relating my education, the manner in which my ideas and sentiments were fashioned, I wish to make it feel unceasingly, that I consider myself a stranger to the world and to its beliefs. I shall turn against the *whole of France* my real talent for insult. My craving for vengeance is like a tired man's craving for a bath. (CB 2:305)[20]

Baudelaire's celebration of the death penalty in *Mon cœur mis à nu* is therefore to be read with an added pinch of salt. It finds itself reintegrated into a wider, self-staging whole designed to antagonize and retaliate against a modern France portrayed as both alien and alienating to the artist.

Some of the hate-filled maxims contained in *Fusées* and *Pauvre Belgique!* further this intent and extend it to Belgium. The latter work echoes and even surpasses the virulence of Baudelaire's anti-*Confessions*. It is replete with vindictive charges that point back to the issue of literary ambition and nonrecognition. From 1863 to 1866, Baudelaire went from disappointment to disappointment while in Brussels, where his lectures turned out to be neither very profitable nor conducive to the coveted publication of his complete works by Lacroix and Verboeckhoven, the publishers of *Les Misérables*. His notes indicate that he considered combining his grievances against Belgium with those concerning France as a debased nation:

> Entremêler les considérations sur les mœurs des Belges d'entremets français.
> *Nadar. Janin. Le réalisme*
> (Guiard) [*sic*];

La peine de Mort, Les chiens.
Les exilés volontaires;
La Vie de César (Dialogue de Lucien)
Pour ceux-ci particulièrement quelque chose de très soigné. Leur révoltante familiarité.
Pères Loriquet de la Démocratie.
Les Coblentz.
Vérités de Télémaque.
Vieilles bêtes, vieux Lapalisse.
Propres à rien, fruits secs.
Elèves de Béranger.
Philosophie de maîtres de pension et de préparateurs au baccalauréat.
Je n'ai jamais si bien compris qu'en la voyant la sottise absolue des convictions.
Ajoutons que quand on leur parle de révolution pour de bon, on les épouvante. (OCB 2:960–61)

Intersperse the considerations on the customs of the Belgians with French treats.
Nadar. Janin. Realism.
(Guiard) [sic];
The Death penalty, dogs.
Voluntary exiles;
The Life of Caesar (Dialogue à la Lucian)
For the following in particular something very special [indeed]. Their revolting commonness.
Jesuits of Democracy.
Avatars of the 1789 émigrés.
Didactic truths *à la* Télémaque.
Old dons, old truisms.
Worthless, dry as can be.
Béranger's pupils.
Philosophy of boarding school teachers and baccalaureate tutors.
I have never understood as clearly as when I saw for myself the utter foolishness of convictions.
Let us add that when they are told about revolution for real, they get scared.

In the last years of Baudelaire's life, the death penalty thus finds itself immersed in a damning hodgepodge of ideas taken to encapsulate France's moral decadence as the poet faces a number of career setbacks. It includes several entities and men he had criticized previously: artists and intellectuals in favor of progress and democracy, photography, the realist movement, the proponents of free education (Auguste Guyard), the exiles who, like Hugo, refused to return to France following Napoleon III's amnesty, and art marked by democratic ideas and a perceived liberal conformism. Baudelaire, who confessed to Narcisse Ancelle that his rhetoric in Belgium was deliberately uncouth ("But here ... you have to be uncouth to make yourself understood"; CB 2:409), lumps them together to symbolize his era's supposedly uncreative imagination, cowardice, truthlessness, intellectual mediocrity, and foolish commitment to social improvement and democracy.

In context, Baudelaire's laudatory evocations of capital punishment and turn to the theme of sacrifice therefore appear to result from his aspiration for artistic originality, a nostalgic stance, and search for forms of moral distinction, but also, increasingly, and following a number of disappointments, from his will to take on the vocal proponents of pro-democratic, progressive politics and to disprove their optimistic convictions. Yet the poet's conception of the death penalty not only depends on these biographical and contextual data. As is beginning to become clear, it also inscribes itself in a related critical quarrel about the relationship between literature and ideology.

CLASH OF THE TITANS: BAUDELAIRE VS. HUGO ON CAPITAL PUNISHMENT

Besides Rousseau, whose *Confessions* he aimed to emulate and subvert in *Mon cœur mis à nu* by proposing a truly ruthless self-portrait, Baudelaire took aim at the liberal Hugo when defending the death penalty.[21] The idolized poet-prophet had conquered publishers and a vast audience, both erudite and popular, and could not be opposed more dramatically than through Baudelaire's promotion of state killing and insistence on man's scarcely redeemable corruption. As noted earlier, one of Baudelaire's most explicit challenges to Hugo's convictions and art is found in his projects of essays and short stories:

L'envers de Claude Gueux. Théorie du sacrifice.

Légitimation de la peine de mort. Le sacrifice n'est complet que par le *sponte sua* de la victime. (OCB 1:598)

Why is *Claude Gueux* to be overturned? This question begs another: what is *Claude Gueux*? Formally, it is the anti–*Dernier Jour d'un condamné* in that it makes no secret of its wish to "save mankind," in Baudelaire's words (OCB 2:936). Just as *Les Misérables* would about thirty years later, it defends social progress and criticizes the death penalty in an overt and didactic way. Inspired by a *fait divers*, the narrative is based on a rather Manichaean plot, sentimentalism, pathos, explicit reflections on the socioeconomic injustices of the day, and a certain heroism. Its eponymous protagonist, who is eventually executed, is the archetype, or rather the prototype, of the exemplary criminal whom Jean Valjean will later duplicate and turn into an icon. In brief, *Claude Gueux* typifies an openly edifying reformist and humanitarian literature.[22]

Published five years after *Le Dernier Jour*, *Claude Gueux* did not pursue the revolutionary representational and narrative techniques tried out in the earlier novel to undermine the legitimacy of state killing. Baudelaire knew *Le Dernier Jour*: he had read it in 1837.[23] But he did not choose it as his target despite the fact that it tackled the issue of capital punishment more clearly than did *Claude Gueux*. "La poésie ne peut pas, *sous peine de mort* ou de défaillance, s'assimiler à la science ou à la morale; elle n'a pas la Vérité pour objet, elle n'a qu'Elle-même" (Poetry cannot, *without risking death* or decay, be assimilated to science or morality; the pursuit of Truth is not its aim, it has nothing outside itself), he stated in 1857 and in 1859, rewriting Poe's "Poetic Principle."[24] For Baudelaire then, *Le Dernier Jour* does not seem to have run the risk of sentencing poetry to death by associating it with explicit practical and moral ends, as opposed to *Claude Gueux*.

Behind this focus on *Claude Gueux* looms a critique of the function and form of literature. What is its primary goal? Where and how do ideology and morality fit into literature? How can or should they emerge in literary works? Is there any room at all for ideology in the literary realm? Baudelaire poses the question in an article on *Les Misérables* of April 20, 1862. The beginning of its second section, in which he refrains from expressing his view too openly, reads:

> L'âge mûr, au contraire, se tourne avec inquiétude et curiosité vers les problèmes et les mystères. Il y a quelque chose de si absolument étrange dans cette tache noire que fait la

pauvreté sur le soleil de la richesse ... qu'il faudrait qu'un poète, qu'un philosophe, qu'un littérateur fût bien parfaitement monstrueux pour ne pas s'en trouver parfois ému et intrigué jusqu'à l'angoisse. Certainement ce littérateur-là n'existe pas; il ne peut pas exister. Donc tout ce qui divise celui-ci d'avec celui-là, l'unique divergence c'est de savoir si l'œuvre d'art doit n'avoir d'autre but que l'*art*, si l'art ne doit exprimer d'adoration que pour *lui-même*, ou si un but, plus noble ou moins noble, inférieur ou supérieur, peut lui être imposé. (*OCB* 2:219)

Conversely, mature age turns to problems and mysteries with anxiety and curiosity. There is something so profoundly strange in this black stain that poverty makes on the sun of wealth ... that a poet, a philosopher, or a man of letters should really be an absolute monster not to feel occasionally moved or intrigued by it to the point of anxiety. Such a literary man surely does not exist; he cannot exist. So the only thing that sets apart this literary man from that literary man, their one divergence lies in knowing whether the work of art should have any goal other than *art*, whether art should express adoration towards *itself* only, or whether a nobler or less noble goal, inferior or superior to it, can be imposed on it.

While the beginning of these considerations, uttered by a writer nineteen years younger than Hugo, sound skillfully derisive (at least in part), the last sentence points to a more fundamental rift between the two authors.[25] A substantial part of Hugo's works indicates that "progress" should be literature's primary goal. Baudelaire disqualifies the "vignette politique" that he believes has characterized these writings by Hugo (*OCB* 2:106; "Théophile Gautier"). He contrasts it with the more "mysterious" parts of his peer's production.[26] The review of *Les Misérables*, a novel that Baudelaire confessed to hating in his private correspondence (254), is therefore at pains not to criticize Hugo for the explicit introduction of morality into his prose. Yet it partly solves the conundrum by returning to the opposition to which "Théophile Gautier" alludes: it praises the "invisible" penetration of some inspired morality into literature, not as a goal but as a function of the richness of "la matière poétique" (217–18).

In sum, Baudelaire's criticism of *Les Misérables*, like that of Gautier inspired by Poe, illuminates his notes on *Claude Gueux*. The object of his discontent is "l'idée d'utilité directe," which, following in Poe's footsteps here again, he perceived as "la grande hérésie poétique des temps modernes" (*OCB* 2:263; "Edgar Allan Poe, sa vie et ses ouvrages"). Like his American model, he resented the "humanitarian poets ... poets of universal suffrage ... poets supporting the abolition of the Corn Laws; poets who want to have workhouses built" (262).

Specific textual exchanges shed further light on the divergence between Hugo and Baudelaire on the question of openly moralizing literature : letters in 1859, first, and, second, a dialogue established in a small number of revealing passages from their literary works. In September 1859, Baudelaire asked Hugo for a preface to his "Théophile Gautier" in a missive containing two prose poems dedicated to the poet-prophet, "Les Sept Vieillards" (The Seven Old Men) and "Les Petites Vieilles" (The Little Old Women). Baudelaire's previous criticism of didacticism put him in an uncomfortable position he felt the need to justify and mitigate:[27]

> So now I owe you some explanations. I know your works by heart and your prefaces show me that I've overstepped the theory you generally put forward on the alliance of morality and poetry. But at a time when society turns away from art with such disgust, when men allow themselves to be debased by purely utilitarian concerns, I think there's no great harm in exaggerating a little in the other direction. It's possible that I've protested too much. But that was in order to obtain what was needed. (*CB* 1:597)[28]

The point made in the above-cited letter to Ancelle about Baudelaire's need for exaggeration (*CB* 2:409) can already be seen here, and may not be purely rhetorical. Yet although Hugo's reply of October 6, 1859 famously complimented the younger poet on the "frisson nouveau" (new shiver) emanating from his writing, *l'homme-siècle* firmly held his ground regarding the association of literature and progressive ideology:

> You are not mistaken in anticipating some dissidence between you and me. I understand your whole philosophy (for, like any poet, you are also a philosopher); I understand it and more, I admit it; but I shall keep mine. I have never said: Art for Art's sake; I have always said: Art for the sake of

Progress. All things considered, it is the same thing, and your mind is too perceptive not to feel it. Onwards! Such is the word of Progress; such is also the cry of Art.... The whole language of poetry is contained therein. *Ite!* ...

Art is not perfectible, I was among the first to say so, I think, so I know it; nobody will surpass Aeschylus, nobody will surpass Phidias; but we can be as good as they were, and to be as good as they were, we must displace the horizon of Art, go higher, further, walk. The poet cannot walk alone, man must also move along. The steps of humanity are thus the very steps of Art.—So, glory to Progress.[29]

Baudelaire soon parodied Hugo's solemn declaration in a letter to Poulet-Malassis. It revealed how unbridgeable the theoretical gap between the two authors remained, and how Baudelaire's formal discourse on and to Hugo differed from his more disapproving private thoughts:

Don't fail to give a fierce punch in De Broise's solar plexus either. This is necessary for the correction of the proofs and the Progress of Typography. It is the Language and the cry of Art. *Ite!*
(Don't print those last lines.) (*CB* 1:608)

Within this debate on the status of literature, its self-sufficiency or, conversely, its functional character, Baudelaire was not the only one who invoked capital punishment—cursing *Claude Gueux*. Hugo in turn used the death penalty as a point of reference. He dubbed it "the most insolent of affronts to human dignity, to civilization, to progress" and a "permanent crime" (*OCH* 12:897), identified the end of lethal justice as the condition sine qua non of progress supported by the first of all human rights (named "l'inviolabilité de la vie humaine"), and insisted that it was incumbent upon the writers of his century to abolish capital punishment.[30] "The writers of the 18th century abolished torture; the writers of the 19th century, I have no doubt, will abolish the death penalty."[31] In other words, while, as Derrida has noted, Hugo anticipated "the right to life" formulated in the 1948 Universal Declaration of Human Rights, Baudelaire defended the right to death—the right to acknowledge man's murderous and suicidal dispositions—and, with it, the right of literature to challenge modernity's abstract and universal humanitarian ideals.[32]

Jean-Marc Hovasse has shown that three works prolong the authors' key epistolary exchange from 1859: the poem from *Les Fleurs du mal* "Le Cygne," a passage of *Les Misérables*, and the prose poem "Le Gâteau." I would argue that capital punishment occupies a privileged place in this intertextual dialogue. The first extract to which Hovasse points is from part 5 of *Les Misérables*. In the presence of two poor children, a bourgeois father feeds two swans in the Luxembourg Gardens, using the brioche his son has spat out crying because he is no longer hungry. When the bourgeois and his progeny then walk away, content with the humaneness they have shown toward the two animals, the children in rags pick up the crumbs. This swan-centered scene operates what Hovasse calls a "déformation transgénérique caricaturale."[33] It reappropriates Baudelaire's "Le Cygne" in a highly critical piece of prose fiction. Not incidentally, Hugo's chilling vignette is preceded by a moral critique about those artists who appear to express indifference toward others:

> Chose étrange, l'infini leur suffit. Ce grand besoin de l'homme, le fini, qui admet l'embrassement, ils l'ignorent. Le fini, qui admet le progrès, ce travail sublime, ils n'y songent pas.... Dieu leur éclipse l'âme. C'est là une famille d'esprits, à la fois petits et grands. Horace en était, Goethe en était, La Fontaine peut-être; magnifiques égoïstes de l'infini, spectateurs tranquilles de la douleur, qui ne voient pas Néron s'il fait beau, auxquels le soleil cache le bûcher, qui regarderaient guillotiner en y cherchant un effet de lumière, qui n'entendent ni le cri, ni le sanglot, ni le râle, ni le tocsin. (*OCH* 12:851–52; part 5, book 1, chapter 16)

> Strangely enough, infinity is enough for them. They ignore that great need in man, the finite, which admits of an embrace. They do not think about the finite, which admits of progress, that sublime toil.... God eclipses their soul. Theirs is a family of minds at once little and great. Homer belonged to it, Goethe belonged to it, La Fontaine possibly; magnificent egotists of the infinite, calm spectators of pain, who do not see Nero if the weather is fine, from whom the sun hides the stake, who would look at a decapitation to seek the play of light therein, who do not hear the cry, nor the sob, nor the death-rattle, nor the bell toll.

Like the bourgeois father in the Luxembourg Gardens, Baudelaire could be seen as a dangerously clueless privileged individual interested in graceful swans, not in starving human beings.

Hovasse demonstrates that Baudelaire responded to this criticism in "Le Gâteau," which pitilessly refutes the existence of human fraternity presumed by the bourgeois—writer or spectator. The poem replaces the generosity preached by Hugo with "une guerre parfaitement fratricide" (a perfectly fratricidal war) between two destitute children fighting over a slice of bread, a "spectacle" said to have "embrumé le paysage" (obscured the landscape) enjoyed by the speaker, ruining "la joie calme où s'ébaudissait [s]on âme" (the calm joy gladdening his soul). Contrary to the aesthetes depicted in *Les Misérables*, Baudelaire's persona in "Le Gâteau" is *not* unaware of the violence that surrounds him. After claiming provocatively to be imperceptibly distracted ("embrumé") by it, he expresses his incredulity at one of the children's use of metaphor: the youngster's hunger is so great that it metamorphoses such basic food as bread into a treat, a "*gâteau*" (italicized in the poem, in addition to being titular). Albeit ironically, Baudelaire signals that he is no Marie-Antoinette.[34] With "Le Gâteau," he bitterly shows that he understands destitution, the persistent possibility of violence resulting from inequality, and the language of violence. For Dolf Oehler, he even encourages those who starve to have recourse to violence in the very presence of a parodied bourgeois audience.[35] This rewriting of *Les Misérables* built into "Le Gâteau" is, in my view, another case of Baudelaire's "envers de Claude Gueux." It shatters Hugo's valorous characters and transforms the exemplary into the amoral or the immoral. Instead of being heroic—poor yet generous—Baudelaire's children are selfish and fierce.

Capital punishment is what ignites this threefold intertextual confrontation. Hugo's vigorous attack on Baudelaire and his fellow aesthetes culminates with a reference to executions, presented as situations in which the writers' blindness—literally—to sociopolitical realities reaches a climax ("qui ne voient pas Néron"). In this powerful caricature, aesthetic passion proves radically incompatible with human solidarity. The text's markers of grandeur ("magnifiques," "tranquilles") become ruthless indictments. By way of oxymoron, Hugo applies them to the aesthetes' selfishness, indifference, and ignorance of their own cruelty. He thereby proposes a monstrous portrayal of the writers who worship beauty: "Dieu leur éclipse l'âme . . . esprits, à la fois petits et grands." In other words, the author turns the scaffold into the sad and ultimate indicator of purely aestheticist literature. Through sarcasm and somber grotesquerie, the nonopposition of poets to lethal justice comes to typify their irresponsibility and, indeed, their inhumanity.

Hugo and Baudelaire's disagreement on the relationship between literature and progressive militancy, which symbolically pivots around the death penalty, points to a deeper divorce. Two antagonistic visions of mankind inform their works. Hugo's remains optimistic, forward-looking, and may even surpass the Christian doctrine itself in a desire for universal charity and forgiveness that does not concern itself with the Last Judgment. For him, who takes the murder of the brother to be the veritable moment of man's Fall, the legal killing of other men is unacceptable in that it replicates this gesture. By contrast, Baudelaire's vision of the human race proves backward-looking and centers on its corrupt nature and intrinsic disposition for evil. What is natural in man is the taste for "demolition," "destruction," and "crime" (*OCB* 1:679).[36] Symptomatically, "Notes Nouvelles sur Edgar Poe" distorts Poe's writings to underscore the latter's supposed belief in "la perversité primordiale de l'homme":

> Il est agréable que quelques explosions de vieille vérité sautent ainsi au visage de tous ces complimenteurs d'humanité, de tous ces dorloteurs et endormeurs qui répètent sur toutes les variations possibles de ton: "Je suis né bon, et vous aussi, et nous tous, nous sommes nés bons!" oubliant, non! feignant d'oublier, ces égalitaires à contresens, que nous sommes tous nés marquis pour [sic] / marqués par le mal! (*OCB* 2:323)

> It is pleasant that a few old-fashioned truths should thus explode in the face of all those who compliment mankind, who mollycoddle and lull us to sleep by repeating with every possible variation of tone: "I was born good, and so were you, and all of us, we were born good!" forgetting, no! pretending to forget, backwards egalitarians that they are, that we were all born as marquis for [sic] / branded with the mark of evil!

Claiming to transcribe Poe's thought, Baudelaire remarks that such "perversité naturelle" "fait que l'homme est sans cesse et à la fois homicide et suicide, assassin et bourreau" (results in man being constantly and simultaneously homicidal and suicidal, murderer and executioner;

OCB 2:323). And for the poet, the scaffold and the figure of the willing condemned man expose this moral duality: they epitomize man's simultaneous criminal and vulnerable natures.

Hugo comes to play a, indeed *the* prominent role in Baudelaire's critique of his era and country's "decadence" identified earlier. Baudelaire's remarks on the supposed hidden goals of the celebration of Shakespeare's birth in the letter he sent to the director of *Le Figaro* in April 1864 are unambiguous in this regard:

> selon ... le *crescendo* particulier de la bêtise chez les foules rassemblées dans un seul lieu, porter des toasts à Jean Valjean, à l'abolition de la peine de mort, à l'abolition de la misère, à la *Fraternité universelle*, à la diffusion des lumières, au *vrai* Jésus-Christ, *législateur des chrétiens*, comme on disait jadis, à M. Renan, à M. Havin, etc. ..., enfin, à toutes les stupidités propres à ce XIXe siècle, où nous avons le fatigant bonheur de vivre, et où chacun est, à ce qu'il paraît, privé du droit naturel de *choisir ses frères*. (*OCB* 2:229)[37]

> depending on ... the particular *crescendo* of idiocy in crowds gathered in a single place, to drink a toast to Jean Valjean, to the abolition of the death penalty, to the abolition of poverty, to *universal Fraternity*, to the diffusion of the Enlightenment, to the *real* Christ, *legislator of the Christians*, as they used to say, to Mr. Renan, to Mr. Havin, etc. ..., and finally, to all the stupid ideas characteristic of this 19th century in which we have the tiring pleasure of living, and in which everyone is, from what it seems, deprived of the natural right to *choose one's brothers*.

The poet accuses a blind humanitarian progressivism and positivism à la Hugo of promoting the monolithic fiction of a universally loving and benevolent mankind, one that eclipses true criminality (Jean Valjean) and places the spiritual leader (Jesus Christ) and the politician (Havin) or the positivist scholar (Renan) on the same moral footing.[38]

In contrast, Baudelaire demands that we be aware of our duality and that we notably acknowledge our active participation in destruction, literal and figurative. The following passage, which concludes a note from *Pauvre Belgique!* cited earlier, can be understood in this light. It both regrets and reclaims the necessary deadly brutality of revolutions:

> MOI, quand je consens à être républicain, *je fais le mal, le sachant*. . . .
> Mais moi, je ne suis pas dupe! je n'ai jamais été dupe! Je dis *Vive la Révolution!* comme je dirais: *Vive la Destruction! Vive l'Expiation! Vive le Châtiment! Vive la Mort!*
> Non seulement, je serais heureux d'être victime, mais je ne haïrais pas d'être bourreau,—pour sentir la Révolution de deux manières!
> Nous avons tous l'esprit républicain dans les veines, comme la vérole dans les os. Nous sommes Démocratisés et Syphilisés. (*OCB* 2:961)

> When *I* agree to be a republican, *I knowingly cause harm*. . . .
> But *I* am not fooled by this! I have never been fooled! I say *Long live the Revolution!* just as I would say *Long live Destruction! Long live Expiation! Long live Punishment! Long live Death!*
> Not only would I be happy to be a victim, but I wouldn't hate to be an executioner,—so as to feel the Revolution from both ends!
> We all have the republican spirit in our veins, like the pox in our bones. We have been made Democratic and Syphilitic.

Here and elsewhere, Baudelaire therefore redefines progress in opposition to Hugo, not as sociomoral improvement but as man facing up to—and, in some cases, surpassing—the depravity that forms part of his nature. The direct, sardonic reference to Hugo's mystic rituals in Jersey in the statement below, from *Mon cœur mis à nu*, confirms it:

> Théorie de la vraie civilisation.
> Elle n'est pas dans le gaz, ni dans la vapeur, ni dans les tables tournantes, elle est dans la diminution des traces du péché originel. (*OCB* 1:697)[39]

> Theory of true civilization.
> It doesn't lie in gas, or steam, or table-turning, it lies in reducing the traces of original sin.

Lessening these traces of the past, Baudelaire argues, depends on such virtues as "dignity" and disinterestedness, on a moral aristocracy of sorts which he claims "the West" (*OCB* 1:697) has largely lost.

Baudelaire's conviction that we are in part viscerally corrupt—a fact that only some men may transcend through moral means—translates into a demand that literature should *show* our fallen and miserable state, whether in his most provocative, parodic projects or in his verse, as the famous epigraph to the first edition of *Les Fleurs du mal*, borrowed from d'Aubigné, confirms.[40] Likewise with the notes to his lawyer for the trial of 1857 in which he rages against the "prudish, uptight, nagging morality" that "would go so far as to say: FROM NOW ON WE WILL ONLY WRITE CONSOLING BOOKS SERVING TO DEMONSTRATE THAT MAN WAS BORN GOOD, AND THAT ALL MEN ARE HAPPY,—abominable hypocrisy!" (*OCB* 1:196).[41] The "envers de Claude Gueux" project is testament to this will to produce works that reveal rather than conceal man's immoral and sometimes criminal penchants. If one is to believe Asselineau, Baudelaire once exclaimed about the blissful portrayal of man presented in *Les Misérables*: "*I* will write a novel in which I will feature a villain, but a real villain, an assassin, a thief, an arsonist and privateer, and it will end with this sentence: 'And under the shade of these trees I planted, surrounded by a family who reveres me, by children who cherish me and by a wife who adores me, I am relishing the fruits of all my crimes in peace!'" (*JIB* 301). For Baudelaire, then, the double immorality resulting from human depravity and from the possibility that society may not punish it is to be explored by literary creation, as opposed to the fabrication of a myth of justice.

Ultimately, a certain kind of Hugolian literature is not just suspected of "functionalism" (i.e., of serving a politico-ideological goal) and paternalism, but also of concealing man's supposed spiritual and anthropological truth, by promoting or promising widespread human happiness. *Pauvre Belgique!* specifically condemns the painter Wiertz, "Christ des humanitaires," whom Baudelaire accuses of foolishness and compares with "Hugo at the end of *Les Contemplations*," before noting: "Abolition de la peine de mort," "Wiertz et V. Hugo veulent sauver l'humanité" (Wiertz and V. Hugo want to save mankind; *OCB* 2:935–36). The end of *Les Contemplations* to which Baudelaire alludes here includes "Ce que dit la bouche d'ombre" (What the mouth of darkness says). This poem portrays a pantheistic *infini* that overflows with life but also evokes God's creation of man as imperfect, and a resulting horrendous human existence plagued by suffering, crime, wandering, and death. It calls for pity, narrates the sympathy of an animated nature, and ends with a hopeful conclusion that heralds the disappearance of evil and pain. *Les Contemplations* thus assures the reader of the transfiguration of darkness into light.

It is this literature celebrating an ascending moral trajectory, either through a confident embrace of redemption and forgiveness postmortem or through the implementation on earth of a more humanitarian law that does away with killing, that Baudelaire vigorously refuses: "All literature derives from sin.—I speak most earnestly," avers a letter to Poulet-Malassis written in late August 1860 (*CB* 2:85). Nevertheless, contrary to what Hugo subtly suggests in the excerpt above from *Les Misérables*, Baudelaire does not promote a literary aestheticism that goes so far as to ignore the fate and pain of the man burned at the stake. Quite to the contrary: while his later texts increasingly indulge in incendiary affront, as early as 1851, he wrote self-critically about the life-threatening risk run by the man of letters obsessed only with beauty and form at the expense of the outside world and his fellow sufferers in a passage from "L'École païenne" (The Pagan School) that is arguably similar to Hugo's text in its forceful tone and content: "The immoderate taste for form results in monstrous and unknown disorders" (*OCB* 2:48–49). But Baudelairean poetry does not promise or promote a moral transfiguration as Hugolian poetry does. Rather, it explores, and exposes, violence, not just on the scaffold but also in what Baudelaire perceives as man's brutal nature as well as in a modern social world plagued by inequalities that idealistic and political discourse may recuperate or fail to fully acknowledge.[42] Baudelaire does not, in this process, turn a blind eye to the executioner's victim, nor to the executioner himself, as chapter 4 will show.

MAISTRE AS MASTER? BAUDELAIRE'S EIGHTEENTH-CENTURY AFFINITIES AND BEYOND

Benjamin Fondane diagnosed Baudelaire's veneration of Maistre and Poe as a means of escape from Hugo.[43] The specific question of capital punishment makes this Hugo vs. Maistre opposition particularly salient. In 1851, Hugo rebuked Maistre's praise of the executioner in a poem entitled "Écrit sur la première page d'un livre de Joseph de Maistre" even though, as a young Ultra-Royalist, Hugo had peppered his early *Han d'Islande* with citations by the counter-Revolutionary thinker.[44]

Prose Praising Sacrifice | 95

Elaborating on Fondane, Jérôme Thélot has argued that Baudelaire's anti–*Claude Gueux* project shows that what he aptly terms the poet's "Maistrean proposition, or posture" is a function of his hatred for Hugo's novels.[45] The context and material examined so far have led us to narrow down this hatred to one that specifically targets the didactic Hugolian novel. The exact modalities of Baudelaire's Maistrean posture also invite further qualification.

Baudelaire claimed to have nostalgic affinities with the eighteenth century of "public executions against a backdrop of libertinism, which were the great festivals of the 18th century," as Georges Blin has put it.[46] While the poet appropriated aspects of the works of the marquis de Sade, whose thought he interpreted as the lucid portrayal of man's evil nature, according to Blin, he simultaneously opposed part of what is commonly remembered of the French eighteenth century, namely the Enlightenment, the promotion of rationality and scientificity over spirituality, and the omnipotence that 1789 claimed to give to the people. The first official evocation of the abolition of capital punishment was formulated during that period, in 1795, in the form of a promise: capital punishment was to be abolished once peace was established, according to article 1 of the *décret du 4 brumaire de l'an IV*. As noted in the introduction, important eighteenth-century authors repeatedly pleaded against the *supplices* and capital punishment. They included Sade—probably unbeknownst to Baudelaire—and Voltaire, an admirer and commentator of Beccaria, who was himself influenced by such French philosophers as Montesquieu.[47] The poet's interest in Joseph de Maistre and his theory of sacrifice is part of an ostentatious resistance to these eighteenth-century roots of French progressivism.

Baudelaire knew Maistre as early as 1850 or 1851 (*JIB*, 284–85) and is likely to have read at least his *Essai sur le principe générateur des constitutions politiques* (*OCB* 1:1513)—which he confused with *Considérations sur la France* (*OCB* 1:709, 2:68, 70)—as well as *Lettres et opuscules inédits* published in 1851 (*OCB* 2:50, 223)[48] and *Les Soirées de Saint Pétersbourg* (*OCB* 2:251, 298; "L'Héautontimorouménos"). Just as Maistre had celebrated bloodshed, the executioner, and the law of destruction in his *Soirées*, Baudelaire repeatedly described mankind as bound to and by carnage.[49] His previously cited offer to contradict *Les Misérables* by narrating the fortune of "un vrai scélérat, assassin, voleur, incendiaire et corsaire" (*JIB* 301) jokingly illustrates this. So do other, more earnest, writings: "Le Voyage" concludes *Les Fleurs du mal* with a lapidary description of

> La chose capitale, . . .
> Le spectacle ennuyeux de l'immortel péché. (*OCB* 1:132)

> The most important thing, . . .
> The tedious spectacle of immortal sin.⁵⁰

and includes glimpses into a modern society saturated with violence and blood:

> Le bourreau qui jouit, le martyr qui sanglote;
> La fête qu'assaisonne et parfume le sang. (*OCB* 1:132)

> The executioner relishing his task, the sobbing martyr;
> The festival seasoned and perfumed with blood.⁵¹

Ghastly cameos reemerge in Baudelaire's anaphoric listing of man's intoxication with violence in *Mon cœur mis à nu*, which refers to his plan to write

> Un chapitre sur l'indestructible, éternelle, universelle et ingénieuse férocité humaine.
> De l'amour du sang.
> De l'ivresse du sang.
> De l'ivresse des foules.
> De l'ivresse du supplicié (Damiens). (*OCB* 1:693; folio 26)

> A chapter on the indestructible, eternal, universal, and ingenious ferociousness of humanity.
> On the love of blood.
> On the intoxication of blood.
> On the intoxication of crowds.
> On the intoxication of the drawn and quartered criminal (Damiens).

This final reference to the man who attempted to assassinate Louis XV and was the last person to undergo drawing and quartering in France confirms Baudelaire's will to foreground an eighteenth century that predates, and is at odds with, humanitarian penal reforms. What better words to gloss the poet's apocalyptic paintings of the human race than Maistre's?

Thus, from the maggot up to man, the universal law of the violent destruction of living things is unceasingly fulfilled. The entire earth, perpetually steeped in blood, is nothing but an immense altar on which every living thing must be immolated without end, without restraint, without respite, until the consummation of the world, until the extinction of evil, until the death of death.

But the anathema must strike down man most directly and most visibly.[52]

In addition to mimicking Maistre's rhetorical and ideological violence, Baudelaire appears to hark back to the latter's "Théorie du sacrifice" when he apprehends the death penalty through the prism of this ritual. The counter-Revolutionary philosopher's *Éclaircissement sur les sacrifices* conceived of the expiatory shedding of blood in a favorable light, on the grounds that *"heaven, angered by flesh and blood, could only be appeased by blood."*[53] In aggrandizing capital punishment through this spiritual model of beneficial sacrifice, Baudelaire opposed both the humanitarian detractors of the death penalty, such as Hugo, *and* its orthodox partisans, who believed in its ability to guarantee society's material safety. Let us recall Baudelaire's statement in *Mon cœur mis à nu*: "La peine de mort n'a pas pour but de *sauver* la société, matériellement du moins. Elle a pour but de *sauver* (spirituellement) la société et le coupable" (*OCB* 1:683). Maistre's theory, which specifically defines moral rescue as the product of sacrifice, is patent here.[54] Baudelaire's recourse to the concept of *sponte sua* also appears to have followed Maistre's definition of the reversibility of merits, according to which a *juste* agent suffers and is thereby promoted from the status of patient to that of victim[55] liable to compensate for men's misdeeds— which echo original sin.[56]

Yet it would be erroneous to assert that Baudelaire thoroughly abides by Maistre's model.[57] *Éclaircissement sur les sacrifices* traces the resort to sacrifice in the ancient world (in Egypt, India, Greece, pre-Columbian America etc.), explaining its persistence and ubiquity by universalizing the notion of the Fall across cultures and periods. The act of shedding blood, Maistre insists, has the crucial function of enabling society to expiate the evil inherent in man. It is beneficial in that it allows for the conversion of his "réité" (or "original . . . degradation").[58] Maistre asserts that, most probably, human sacrifices were originally carried out against condemned men and that this procedure was seen as one of common sense: the elimination of a criminal supposedly led to his salvation and, more important perhaps, to the protection of the community, since his execution signaled its members' will to not be complicit with his acts.

To this economy of "compensation" Maistre adds another configuration of sacrifice in which the victim is innocent. Following the process of reversibility, the blood of a chosen member of the community can be shed to make up for the crimes of guilty men, the underlying "logical" connection being that we are all fallen beings and therefore potential culprits liable for the offenses of our fellow creatures.[59] In this second sacrificial configuration, Maistre notably refers to the ritual killing of animals, whose blood serves as a symbolic substitute for that of man. The philosopher severely condemns human sacrifices within this framework. But he enthusiastically evokes a third configuration to be distinguished from these unacceptable human sacrifices. In it, a "propitiatory victim" belonging to mankind volunteers to die for his brothers' redemption.[60] Maistre argues that this supposedly laudable case of sacrifice is Christian and corresponds to a true understanding of how the institution functions.[61] Jesus Christ—followed by others, such as Louis XVI—is taken to exemplify this superior sacrificial model.

The figure and concept of the *sponte sua* Baudelaire proposes differ from the various sacrificial scenarios envisaged by the philosopher. It situates itself at the crossroads of two types of Maistrean sacrifice: (a) the one in which society executes a criminal condemned to death and thereby transforms him into an agent of both individual and collective redemption; (b) the one in which an innocent man willfully dies for the redemption of the human race, by way of reversibility—"the righteous [le juste], suffering willingly, fulfill their duty not only towards themselves, but towards the guilty, who, on their own, could not expiate their own sins."[62] Both Baudelaire's framework and new willing hero are hybrid and subversive. They destabilize the Maistrean typology of sacrifice in several ways. First, they establish the moral grandeur of the "coupable" (*OCB* 1:683; folio 12) condemned to death, whereas the philosopher attributes this grandeur only to the innocent victim. Second, they make "reversibility" take on new meaning: the metamorphosis of a criminal into a saint.

In reinventing the *sponte sua*, Baudelaire undoes both the strict hierarchy of sacrifices and the history of their evolution as established by Maistre, who argues that, from Jesus Christ to Louis XVI, willing victims incarnate the ultimate refinement of the sacrificial institution in Christian civilization. The modern poet, for his part, has criminality and martyrdom coincide. This association of guilt and saintliness within a single being blurs, indeed tarnishes, the Maistrean typology in which propitiatory executions are revered. While Baudelaire borrows key notions from the reactionary philosopher—among which the correlation of condemned man and sacrificial victim, the notion of voluntary death, the superior status of the executioner, and the sanctity of the propitiatory *sacrifié*—he inserts them in a unique development that moves away from Maistre's tortuous but resolute reflections on the superiority of Christian sacrifice. This shatters the sense of order and metaphysical confidence the counter-Revolutionary thinker seeks to establish.

A logical lacuna in the passage of Mon cœur mis à nu that centers on the spirituality of the death penalty corroborates the idea that Baudelaire alters Maistre's methodical teachings on sacrifice. This passage ("La peine de mort est le résultat d'une idée mystique..." *OCB* 1:683) is both preceded and followed by ones in which the poet reflects on torture. He despises it as an "art de découvrir la vérité" (art of discovering the truth) on the grounds that it relies on the "application d'un moyen matériel à un but spirituel" (application of a material means to a spiritual end). But Baudelaire's sacrificial (re)conception of capital punishment echoes this very shortcoming. The transcendental process it supposedly represents depends on the protagonist's physical suffering and, eventually, annihilation. The sandwiching of Baudelaire's reflection on the death penalty between two critical remarks on torture—"niaiserie barbare" (barbaric nonsense) "née de la partie infâme du cœur de l'homme" (originating in the vile part of man's heart)—further warns against an excessively literal, or Maistrean, reading of his apology for the scaffold. Likewise, Baudelaire's exaggerated portrayal of the willing condemned man's "assentiment et joie" (consent and joy) during the execution and his general skepticism regarding redemption deepen the partly ironic character of his sanctification of capital punishment through sacrifice.

Baudelaire's taste for eccentricity, his "idée fixe de la Différence," as Blin would have it, and preoccupation with the sociomoral de-hierarchization produced by the egalitarian ideals that developed in the nineteenth century appear to have moved him to revisit capital punishment as a desirable form of sacrifice.[63] From the late 1850s onward in particular, the poet vigorously challenged the proponents of social progressivism through the redefinition and praise of the death penalty as sacrifice. This archaic practice conveniently went against the forward-looking imperative of the "inviolabilité de la vie humaine" (inviolability of human life) defended by Hugo and his peers at the same time as it refuted the latter's demand that art should contribute to society's improvement. In this respect, Baudelaire's praise of sacrifice may be read as the culmination of an anti-Hugolian enterprise—literary, but also deeply ideological in nature. Beyond the refusal to "functionalize" works of art in flagrant ways, the modern poet, through the provocative defense of executions, expresses his belief in man's indelible violence. He turns to the eighteenth century of sadism, the *supplices*, and the counter-Enlightenment to bolster this stance. Maistre's concepts, rhetoric, and imaginary are used in his reconception of the death penalty for this very reason. Nevertheless, Baudelaire does not follow them *à la lettre*, far from it. He associates the figure of the *juste* with that of the criminal and rejects torture because it relies on the very material-spiritual dynamic he applies to the *sponte sua*. Baudelaire thereby subverts both Maistre's purportedly reassuring typology of sacrifice and his own defense of capital punishment. The condemned man, *sponte sua*, is both criminal and saint, impure and pure.[64] He points back to the contradictory etymology of "sacred" and to Baudelaire's insistence that a "double postulation," one toward God, the other toward Satan (*OCB* 1:682), structures the human psyche. Baudelaire embraces the duality of the sacred in opposition to a false, adulterated modern sacredness that has moved away from this complexity. In *Fusées*, this repugnant, self-celebrating "sacerdoce," this loss of a genuine sacred, is incarnated by none other than Hugo:

> Hugo pense souvent à Prométhée. Il s'applique un vautour imaginaire sur une poitrine qui n'est lancinée que par les moxas de la vanité. Puis, l'hallucination se compliquant, se variant, mais suivant la marche progressive décrite par les médecins, il croit que, par un *fiat* de la Providence, Sainte-Hélène a pris la place de Jersey.
>
> Cet homme est si peu élégiaque, si peu éthéré, qu'il ferait horreur même à un notaire.
>
> Hugo-Sacerdoce, a toujours le front penché,—trop penché pour rien voir, excepté son nombril.
>
> Qu'est-ce qui n'est pas un sacerdoce aujourd'hui? La jeunesse, elle-même, est un sacerdoce,—à ce que dit la jeunesse.
>
> Et qu'est-ce qui n'est pas une prière? Chier est une prière, à ce que disent les démocrates, quand ils chient. . . .

> L'homme, c'est-à-dire chacun, est si naturellement dépravé qu'il souffre moins de l'abaissement universel que de l'établissement d'une hiérarchie raisonnable. (*OCB* 1:664–65)

> Hugo often thinks of Prometheus. He places an imaginary vulture onto a chest that nothing lacerates other than the moxa of vanity. Then, as his hallucination becomes increasingly complex and varied, but following the progression described by the doctors, he believes that, through a fiat of Providence, the island of Saint Helena has replaced Jersey.
> This man so lacks any sense of the elegiac and the ethereal that even a notary would be appalled by him.
> Sacerdotal Hugo, always with his forehead leaning forward—too bent over to see anything, except for his own navel.
> What isn't sacerdotal nowadays? Young people themselves are sacerdotal,—according to what young people say.
> What isn't a prayer? Crapping is a prayer, according to what the Democrats say, when they have a crap. . . .
> Man, that is to say everyone, is so naturally corrupt that universal debasement makes him suffer less than the establishment of a reasonable hierarchy.

Baudelaire's laudatory remarks on lethal justice therefore constitute a discourse of reaction against a perceived modern moral corruption and liberal doxa. Opposing Hugo, he sets out to highlight the extremities that coexist in man, away from both didactic progressive art and art for art's sake. Yet like any "system," which the poet himself deemed bound to abjuration (*OCB* 2:577), Baudelaire's recasting of the death penalty as sacrifice in his prose is ultimately disavowed, not least by his poetry.

CHAPTER 4

Poeticized Slaughter?

Execution in Les Fleurs du mal

La tête se détachait du cou, une grosse tête blanche et rouge, et roulait avec bruit devant le trou du souffleur, montrant le disque saignant du cou, la vertèbre scindée, et tous les détails d'une viande de boucherie récemment taillée pour l'étalage.

His head was severed from his neck, a big white and red head, which rolled down loudly in front of the prompter's box, exposing the bleeding disc of the neck, the severed vertebra, and all the details of a piece of butcher's meat freshly cut for the stall.

—Charles Baudelaire, "De l'essence du rire et généralement du comique dans les arts plastiques," in *Œuvres complètes*

"Poetry of mass graves and slaughterhouses." This is the phrase that Louis Goudall used to summarize the eighteen poems Baudelaire published under the title *Les Fleurs du mal* in the June 1855 issue of the *Revue des Deux Mondes*.[1] That same year, with an essay titled "De l'essence du rire et généralement du comique dans les arts plastiques," the poet took full responsibility for his peculiar thematic and imagistic tastes and anticipated by the aim of his verse as he would later describe it, "extraire la beauté du mal" (to extract beauty from evil):[2] "Chose curieuse et vraiment digne d'attention que l'introduction de cet élément insaisissable du beau jusque dans les œuvres destinées à représenter à l'homme sa propre laideur morale et physique!" (The introduction of this elusive element of beauty, even into works destined to show men their own moral and physical ugliness, is a thing [that is] both curious and truly worthy of attention!; *OCB* 2:526). Once it was published as a complete book of poems in 1857, and then again in 1861, *Les Fleurs du mal* thoroughly confirmed this premise

103

that beauty seeps into the figuration of man's physical and moral vileness, notably through the most graphic poems that so displeased Goudall. In them and others, chopped flesh, severed heads, killers, and executioners abound. These compositions that elaborate on the imaginary of capital crime and punishment allow for a better understanding of Baudelaire's literary use of execution, across its literal and artistic meanings. They also shed a critical light on the poet's—already problematized, as we have seen—turn to Maistre in his prose pieces claiming to legitimize the death penalty as sacrifice.

BLOODY AESTHETICS

As something of a "boucherie," Baudelaire's poetry brings grist to Goudall's mill. *Le Grand Dictionnaire universel du XIXe siècle* first defines *boucherie* as the "abattoir, endroit où l'on tue les animaux, dont la viande se vend ensuite en détail" (slaughterhouse, place where animals are killed and where the meat is then sold) and second as the "établissement où l'on vend au détail la chair des mêmes animaux" (establishment in which the flesh of these animals is sold).[3] While executions take on a variety of forms in *Les Fleurs du mal*—from hanging to poisoning and strangulation—they frequently emphasize some of the procedures and attributes reminiscent of the slaughterhouse and the butcher's shop: the slaying of bodies, the use of the knife, the presence of blood, and the display and commerce of dead flesh.

Some of the most memorable quatrains from "Une charogne" (A Carcass) foreground this dead flesh:

> Les mouches bourdonnaient sur ce ventre putride,
> D'où sortaient de noirs bataillons
> De larves, qui coulaient comme un épais liquide
> Le long de ces vivants haillons.
>
> . . . .
>
> Alors, ô ma beauté! dites à la vermine
> Qui vous mangera de baisers,
> Que j'ai gardé la forme et l'essence divine
> De mes amours décomposés! (*OCB* 1:31–32)

> The flies were buzzing on that putrid belly,
> From which issued black battalions

Of larvae, flowing like a thick liquid
Along those living rags.
. . . .
Then, o my beauty, say to the vermin
Who will devour you with kisses,
That I have kept the form and the divine essence
Of my decomposed loves![4]

Decay, rather than slaughter, affects the animal body here. Nevertheless, the well-known *ars poetica* this poem constitutes is a useful point of departure in that Baudelaire specifically constructs it around the reality of dead flesh. In keeping with the observation from "De l'essence du rire," this flesh, which attracts swarms of flies and in which ugliness proliferates, is associated with aesthetic blossoming. Carnal decomposition conditions poetic composition: the carcass that elicits horror acts not just as a prolepsis for the future death of the beloved, as becomes clear in the last three quatrains, but also, both directly (in and of itself) and by analogy (through this prolepsis), as the subject and matrix of the perennial poetic form with which we are presented and on which the speaker eventually prides himself. While the meat is rotten, *boucherie* does operate at a symbolic level: speaker and text are able to preserve the body of the dead animal—and, soon, that of the woman—despite its disintegration (stanza 8) and "sell" it to the beloved and to the scene's other witness, the reader. It finds itself consumed visually and aurally by them.

Other poems feature both the literal brutality and the figurative sense of *boucherie* more directly. In the sonnet "Le Tonneau de la haine" (The Cask of Hate), two quatrains stage an allegorized "Vengeance" whose "bras rouges et forts" and "grands seaux" of blood evoke the archetypal butcher—before the two tercets turn revenge into another prosaic figure, that of a drunkard in a tavern:

> La Haine est le tonneau des pâles Danaïdes;
> La Vengeance éperdue aux bras rouges et forts
> A beau précipiter dans ses ténèbres vides
> De grands seaux pleins du sang et des larmes des morts,
>
> Le Démon fait des trous secrets à ces abîmes,
> Par où fuiraient mille ans de sueurs et d'efforts,
> Quand même elle saurait ranimer ses victimes,
> Et pour les pressurer ressusciter leurs corps. (*OCB* 1:71)

Hate is the cask of the pale Danaïdes;
Vengeance distraught has red and brawny arms
With which she hurls into her empty dark
Buckets of blood and tears from dead men's eyes,

Satan makes secret holes in these depths
Through which would seep out a thousand years of pain and toils,
Even if she knew how to bring her victims back to life,
And to resuscitate them before squeezing them dry.[5]

This Vengeance-butcher works not in a shop but in hell. Combining myth and raw materiality, Baudelaire's allegorical vision takes on an especially gory quality. It substitutes the water that the daughters of Danaus are condemned to carry and pour for eternity with epic quantities of human bodily fluids—blood, tears, and sweat, all synonymous with pain. Both the opening portrait of the exsanguine Danaids, marked by a chromatic contrast (whiteness, redness, blackness of the "ténèbres"), and the elongated and ruptured syntax of the second sentence, stretched by six consecutive enjambments and punctured by an inversion in line 8 which together mirror uncontainability and violence, further hyperbolize the figuration of death, violence, and suffering. Expanding on the poem's inaugural metaphor about the insatiability of hate ("La Haine *est* le tonneau des pâles Danaïdes"), this dramatic tableau climaxes in the hypothesis of a useless "resuscit[ation]" of the deceased. The image is doubly blasphemous, since hell is no place for resurrection and since this resuscitating would serve to kill again ("pour les pressurer"). A veritable liquidation of human shadows thus activates the meaning by extension of the term *boucherie*, which refers to the "mort sanglante et assurée d'un grand nombre de personnes" (bloody and assured death of a great number of individuals).[6]

Exalted killing also pierces through "L'Héautontimorouménos" (The Self-Tormenter):

Je te frapperai sans colère
Et sans haine, comme un boucher,
Comme Moïse le rocher!
Et je ferai de ta paupière,

Pour abreuver mon Sahara,
Jaillir les eaux de la souffrance.

Mon désir gonflé d'espérance
Sur tes pleurs salés nagera. (*OCB* 1:78)

I'll strike you without rage or hate,
The way a butcher strikes his block,
The way that Moses smote the rock!
So that your eyes may irrigate

My dry Sahara, I'll allow
The tears to flow from your distress.
Desire that hope embellishes
Will swim along the overflow.[7]

The opening stanza denies the literal meaning of *boucher*, that of an impassive, "hateless" worker, as claimed in line 2 and brings out its figurative sense instead: the spectacle of an eminently hostile violence imposes itself from the poem's first words ("Je te frapperai"). As in "Le Tonneau de la haine," aquatic images hyperbolize the scene. Mythological and epic overtones characterize the destruction of the other. This time, they are biblical. Comparing the aggressor's action with that of Moses in line 3, Baudelaire subverts the Old Testament to underscore the speaker's brutality as well as the close association—indeed, the possible substitution—of word and violence. Where, in both Exodus and the Book of Numbers, Moses hits the rock to give water to his people, that is to say sustains them with a stone that stands for Christ (Corinthians 10), the poem's speaker, on the other hand, plans to hit the woman, that is to say destroy a being that stands for carnal, rather than spiritual, love (l. 7). And where, in the Book of Numbers, Moses fails to follow God's orders, using his stick instead of speaking to the water-bearing rock, Baudelaire's protagonist uses speaking, but to promise hitting. In so doing, he restores confidence in language, but a language that is human, not divine, and that heralds violence against humanity. In the third sentence ("Mon désir gonflé d'espérance / Sur tes pleurs salés nagera"), the sadistic perversity of the speaker's premeditation becomes so overwhelming that it sets it into motion. Metaphors of swelling, gushing, and swimming animate his larger-than-life plan, and a vitalist aesthetic paradoxically emerges from the vicious, and potentially fatal, molestation he plots.

"À une Madone" (To a Madonna) epitomizes this inscription of cruelty within a slow, excruciating process of planned execution:

Enfin, pour compléter ton rôle de Marie,
Et pour mêler l'amour avec la barbarie,
Volupté noire! Des sept Péchés capitaux,
Bourreau plein de remords, je ferai sept Couteaux
Bien affilés, et, comme un jongleur insensible,
Prenant le plus profond de ton amour pour cible,
Je les planterai tous dans ton Cœur pantelant,
Dans ton Cœur sanglotant, dans ton Cœur ruisselant! (OCB 1:59)

Finally, to complete your role as Mary,
And to mingle love with barbarity,
Black delight! From the seven deadly Sins,
I shall, an executioner filled with remorse, make seven well-honed knives,
And like an unheeding juggler,
Taking the deepest springs of your love as my target,
I shall plant every one of them in your panting Heart,
In your sobbing Heart, in you streaming heart![8]

In these final lines, an alliterative network composed of hard consonants [p / k / t], the antiphrastic periphrasis "Bourreau plein de remords," and the epizeuxis "dans ton Cœur" cap the gradation in violence that structures the poem. Together, they seal the triumph of a murderous desire presented as irrepressible and ironically mystical.[9]

To understand better this recourse to knives, flesh, blood, and the exhibition of dead bodies characteristic of the imaginary of butchery and execution in some of *Les Fleurs du mal*, it is helpful to return to "De l'essence du rire." This essay, which takes as its subject matter the habilitation of caricature as a pictorial genre and the examination of the mechanics behind human laughter, establishes a hierarchy of comic forms that consecrates the "comique absolu" (absolute comic; OCB 2:535). For Baudelaire, the "comique absolu" is the alternate name of the grotesque, "une création ... une idéalité artistique" (a creation ... an artistic ideality; 535) that contrasts with vile imitation. He considers the first English pantomime he saw performed as its quintessence. Pierrot, the protagonist, finds himself guillotined at the end of the show:

Après avoir lutté et beuglé comme un bœuf qui flaire l'abattoir, Pierrot subissait enfin son destin. La tête se détachait du cou, une grosse tête blanche et rouge, et roulait avec bruit devant le trou du souffleur, montrant le disque saignant du cou, la vertèbre scindée, et tous les détails d'une viande de boucherie récemment taillée pour l'étalage. Mais voilà que, subitement, le torse raccourci, mû par la monomanie irrésistible du vol, se dressait, escamotait victorieusement sa propre tête comme un jambon ou une bouteille de vin, et, bien plus avisé que le grand saint Denis, la fourrait dans sa poche! (OCB 2:539)

After struggling and bellowing like an ox that senses the slaughterhouse, Pierrot was finally subjected to his destiny. His head was severed from his neck, a big white and red head, which rolled down loudly in front of the prompter's box, exposing the bleeding disc of the neck, the severed vertebra, and all the details of a piece of butcher's meat freshly cut for the display. But then, all of a sudden, the truncated torso, driven by the irresistible monomania of theft, drew itself up, triumphantly snatched its own head like a ham or a bottle of wine, and, much wiser than the great Saint Denis, shoved it in its pocket!

In this scene of "boucherie-charcuterie," *guignolesque* gestures, noises, forms, and colors contribute to a saturated sensory landscape. Comparing this caricatural mime show and literature, Baudelaire laments the weakness of words to convey the energy that emanates from grotesque theatrical representation. "Avec une plume tout cela est pâle et glacé. Comment la plume pourrait-elle rivaliser avec la pantomime?" (With a quill, all this is pale and icy. How could the quill compete with pantomime?; OCB 2:540).

Arguably, the *boucherie* present in some *Fleurs du mal* as both a motif and a trope enables Baudelaire to equal "le vertige de l'hyperbole" (OCB 2:539) he perceives in this absolute comic, the "appanage des artistes supérieurs" (prerogative of superior artists; 536). It brings out violence, colorfulness, and crudity.[10] It also allows the writer to re-create the motion and life of dramatic performance, as well as what he deems to be the extreme ferocity of the grotesque (538). Baudelaire's portrait of Pierrot as a raw, vivacious, and excessive figure illustrates the "artistic ideality" (535) of the absolute comic and illuminates these characteristics he cultivates through the bloody aesthetics of some poems:

Par-dessus la farine de son visage, il avait collé crûment, sans gradation, sans transition, deux énormes plaques de rouge pur. La bouche était agrandie par une prolongation simulée des lèvres au moyen de deux bandes de carmin, de sorte que, quand il riait, la gueule avait l'air de courir jusqu'aux oreilles.

Over his face's white makeup, he had pasted crudely, without gradation, without transition, two huge blotches of pure red. The mouth was widened by a feigned prolongation of the lips, by means of two crimson stripes, so that, when he laughed, the mouth seemed to run from ear to ear. (*OCB* 2:538–39).

The most graphic *Fleurs du mal* integrate this coarse redness—a synthetic metonymy for violence, colorfulness, and crudity—caricatural traits, and dynamism ("collé," "agrandie," "riait," "courir"). But they do so away from the clownish potential of this pantomime that dampens cruelty and pathos. Instead, they combine these traits with the palette and "desolation" (760) of Eugène Delacroix's massacres and Francisco Goya's monstrous gloom.[11] The wealth of blood, limbs, and organs (human hearts, intestines, eyes, trunks, shoulders), red blotches, and quartered contours found in *Les Fleurs du mal* thus constitutes the site and the means of a visual and theatrical emulation, but one that undergoes sinister adaptation. Baudelaire's *ut pictura poesis* must be *in sanguinem* and leaves no room for laughter.

This exacerbated dialogue with the visual and performing arts translates into the simultaneous magnification and deconstruction of pictorial elements in the poems, as is manifest in the texts I have begun to examine. "À une Madone" encloses in a full-length portrait a statue-like virgin saturated with finery that is turned into a series of vices and failings that soil her increasingly before the final murder. Through a syntax made up of accumulations, a prosody fraught with alliterative redundancies, and the imbrication of incriminating metaphors, Baudelaire transposes in writing the density characteristic of baroque iconography. A materiality "dans le goût espagnol" that comes to verge on the rococo gradually entraps and crushes the Madonna-like mistress, wrapped in "un Manteau . . . / Barbare, roide et lourd, et doublé de soupçon" (a Cloak . . . / Of barbarous fashion, stiff and heavy and lined with suspicion; *OCB* 1:58). The poem's closing homeoptoton, "pantelant," "sanglotant," "ruisselant," introduces a trembling and ominous motion into this artistic production.

Likewise, "L'Héautontimorouménos" destroys the subject through a sophisticated and dynamic visual demonstration. Its highly rhythmic penultimate quatrain magnifies the vision of a body undergoing dismemberment through a kaleidoscopic perspective:

> Je suis la plaie et le couteau!
> Je suis le soufflet et la joue!
> Je suis les membres et la roue,
> Et la victime et le bourreau! (*OCB* 1:79)

> I am the wound, and rapier!
> I am the cheek, I am the slap!
> I am the limbs I am the rack,
> The prisoner the torturer![12]

A fixed and bare grammatical structure (subject, copula, attribute), which Baudelaire mechanizes further with an anaphora and in which only one paradigmatic component changes, makes the reader visualize the swift circulation of body parts and lethal utensils. That they are different yet unchanging is symbolically reinforced by alternating feminine and masculine nouns of one and two syllables ("plaie" and "couteau," "soufflet" and "joue," "membres" and "roue"). The diffraction effect thereby created heightens the dynamism of the tableau that emerges from the close-up on the eyelid at the beginning of the poem.

"Une martyre," which bears the revealing subtitle "dessin d'un maître inconnu" (drawing by an unknown master), offers a final and most telling instance of how Baudelaire maximizes his poems' pictorial and performative potential through butchery:

> Au milieu des flacons, des étoffes lamées
> Et des meubles voluptueux,
> Des marbres, des tableaux, des robes parfumées
> Qui traînent à plis somptueux,
>
> Dans une chambre tiède où, comme en une serre,
> L'air est dangereux et fatal,
> Où des bouquets mourants dans leurs cercueils de verre
> Exhalent leur soupir final,

Un cadavre sans tête épanche, comme un fleuve,
Sur l'oreiller désaltéré
Un sang rouge et vivant, dont la toile s'abreuve
Avec l'avidité d'un pré. (*OCB* 1:111–12)

Surrounded by flasks, and by spangled lamés,
All matter of sumptuous goods,
Marble sculptures, fine paintings, and perfumed peignoirs
That trail in voluptuous folds,

In a room like a greenhouse, both stuffy and warm,
An atmosphere heavy with death,
Where arrangements of flowers encoffined in glass
Exhale their ultimate breath

A headless cadaver spills out, like a stream,
On a pillow adorning the bed
A flow of red blood, which the linen drinks up
With a thirsty meadow's greed.[13]

An actual frame, in the form of a pillow (made of "toile," which revealingly means both "cloth" and "canvas"), girds the woman's severed and bleeding neck. The reader-viewer discovers it only after glimpsing the picture's rich background and decorative components. In yet another remarkable *mise en abyme*, these include pictures. In this still life, or rather this still death, the blood of the female body is paradoxically presented as being in motion. Like the bouquets, the reader is trapped in the airless bedroom and made to absorb its increasingly deadly material abundance. Placed next to the headless corpse in the third stanza, and in a highly visible and vulnerable space (where glass and entrapment—"serre" and "verre"—rhyme and prevail), we symbolically become a potential murder suspect. I will return to this poem's subsequent stanzas later. For now, suffice it to note that Baudelaire's bloody aesthetics finds itself caught up in such an intense bid to capture, or outdo, the efficiency of the visual and performing arts that it may absorb the reader into its violence. He may make us dangerously complicit with it, as we walk a thin line between voyeur and actor, between collaborator and (second) victim.

POÉSIE-BOUCHERIE: FROM THE OUTSIDE IN

The pain and horror of Baudelaire's poetic butchery is aesthetically productive. An apparent indifference toward the politics of killing and unconcern for the suffering of the Other—the victim in the poem and, to some extent, the reader—accompany this visual feast. Under the emphatic heading "POLITIQUE," *Mon cœur mis à nu* claims that Baudelaire did not to have any "convictions, comme l'entendent les gens de [s]on siècle" (convictions, as the people of [his] century understand them; *OCB* 1:680).[14] The folio of *Mon cœur* that provocatively lauds the supposed moral nobility of capital punishment and the related need for the condemned man to suffer "with joy" (folio 12; 683) also offers a critical reflection on torture that associates "cruauté et volupté," presenting them as identical sensations for which man's basest instincts yearn, "comme l'extrême chaud et l'extrême froid" (like extreme heat and extreme cold). The exaltation of brutality in both these citations and Baudelaire's narrative projects featuring the death penalty (598) appear to fit neatly with the imagery of bloodshed in which some *Fleurs du mal* indulge.

Upon closer examination, however, there are limits to this aesthetic celebration of executions in Baudelaire's verse. They certainly allow Baudelaire to "glorifier le culte des images ([sa] grande, [son] unique, [sa] primitive passion)" (glorify the cult of images, [his] great, [his] only, [his] primitive passion; *OCB* 1:701). But they also disclose a profound discomfort in the face of killing. The figuration of *boucherie* functions as a crude and strategic call for ethics, or what the poet himself termed a "terrible moralité" (193).[15] Several clues testify to the difficulties that undermine the poems' affected posture of detachment vis-à-vis death, blood, and slayed flesh. Through moments of interpellation, the distance and distinction between the butcher and his meat—or their analogues, the executioner and his or her victim—collapse.[16]

Doubt, irony, and laughter make this suspension of clear differentiation manifest. "L'Héautontimorouménos" illustrates each of these forms of fracture. A searing negative interrogation placed at the center of the poem turns it on its head as the speaker who initially presented himself as a *boucher-bourreau* declares:

Ne suis-je pas un faux accord
Dans la divine symphonie,
Grâce à la vorace Ironie

> Qui me secoue et qui me mord?
> Elle est dans ma voix, la criarde!
> C'est tout mon sang ce poison noir!
> Je suis le sinistre miroir
> Où la mégère se regarde. (*OCB* 1:78)

> But am I not a false accord
> Within the holy symphony,
> Thanks to voracious Irony
> Who gnaws on me and shakes me hard?
>
> She's in my voice, in all I do!
> Her poison flows in all my veins!
> I am the looking-glass of pain
> Where she regards herself, the shrew.[17]

Robert Wilcocks and Debarati Sanyal have shown the deep investment of the "je" in the processes of pain infliction and killing depicted by this poem. Wilcocks refutes a traditional reading according to which "L'Héautontimorouménos" combines sadistic eroticism with "a dash of self-flagellation at the end." Instead, he argues, the progression of the stanzas points to a divided poetic self.[18] Sanyal takes up this thesis and qualifies it. She notes that the poem reveals a wounded "je": in the central stanza, the speaker is annexed by a personified irony and finds that his initial victim, his Other, is in fact constitutive of himself, enclosing both his subjectivity and the poem in a self-reflexive spiral.[19]

In "L'Héautontimoroumémos," reflection and reflexivity are thus twofold. On the one hand, they pertain to the self and the Other, with this Other taking on various forms: that of the "t[u]" whose alterity one presupposes before it merges with the "je," and, at the end of the piece, that of the collective marginal figure formed by the "grands abandonnés."[20] On the other hand, reflexivity and diffraction are to be found within the "je" itself. Sanyal asserts that, ultimately, Baudelaire maintains a distinction between subject and object, or between executioner and victim, by resorting to intertextuality, irony, and interpellation.[21] Although such strategies are set up in the poem, its progression nevertheless both implements and stresses an endlessly unstable and multiple identity torn between destructive agency and passive victimhood: "Je suis de mon cœur le vampire . . . / Au rire éternel condamnés" (I am of my own heart the vampire . . . / To eternal laughter condemned).[22]

Elsewhere in *Les Fleurs du mal* ("Le Vampire," "Les Métamorphoses du vampire"), the vampire is the beloved woman, who initially emerges as the speaker's prey in "L'Héautontimorouménos." Such interchangeability of positions at the level of the collection as a whole reinforces the volatility of the speaker's self in this poem. In addition, the sixth stanza ("Je suis la plaie . . ."), whose anaphoric structure, multiple exclamations, and revelation of a paradox regarding identity simultaneously strike eye, ear, and mind, combines with the closing quatrain to seal a self-enclosed space within which a vertiginous waltz takes place. In a manner that is both chaotic and hermetic, the text's two alterities—the external other (the initial "tu" and the "grands abandonnés") and the split self—ultimately merge in the all-absorbing image of an autophagous and prostrate speaker.

As "L'Héautontimorouménos" gradually morphs from a brutal love poem into one that explores self-suffering and self-alienation, one may think that it returns to the psychological examination conducted in the classical plays by Menander and Terence whose title Baudelaire borrows—Ἑαυτὸν τιμωρούμενος / *Heauton Timorumenos*.[23] Yet Terence's comedy about a "self-tormenter" differs quite markedly from Baudelaire's homonymous creation. Its protagonist, Menedemus, experiences remorse and guilt after he has disapproved of his son's love life. Menedemus's self-inflicted tough life enables him to appease his culpability, and he eventually converts to benevolence, approving his son's wedding.[24] His moral evolution contrasts with the tragic trajectory of Baudelaire's piece. "L'Héautontimorouménos" ends with the image of ceaseless "laughter," which "De l'essence du rire" defines as the symptom of the illusory superiority of one subject over another. This hilarity is all the more synonymous with the malaise of delusion as it caps the poem's dramatic power reversal of the molester into a sufferer. The speaker irreversibly moves away from the comfort of smiling ("sourire," l. 28), whereas Terence's socially and morally harmonious denouement calls for it.

The other intertext of "L'Héautontimorouménos," Maistre's *Les Soirées de Saint-Pétersbourg*, is subject to inflection as well. As noted in chapter 3, Maistre prescribes redeeming the sins of mankind and the guilty through the execution of a "juste."[25] Elements of this theorization of sacrifice might seem to be at work in Baudelaire's poem: it emphasizes, and even appears to celebrate, pain (stanzas 1 and 2), highlights various means of execution (stanza 6), and features the figure of the victim both at the beginning and at the end. Yet Baudelaire departs from

Maistre here as he does in his prose writings. He proposes a definition of reversibility distinct from the eighteenth-century philosopher's in that it metamorphoses the perpetrator of lethal violence into its object, takes place within the subject, and forgoes the purity of the victim. In addition, his poem undoes the superior status that Maistre typically conferred on the executioner, and makes no reference to redemption.[26] What prevails in "L'Héautontimorouménos" is an unsteady configuration, a principle of nonsuperiority of one being over another, and the forced distribution of violence and pain. Terence and Maistre thus make the inner desperate violence of Baudelaire's speaker only stand out more.

Be it less overtly, other poems point to the *boucher-bourreau*'s vulnerability and the impossibility of absolute alterity vis-à-vis his victim. Recurring themes and figures throughout *Les Fleurs du mal* reinforce this inflected portrayal of the violent subject: that of a general damnation, borne out by frequent reminders of human sinfulness and incorrigibility, and the specific persona of the poet-martyr, for instance. "Bénédiction," "L'Albatros," and "La Fontaine de sang" are cases in point. The speaker of "La Fontaine" falls prey to a hemorrhage whose cause and reality he cannot verify. The world around him takes advantage of his abundant bleeding, through which it literally quenches its thirst:

> Il me semble parfois que mon sang coule à flots,
> Ainsi qu'une fontaine aux rythmiques sanglots.
> Je l'entends bien qui coule avec un long murmure,
> Mais je me tâte en vain pour trouver la blessure.
>
> À travers la cité, comme dans un champ clos,
> Il s'en va, transformant les pavés en îlots,
> Désaltérant la soif de chaque créature,
> Et partout colorant en rouge la nature. (*OCB* 1:115)

> I sometimes feel that my blood is flowing in waves,
> Like a fountain with its rhythmical sobs.
> I can hear it clearly, flowing with a long, murmuring sound,
> But I touch my body in vain to find the wound.
>
> Through the city, as if in an enclosed field,
> It goes, turning the paving-stones into islets,
> Slaking the thirst of every creature,
> And everywhere colouring nature red.[27]

Both imaginary and real in its materiality, the sacrifice of the Christlike "I" benefits the insatiable "cité," which recomposes its geography and drapes itself with color and exoticism ("îlots") by vampirizing its victim. Pichois links this gradual loss of blood and life to Baudelaire's idea of the poet's "moral hemophilia" (*OCB* 1:1065) in the sonnet "À Théodore de Banville": "—Poète, notre sang nous fuit par chaque pore—" (Poet, our blood seeps out from every pore we have; 208). But the figure of the poet who risks self-loss in researching and producing his art arguably looms over *Les Fleurs du mal* in its entirety. The very structure of the collection underscores his experimenting with various perilous modes of escape from boredom and "spleen" (wine, damned loves, revolt, and death), and the famous closing lines of "Le Voyage" suggest that he is prepared to sacrifice his life for the benefit of poetry's renewal:

> Plonger au fond du gouffre, Enfer ou Ciel, qu'importe?
> Au fond de l'Inconnu pour trouver du *nouveau*! (*OCB* 1:134)

> To plunge into the depths of the abyss, Hell or Heaven, what does it matter?
> To the depths of the Unknown to find something *new*![28]

This poet figure who oscillates between cruelty and vulnerability reappears in "À une Madone" and "Une martyre," complicating the sadistic or voyeuristic enthusiasm apparent in the poems' portrayal of bloodshed. "À une Madone" recalls the intimate union and the tension that bring together the pronouns "Je te" from the first line of "L'Héautontimorouménos" onward. It traces a specular ballet in which the idolized woman's clothes, that is to say her second skin, originate from an unexpected fabric: the speaker's inner self. Through a unique and metaphorical spatial configuration ("au fond de ma détresse" [in the depths of my anguish], "dans le coin le plus noir de mon cœur" [in the blackest corner of my heart], "dans ma Jalousie" [from my Jealousy]), the "je" merges her body with his vengeful affectivity turned into a figurative altar. The tyrannical subject refuses to live alone in his suffering and therefore entraps and mates with a "toi" whom he eventually kills in fury.[29]

Yet this murder is also a suicide.[30] The seven knives viciously planted in the idol's heart toll the bell for both victim and slayer, as the human anatomy that Baudelaire here recasts interweaves the two individuals.

The other's blood and death are built—engraved—into the speaking subject. Like "L'Héautontimorouménos," of which this poem may be said to provide a bi-subjective version, "À une Madone" is engineered around an incessant pronominal alternation, reinforced by two crisscross alliterative networks. The first centers on the plosive [t], reminiscent of the aggressed "toi" and its cognates; the second on the softer phoneme [m] and its derivatives, which echo the "moi." Their co-presence and increasingly irregular alternation symbolize a chaotic interdependence:

> Je veux bâtir pour **t**oi, Madone, **m**a **m**aîtresse,
> Un au**t**el sou**t**errain au fond de **m**a dé**t**resse,
> Et creuser dans le coin le plus noir de **m**on cœur,
> Loin du désir **m**ondain et du regard **m**oqueur,
> Une niche, d'azur et d'or tout émaillée,
> Où **t**u **t**e dresseras, S**t**a**t**ue émerveillée. (*OCB* 1:58)

> I mean to build for you, Madonna, my mistress,
> An underground altar in the depths of my anguish,
> And to hollow out, in the blackest corner of my heart,
> Far from worldly desires and mocking eyes,
> A niche all enameled in azure and gold,
> Where you will stand, a wonder-struck Statue.[31]

Albeit less conspicuously, this interconnectedness of speaker and victim and suspended omnipotence of the perpetrator of violence also transpire in "Une martyre." While the "I"-voyeur does have the capacity to contemplate and recompose freely the bloody crime scene he portrays, thereby controlling it from an empirical and intellectual standpoint, the victim is also shown to have power as, in turn, she magnetizes both him and the reader:

> Semblable aux visions pâles qu'enfante l'ombre
> Et qui nous enchaînent les yeux,
> La tête, avec l'amas de sa crinière sombre
> Et de ses bijoux précieux,
>
> Sur la table de nuit, comme une renoncule,
> Repose; et, vide de pensers,
> Un regard vague et blanc comme le crépuscule
> S'échappe des yeux révulsés. (*OCB* 1:112)

> Like pale apprehensions born in the dark
> And that enchain the eyes,
> The head—the pile of its ebony mane
> With precious jewels entwined—
>
> On the night table, like a ranunculus,
> Reposes; and a gaze,
> Mindless and vague and as white as the dusk
> Escapes from the pallid face.[32]

In these quatrains, the viewer falls prey to captivity (chained eyes) whereas the dead woman's revulsed and "empty" gaze unexpectedly associates itself with mobility and emancipation through the collocation "s'échappe." Her very inertia and silence paradoxically subjugate speaker and reader. We first scan her body and undress her visually; the eye then slides vertically from her head to her torso down to her leg before staring at her body's contours ("épaule au contour heurté, / La hanche un peu pointue et la taille fringante" [the shoulder lean and lithe, / The haunch a bit pointed]). Poe's 1831 poem "The Sleeper" unfolds in a strikingly similar fashion. Both poems are built around a double visual infiltration—of the bedroom and of the dead woman's body. Both feed on the mystery that surrounds the inert lady and fascinates the speaker. In each poem, the speaker also calls for her peaceful rest, but not without cruel overtones.

Nevertheless, "Une martyre" differs from "The Sleeper" in its twelfth and thirteenth stanzas, which add verbal aggression to scopic penetration. Curiosity and desire prompt the speaker, whose initial position in the poem was one of mere observer, to become an actor of the scene. He addresses the female corpse with malice:

> L'homme vindicatif que tu n'as pu, vivante,
> Malgré tant d'amour, assouvir,
> Combla-t-il sur ta chair inerte et complaisante
> L'immensité de son désir?
>
> Réponds, cadavre impur! Et par tes tresses roides
> Te soulevant d'un bras fiévreux,
> Dis-moi, tête effrayante, a-t-il sur tes dents froides
> Collé les suprêmes adieux? (*OCB* 1:113)

> That intractable man whom alive you could not,

> Despite so much love, satisfy,
> Did he there, on your still and amenable corpse,
> His appetite gratify?
>
> Tell me, impure cadaver! and by your stiff hair
> Raising with feverous hand,
> Terrible head, did he paste on your teeth
> His kisses again and again?[33]

The insulting apostrophes ("cadavre impur!" "tête effrayante") and repeated questions that suggest the woman may have been subjected to acts of necrophilia symbolically put the speaker in the position of aggressor. Once more, nonetheless, the aggressor is not independent from his victim: the reference to the "vindictive[ness]" of a man, whom we later discover is the victim's spouse, as well as the imperious tone of the stanzas suggest that the speaker could be the woman's lover, consumed by jealousy. The closing quatrain—keeping the form of a direct address—seems to eclipse his closeness to the female protagonist through the image of the two spouses being faithful until death. Yet the remark is bitterly ironic in light of her implied infidelity. Besides, because of a remarkable intertextual detail, the speaker is not altogether removed from the stanza:

> Ton époux court le monde, et ta forme immortelle
> Veille près de lui quand il dort;
> Autant que toi sans doute il te sera fidèle,
> Et constant jusques à la mort. (*OCB* 1:113)
>
> Your bridegroom may roam, but the image of you
> Stands by him wherever he rests;
> As much as you, doubtless, the man will be true,
> And faithful even till death.[34]

The closing reference to the woman's "forme immortelle" that accompanies the husband strikingly echoes "Une charogne," whose last two lines read, "Que j'ai gardé la forme et l'essence divine / De mes amours décomposés!" (That I have kept the form and the divine essence / Of my decomposed loves!). The woman who was a victim at the beginning of "Une martyre"—and at the end of "Une charogne"—now actively replaces the curator of deadly form found in "Une charogne." Her "forme immortelle" is no longer "kept" by the speaker-poet, as was the case in the other poem, but has gained agency. It "watches over" the spouse. In other words, after hinting at the victim's subduing power throughout, "Une martyre" concludes with its female protagonist playing the part reserved for the "I"-poet earlier in the collection.

Although the spectacle of slaughter may seem to be observed from the outside in Baudelaire's *poésie-boucherie*, this exteriority therefore is not durable.[35] The other's pain becomes one's own, homicide turns into suicide, and a remarkable proximity, if not an identity or interchangeability, between the actual or symbolic perpetrator of violence and the victim, whose status turns out to be flexible, often imposes itself.[36] Baudelaire's slaughters tend to conceal Siamese twins. They greatly qualify the sense that his *poésie-boucherie* is one of sadism or one of sheer aestheticism.[37]

ESSENTIAL VIOLENCE AND SELF-CRITICISM

If Baudelaire's most graphic poems inflect Maistre's concept of reversibility, and if the masochism that lies behind their sadism calls for a reconsideration of the sacrificial dynamic that sometimes appears in his *poésie-boucherie*, of what nature, we may ask, is the violence at play in this verse?

The modalities of this violence examined so far include its ability to spread, conveyed by rampant liquid metaphors ("Le Tonneau de la haine," "L'Héautontimorouménos," "La Fontaine de sang," "Une martyre"); a principle of embedding ("L'Héautontimorouménos," "À une Madone," "Une martyre") or closeness that troubles, and sometimes levels out, the distinct positions of the "je" and the "tu" (victim and executioner, or flesh and butcher); and the removal of the reader's privileged status through these processes of contagion, imbrication, or equalization. These characteristics point to man's destructive, frail, and finite condition, which emerges at the outset of *Les Fleurs du mal* as the inaugural "Au lecteur" establishes an identity pact of sin and misery between speaker and reader, "semblable" and "frère." Besides, from a metaphysical standpoint, Baudelaire's writings repeatedly assert mankind's fundamental violence, presented as the fruit of an innate malevolence. Catherine Toal has rightly noted how they distort Poe's ideas on human perversity to that end.[38] Baudelaire reads the American writer as affirming that human wickedness is natural, emphasizing man's fundamental evil, whereas Poe merely observed that all individuals may be haunted by a desire for transgression.

Baudelaire's insistence on this impossible escape of the subject—whether victim, executioner, or reader-viewer—from an evil that notably takes the form of ruthless violence leads me to name the latter "violence essentielle," following René Girard's expression.[39] For Girard, such violence is born of an infinite contagion of brutality and vengeance, of an "escalade cataclysmique" that sacrifice sometimes fails to curtail, resulting in a sacrificial crisis.[40] Beyond an aesthetic exercise, what the frequent figuration of slaughter in Baudelaire's poems reveals is such a crisis. Sacrifice aims to establish a sociopolitical stability that benefits a given human community in allowing for the evacuation of the latent violence that pervades it and for a communion around a sacred order.[41] It works toward concord. Maistre's *Soirées de Saint-Pétersbourg* and *Éclaircissement sur les sacrifices* play up this beneficial mechanics supposed to underlie spectacular bloodshed. Sacrificial crisis, on the other hand, marks the failure of this model. Girard provides two possible causes for it: a complete rupture between victim and community or, conversely, an excessive continuity between the two.[42] In both cases, he argues, the sacrificial victims cannot purge violence because of the unfitting distance that relates them to the community.

I noted earlier that Baudelaire redefines Maistre's concept of reversibility and subverts the sacrificial ritual. In light of Girard's analysis, it appears that the poet foregrounds the failure of sacrifice in the second of two ways. By ultimately federating the "je," the "tu," and sometimes the reader, he replaces what the critic names the necessary "contiguity" between the victim who is actually killed and the human beings for whom it is substituted by an explicit or symbolic interlocking of actors bound to unsettle a sacrificial process that requires difference.[43] The incongruous reconfiguration of spaces and beings in the poems analyzed earlier—imbricated bodies, dispersed limbs, enlarged fragments, role reversals—symbolizes this uncontrolled and proliferating violence.

For Girard, this infinite contamination, or "violence essentielle," occurs between different members of a given community. Baudelaire goes further. The contamination he represents is total, at once pandemic and endemic, developing also within the limited space of the alienated self. Even inanimate objects morph into the perpetrators or recipients of extreme violence. In "L'Héautontimorouménos," the speaker mixes, and thereby seems to align, not only the actors of violence ("victime" and "bourreau") but also the tools that carry it out ("le couteau," "la roue"), the act that incarnates it ("le soufflet"), and the aftermath it produces ("la plaie"). Within this fundamental undifferentiation between being, object, and gesture, between patient and agent, and cause and consequence, a loss of meaning looms. Indeed, the poem's final stanzas, in which violence generates a dissolution of identity, a hallucinatory delirium, self-enclosure, and annihilation, are reminiscent of the radical figuration of man's atomization found in *Le Dernier Jour d'un condamné*.[44]

Baudelaire and his poems do expose this abysmal spectacle. Although this exposure often comes from within and thus seems akin to a testimony, many remarkable self-referential moments signal the poetic mastery of the speaker-poet as he displays flesh and blood. What, then, becomes of the collection's ethics of negative equality, of the inclusion and indistinction of all in essential violence, of a supposedly shared pain and violence?[45] In "Une martyre," the severed head on the nightstand resembles a "renoncule" (buttercup), that is to say a "fleur du mal" ready for public consumption, as Sanyal has rightly remarked.[46] A similar self-referential move can be found in "Duellum," which has the skin of two lovers fighting to the blood "fleuri[r] l'aridité des ronces."[47] This poetic gain permitted by bloody violence resurfaces in "À une Madone." Here, poetry serves as the sophisticated tool used for the slaughter. It participates in the murderous monumentalization of the icon through its "Vers" and "rimes" (ll. 7 and 8):

> Avec mes Vers polis, treillis d'un pur métal
> Savamment constellé de rimes de cristal,
> Je ferai pour ta tête une énorme Couronne. (*OCB* 1:58)

> Of my polished verse, cunningly bestarred
> With crystal rhymes,
> I shall make for your head an enormous Crown.[48]

The speaker-poet then refers more broadly to his "art diligent" (line 23). It gradually aggregates allegories (his "Jalousie," "Désir," "Respect") around the Madonna to immobilize and entrap her before the final stabbing, thereby giving birth to the poem as a whole. Let us also return to the early lines of "L'Héautontimorouménos":

> Et je ferai de ta paupière,
>
> Pour abreuver mon Sahara
> Jaillir les eaux de la souffrance.

Mon désir gonflé d'espérance
Sur tes pleurs salés nagera

Comme un vaisseau qui prend le large, (OCB 1:78)

So that your eyes may irrigate
My dry Sahara, I'll allow
The tears to flow of your distress.
Desire, that hope embellishes
Will swim along the overflow.

As ships set out for voyaging,[49]

Massacre and bodily dismantlement find their formal echo in the enjambment and blank space that follow "paupière," as well as in the inverted structure "Et je ferai de ta paupière, / . . . / Jaillir les eaux de la souffrance" and in the early insertion of the purpose clause "Pour abreuver mon Sahara." But this physical and formal dislocation results in the graceful image of marine flight, that is to say in one of the richest imagistic networks of *Les Fleurs du mal* that the author associates with poetic and aesthetic ideality (OCB 1:663–64, 696).

The profit that art may derive from killing is a topos present elsewhere in Western literature of the nineteenth century. It often focuses on painting, from Balzac's "Le Chef d'œuvre inconnu" to Poe's "The Oval Portrait." But Baudelaire underscores the fact that the *poet* is the one who manages this transaction. Walter Benjamin has shown how Baudelaire's writings engaged with modern materialism and capitalism. The specific background paradigm of the *boucherie*, literal or figurative, could be read as the caricatural illustration of this materiality and commercial spirit: like the symbolic butcher of "Une charogne," the protagonists of "Le Tonneau de la haine" and "L'Héautontimorouménos" chop up flesh, preserve it, and put it on display. More generally, Baudelaire's bloodiest poems stage a constant business of production and gain based on slayed bodies, formal violence, and the reader's attention and consumption: the instances above attest that essential violence produces prominent Baudelairean allegories and metaphors, and vice versa. In other words, contagious violence results in and from the devices that define the poetic genre in general, and the substance of Baudelaire's collections in particular: the imagery of alienation, the voyage, and escape that the figuration of slaughter generates constitutes the heart of *Les Fleurs du mal*.

The modern poet, then, is a dealer in human executions of a sort. The spectacle of bloodshed enables his art to prosper. In this respect, he is not unlike the writer-merchant who, at the beginning of the *Salon de 1846*, pretends that he sympathizes with bourgeois readers taken to wish that their work and wealth will be repaid by the "enjoyment ... of the imagination" literature offers (*OCB* 2:417). But just as biting irony undermines this address "to the bourgeois" in the *Salon*, in the poems the speaker distances himself from this trade: the self-referentiality noted earlier also functions as a self-denunciation. It signposts his own exploitation of slaughter, which in turn further establishes the failure of sacrifice. A basely secular, exploitative, and (self-)criticized violence emerges from behind or within the violence whose vaguely ritual appearance at times prefigured spirituality. No transcendent order ultimately ennobles bloodshed in *Les Fleurs du mal*, not even that of aesthetic ecstasy. The somber visual and dramatic excess that characterizes Baudelaire's poetic executions, like Baudelairean laughter, remains inextricably tied to a persistent disquiet and to a deceptively powerful subjectivity.

While in his prose Baudelaire claims to present the death penalty as a noble sacrificial act, and while numerous poems stage a persona indifferent to or responsible for the agony of others, the depths of *Les Fleurs du mal* show that bloody executions are acts and spectacles that can be neither related nor exalted without difficulty. Gory killing and corpses constitute a reservoir of powerful images that enables Baudelairean poetry to rival other modes of representation, dramatic and visual. Yet the imaginary of butchery is not solely a privileged point of access to "la beauté dans le mal" (beauty in evil/pain) and to artistic ideality. Baudelaire also turns it into an uneasy ethical site. What looms behind the garishness of Baudelaire's scenes of slaughter and tableaux of dismantled flesh is an impossible distancing from killing. He proposes configurations of lethal violence in which the Other points to the self—the self of the speaker-poet or of the reader. They institute a painful equality between subjects that one thought to be distinct from, if not at odds with, one another. Any semblance of the sacrificial in *Les Fleurs du mal* should therefore be relativized. Baudelairean violence is contagious. It is not a source of stability resulting from the efficient functioning of sacrifice; conversely, it bears witness to a sacrificial rout. Even when the poet seems to extricate himself from a ubiquitous essential violence by laying out a space from which he can signal that he is exploiting it, he reinforces the failure of the sacrificial dynamic: far from generating salvation or appeasement, the violence of his poetic slaughter remains terribly worldly. With Baudelaire, poetic execution both explores and rivals the actual practice of execution under the persistent banner of anthropological and metaphysical angst.

* * *

Capital punishment plays a crucial role in Baudelaire's opposition to Hugo and to what the latter represents in the eyes of the modern poet. It acts as a nerve center through which Baudelaire emphasizes major literary but also political and ideological differences. To be sure, Baudelaire conceived the sanctification of the death penalty as an efficient *faire-valoir* of his artistic originality and talent for provocation. But his defense—and redefinition—of capital punishment as sacrifice also plunges its roots into a deeper substrate, at once reactionary and critical. The rejection of Hugo's abolitionism and didactic fiction is a means of invalidating both a sociopolitical platform, promoting equality among men and an optimistic vision of mankind, and a literary doctrine, favoring progressive art that is explicitly political and moral. In this respect, the death penalty as conceived by the two writers can be said to illuminate irreconcilable anthropological reflections *and* theoretical takes on the function of literature and the writer within society.

While capital punishment crystallizes certain antagonisms between Baudelaire and Hugo, it also complicates them. The close examination of Baudelaire's laudatory statements on the death penalty as sacrifice and the analysis of his execution-centered poetry reveals a departure from Maistre and a dissatisfaction with bloodshed despite the aesthetic ideality that its imaginary is shown to allow. The most brutal poems of *Les Fleurs du mal* point to the failure of controlled violence and display the symptoms of a sacrificial crisis. Baudelaire's verse at once exploits and denounces the spectacle—real or poetic—of killing. Thus, on the one hand, Baudelaire's writing sharply contrasts with that of Hugo in *Le Dernier Jour d'un condamné*, whose call for abolition and defense of "l'inviolabilité de la vie humaine" are as strong as they are indirect—these strategies of indirection in fact appear to have spared it the furious critique Baudelaire reserves for Hugo's openly edifying fiction; on the other hand, however, Baudelaire's "poésie-boucherie" undermines his own promotion of the death penalty as sacrifice: the bloody imagery of *Les Fleurs du mal* underlines the negativity of the social contract that unites mankind, sheds light on our dual nature as both victim and executioner, and exposes the essential and exponential violence that pervades modernity.

In differing ways, and despite profoundly dissimilar ideological stances, Hugo and Baudelaire thus critique key claims of lethal justice through poetics: the alleged painlessness and humanitarianism of decapitation for the former, and the theoretical ability of executions to federate a community and regulate violence for the latter. This critique through poetics inflects the monolithic and competing categories of "L'Art pour le progrès" and Art for Art's sake that the two writers are usually considered to represent, and that they sometimes do represent—often not without caricatural insistence on and an awareness of the artificiality of such a dichotomy. Part III further investigates the role played by this poetic mode of *engagement* and the crucial part it plays in conceiving and critiquing modern state killing, its imaginary, and literature itself.

PART III

Camus's Capital Fiction and Literary Responsibility

Shelley: "Les poètes sont les législateurs non reconnus du monde."

Shelley: "Poets are the unacknowledged legislators of the world."

—Albert Camus, *Carnets* (1945), in *Œuvres complètes*

SPEAKING THE TRUTH, LOVING LIFE, AND THE ULTIMATE "RÉVOLTÉ"

Multiform and relentless, Albert Camus's abolitionism was to the twentieth century what Victor Hugo's was to the nineteenth. Recent scholarship, published from the late 1990s to the early 2010s, has revealed the depth and breadth of this commitment. It manifested itself in the writer's public speeches as well as in his articles and editorials, fiction, and essays.[1] Importantly, it also led him to write numerous letters in support of condemned men irrespective of their national, sociopolitical, and cultural identities. Having edited and examined these contributions elsewhere, I will not return to all of them here, but instead point to a few key moments and traits of Camus's lifelong fight against the death penalty that provide an informative background against which to analyze his works of fiction that feature state killing.

As early as 1931, the young Camus took Hugo's *Le Dernier Jour d'un condamné* as a point of reference in the first short story he published, "Le Dernier Jour d'un mort-né" (The Last Day of a Still-Born). The plot bore no trace of the guillotine, but it did relate a young man's sudden sensual attachment to life and desperate anger at the thought of his imminent death—as predicted to him by a doctor. Beyond the autobiographical echoes this novella may have had for the tubercular Camus, the affects it stages recur in his subsequent writings on the death penalty. The first book he published, the collection of essays *L'Envers et l'endroit* (Betwixt and Between; 1937), addressed the question of lethal justice directly, warning: "Qu'on ne nous raconte pas d'histoires. Qu'on ne nous dise pas du condamné à mort: 'il va payer sa dette à la société,' mais: 'On va lui couper le cou.' Ça n'a l'air de rien. Mais ça fait une petite différence" (Don't let them tell us stories. Don't let them say about the man condemned to death: "he is going to pay his debt to society," but: "We're going to cut off his neck [*sic*]." It may seem trivial. But it makes a small difference; *OCC* 1:54). Capital punishment is associated here with a demand for truth and lucidity. As a falsely casual irony indicates, and as the subsequent chapters will show in greater detail, one of Camus's contributions to the critique of modern state killing following in Hugo's footsteps lies in exposing the crucial role played by representation, and more particularly by language, in the conception and reception of this institution.

Le Mythe de Sisyphe (1942) elaborated on the rejection of capital punishment perceptible in the previously cited injunction to lay bare the brutality of executions. This time, Camus disqualified the death penalty through the philosophical apparatus developed in his reflections on the Absurd—part of which grew out of his earlier demand for lucidity. He claimed that, while we are all sentenced to death in that we are all mortal, our active, obstinate existence undiminished by the clear awareness of our tragic condition should respond to this harsh reality. Such is, in part, his definition of "la révolte." In Camus's metaphysical framework, the man on death row epitomizes this attachment to the "pure flame of life," "a life without consolation": he wishes to live even as his execution is impending (*OCC* 1:260). The condemned man becomes the ultimate, and respectable, incarnation of the "révolté" in that despite the programmed death that society imposes on him in addition to, and before, the death that awaits all of us, he clings to terrestrial life and refuses suicide (256).

THE UNACCEPTABLE "MEURTRE LÉGITIMÉ" AND THE TEST OF HISTORY

The mass murders perpetrated under the aegis of Nazism, Fascism, and Stalinism intensified Camus's rejection of what he called "legitimized murder."[2] So did Franco's dictatorial regime after the Spanish Civil War (1936–39) and the use of capital punishment overseas by colonial France and imperial England—in Algeria during the War of Independence (1954–62) and in Cyprus, Tunisia, and Madagascar. In the 1940s and 1950s, Camus became the implacable foe of the organized and legitimized killing of civilians by the state or political parties, regardless of the forms such killing took. He distinguished it from "crimes of passion" (OCC 3:63) and from the recourse to killing as an exceptional transgression designed to protect both justice and freedom.

In 1946, the politics of extermination that had characterized World War II, as well as contemporary world politics, led him to aver: "There is but one problem today which is that of murder" (OCC 2:687). In the middle of the twentieth century, murder, he argued, had come to elicit a "feeling of indifference or friendly interest or experimentation, or of mere passivity" (739), resulting in a veritable "Crisis of Man." Camus's "cycle of Revolt" (*La Peste, Les Justes, L'Homme révolté*) as well as his many postwar editorials, articles, speeches, and an abundant correspondence picked apart both the right to kill that states and institutions may arrogate for themselves and our passive or active condoning of murder. *L'Homme révolté* (1951) encapsulates this anxiety: "We will know nothing as long as we don't know whether we have the right to kill this other man standing before us or to consent to his killing" (OCC 3:64). It also examines in detail the Reign of Terror as a specific moment in French history when, in Camus's view, authentic "revolt" ended and was perverted by a bloodthirsty revolution sanctified by the scaffold (155).

One exception to Camus's sustained abolitionist reflections is the period of the Épuration (postwar purges). Haunted by the war and the loss of his friends from the Resistance, among them the journalist René Leynaud, Camus supported the executions of the most active French Collaborationists from May to November 1944.[3] He accounted for this stance, which contradicted both his long-standing opposition to the death penalty and some authoritative figures such as François Mauriac, in articles and editorials that called for "the immediate repression of the most obvious crimes" through "a justice that is prompt and limited in time" (OCC 2:558):

> It is not the judgment coming from a class or an ideology, it is not the verdict reached in the name of an Abstraction that is at work here. It is the general cry, the call, the language replete with flesh and vivid images, the demand from the accused that we have all been for the past four years, [and who have] suddenly become strong enough to judge their

own judges and to do so without hatred, but without pity [either]. (*OCC* 1:923)[4]

The language of truth that Camus had previously advocated to lay bare the violence of capital punishment was now trumped by a "language replete with flesh and vivid images" that he claimed had emerged from the experience of "four years" of Nazi and Collaborationist ferocity, and that now demanded that justice be done "without hatred, but without pity [either]." When faced with the reality of the purges, Camus changed his mind, however; in his opinion, they spared talented rhetoricians while sentencing to death journalists who did not deserve it (*OCC* 2:592). In early January 1945, he asserted that the Épuration had failed and returned to his vigorous rejection of execution (407–8). He even supported the campaign for the pardoning of Collaborators he profoundly despised, such as Robert Brasillach (733–34).

Camus's returning revulsion at legitimized murder after the Épuration, as well as the progressive roots of European penal philosophy and the observation of the politics of both the recent past and the present, also led him to develop his argument and activism against the death penalty on the international scene.[5] While in New York City on March 28, 1946, he pleaded for the universal abolition of capital punishment by the United Nations (*OCC* 2:744). An article entitled "Un nouveau contrat social" (A New Social Contract) reiterated his proposal in November. During the second half of the 1940s and at the beginning of the 1950s, Camus further clarified his refusal of institutionalized violence, arguing that if brutality may be necessary at particular historical moments, it should always remain extraordinary: "I believe that violence is inevitable, the years of Occupation taught me as much. To be frank, there was, at that time, terrible violence which posed no problem for me. . . . Violence is both inevitable and unjustifiable. I believe we should preserve its exceptional character and keep it confined within limits as much as possible" (457).[6] The death penalty contradicts this principle: its violence is inscribed within the law, unexceptional, and consequently strikes the author as indefensible. In a sense, it grants institutional legitimacy to what Camus called man's "death instinct" (*OCC* 4:138).

"LA SOLIDARITÉ CONTRE LA MORT"

Camus's work of nonfiction that deals with lethal justice most explicitly and extensively, the essay "Réflexions sur la guillotine," originally came out as a two-part article in 1957. It was soon included in a multiauthored volume entitled *Réflexions sur la peine capitale* to which Arthur Koestler and Jean Bloch-Michel also contributed. Camus's tightly argued "Réflexions" invalidate the traditional arguments leveled by the supporters of capital punishment and dissect the violence imposed on the condemned man's body and mind. They partly follow in the footsteps of Hugo's 1832 preface to *Le Dernier Jour d'un condamné*, pointing to the inefficiency, preventive or retributive, of capital punishment; to the confusion of man's vengeful impulses with the duty of the law, which is to place itself above individual instincts; and to the fact that the bloody spectacle of execution may in fact invite some individuals to indulge in violence. Camus's essay is profoundly critical of the state. Defining executions as premeditated and organized killing, he condemns the state's erroneous logic according to which they constitute an appropriate punishment for crimes driven by passion or pathology. In addition, he holds the state partly responsible for certain murders committed by individuals whom he views as the victims of criminogenic socioeconomic factors, including the commercialization of alcohol facilitated by the law. Camus argues that, although punishment is necessary, individual responsibility exists, and the killer and his victim should never be confused, state justice cannot have recourse to a penalty that is absolute and irreversible, when, as a human institution, it is bound to be fallible. Instead, it should be relative and aware of its potential shortcomings and inconsistencies. Lastly, the essay insists that, in the first half of the twentieth century, the state committed many more murders than individuals did and was therefore not well placed to judge and condemn them in a definitive manner.

"Réflexions sur la guillotine" and Camus's prior and subsequent articles, novels, plays, and letters on capital punishment tend to put forth life as an ultimate value. They stress the fact that significant external factors or uncontrollable passions may partly account for individual capital crimes, and, to a lesser extent, signal the potential perfectibility of human beings. Camus's ethics and reasoning are partly reminiscent of Hugo's abolitionism. Unlike Hugo, however, the Nobel laureate does not conceive them in a progressive Christian perspective—especially as, in his view, such a perspective could support the death penalty by positing eternal life and the existence of a divine justice liable to correct the errors of man's capital justice (OCC 4:161). Camus situates the inviolability of human life on a secular, antemortem plane where, he argues, a fundamental, "indisputable" solidarity should prevail: our solidarity against death (159, 161). Other significant representational and ethical dimensions of Camus's fiction are in dialogue with Hugo's—and Baudelaire's—reflections and literary works on capital punishment. What follows sheds light on these contact zones, after analyzing the way in which Camus's major narratives stage lethal justice.

CHAPTER 5

Ad nauseam

Camus's Narrative Roads to Abolitionism

Patrice raconte son histoire de condamné à mort: "Je le vois, cet homme. Il est en moi. Et chaque parole qu'il dit m'étreint le cœur. Il est vivant et respire avec moi. Il a peur avec moi. . . .

"Je sais maintenant que je vais écrire."

Patrice tells his story about the man condemned to death: "I can see this man. He is in me. And each word he says grabs my heart. He is alive and breathes with me. He is afraid with me. . . .

"I now know I am going to write."

—Albert Camus, preparatory notes for *La Mort heureuse*, *Carnets* (1936), in *Œuvres complètes*

Camus's novels give life to the death penalty. They stage characters who are directly or indirectly confronted with judicial and penitentiary institutions or with execution. In *L'Étranger*, *La Peste*, and *Le Premier Homme* in particular, the role played by capital punishment, and the portrayals to which it is subject, call for examination. *L'Étranger*, Camus's first published novel, came out in 1942, following several semi-autobiographical projects. Among them was *La Mort heureuse*. In the author's preparatory notes from 1936 cited in the epigraph, the protagonist of *La Mort heureuse* and forebear of Meursault, Patrice Mersault, expresses the wish to become a writer in order to voice the compassion and fear he feels for a condemned man (*OCC* 2:810–11); he also imagines a priest attempting to change the mind of this condemned man with whom he identifies. A foretaste of *L'Étranger* appears in this preliminary work: Camus's best-seller returns to this close interest in the condemned man's experience, his *face à face* with religious authority, and a reflection on, as well as the thematization of, a thirst for life and happiness. Distinct from Camus's earlier prose, *La Peste* (1947), which presents itself as an allegorical fiction in the form of a chronicle, also features lethal justice.

135

By way of analogy, the plague epidemic allows for the representation of life in Nazi-occupied territories during World War II. In the third part of the novel, the narrator, Dr. Bernard Rieux, mentions in passing two exemplary executions in Oran (152). In part 4, Jean Tarrou confides in the doctor that, as a teenager, he attended a capital trial at the court of assizes. This event, during which his father called for a capital sentence, is presented as having deeply affected Tarrou, who also explains that he witnessed an execution a few years later. *Le Premier Homme* (1994), an unfinished novel of autobiographical inspiration commenced in the early 1950s, found in Camus's briefcase upon his accidental death in January 1960 and published posthumously, returns to the question of witnessing legal killing. In its current form—a fraction of what the author planned to write—the narrative consists of two parts, entitled "Recherche du père" (Search for the Father) and "Le Fils ou le premier homme" (The Son or The First Man).[1] The latter part echoes the novel's title and chief subject, namely the reconstitution of, and quest for, the identity and humble origins of a protagonist named Jacques Cormery. On the eve of the Algerian War of Independence, Jacques, Camus's alter ego, pieces together the story of his parents, and more particularly that of his long-deceased father, Henri Cormery. This leads to glimpses into the lives of the poorer "pieds-noirs" in colonial Algeria from the mid-nineteenth century onward. Jacques's investigation alternates with an account of his childhood and youth—based on Camus's memories rendered in a fictional guise.[2] At the crossroads of these narrative planes lies an anecdote about the late Henri Cormery that his son had heard in his youth and about which his adult self inquires: Henri once attended the execution of a farm laborer named Pirette, who had murdered a whole family before going home and vomiting repeatedly. Closer examination of these references to the death penalty in all three novels shows it to be essential to their storylines. They converge to chart an original path toward the rejection of lethal justice that brings together the physical, the mythical, and the ethical.

STATE KILLING AND STORYTELLING

That the death penalty occupies a privileged place in Camus's fiction becomes apparent when state killing is situated within the overarching structure of each novel. A capital crime lies at the heart of *L'Étranger*. After shooting an Arab man dead—at the end of part 1—Meursault is sentenced to death. The narrative's elliptic denouement has him await and fantasize about his imminent execution, which mirrors the murder he has committed in the middle of the narrative. Camus's fiction thus presents capital punishment as both a pivot and the point of arrival reached, and somehow surpassed, by an everyman who has unexpectedly become a murderer.[3] Quantitatively, capital justice makes up the whole second half of *L'Étranger*, which depicts the actors, reasoning, and human and judiciary mechanisms that contribute to Meursault's death sentence.

In this second part of the novel, institutional justice rereads the events and affects that the first part had already presented through the perspective of an individual indifferent to a number of social codes. From his meeting with the examining magistrate to the verdict, the protagonist finds himself immersed in the "world of the trial," where displacement and distortion prevail.[4] So does the reader. The crime for which Meursault is condemned is not the murder he has committed as much as his rejection of Christian ideology and his inability to conform to behavioral norms and to small, commonplace lies. A witness (Marie) declares that she is made to say the opposite of what she thinks (*OCC* 1:196), and the parricide committed by a man who is to be judged after Meursault is conflated with his crime (200).

Both within the novel's overall architecture and within this particular judicial space marked by deformation, a moral and penal role reversal occurs. The men of law become guilty as they fail to judge the protagonist for his actual crime. For his part, the accused—and culprit—comes across as innocent insofar as the crime for which he is eventually sentenced, "murder[ing] his mother morally" (200), is not one.[5] No longer associated with justice, the death penalty is part of a series of entities and figures that are implicitly disqualified in *L'Étranger*. They are the very entities and figures that construct the strangeness of the stranger: the social codes to which individuals usually subject themselves, judiciary authorities shown to be influenced by ideology, fatigue, and amalgam (as we will see in chapter 6), and a Christian spirituality presented as unconvincing and ineffective in Meursault's perspective.

In *La Peste*, the previously cited passages in which Tarrou encounters lethal justice lead to the full disclosure of the novel's allegorical meaning, to which the next section will return. But its narrative canvas as a whole also relies on capital sentencing understood in both a somewhat inflected literal sense and in a metaphorical one. Oran's inhabitants are portrayed as prisoners (*OCC* 2:83) who are soon likened to men condemned to death. The narrator describes himself as follows: "Impatients de leur présent, ennemis de leur passé et privés d'avenir, nous ressemblions bien ainsi à ceux que la justice ou la haine humaines font vivre derrière les barreaux" (Impatient with the present, hostile to the past, and deprived of our future, we were much like those whom human justice, or hatred, has forced to live behind bars; 83). The comparison resurfaces in his account of Father Paneloux's sermon, which is presented as making some Oranians more fully aware of their "claustration" in the prison-like city (102). This partly figurative confinement of the inhabitants soon becomes literal, when going out is punished by incarceration (110).

Tarrou himself later connects this status of prisoner with that of condemned man.[6] Disapproving of the use of convicts for "les gros travaux" (the heavy lifting) that the epidemic requires from a sanitary standpoint, he blurts out, "'J'ai horreur des condamnations à mort'" (I loathe death sentences; OCC 2:119). As the disease spreads, capital sentencing takes on a metaphorical value, but without altogether losing its literal meaning. While this passage does not refer to any judicial process resulting in a death sentence, for example, Oran's administration does know that the measures that have been adopted will lead to the contamination of the prisoners. The authorities therefore deliberately send them to their deaths. Elsewhere, the metaphorical and the literal senses of "the death penalty" also coexist given "la certitude commune à tous les habitants qu'une peine de prison équivalait à une peine de mort par suite de l'excessive mortalité qu'on relevait dans la geôle municipale" (the certainty shared by all the inhabitants that being sent to prison was tantamount to a death sentence due to the disproportionately high mortality in the city jail; 151). Again, no capital trial leads to the violent demise of the incarcerated population, but a certain death penalty is at work in that nonlethal punishment (imprisonment) is requalified as an assured death.

Midway between image and reality, capital sentencing in fact applies to the population as a whole: "Avec la peste, plus question d'enquêtes secrètes, de dossiers, de fiches, d'instructions mystérieuses et d'arrestation imminente. À proprement parler, il n'y a plus de police, plus de crimes anciens ou nouveaux, plus de coupables, il n'y a que des *condamnés* qui attendent la plus arbitraire des grâces, et, parmi, eux, les policiers eux-mêmes" (With the plague, gone are the secret inquiries, the files, the records, the mysterious investigations and imminent arrests. Strictly speaking, there are no police left, no more crimes old or new, no more guilty individuals, there are only *condemned* people awaiting the most arbitrary pardon, and among them are the police officers themselves; 168; my emphasis). The plague is justice gone wrong, turned arbitrary through the stripping of the procedures designed to check its capriciousness. Tarrou's negative syntax and judicial lexicon confirm this corruption and annihilation of institutional protocols and methods, which random condemnation alone replaces and to which the very guarantors of the state may fall prey.

In *Le Premier Homme*, the death penalty takes on particular importance insofar as it simultaneously problematizes and structures remembrance, that is to say the core of the novel. The anecdote of Pirette's execution is linked to the faint memory of Henri Cormery's life. The fifth chapter, titled "Recherche du père," reveals that Henri died after being hit in the head by shrapnel during the Battle of the Marne, when his son was still an infant (*OCC* 4:778, 781–83). As a consequence, Jacques knows very little about his father, whom the narrative presents as a man of few words. This motivates the genealogical search of the novel's first part and inscribes Pirette's decapitation within the transversal problematic of deficient memory. In addition to Jacques's lack of familiarity with and memories of his father, the episode of the beheading both reveals and transcends a double dysmnesia: that of Catherine Cormery, Jacques's mother, who struggles to recall this episode at her son's request, and, more broadly, that of poor people, which is described as tenuous. Chapter 6, "La famille," introduces various portraits of the protagonist's relatives, beginning with Catherine. Jacques's conversation with her about the murderer Pirette leads to a critical argument: the narrator, whose voice merges with the protagonist's, claims that the memory of lowly people is less detailed than that of the wealthy. Their monotonous existence is said to prevent them from isolating from their daily routines particular moments for recollection. The arduous life of the *taiseux* (quiet ones) also results in a fatigue that favors faster forgetting, according to the narrator. In addition, dysmnesia is presented as a protective strategy that helps poor people cope with their harsh lives (788).

Such a thesis, which diagnoses the supposedly flawed or impoverished memory of modest people as both a social injustice and a necessary evil, sheds new light on the narrative as a whole. It increases the value of any fragment of memory to which Jacques—and the reader—might have access. Camus adds the following note to his chapter title: "Un livre sur le *manque de mémoire*. Le Proust des pauvres vies mais le temps y est toujours perdu" (A book about the *lack of memory*. The

Proust of poor people but in which time is always lost; OCC 4:786). The main text itself insists on the impossibility of a *Temps retrouvé* (Time Regained): "Le temps perdu ne se retrouve que chez les riches" (Time can be regained only by the wealthy; 788). The reader of *Le Premier Homme* is thus presented with both a Proustian text in that it seeks to resuscitate the past and piece together an identity, and with a non-Proustian text insofar as it simultaneously denies the possibility of conjuring up the past of the Cormery parents in its completeness and complexity, and the satisfaction that may be derived from such a process. De facto, in chapter 5, Catherine is unable to identify her late husband's middle names, her own birth year, their exact age difference, or the year when Henri lost his parents or when his sister left him in an orphanage (776–77).

Catherine Cormery's relative muteness and "demi-surdité" (semi-deafness; OCC 4:775) further complicate the challenging "memorial quest" that frames the anecdote of the decapitation, a rare vestige of the father figure.[7] She is the alter ego of the author's mother, Catherine Camus, who appears in the paratext as the novel's beloved and impossible—for illiterate—dedicatee, designated by the two periphrases "Vve Camus" (Widow Camus) and "toi qui ne pourras jamais lire ce livre" (you who will never be able to read this book; 741). In addition to underscoring her uneasy relation to language (786–87), the novel portrays Catherine as petrified and inclined to silence.[8] Jacques's interactions with her are further complicated by her incoherent answers when he asks about his father and the execution he attended. After affirming that she and her husband never lived in Algiers, she confirms to her son that Jacques Cormery indeed witnessed Pirette's beheading in the city's prison, Barberousse. Jacques points out this contradiction, and she concurs somewhat haphazardly:

> Elle disait oui, c'était peut-être non, il fallait remonter dans le temps à travers une mémoire enténébrée, rien n'était sûr. . . . Cette maladie de jeunesse . . . l'avait laissée sourde avec un embarras de parole, puis l'avait empêchée d'apprendre ce qu'on enseigne même aux plus déshérités, et forcée donc à la résignation muette, mais c'était aussi la seule manière qu'elle ait trouvé de faire face à sa vie, et que pouvait-elle faire d'autre, qui à sa place aurait trouvé autre chose? (OCC 4:788)

She said yes, maybe it was no, she had to travel back in time through a clouded memory, nothing was for sure. . . . A childhood disease . . . had left her deaf with a speech impediment, then had prevented her from learning what even the most underprivileged are taught, and hence had forced her into this mute resignation, but it was also the only way she had found to face up to her life, and what else could she do, who in her position would have found another way?

The mother's failure to understand some of her son's sentences and her somewhat fearful confusion (*OCC* 4:787) trigger speculative and compensatory thoughts in Jacques—and, *en abyme*, the writing of the semi-autobiographical novel as a whole.

This section of the novel reports on a critical *nœud de mémoire*, sees the protagonist attempt to disentangle it through a precarious dialectical method, and makes perceptible the disheartening effect that Catherine's inability to tell or clarify the desired story has on him. Doubt mixed with despair and understanding follows the failure of Jacques's investigation. Free indirect speech discreetly translates his emotional state, and he notes that he cannot even know the exact disease that has caused his mother's speech and hearing impediments: "Là, encore, c'était la nuit" (There again, it was dark as night; *OCC* 4:788).

A gradation then occurs, culminating in identity trouble. As if by way of contagion, Jacques goes so far as to question the very love and life his parents once shared, and comes to mirror his mother's partial aphasia before her (*OCC* 4:788). The collapse of both past and present intensifies, and he eventually acknowledges that he has reached a dead end: "Il fallait renoncer à apprendre quelque chose d'elle" (He had to give up on learning anything from her; 788). In making him question his parents' relationship, the mother's inability to talk much about the past comes to endanger his own identity, already destabilized by his awareness that, at the age of thirty-nine, he is older than his father at the time of his death on the battlefield and is thus placed in an unnatural position. Conversely, the mother in front of whom the son stands is infantilized in the sense that she does not speak—in accordance with the term's etymology (*infans*).

Although the anecdote of Pirette's execution crystallizes the mother's dysmnesia, communication failures, and, to some extent, the narrator's theory of the memorial impoverishment from which the proletariat suffers, and although these combined phenomena obstruct the recovery of his roots, the story of the beheading that Henri Cormery is reported to have attended sporadically transcends these shortcomings, nevertheless. This event is one of the few that the mother is able to corroborate when pressed by her son, who ends up resorting to a hand gesture (mimicking the decapitation) to make himself understood. While Catherine's confirmation occurs in the midst of a sluggish and sometimes inconsistent dialogue, it takes the form of an immediate response ("elle répondit aussitôt" [she answered straight away]) and of one of the longest and most specific sentences she manages to utter: "Oui, il s'est levé à 3 heures pour aller à Barberousse" (Yes, he got up at 3 a.m. to go to Barberousse; OCC 4:787). With this confirmation, the widowed mother does briefly act as the "intercesseur" between her son and his unknown father, in keeping with the novel's dedication (741).

Ultimately, therefore, it is through what could be called an archaeological, anamnestic approach that markedly differs from the spontaneous Proustian *mnèmè* that a small but meaningful whole (the anecdote of Pirette's execution) is laboriously reconstituted from a fragment: the narrative presents the image of the father going to Barberousse and subsequently suffering from nausea as the only "détail" (OCC 4:788) that Jacques has carried with him since childhood, after hearing his grandmother talk about it. However imperfectly—the grandmother's and the uncle's versions of the story are discordant, and the mother seems unable to relate the whole event and to recall the nausea—the story of the execution functions as the medium that enables Jacques to recover a meaningful piece of the past. Through the effect that both the crime (the murder of a family) and the scaffold are said to have had on Henri, namely indignation and revulsion (789), the father's psyche and values can be better identified. Additionally, Jacques manages to recompose a second story on the basis of this narrative fragment: that of the evening when, as a child, he himself felt terror when he heard this narrative for the first time, and that of the recurring nightmare it caused.

Camus doesn't just turn the death penalty into a keystone of the architecture of his three novels. They rehash various aspects of capital justice, with both difference and repetition. From one work to the next, the writer dissects and returns to the various moments that precede, trigger, and follow the death sentence. *L'Étranger* stages a man's crime, his sentencing, the wait before his execution, but forgoes the (actual, not the fantasized) moment when he is decapitated. *La Peste* goes back to the world of the trial, yet this time, the narrative does evoke execution, twice: it briefly mentions the use of firing squads due to the city's state of siege (*OCC* 2:152) and, later, provides a clinical account of the shooting of a likely political prisoner (207). As for *Le Premier Homme*, after evoking indirectly the spectacle of the scaffold, it narrates in detail the quintuple murder perpetrated by a "bewildered" man:

> Il avait tué à coups de marteau ses maîtres et les trois enfants de la maison. "Pour voler?" avait demandé Jacques enfant. "Oui," avait dit l'oncle Étienne. "Non," avait dit la grand-mère, mais sans donner d'autres explications. On avait trouvé les cadavres défigurés, la maison ensanglantée jusqu'au plafond et, sous l'un des lits, le plus jeune des enfants respirant encore, et qui devait mourir aussi, mais qui avait trouvé la force d'écrire sur le mur blanchi à la chaux, avec son doigt trempé de sang: "C'est Pirette." (*OCC* 4:788–89)

> He had killed his employers and the three children in the house with a hammer. "To rob them?" Jacques had asked as a child. "Yes," his uncle Étienne had said. "No," the grandmother had said, but without any further explanation. The disfigured corpses had been found, the house blooded as far up as the ceiling and, under one of the beds, the youngest of the children still breathing; he too was to die, but had found the strength to write on the whitewashed wall, with his blood-soaked finger: "It's Pirette."

Desperate, sinister, and primitive, the writing of the murderer's name on the wall symbolically mirrors Camus's rewriting of a childhood memory that is also grim. This symmetry dramatizes the horror of killing. So does the fact that it is perceived through a child's eyes, twice: Pirette's victim and the young Jacques. Besides, although a narrative ellipsis conceals Pirette's decapitation, the chapter zeroes in on the reaction it elicits in one of its witnesses: Jacques's father, "revenu livide, s'était couché, puis relevé pour aller vomir plusieurs fois, puis recouché" (livid upon his return, had gone for a lie-down, then got up again to vomit several times, before lying down again; *OCC* 4:789). Mimicking Henri Cormery's shocked mind and body, this sentence staggers by repeating the same prefixes and prepositions and is reduced to a bare grammatical minimum, eventually omitting two auxiliary verbs. Camus's fiction thus appears to explore and absorb the multiple phases of the capital experience relentlessly.

The individual and historical perspectives provided in each novel also prove complementary. In *L'Étranger*, the condemned man is the subjective filter through which the reader perceives capital justice. With *La Peste*, our attention turns to the spectator of a capital trial and, later, of an execution in Hungary. Tarrou encounters the death penalty in a somewhat fortuitous way: his father invites him to observe his performance in court. In *Le Premier Homme*, Henri Cormery is the counterpoint of this middle-class figure who witnesses a capital case by chance. Jacques's father, who, at first, believes that the punishment inflicted on Pirette is deserved, *chooses* to go to Barberousse to attend the execution. He observes it with the eyes of a humble man to whom the judicial world is thoroughly foreign and subsequently abstains from commenting on it, as opposed to Tarrou, who, as an adult, is eventually able to verbalize his rejection of capital justice. The geopolitical contexts that surround lethal justice also vary greatly, from the beheading of two *pieds-noirs* in colonial French Algeria (*L'Étranger* and *Le Premier Homme*) to the exemplary shooting of thieves in the midst of an epidemic analogous to Nazi totalitarianism and the Occupation, which tends to eclipse Oran's particular identity as a colonial city in "194." (*La Peste*), to an execution carried out in a satellite state of the Soviet Union (*La Peste*). The persistent reality of state killing is portrayed as outdoing, and in a way as leveling out, this contextual heterogeneity.

Across Camus's narratives, these iterations, overlaps, and alternating focalizations and circumstances add up to form a kaleidoscopic picture. He does not neatly separate the writings in which he represents lethal justice. Instead, through intertextual echoes, his works appear to weave a macro-narrative, or what could be called transtextual representations of the death penalty. *La Peste* mentions Meursault's condemnation in passing (OCC 2:71). The anecdote of the father who vomits after seeing a beheading surfaces in *L'Étranger* (OCC 1:205), is revisited in *Le Premier Homme* in more detail, and reappears at the outset of "Réflexions sur la guillotine," in the form of a brief factual narrative (OCC 4:127). It thereby becomes a landmark scene. Likewise, the observation according to which one should not say of the condemned man "Il va payer sa dette à la société" (He is going to pay his debt to society) but rather "On va lui couper le cou" (We're going to cut off his neck) reemerges in multiple forms, from *L'Envers et l'endroit* (OCC 1:54) to Camus's *Carnets* from 1938 (OCC 2:871), *La Peste* (206), *Le Premier Homme*, where the clinical image of head severance reappears, dramatized by Jacques's miming as he asks his mother "Mais alors quand papa est allé voir couper le cou à Pirette" (But then what about the time when dad went to see them cut off Pirette's head; *OCC* 4:787), and "Réflexions sur la guillotine" (*OCC* 4:132). This transtextual network both insists on the crude reality of the death penalty and makes this punishment stand out against a backdrop that features death under other guises.

For Camus's three "capital novels" emphatically thematize death beyond capital punishment. It dominates their plots. "Aujourd'hui, maman est morte" (Mom died today; *OCC* I:141) reads as one of the most famous opening sentences of French literature. What follows is the account of successive rituals that make this liminary loss stretch in time: a night of vigil around the mother's corpse in an old people's home, a long walk during which Meursault accompanies the mortuary convoy, the religious ceremony, and the burial. Meursault's own name contains a conjugated form of the verb *mourir*. Death pervades *La Peste* too, from the rampant epidemic to Cottard's attempted suicide, his random shooting from his window, and the analogy between the disease and the Nazi regime, which Camus highlighted in 1955, when Roland Barthes accused his novel of antihistoricism (*OCC* 2:286). Ultimately, *La Peste* could be said to stage deadly absolutism.[9] As for *Le Premier Homme*, its first part, "Recherche du père," sets out to remedy Henri Cormery's premature death and relative anonymity. Maurice Weyembergh has remarked that, more broadly, Camus's unfinished novel interrogates the death of the dead themselves, that is to say the forgetting of the deceased *pieds-noirs* such as Jacques's father, who is indeed presented as lacking forebears and remembrance (*OCC* 4:914).[10]

In parallel to these "natural" deaths, the novels foreground murder. In *L'Étranger*, the murder of the Arab overturns Meursault's life, the plot, as well as the reader's previous perception of an a priori peaceful protagonist. This crime also has two mirror images in the novel: "l'histoire du Tchécoslovaque" (the Czechoslovakian's story; *OCC* 1:187), a man murdered by his mother and sister when he returns home to surprise them after making money—Meursault specifies that he has read this story (that of Camus's play *Le Malentendu*) "des milliers de fois" (thousands of times); and the story of the parricide evoked during Meursault's trial (200). Colin Davis has rightly argued that an attraction to altericide and gratuitous violence seeps through Camus's fiction.[11] Beyond the well-known case of *L'Étranger* in which murder is triply present—without being systematically gratuitous, nevertheless— *La Peste* and *Le Premier Homme* do interrogate a society in which murder, or assassination, persists. Tarrou asserts that this is precisely what he is fighting against (OCC 2:207). Henri Cormery despises murder too: as a *zouave* sent to Morocco in 1905, he comes across the corpse of a fellow soldier whose throat has been slit and whose severed penis has been placed in his mouth. "Un homme ne fait pas ça. . . . Non, un homme, ça s'empêche" (A man doesn't do that. . . . No, a man keeps himself under control), he shouts (OCC 4:779).

These prominent themes of natural death and homicide have a contrastive and critical effect. On the one hand, capital punishment is shown to distort mortality as an inevitable component of the human condition. Camus is familiar with Pascal's famous use of the figure of the "condamnés à mort" to depict this condition. In the philosophy thesis written in his youth, "Métaphysique chrétienne et néoplatonisme," he cites it and interprets its pessimism as a way of underscoring Pascal's subsequent "adherence" to Christianity: "Let us imagine a number of men in chains, and all of them condemned to death, some of whom have their throats slit in plain sight of the others each day, those who remain see their own condition in that of their fellow prisoners, and, looking at one another with pain and without hope, await their turn. This is the image of the human condition" (OCC 1:1009).[12] Camus's notes from 1949 present a tableau that may be read as a rewriting of Pascal's fragment. It replaces the condemned men with tortured men and adds a significant chronology to the original analogy: after "millennia" of looking away with "the most perfect distraction," Camus remarks, all men eventually watch the persecution of their peers (OCC 4:1062–63). In the aftermath of World War II, the author thus replaces the image of man's suffering and hopeless condition that precedes Pascal's apology of Christianity with another in which man's long-standing indifference toward the pain (and, implicitly, the death) of others gives way to a sense of concern and responsibility and to a focus on the terrestrial world and human agency.

That the worst human torments, and some deaths, are generated—and can be prevented—by mankind *aside from* or *in addition to* man's mortal condition is precisely what Camus's fiction stresses. The individual murders in the novels at once illustrate this idea and serve as points of contrast with state killing. The narratives show capital punishment to be death decided and organized by society in order to intimidate or fascinate the people (OCC 1:189, 206; 4:790), as opposed to an inexplicable or a vengeful murderous gesture, such as that of Meursault in *L'Étranger* or that of colonized men mutilating an enemy soldier in *Le Premier Homme*. Neither novel justifies these individual acts, but both do represent them with a certain understanding, whereas, conversely, they clearly delegitimize capital punishment.[13]

Lethal justice is presented as unstoppable once launched, eliminating the exceptional and transgressive character of individual violence: "La mécanique écrasait tout" (The mechanics crushed everything), says Meursault (*OCC* 1:206), who also repeatedly underscores the "rite implacable" (204) and "déroulement imperturbable" (an unfolding that nothing could disturb; 205) of the capital sentence.[14] "Keep the sense of rupture, of crime in violence—that is to say admit it only insofar as it relates to a personal responsibility. Otherwise it stems from a command, it follows a rule—be it the law or metaphysics. It no longer is a rupture" (*OCC* 2:1093), noted Camus in 1947, anticipating the argument he was to develop in *L'Homme révolté* a few years later. In their own right, his works of fiction that feature the death penalty hint at the failure of this containment of violence. By way of narrative construction, intertextuality, and symbolic contrasts, they aggregate to elicit a systematic mistrust in lethal justice.

REVELATIONS AND VISIONS IN THE FACE OF EXECUTION

State killing is also instrumental to the characterization of Camus's novels. Meursault, Tarrou, and Jacques all undergo metamorphoses in the face of the death penalty. This process is most patent in *La Peste*. Its fourth section associates capital justice with several epiphanies: it narrates how death sentences make manifest to Tarrou what was previously invisible and unknown to him, and, by ricochet, it discloses the polysemous allegory that underlies the novel.[15]

Tarrou's first epiphany occurs when he is seventeen and attends a trial at the court of assizes; the second one takes place once he has become an adult and witnesses an execution. Retrospection and a first-person account dramatize these two revelations, along with the fact that, through this "confession d'un pestiféré" (confession of a plague-stricken man; *OCC* 2:1196), both Tarrou's interlocutor, Rieux, and the reader further "discove[r]" (202) a protagonist about whom little is known at this point in the novel.[16] Tarrou's self-unveiling symbolically occurs in a postapocalyptic atmosphere associated with spiritual purgation. He and Rieux are atop the city, on a terrace, in a "lumière pure et glacée" (pure and frozen light), against a cloudless sky that has been cleansed by a "deluge" of downpours (202). A cryptic remark inaugurates Tarrou's narrative: "Je souffrais déjà de la peste bien avant de connaître cette ville et cette épidémie" (I already suffered from the plague long before encountering this city and this epidemic; 204). Still enigmatically, he emphasizes the will he has always had to "get out of" the plague ("sortir [de la peste]"; 204). At the end of his confession, the mystery that surrounds these statements is solved.

What follows Tarrou's mystifying introduction is a portrayal of his father. A lawyer and an "honnête homme" (honest man; OCC 2:205), at once harmless and imperfect—pernickety, unfaithful, and proud— he undergoes a radical transformation during a capital trial that he invites his son to attend in the hope of impressing him. The death penalty here functions as a developer in the photographic sense. While in court, Tarrou's father demands that the accused be sentenced to death, and, through his son's eyes, the narrative shows his figure, hitherto described as deeply human, to metamorphose into a monstrous one. Dressed in a blood-red robe, he utters "des phrases immenses" (endless sentences), "grouill[ant] . . . comme des serpents" (swarm[ing] like snakes; 206). An anacoluthon symbolically dislocates the sentence that describes this transformation. Infernal imagery takes over the description, and, just as in *L'Étranger*, the man of law becomes the culprit.[17] The depersonalized speech of the father, who invokes "la société" as an indeterminate and abstract agent justifying his call for the defendant's decapitation, as well as the euphemizing language he uses ("ce qu'on appelait poliment les derniers moments et qu'il faut bien nommer le plus abject des assassinats" [what was politely called the last moments and which should instead be called the most abject of murders; 206]) portray human justice as ignoring the responsibility and the reality of punishment. Tarrou's confession also presents the death penalty as the "developer" of *his* conscience: his experience of the assizes triggers a sudden and forced maturation after which he breaks away from his careless, disengaged perception of the world, perceives the duplicity of the words that decree or describe lethal penalties, and decides to leave home.

This first epiphany relies on an unexpected, close connection between Tarrou and the defendant. If, in *Le Dernier Jour d'un condamné* and, as we will see, in *L'Étranger*, the condemned man and Meursault are animalized in their cells, *La Peste* accentuates the assimilation of accused and beast in the courthouse. "Ce petit homme au *poil* roux et pauvre" (This little man with thinning red *hair*; OCC 2:205; my emphasis), a nameless "hibou effarouché par une lumière trop vive" (owl frightened by too harsh a light; 206), is soon referred to as "le hibou roux" (the red-haired owl; 207, 209) only. These periphrases do not only highlight the way in which the extreme fear of punishment erases the condemned man's humanity or merely serve a characterization that is both pathetic and realistic from a psychological perspective. Beyond these functions, the animality of the accused becomes a *positive* property: in Tarrou's eyes, it testifies to the fact that the criminal belongs to the world of the living.

This world contrasts with both that of the father—a deadly figure associated with chthonic images during his speech for the prosecution— and "la catégorie commode d'"inculpé'" (the "accused" as an all-too convenient category; OCC 2:206) through which Tarrou abstractly thinks of the "petit homme" (little man) before he witnesses his condemnation. Such is the foundation of Tarrou's first epiphany, emphasized by the suddenness of his realization and the rupture it brings about: "À partir de ce jour, je m'intéressai avec horreur à la justice. . . . Ce qui m'intéressait, c'était la condamnation à mort" (From that day onward, I took a horrified interest in justice. . . . What interested me was the death sentence; 206–7). Alive just like the defendant in front of him, Tarrou feels a solidarity so great that a symbiosis appears to connect him to the defendant: he has stomach cramps when watching the accused and feels "blind[ly]" drawn to his "côtés" (side) by "un instinct formidable" in an "intimité . . . vertigineuse" (206).

A second epiphany both echoes and deviates from the assizes scene. As an adult, Tarrou joins "les autres" (other men; OCC 2:207), who, like him, have grown critical of society. The group of which he is part is reported to sentence individuals to death on occasion: "Mais on me disait que ces quelques morts étaient nécessaires pour amener un monde où l'on ne tuerait plus personne" (But I was told that these few deaths were necessary to bring about a world in which no one would be killed anymore; 207). Tarrou initially convinces himself that these condemnations are legitimate by thinking of none other than the "hibou roux."[18] Yet the spectacle of the execution soon leads him to reject it. The disrupted syntax and prosody used to narrate this episode duplicate those of the previous anecdote. And just as Tarrou had earlier shed light on the discrepancy between euphemistic language and the reality of decapitation, here he underscores the way literature and iconography may mask the crude reality of firing squads. In this second revelation, nevertheless, the primary target of criticism no longer is the judicial institution and its actors. Tarrou's realization is self-critical. The condemned man, turned into the mere synecdoche of "le trou dans la poitrine" (the hole in the chest), that is to say sheer vulnerability and disfigurement, makes him understand that, despite his good intentions, he too is a murderer, "à [s]on tour" (in turn) (209).

The establishment of an ethics whose content and formulation are both negative and minimal results from this second realization: "n'être l'ennemi mortel de personne ... soulager les hommes et, sinon les sauver, du moins leur faire le moins de mal possible et même parfois un peu de bien ... renonc[er] à tuer ... refuser d'être avec le fléau" (to be nobody's mortal enemy ... to bring relief to men and, short of saving them, at least to do as little harm as possible to them and even, sometimes, a little good ... to refuse to kill definitively ... to refuse to be on the same side as the plague; OCC 2:209–10). Yet this simple ambition constitutes a trying, if not an impossible task, as suggested by the intertwined analogies of physical and military battle (against the disease and against a tempest) that Tarrou uses and by the oxymoron to which he aspires: to be a "meurtrier innocent" (innocent murderer; 210).[19] He also admits that this ethics is temporary and imperfect in a community whose moral categories—from the active executioner to the "vrai médecin" (real doctor) or the "meurtrier innocent"—are permeable and whose members may act in contradiction to their intentions. This second face-to-face with the death penalty therefore complements the first and modifies the analysis to which it had led. Legal murder is no longer represented or experienced as exterior and collective. Tarrou reconceives it as a responsibility that is also interior and individual. Furthermore, state killing ceases to be localized and sporadic. Instead, it emerges as virtually ubiquitous and permanent, leading Tarrou to adopt a principle of constant self-suspicion so as to avoid any legitimation of capital condemnation. "Je me disais alors que, si l'on cédait une fois, il n'y avait pas de raison de s'arrêter" (I then told myself that, if you gave in once, there was no reason to stop; 208).

As a consequence of this solidarity with the condemned, discovered in two successive stages, Tarrou engages in a vast fight for life and, at the metanarrative level, unveils the novel's meaning and allegorical layering. He strives to "refuser tout ce qui, de près ou de loin, pour de bonnes ou de mauvaises raisons, fait mourir ou justifie qu'on fasse mourir" (reject all that which, in one way or another, for good or bad reasons, makes people die or justifies that they be made to die; OCC 2:209). The reader therefore learns that, beyond its literal acceptation, the plague refers both to death itself, following a disease or human intervention, and to any active contribution to *or* mere inaction in the face of killing ("tuer ou ... laisser tuer"; 209). In other words, the rejection of the death penalty leads to a rejection of a broader deadly paradigm that comprises pathology, penalty, and crime—individual or collective, political or not.[20] This cluster that brings together all that kills consolidates the novel around a categorical moral imperative, namely the maximal protection of human life. And in identifying active or passive killing as highly suspicious means that may be used to serve a cause believed to be legitimate, it also activates a political critique.[21]

Like *La Peste*, albeit more indirectly, *Le Premier Homme* has the identity of a protagonist develop through a capital scene associated with the father figure. In contrasting ways, this figure who conventionally incarnates the law brings about the rejection of lethal justice in both novels. In the case of the Cormerys, the two recomposed stories mentioned earlier (the Pirette anecdote and Jacques's reaction upon hearing it) symbolically represent the rebirth of both father and son: as the account of the Barberousse scene gives life to Henri as an agent, endowed with moral judgment and a reactive body, it confirms the existence and nature of Jacques's origins. In other words, the recollection of Henri Cormery's nausea provides the father with a reality and humanity that allows his son to authenticate his own filiation, confirming the resemblance between father and son briefly pointed out by the mother in chapter 5 (OCC 4:776). A violent physical and moral mimesis actually consecrates Jacques and Henri's likeness and relationship: just as the late father is reported to have vomited after the execution, a "nausée d'horreur" (nausea of horror) affects the young Jacques. Although he manages to "raval[er]" (swallow back) his disgust, the narrator presents it as haunting him "sa vie durant" (throughout his life) and consecrates it as his "seul héritage évident et certain" (only obvious and definite legacy; 789).

What Jacques relies on as he restores this genealogy is a *vision* of capital punishment rather than the actual spectacle of the beheading, about which his father is said not to utter a word (OCC 4:789). The "images" (789) that haunt the child result from an oral narrative created by his whole family—with several variants—and upon which he elaborates in his mind's eye (789).[22] This narrative provides Jacques with a moral foundation. It also reportedly "impresses" him, "distresses" him, and invades his "dreams" (788) and "nightmares" (789). At once an ever-repeated story that inspires fear, a collective representation, and a personal appropriation that enables the individual to situate or orient himself, Pirette's story arguably operates as a founding myth.²³ It doesn't contradict reality altogether—an illusion to which the young Jacques himself clings (789). Rather, it informs reality in a decisive manner. The last part of the section titled "La famille" focuses on Jacques once he has reached adulthood ("l'âge d'homme"), much like Tarrou in the second half of his confession. The "history" and "events" that surround him at that point in time are presented as corroborating the meaning of the founding myth in which the scaffold makes the father sick: they invalidate the desirability of decapitation established by the law and the vox populi (789), suggesting that any man, even Jacques himself, could be executed (789).

In 1942, *L'Étranger* already linked the death penalty both with the experience of an epiphany as highlighted in *La Peste* and with that of a vision perceptible in *Le Premier Homme*. At the end of the novel, Meursault's acceptance of his fate and apparent metaphysical emancipation (he claims that he is ready to relive an existence marked by finitude and absurdity) come across as a coup de théâtre. Critics have read this plot twist in various ways. For Blanchot, it was a failure in that it contradicted the protagonist's quasi-subjectlessness throughout the narrative.²⁴ For Sartre, the dénouement illustrated the argument of *Le Mythe de Sisyphe*, which simultaneously asserts the senselessness of terrestrial life and the will to embrace it without recourse to either God or suicide. *Le Mythe de Sisyphe* also finds exemplarity in the man condemned to death and his "divine availability" (OCC 1:260) on the day of his execution.²⁵ "It is with a view to making us relish this dawn and this availability [of the condemned man] that Mr. Camus sentenced his hero to the death penalty," says Sartre.²⁶ His interpretation of *L'Étranger* as the fictional pendant of Camus's conceptualization of the absurd still prevails today—and Camus himself classified his novel in the "cycle of the Absurd." Yet this tends to simplify the complex representation of Meursault's thoughts and behavior as his execution is impending.

Meursault experiences a tortuous mental process at the end of *L'Étranger*. Its progression makes his final "liberation" ambivalent. First come imaginary scenarios whereby the protagonist attempts to counter the inevitability of his execution: he envisions legal and medical arrangements—bills and drug combinations—that could save him from death. The failure of this speculative strategy and Meursault's concomitant criticism of his own inability to be "raisonnable" (OCC 1:205) dryly underscore the irreversible, tragic situation in which he finds himself. Irony ensues, as the condemned man *doubly* adheres to lethal justice. First, when imagining that he could be freed, he expresses the wish to be able to attend all future executions (205). Here, the spectacle of another's death is shown to trigger Schadenfreude rather than deterrence. Second, the protagonist must admit that it is in the condemned man's best interest that his own beheading unfold smoothly, for a prompt and less painful death (206). Dark humor characterizes a further consideration. Meursault notes that, in contrast with the iconic status given to the guillotine by the popular imagination since the French Revolution, the scaffold is not the site of an apotheosis. Instead of experiencing a transcendent "ascension en plein ciel" (ascension into the sky; 206), man faces a prosaic device of average size, placed on the ground, and even personified as a mere fellow man toward whom the condemned man is to walk. Initially believed to be somewhat grandiose, decapitation turns out to be demystified by three adverbial qualifiers: "On était tué discrètement, avec un peu de honte et beaucoup de précision" (They killed you discreetly, with a little shame and much precision; 206). In this sequence, tragedy, irony, and the grotesque follow one another.

The novel's dénouement then takes a pathetic turn when Meursault comes to detail the mental efforts through which he prepares himself for his decapitation. That he needs to invert the natural succession of day and night to better face his punishment symbolizes its brutality and inhumanity. He is on the lookout after midnight, as this is the time after which he may be taken to the scaffold. With remarkable psychological realism, the narrative dissects the protective coping mechanisms he deploys at that point: his anticipation of the moment when he will be forced out of his cell, his rationalization of death, attempt to domesticate the image of the execution despite his lack of imagination, and the restraint he imposes on himself by thinking about his pardon only *in fine*. What this internal close-up highlights is the convict's failure to control his terror:

> Passé minuit, j'attendais et je guettais. Jamais mon oreille n'avait perçu tant de bruits, distingué de sons si ténus. . . . J'aurais pu entendre des pas et mon cœur aurait pu éclater. . . . Le moindre glissement me jetait à la porte. . . . L'oreille collée au bois, j'attendais éperdument jusqu'à ce que j'entende ma propre respiration, effrayé de la trouver rauque et si pareille au râle d'un chien" (*OCC* 1:207)

> After midnight, I waited and listened out for them. Never before had my ears perceived so many noises, heard such faint sounds. . . . I could have heard footsteps and my heart might

have burst. . . . The slightest slipping sound made me rush to the door. . . . My ear pressed against the wood, I waited desperately until I could hear my own breathing, scared to find that it sounded hoarse and so much like the groaning of a dog.

Meursault metamorphoses into an animal despite his best efforts, but this animalization differs from that of *La Peste*: it is entirely negative. Camus takes up the strategy used by Hugo in *Le Dernier Jour d'un condamné* over a century earlier.[27] The individual who awaits a certain death is portrayed as progressively losing his full human status. "Réflexions sur la guillotine" summarizes this transformation during which, before the execution, "torture through hopefulness alternates with the throes of animal despair" (*OCC* 4:145), "round[ing] off [the condemned man's] condition as an object." "According to all witnesses, the skin color changes, fear acting like an acid. . . . The actor that resides in every man could come to the rescue of the scared animal then and help it put on a brave face, even to himself. But the night and the secret are without any recourse" (145, 147–48). On the verge of cardiac "éclate[ment]" (bursting; *OCC* 1:207) that renews itself every twenty-four hours, Meursault precisely suffers this degenerative state and dehumanization. The disavowal of the intellect, and of courage, is prolonged by that of spirituality: the idea that all men die sooner or later, whether or not they have been sentenced to death, only convinces Meursault temporarily (207); he rejects this argument when the chaplain formulates it, just as he resolutely, and ultimately angrily, rejects the Christian framework that could alleviate his ordeal by giving him hope (204, 208–12).[28]

These antecedents potentially complicate Meursault's subsequent embrace of "cette vie absurde" (this absurd life; *OCC* 1:212), that is to say his apparent metaphysical emancipation at the very end of the novel. The dénouement seems to constitute a moment of revelation: Meursault declares himself calm, "purgé du mal" (purged of evil), and in touch with "la tendre indifférence du monde" (the tender indifference of the world; 213) at a liminal moment ("à la limite de la nuit"). But the psychological ordeal and dehumanization that precede this could lead one to read these remarks and his final masochistic wish that hateful shouts "welcome" him when he is put to death (213) as emanating from an impaired consciousness, as the paroxysm of despair ("vidé d'espoir") and "épuis[ement]" (exhaustion) for a mind that can no longer cling to anything and is thoroughly alienated. The metaphors that pervade the beginning of the novel's closing paragraph could confirm this interpretation. Meursault appears to lose the sense of time and reality: "*Je crois que j'ai dormi*" (*I think* I must have slept; 212; my emphasis). He also lets go of the prosaism that has largely characterized his self-expression hitherto: as in the murder scene, a highly figurative language replaces it and appears to signal an *état second*.

What is more, these metaphors present Meursault as unable to distinguish his being from his environment. He fuses the two: "Je me suis réveillé avec des étoiles sur le visage. Des bruits de campagne montaient jusqu'à moi. Des odeurs de nuit, de terre et de sel rafraîchissaient mes tempes. La merveilleuse paix de cet été endormi entrait en moi comme une marée" (I woke up with stars over my face. Countryside sounds were rising up toward me. Scents of the night, earth and salt were cooling my temples. The wonderful peace of this sleeping summer flowed into me like a tide; OCC 1:212). One may doubt the possibility of such a sensorial symbiosis from within a prison cell and wonder if delusion doesn't underlie or cloud Meursault's inner liberation. Earlier in the narrative, what covers his "face" at night in the jail are not "stars" but "des punaises" (bugs) "cour[ant] sur [s]on visage" (crawling over [his] face; 183). Could the condemned man be confusing the latter with the former in a psychotic moment? There is no need to choose an ultimate reading. But it seems necessary to acknowledge that the very language used to express the protagonist's final stance prevents the reader from being sure of his lucidity, and hence of the value that his metaphysical epiphany should be given.

Regardless of how one interprets the novel's closing paragraph, Meursault's end marks the failure of the modern death penalty. Either the condemned man's atomized psyche bears witness to the unbearable pain caused by the guillotine, contravening the machine's aim, as we have seen; or capital punishment operates as the catalyst for an interior deliverance and, in so doing, reveals the inefficacy of the negative retribution that the judicial authorities and society at large aim to impose on the criminal.

Subversion and irony cap Meursault's ambiguous epiphany through a final vision. The scene strikingly echoes that of the crucifixion of Christ on Golgotha, a scandalous execution par excellence, concerning as it does an innocent figure.[29] Meursault states, "Il me restait à souhaiter qu'il y ait beaucoup de spectateurs le jour de mon exécution et *qu'ils m'accueillent avec des cris de haine*" (What was left for me to hope was that there should be many spectators on the day of my execution and *that they should greet me with cries of hatred*; OCC 1:213; my emphasis). In French, John's gospel reads:

> Jean XIX, 5.... Pilate leur dit: Voilà l'homme.
> Jean, XIX, 6. Quand les grands prêtres et les gardes le virent, ils *crièrent: Crucifie! Crucifie!* ...
> Jean XIX, 15. Alors ils *crièrent: Enlève, enlève, crucifie-le.*[30]

> John XIX, 5.... Pilate told them: Behold the man.
> John XIX, 6. When the great priests and the guards saw him, they *cried out: Crucify! Crucify!* ...
> John XIX, 15. Then they *cried out: Take him away, take him away, crucify him.*

Through this implicit intertext, Camus associates Meursault with a sacred figure in whom his character does not believe, who may have saved him had he pretended to "se confier à lui" (confide in him [Christ]; OCC 1:181), and whose redeeming potential morphs into a damning one: his judges, one of whom calls himself "chrétien" (181), condemn the protagonist to death (a death devoid of a possible resurrection, contrary to that of Jesus, according to Meursault) *because* he refuses to recognize Jesus. The stranger who, in the magistrate's eyes, resembles an "Antéchrist" (182), expires like Christ.[31] The novel's ultimate revelation therefore is that of the carnivalesque, or perverse, potential of capital justice.[32]

In Camus's three novels, the death penalty could ultimately be said to be part of a rite of passage. It leads the protagonists to be temporarily separated from their community, marginalized, and subsequently reintegrated into the particular, elective community of those who valorize terrestrial—and human—life above all else. The characters are represented as experiencing a coming of age when embracing this stance: Tarrou develops his *conscience résistante*, Jacques experiences a revulsion that we learn stays with him throughout his adult life, and Meursault's revelation, however equivocal it remains, makes him decide that he is "prêt à tout revivre" (ready to relive everything; 213) in true Nietzschean fashion. The representation of this moral and existential maturation goes hand in hand with the discrediting of the edifying, deterrent, or retributive vocation of the death penalty, and the repeated use of visions and epiphanies to stage this critique provides it with a sacred aura. And indeed, the stranger resembles Christ, Tarrou wonders about the possibility of being a saint without God, and Jacques finds in the Pirette anecdote the "lien mystérieux" (mysterious bond; OCC 4:789) that connects him to his father. This implicit sacralization no longer belongs to an intradiegetic myth, as is the case with the young Jacques. Instead, the novels sketch an abolitionist mythography of their own through a chorus of characters.

PHYSICAL JUSTICE AND INVOLUNTARY ETHICS

The systematic critique of the effectiveness or rightfulness of capital punishment, as well as the quasi-transcendental character of the protagonists' "abolitionist moments," may lead to the conclusion that the death penalty is the site of moral didacticism and exemplary heroism in Camus's fiction. To some extent, this is true. While Meursault the discreet clerk, prone to indifference and gratuitous murder, seems more akin to an antihero than a hero, his "absolute respect for truth," "surprising determination," and "veritable heroism of lucidity" outdo this first impression, as Rachel Bespaloff has noted.[33] The stranger is also heroic insofar as he is subjected to a greater, irresistible force—the sun—presented as the agent that makes him commit murder. Meursault lives his *fatum* fully. Even his most innocuous deeds are fatal to him when examined by the law.[34] Tarrou flirts with heroism more explicitly than does Meursault, and through another prism: that of a new saintliness paradoxically aspiring to atheism ("être un saint sans Dieu"). A host of heroes also surround Tarrou: Rieux, who asserts that he has no "goût ... pour l'héroïsme et la sainteté" (taste ... for heroism and saintliness; OCC 2:211) but nevertheless shows extraordinary dedication, Grand, Rambert, and Castel.[35] This characterization, the overt and dramatic promotion of positive values such as solidarity and perseverance, and the triumph of a certain humanism over "religious tradition, the demand for happiness, and the desire for absolutes," in Bespaloff's words, turn *La Peste* into an edifying narrative.[36]

However, the novels also problematize this clear-cut moral trajectory and exemplarity. The condemnation of the death penalty by Camus's *résistants* is not devoid of difficulty, uncertainty, and, sometimes, contradiction. As mentioned earlier, Meursault's designation of mortal life as the supreme good during his (ambivalent) epiphany occurs after a paralyzing fear has assailed him. Bedridden and crushed by anguish, he observes his own febricity: "J'avais si affreusement froid que je me recroquevillais sous ma couverture. Je claquais des dents sans pouvoir me retenir" (I was so horribly cold that I curled up under my blanket. My teeth were chattering uncontrollably; *OCC* 1:205). Remarkably, the young Jacques, struck by "horror" in imagining the scaffold, curls up in his bed just like Meursault (*OCC* 4:789). The narratives often highlight the status of *patient* of those who face or witness the death penalty, even if this status is represented as temporary. Camus's capital scenes establish a maximal proximity with their tormented interiority in ways that question their heroism—or even their abolitionism, as in the case of Meursault, who wishes to see someone else be decapitated.

Not only do some of Camus's protagonists turn out to be passive and crippled by distress; when in a position to judge whether the ultimate punishment inflicted on a fellow man is acceptable or desirable, they fall prey to doubt and criticism, including self-criticism. Such is the case for Tarrou and Henri Cormery. *La Peste* and *Le Premier Homme* point to their indifference or to the beliefs that lead them to support the killing of others, thereby further inflecting the model of the abolitionist hero. Tarrou must acknowledge his participation in murder, and he is forced to embrace a most modest moral imperative ("soulager les hommes et, sinon les sauver, du moins leur faire le moins de mal possible"). Jacques's father is initially attracted to the spectacle of the scaffold and convinced of its legitimacy before rejecting his vengeful inclination. Both therefore don't articulate a magisterial critique of lethal justice. On the contrary, they highlight human fallibility and the difficulty one may encounter in establishing one's ethics.

A somewhat unexpected moral compass orients these protagonists on their challenging ethical journey: the human body. It acts as a common denominator that homogenizes the rejection of the death penalty across the three narratives. Critics and the novelist himself have underscored the preeminence of physical sensations in *L'Étranger*.[37] The body rules Meursault's life, from pleasure to murder (he clenches his gun and pulls the trigger because the sun overwhelms him). Whether delusional or not, heightened physical perception also characterizes what he presents as the inner liberation through which he eventually surpasses, or claims to surpass, his sentence. The body plays a key role in the episodes under consideration in *La Peste* and *Le Premier Homme* as well. With these later works, it undergoes the marked "evolution toward solidarity and participation" (*OCC* 2:286) identified by Camus when he compared

L'Étranger with *La Peste*. From *La Peste* onward, the vulnerable body of the Other matters. Rieux and Tarrou aim to "sauver les corps" (save the bodies), to take up Camus's phrase in an editorial from November 20, 1946. For the protagonists, the death of ailing bodies—on whose materiality the text continually insists—must be prevented at all costs.

Additionally, the body matters in that a major symptom of the plague is "décharnement" (emaciation; OCC 2:159), understood as the physical wasting away of the epidemic-stricken Oranians but also as the paralysis of memory and the imagination that takes away their ability to *picture* the physiognomy of their loved ones.[38] This notion of "décharnement" illuminates Tarrou's double epiphany. The trial and execution he witnesses, and more particularly his *face à face* with both the "hibou roux" (OCC 2:206) and the "hole" (209) in the chest that 'metonymizes' the Hungarian condemned man, overturn the "abstraction" through which he conceived justice in his youth. "Un mort n'a de poids que si on l'a vu mort" (A dead man has real meaning only if you have actually seen him dead; 60), Rieux writes in his chronicle, before noting that closing one's eyes in the face of death and thereby ignoring cruelty and pain is sorely tempting. *La Peste* and *Le Premier Homme* defend a related argument: a condemned man "has real meaning" only if one has seen him be sentenced to death or executed.

There is more. A particular emotional response grounded in the body, namely disgust, overwhelms the individual who *observes* the condemned man's experience or who pictures it with sufficient imagination. Tarrou for one suffers from dizziness, feels "un dégoût abominable" (abominable disgust; OCC 2:206), and has "le cœur malade" (an upset stomach; 207) as well as a "mauvais goût ... dans la bouche" (bad taste ... in his mouth; 208) in the presence of the firing squad. Later, he notes that he has a "gorge nouée" (lump in his throat) and "n'arriv[e] pas à déglutir" (cannot swallow; 208). Henri Cormery too vomits after attending Pirette's execution, and his son inherits this nausea, which haunts him throughout his life, as we have seen. Opposite the condemned body stands the disgusted body of the witness. Although disgust, and sometimes, more broadly, the valorization of biology, is commonly used in discourses and reactions that portray the body of the criminal as an abject entity whose exclusion or elimination is presented as necessary, the sickened bodies of Tarrou, Henri, and Jacques provide the foundation for the rejection of—in Camus's words, one might say a *revolt against*—the fate of the condemned individual and for his preservation.

Disgust in the face of state-imposed death surfaces in much of Camus's *nonfiction* as well. In an interview with Carl Viggiani, the author referred to "an organic refusal [of the death penalty] when the thought of [capital punishment] occurred to [him]" in his youth (OCC 4:642). Following the execution of Philippe Pétain's minister of the interior Pierre Pucheu on March 20, 1944, Camus published an editorial in which he repeated that executions had "always filled him with disgust and revolt" (OCC 1:921), but this time, he confessed that, "for the first time," and precisely because he had "experienced [this feeling] to the point of fury" over the previous four years, the death of this *Vichyste* senior official had not moved him. On January 21, 1948, in a letter to Jean Grenier, Camus also underscored "the gut reaction that ma[de him] stand up against punishment [le châtiment]" again before recounting that, at the time of the Épuration, he had attended a trial during which he felt solidarity with the accused whose guilt he nevertheless believed to be established.[39]

Until the late 1950s, that is to say until shortly before his death, the feeling of disgust continued to pervade Camus's publications and speeches about the use of legitimized, rationalized killing by states and political parties. These contributions included his criticism of Franco's Spain being admitted to UNESCO in 1952 (OCC 3:435), that of the "terrorist" and counterterrorist tactics used by the Front de Libération Nationale and the French state during the Algerian War of Independence (934), and that of the execution of Imre Nagy, after the Hungarian politician attempted to break free from Moscow and withdrew from the Warsaw Pact (OCC 4:599). In 1957, "Réflexions sur la guillotine" also insisted on the "disgusting butchery" of execution (166): "No nobility whatsoever around the scaffold, but rather *disgust*, contempt or the basest kind of enjoyment" (141). Throughout these texts, the physical sensation of revulsion causes the rejection of capital punishment, but it also tends to blur the difference between capital punishment and political assassination.[40] *La Peste* itself gestures toward this conflation by not specifying whether the shooting that Tarrou witnesses in Hungary is extrajudicial, following a sham trial, or results from due process.

If the disgusted body of the witness functions as a moral compass so powerful that it occasionally suspends the difference between various kinds of state- or party-sponsored execution, conversely, the intellect as a moral guide elicits some suspicion. *La Peste* and *Le Premier Homme* stage the ability of logic or dogma to legitimize the death penalty wrongly. Henri initially believes that retaliation is in order for Pirette, and, once an adult in Hungary, Tarrou endorses a certain historicism. Camus's "capital fiction" suggests that the primacy of reasoning should give way to a spontaneous, body-based movement of revolt.[41] Rieux exemplifies this. While he doesn't reject reasoning altogether, he turns it into a secondary process: "Pour le moment, il y a des malades et il faut les guérir. *Ensuite, ils réfléchiront, et moi aussi.* Mais le plus pressé est de les guérir. Je les défends comme je peux, voilà tout" (For now, there are sick people and they need curing. *Then, they will think things over, and so will I.* But the most pressing task is to make them better. I stick up for them as best I can, that's all; *OCC* 2:121; my emphasis). Camus's correspondence with Jean Grenier insists: "What Rieux (I) wants to say is that we must cure everything that can be cured—while waiting to *know*, or see."[42] This relative demotion of the mind recalls Nietzsche, whom Camus revered.[43] Yet Nietzsche viewed human compassion as a physiological weakness and a sign of moral decadence in *Twilight of the Idols*. For Camus's characters, quite to the contrary, the sickened body constitutes the foundation of an empathy (in the original sense of suffering *in* the other) that may lead them to correct their judgment, as in the case of Tarrou and Henri.[44]

A kind of physical justice surfaces in both *La Peste* and *Le Premier Homme*, then. Camus himself used this concept when commenting on Pucheu and his peers during the purges: "For us, their biggest crime is to never have gone near a dead body, be it a tortured body like Politzer's, with the eyes of the body and what I would call *the physical notion of justice*" (*OCC* 1:922; my emphasis).[45] Conversely, Henri, Jacques, and Tarrou do perceive capital justice "with the eyes of the body." All three somatize *because* they see or picture the executions all too well:

> Savez-vous que le peloton des fusilleurs se place au contraire à un mètre cinquante du condamné? Savez-vous que si le condamné faisait deux pas en avant, il heurterait les fusils avec sa poitrine? Savez-vous qu'à cette courte distance, les fusilleurs concentrent leurs tirs sur la région du cœur et qu'à eux tous, avec leurs grosses balles, ils y font un trou où l'on pourrait mettre le poing? (*OCC* 2:208)

> Do you know that the firing squad instead stands a yard and a half away from the condemned man? Do you know that if the condemned man took two steps forward, his chest would brush up against the rifles? Do you know that at this

short distance, the shooters aim their fire at the area of the heart and that together, with their big bullets, they make a hole in it, a hole large enough to put your fist into?

Tarrou's pounding anaphora, gradual close-up, emphasis on the disproportionate number and destructive power of the weapons and gunmen used to target the heart—a symbol of vulnerability—as well as the almost grotesque detail of the gaping hole in the man's chest bring home the reality of what Camus calls the "corps supplicié." Remarkably, Jean's *écœurement* (sickness, the bad taste in his mouth that he notes is persistent) is sparked by the victim's literal *écœurement*, in the etymological sense of the term, that is to say the removal of his heart. In the sentences that follow, the "bad taste" in Tarrou's mouth ironically echoes and responds to the "bad taste" that society associates with talking about executions.

It should be noted that this physical justice represented in Camus's post–Second World War novels is not reciprocal. The look that the narratives underscore or imply goes only from the witness, direct or indirect, to the condemned man. It is unilateral, and, contrary to the dynamic of the Levinasian *face à face* ("autrui me regarde" [the Other concerns/looks at me]), the Other concerns Tarrou, Henri, and Jacques *without* looking back at them.[46] In the court of assizes, Tarrou observes the nervous "hibou roux" without the defendant noticing. The accused is actually described as an animal *blinded* by an excessively strong light (OCC 2:206). Interestingly, the focus of Tarrou's eyes is not just the defendant's face but his whole body insofar as it is marked by human banality and imperfection—his right hand, his ill-fitting clothes, his bitten nails. As for Henri Cormery, we know only about his reaction to the decollation. No mention is made of a visual exchange between him and Pirette. Here again, a centrifugal ethics that originates in the witness operates. The ellipsis of the decapitation in the narrative and the fast-forwarding to Henri's nausea highlight the shocking nature of the spectacle and the irresistible physiological response elicited by a legal system that operates through pure force. Camus focuses on the loss of agency of the witness—mirroring that of the executed man, which is so great that the scene symbolically obliterates him.

The body as bearer of justice is not universal either.[47] The ubiquity of murder throughout Camus's novels, the "cries of hatred" emanating from the crowd around the scaffold that Meursault imagines at the end of *L'Étranger*, and the fact that most Oranians don't join the Resistance against the plague confirm this nonuniversality. Furthermore, the sickened body of the witness does not guarantee any rescue either. Even if Rieux sometimes succeeds in securing it, and if Tarrou's mantra as an adult focuses on preserving human lives, in the capital scenes we have examined, the body that is exposed to and disgusted by the execution is in fact powerless. Nevertheless, its recurring presence, which leads to the humble and inevitable acknowledgment of a living status common to the man who is killed and the witness, is meaningful. Through the detailed description of this *corps justicier*, *La Peste* and *Le Premier Homme* represent an organic, physiological ethics that is not an end in and of itself but constitutes the precursor to a *possible* solidarity (for the better "médecins de la peste") or, more modestly, a possible partaking in the suffering of the other and the radical rejection of his elimination (*Le Premier Homme*). What the Camusian novel sketches after 1947 through the original notion of physical justice is an involuntary and nonunanimous ethics of solidarity with the condemned that is both uncomfortable and resolute.

In his notebooks of 1949 and in 1957, when he was awarded the Nobel Prize in Literature, Camus referred to the seemingly paradoxical concept of "engagement involontaire" (OCC 4:247, 1066). To develop this idea, he used the metaphor of the artist as forcibly "embarked" on the "ship of his era," thereby taking up the image of Pascal's wager: "Cela n'est pas volontaire, vous êtes embarqué" (That is not voluntary, you are forcibly taken on board; *Pensées*). This notion of *embarquement* enabled Camus to distance himself from the Sartrian notion of *littérature engagée* all the while expressing his interest in contemporary social and political realities; for if, like Camus, Sartre employed the image of embarking in *Qu'est-ce que la littérature?*, he did so to promote a particular literary model in which political prescription, or dogmatism, prevailed.[48] Camus begged to differ, as his notebooks from 1950 make clear: "*Engagement*. I have the most noble, and most passionate, idea of art. Much too noble to consent to subjecting it to anything. Much too passionate to want to separate it from anything" (1094). Camus's concept of "involuntary engagement" and his commitment not to separate literature from anything—or anyone—while at the same time resisting the rigidity of dogmatism illuminate his fictional representations of lethal punishment. His novels' physical justice, which acts as the foundation for a possible ethics of solidarity with the condemned man, converges with involuntary engagement: it puts forth the visceral inability of some characters to ignore or support state killing, all the while steering clear of universalizing this body-based rejection of capital punishment, of celebrating reciprocity, and of ignoring man's interest in murder.

Camus's narrative prose fiction carves out a space in which to critique the death penalty. It complements the argumentative and normative forms of abolitionist discourse that the writer develops in his essays, editorials, speeches, and correspondence. To some extent, it anticipates the Kantian reasoning which, as Philippe Vanney and Denis Salas have noted, appears in "Réflexions sur la guillotine" through the moral imperative of preserving human life *a maxima*.[49] In *L'Étranger*, *La Peste*, and *Le Premier Homme*, the death penalty functions as a key architectural component: it structures the narratives in depth. It is also subject to a veritable *ressassement* and to transtextual representations that stress the rejection of state killing. While the capital scenes take on various forms, they all include revelations or visions in the face of execution. Camus portrays the confrontation with capital punishment as causing a somewhat mysterious, if not mythical, maturation in his protagonists. Related in detail, decomposed, and repeated, these "capital episodes" nonetheless eschew conventional heroism through a dramatic emphasis on fear, doubt, (self-)critique, or thoughtlessness. After the Second World War, Camus turns the body of his characters into an instrument that enables them to contest the death penalty or, rather, into one that makes it impossible for them to ignore—or support—its violence. It is from the acknowledgment of the condemned man's vulnerable flesh by the (direct or indirect) spectator of his execution that a profound but unilateral connection to the Other emerges in the unexpected form of an overwhelming nausea. Both literally and figuratively, this vomiting marks the rejection of the organized, bloody, and irreversible exclusion of a fellow man from society by the state or a political party. With this spontaneous, corporeal, nontheoretical, and nonuniversal reaction of his protagonists, Camus puts forth an involuntary ethics that actualizes the notion of "engagement involontaire" he uses to designate the intermediary place he assigns to literature: a place in which fiction is neither programmatic nor blind to the outside world. The resistance to lethal justice occurs against the grain of society *and* against the self, whose penchant for indifference, homicide, revenge, or morbid fascination, that is to say for various kinds of "de-solidarization" the narratives also acknowledge.

CHAPTER 6

Poetic Accountability

Critical Language and Its Limits

Tolstoï, dans l'affaire Chibounine plaide devant le tribunal pour le malheureux, coupable d'avoir frappé son capitaine—fait appel pour lui après la condamnation—écrit à sa tante pour lui demander d'intervenir auprès du ministre de la guerre. Celui-ci remarque seulement que Tolstoï a oublié de donner l'adresse du régiment, ce qui l'empêche d'intervenir. Le lendemain du jour où Tolstoï reçoit la lettre qui lui demande de combler cette lacune, Chibounine est exécuté *par la faute de Tolstoï*.

Tolstoy, in the Chibounine affair, pleads in court in favor of the poor man, guilty of hitting his captain—appeals on his behalf after the sentence—writes to his aunt, asking her to intervene with the Minister of War. The latter simply remarks that Tolstoy has forgotten to give the regiment's address, which prevents him from interceding. The day after Tolstoy receives the letter asking him to remedy this omission, Chibounine is executed *through Tolstoy's fault*.

—Albert Camus, *Carnets* (1949)

Camus's narrative fiction chimes with Hugo and Baudelaire in providing glimpses into the human inclination to support executions, be it motivated by hatred, Schadenfreude, curiosity, or a spirit of revenge. The endings of *Le Dernier Jour d'un condamné* and of *L'Étranger*, as well as Baudelaire's verse and *Mon cœur mis à nu* (OCB 1:132, 693) all highlight the popular ecstasy that the spectacle of state killing may elicit. Where and how do the writers situate themselves within this anthropological landscape where the crowd responds to lethal justice with fervor? What does their craft do with and to these responses? Camus's "Réflexions sur la guillotine" are based on the premise that "speaking crudely" (OCC 4:128) about capital punishment is a precondition to thinking about it critically for state killing is subject to silence and rhetorical manipulations that thwart our understanding of its reality. This argument implies that authors, whose raw material is language, take on a major responsibility in representing the death penalty. The role played by words in this institution is all the greater as, more dramatically than any other punishment, the death penalty is born out of the performative utterance "Condamné à mort!" Camus, Hugo, and Baudelaire thus have reason to reflect on their positioning and potentially participate in "capital violence" on two counts: as members of a human collectivity that they portray as easily captivated by or supportive of state killing, and as the artisans of a language that not only brings about capital punishment but also shapes its reception. This closing chapter examines Camus's fiction and its anxiety about the shortcomings of the words chosen to paint the death penalty, before comparing his poetic strategies and critique of the writer's responsibility vis-à-vis the scaffold to those of Hugo and Baudelaire.

DUBIOUS TONGUES: CAMUS BETWEEN METAPHOR AND SILENCE

Camus's evocations of capital punishment insistently return to the fact that language tends to mask this institution. Hugo had already denounced the danger—and indecency—of such rhetorical concealment in his mordant 1832 preface to *Le Dernier Jour d'un condamné*. He argued that the royal prosecutor made his case as if he were a writer and usurped the tools of this profession:

> Son réquisitoire, c'est son œuvre littéraire, il le fleurit de métaphores.... Il gaze le couperet. Il estompe la bascule. Il entortille le panier rouge dans une périphrase. On ne sait plus ce que c'est. C'est douceâtre et décent.... Remarquez-vous comme il fait infuser dans un gâchis de tropes et de synecdoches deux ou trois textes vénéneux pour en exprimer et en extraire à grand'peine la mort d'un homme? (*OCH* 4:491–92)

> His summing up for the prosecution is his literary work, and he adorns it with metaphors.... He puts gauze on the blade. He fades out the bascule. He puts ribbons of periphrases around the red basket. One no longer knows what it is. It

is sickly sweet with decency.... Do you notice the way in which he has two or three poisonous texts brewing away in an overabundance of tropes and synecdoches so as to press out and extract from with much effort the death of a man?

With Camus, this blame *ad professionem* morphs into a broader concern about the power of speech to legitimize executions through formal pirouettes. His "Réflexions sur la guillotine" begin with a condemnation of the stock and dissimulative language used by "journalists and state employees" to refer to the death penalty before widening the accusation to the all-inclusive subjects "on" and "tout le monde" (everyone; 128).[1] While Hugo's denunciation of the prosecutor's cosmetic metaphors ("raffinements," "gaze," "déguisements"), and witch-worthy stylistic devices ("fait infuser... deux ou trois textes vénéneux") itself relies on figurative language, Camus uses direct turns of phrase to command adherence to a sort of linguistic transparency, as his previously cited injunction confirms: "Qu'on ne nous raconte pas d'histoires. Qu'on ne nous dise pas du condamné à mort: 'Il va payer sa dette à la société,' mais: 'On va lui couper le cou.' Ça n'a l'air de rien. Mais ça fait une petite différence" (*OCC* 1:54).[2]

I noted in chapter 5 that there exist numerous variants of this argument in Camus's notebooks, fiction, and nonfiction. They make explicit the reason euphemistic expressions about lethal punishment are unacceptable to him: in Meursault's words, "Cela ne parle pas à l'imagination" (That doesn't speak to the imagination; 204). Camus's "Réflexions sur la guillotine" reread the recurrent anecdote of the father's nausea in this light (*OCC* 4:129), asserting that "grand formulae" had concealed the reality of beheading from Lucien Camus until he witnessed it (127). Camus argues that language has the ability to render the materiality of state killing (129), which is itself a precondition to our full understanding of the punishment. According to this logic, language is responsible for our a priori acceptance of the death penalty when it eclipses the latter's violence from our mental representations. In other words, and as Camus reiterates in his reflections on the Second World War and the rise of totalitarian ideologies in *L'Homme révolté* (*OCC* 3:304), a language that distances itself from direct referentiality—notably through a certain use of metaphor—makes killing possible.

While the Nobel laureate places embellishing metaphors and nonspecific phrasing at one end of the spectrum of dubious language, the other end of this spectrum features silence: not the silence that the writer associates with profound affection—the silence through which a mother and her son can communicate, for instance—but the silence that may cover up violence, deliberately or not.³ Meursault's father in *L'Étranger*, Camus's father in "Réflexions," Jacques's father in *Le Premier Homme* do not utter a word after witnessing an execution (*OCC* 1:205; 4:127, 789). They are unable to. That ellipses prevail when it comes to representing the beheadings they attend reinforces this sense of unsayability. Another form of obliteration, bourgeois propriety, is found in Tarrou's family. They avoid the topic of capital punishment, despite the fact that it causes the young man to leave his home (*OCC* 2:206, 207).

La Peste likewise warns against the danger of silence after individuals have witnessed (preventable) death and may be tempted to then forget (248) it: as the novel eventually discloses the narrator's identity, it stresses that Rieux's chronicle originates in the desire to puncture or compensate for such muteness. Rieux's perspective converges with the idea expressed by Camus in 1948, that "to act, man must speak" (478), even if part of his fiction suspends this means-end relation between word and action and has action trump words through highly likable characters who do not fully master language, from Grand in *La Peste* to Jacques's uncle in *Le Premier Homme*. The novels' reflections on silence as allowing for the smooth functioning or persistence of capital punishment (represented both literally and allegorically in *La Peste*) certainly have some basis in fact. The guillotine was not named in the article of the French penal code that implicitly prescribed its use ("Any person sentenced to death shall have their head cut off"), and the omission of this key word went hand in hand with a certain discretion and the absence of investigative publications after executions took place. Until the 1970s, the French state punished any breach of the muteness it prescribed.⁴

How do Camus and some of his protagonists propose to undercut both the concealing metaphors and the (self-)censorship that surround the scaffold? How do they expose what the writer perceives as "the obscenity that is hiding under the cloak of words" (*OCC* 4:128)? By resorting to "le langage clair, le mot simple" (clear language, the simple word; *OCC* 3:304), answer both *La Peste* and *L'Homme révolté*. Tarrou's most famous declaration in the novel echoes Camus's journalistic publications during the war: "J'ai entendu tant de raisonnements qui ont failli me tourner la tête, et qui ont tourné suffisamment d'autres têtes pour les faire consentir à l'assassinat, que j'ai compris que tout le malheur des hommes venait de ce qu'ils ne tenaient pas un *langage clair*.

J'ai pris le parti alors de *parler et d'agir clairement*, pour me mettre sur le bon chemin" (I've heard so many arguments that almost turned my mind, and that made a large enough number of other people lose theirs and had them approve of murder that I've come to understand that all human unhappiness stems from men's failure to use *plain language*. So I've resolved *to speak and to act clearly*, to put myself on the right path; *OCC* 2:210; my emphasis).⁵ By "langage clair," a number of Camus's characters, and, *en abyme*, the author himself, seem to mean a strict relation of facts.

This aspiration to factual reporting infuses all of the author's "capital writings." In *L'Étranger*, "Réflexions sur la guillotine," and *Le Premier Homme*, the founding scene of the father's nausea is reported in short, unadorned narrative sequences—voiced by Meursault's mother and himself, by Camus, and by Jacques, who acts as his mother's substitute.⁶ In *La Peste*, Rieux glosses the genre chosen for his testimony, the chronicle—also the form of the book itself—underscoring the need for what he calls the "objective" tone of the voice of the "witness" and for a relation of facts that steers clear of both hostility and sensationalism (*OCC* 2:128–29). Later, the narrative advocates "restraint" and the avoidance of speculation (243). Throughout the novel, counterexamples make this demand stand out by contrast. They include the epic tone of newspapers and radio news (129), the prophecy that capitalizes on men's despair and is relayed by opportunists (186–87), the sermon, or even notebooks that indulge in obscure remarks and give in to personal curiosity.⁷

"Le langage clair" emerges through other forms and devices, but all of them conform to the same aesthetic principles, which are also ethical principles. Camus may render state killing through photographic capture, as with his close-ups on particular parts of the condemned body (the "hibou roux"'s right hand and nails, for instance), through asyndetic parataxis, or stichomythia. The way in which the execution of the Russian Revolutionary hero Kaliayev is related at the end of *Les Justes* is a case in point:

> DORA, *la tête dans les mains*: Un peu de boue!
> ANNENKOV, *brusquement*: Comment sais-tu cela?
>   *Stepan se tait.*
> Tu as tout demandé à Orlov? Pourquoi?
> STEPAN, *détournant les yeux*: Il y avait quelque chose entre
>   Yanek et moi.
> ANNENKOV: Quoi donc?

STEPAN: Je l'enviais.
DORA: Après, Stepan, après?
STEPAN: Le père Florinski est venu lui présenter le crucifix. Il a refusé de l'embrasser. Et il a déclaré: "Je vous ai déjà dit que j'en ai fini avec la vie et que je suis en règle avec la mort."
DORA: Comment était sa voix?
STEPAN: La même exactement. Moins la fièvre et l'impatience que vous lui connaissez.
DORA: Avait-il l'air heureux?
...
STEPAN: Il a marché. On chantait sur le fleuve en contrebas, avec un accordéon. Des chiens ont aboyé à ce moment.
DORA: C'est alors qu'il est monté...
STEPAN: Il est monté. Il s'est enfoncé dans la nuit. On a vu vaguement le linceul dont le bourreau l'a recouvert tout entier.
DORA: Et puis, et puis...
STEPAN: Des bruits sourds.
DORA: Des bruits sourds. Yanek! Et ensuite...
Stepan se tait.
DORA: *avec violence*: Ensuite, te dis-je. (*Stepan se tait.*) Parle, Alexis. Ensuite?
VOINOV: Un bruit terrible. (OCC 3:50–51)

DORA, *her head in her hands:* A bit of mud!
ANNENKOV, *abruptly*: How do you know all this?
Stepan falls silent.
You asked Orlov about all this? Why?
STEPAN, *looking away*: Something came between Yanek and me.
ANNENKOV: What was it?
STEPAN: I envied him.
DORA: What happened next, Stepan, what next?
STEPAN: Father Florinski came up to present him with the crucifix. He refused to kiss it. And he said: "I've already told you that I'm done with life and I'm at peace with death."
DORA: How did he sound?
STEPAN: Exactly the same as usual. Minus the fever and his characteristic impatience that you know of.

DORA: Did he seem happy?
...
STEPAN: He walked. People were singing down by the river, with an accordion. Some dogs barked at that moment.
DORA: That's when he went up the steps . . .
STEPAN: He went up. He walked into the night. We caught a glimpse of the shroud with which the executioner had covered him up entirely.
DORA: And then, and then . . .
STEPAN: Muffled sounds.
DORA: Muffled sounds. Yanek! And then . . .
Stepan falls silent.
DORA, *forcefully*: Then, do tell me. (*Stepan keeps quiet.*) Speak, Alexis. Then?
VOINOV: A horrible sound.

Dora's character leads the interrogation that allows Yanek's relatively clandestine end to be reconstituted. Stepan (Kaliayev's former contradictor and competitor) and she are, respectively, two and three steps removed from the hanging: we are made to understand that Stepan has already asked Orlov about it in detail as Dora presses the former and, to a lesser extent, Voinov to report the scene to her. The shape taken by the account is plain, clinical, and chronological. She and the spectator are therefore not in direct contact with the event but close enough to it through the interface of a minimal form of language. It foregrounds fragments of perception (the image of the mud stain, that of the unkissed crucifix, the tone of Yanek's voice, the surrounding noises) and microfacts that take on dramatic and symbolic significance, from the hangman's gestures before the execution to the shroud in which he is wrapped. This language achieves directness and precision, although the relation of Kaliayev's last moments remains filtered by multiple perspectives: that of the witnesses Orlov and Annenkov implicitly, and, explicitly, that of Stepan, whose subjectivity is acknowledged by his avowal that he "envied" Yanek. Here again, the unbearable (albeit indirect) witnessing of the death penalty results in silence. "Stepan se tait" (Stepan falls silent) twice. Yet this silence is symbolically broken as Voinov takes up where Stepan left off and as the triple repetition of the telling noun "bruits" by the three characters creates an echo effect.

This tentative poetics of clarity fulfills several functions. It forms part of Camus's quest to "always be a little understated in one's expression"

(OCC 2:856), a strategy designed to increase the suggestiveness of writing. In the specific case of capital punishment, restrained and factual language exposes pure violence and suggests a certain gratuitousness, as the closing scene of *Les Justes* illustrates.[8] In addition, it presents this violence as irrefutable. Rieux insists on the need to leave a written trace of the plague (37) in a city prone to denial: "Ils niaient tranquillement, contre toute évidence, que nous ayons jamais connu ce monde insensé où le meurtre d'un homme était aussi quotidien que celui des mouches" (They calmly denied, despite all evidence to the contrary, that we had ever known that senseless world in which men were killed off as commonly as flies; 240). In barring "peace[ful]" denial, straightforward language serves as a first precondition to remembrance, a process on which the novel's cautionary ending insists, pointing to itself and to literature at large in a self-reflexive climax: "On peut lire dans les livres, que le bacille de la peste ne meurt ni ne disparaît jamais" (Books tell us that the plague bacillus never dies or disappears for good; 248).

Last but not least, Camus's poetics of clarity actively de-romanticizes state killing. The dénouement of *Les Justes* divulges the stages, banal details, and sinister sounds that characterize a hanging. In doing so, it completes the play's increasing de-idealization of killing—Yanek gradually loses his naïveté as a young revolutionary enthusiast in accordance with Dora's gentle warning in Act I; in *L'Étranger*, Meursault's final delusion of grandeur as he pictures his persecution on the scaffold is undermined by the hour-by-hour account of the nightly anxiety from which he suffers and by his detailed reflections on the logistics of the guillotine. Both in this novel and in *La Peste* and *Le Premier Homme*, the terse reporting of the father's vomiting also annihilates the idealized representation of which the condemned individual may be the subject—as seen in much of the literature and iconography of the nineteenth century.[9]

Evidently, the notion of a "langage clair" is nevertheless problematic, if not utopian. While Camus's literary works promote this model and repeatedly actualize it, they also reveal its shortcomings.[10] There are many, beginning with the fact that the mediating nature of language forecloses the translucence of the "diamond" that Camus uses as an analogy for the writing, and the œuvre, to which he aspires (OCC 2:862). To this fundamental issue, *La Peste* adds the fact that "le langage conventionnel" (129) is inadequate to express the subtlety and complexity of human behavior and affectivity, a fortiori in extreme situations where life is at stake. But equally, a language that considers itself to be "sans réserves" (41) runs the risk of deadly absolutism, as Rambert teasingly points out to Rieux, comparing his rhetoric to "le langage de Saint-Just" (41). The doctor himself concedes that his demand that the journalist be able to tell nothing but the truth in a "total" manner is more strategic than literal.

Speaking plainly also proves challenging and, at times, undesirable in *La Peste*:

> —Allons, dit Rieux, il faut peut-être se décider à appeler cette maladie par son nom. Jusqu'à présent, nous avons piétiné. . . .
> —Oui, oui, disait Grand en descendant les escaliers derrière le docteur. Il faut appeler les choses par leur nom. Mais quel est ce nom?
> —Je ne puis vous le dire, et d'ailleurs cela ne vous serait pas utile.
> —Vous voyez, sourit l'employé. Ce n'est pas si facile. (*OCC* 2:62)

> "Now," said Rieux, "we should perhaps resolve to call this disease by its name. So far we've not got very far." . . .
> "You're right, you're right," said Grand as he followed the doctor down the stairs. "We should call things by their name. But what is this name?"
> "That I can't say, and anyhow it wouldn't be of use to you."
> "You see," smiled the employee. "It's not that easy."

Rieux, who is the very proponent of the truth—and an individual whose intellectual and social status should enable him to use a wealth of words with precision—declines to name the epidemic at this stage of the narrative. Although he has identified the disease, he chooses to spare Grand and prevent the spread of panic. The town hall employee gently points out that the doctor paradoxically fails to abide by his own standards of clarity. Elsewhere, the narrator of *La Peste* also reveals the difficulty, if not the impossibility, of the claim to objectivity that underlies the chronicle. Tarrou's notebooks are said to forgo neutrality intermittently and lapse into personal considerations (*OCC* 2:224–25), for instance. They symbolically signal the tension that lies at the heart of the novel as it attempts to reconcile the promotion of objectivity with an emphasis on the vital role of witnessing, which necessarily implies subjectivity.[11] The very structure of *La Peste*, which invites rereading as it ends with the revelation of the narrator's identity (243), acknowledges this rift. Furthermore, a crucial scene radically disavows truthful language and objectivity. To spare Othon, Tarrou denies that the death of his young son, Philippe, was excruciating (201), after an extensive description has detailed the boy's agony through the combined dramatic analogies of a shipwreck and a "grotesque" crucifixion (180–82).

In sum, Camus's capital fiction features forms of "langage clair" and conspicuously problematizes this poetico-ethical ideal upheld by the author and several of his characters. Between the lines, the narrator of *La Peste* himself acknowledges the impossibility of an entirely direct and unadulterated relationship between experience and language: "C'est ainsi, soit dit entre parenthèses, que pour ne rien trahir et surtout pour ne pas se trahir lui-même, le narrateur a tendu à l'objectivité. Il n'a *presque rien* voulu modifier par les effets de l'art, *sauf* en ce qui concerne les besoins élémentaires d'une relation à peu près cohérente" (That is why, it may be noted in passing, in order not to betray anything and in particular not to betray himself, the narrator has striven for objectivity. He has *hardly* wanted to make changes to *anything* for the sake of artistic effect, *except* for the basic adjustments needed to present a coherent enough narrative; *OCC* 2:158–59; my emphasis). At the diegetic level, Rieux is forced to concede that objectivity is a relative goal rather than an absolute one ("a tendu à"), that it is first and foremost a strategy of self-discipline ("pour ne pas se trahir lui-même"), and that the strict transcription of facts is a fiction ("les besoins élémentaires ... à peu près cohérente"). At the metafictional level, the doctor's admission is of course magnified by the fact that his "relation" *is* the novel. In it, "les effets de l'art" are omnipresent—from careful narrative construction to intense dramatization and the juxtaposition of discursive types, tonalities, and subjectivities. Above all, the "art" of this novel lies in its allegorical character, that is to say in a most indirect form of language whereby one reality is represented by another, as the epigraph by Defoe avers.

Although *La Peste* may be more visibly critical of Camus's own model of linguistic transparency than his other works, the claim that language should be the bearer of truth, maximal limpidity, and objectivity coexists with a distancing from this model in the rest of his "capital fiction." Camus's own poetics of clarity is thus represented as both necessary and relative. It is not an absolute and cohabits with strategies of indirect expression deemed liable to render the intensity of lethal violence and the unacceptability of state killing. Metaphor itself finds itself relegitimized in this context, under specific conditions.

STRATEGIES OF EXPOSURE IN HUGO AND CAMUS

While, for both Camus and Hugo, metaphors and periphrases are unacceptable ways of referring to capital punishment, both writers do sometimes mobilize these very tropes and other representational strategies that move away from literality and "le mot simple" (OCC 3:304). Their capital fiction turns to these transformative devices in two main contexts: the disclosure of the condemned man's perspective, and the portrayal of the judicial world.

Drawing a parallel between the poetic strategies developed in Hugo's and Camus's writings on capital punishment may seem unwelcome given the latter's misgivings about the representation of criminals on which his predecessor based part of his abolitionist argumentation. Apparently referring to *Les Misérables*—as Baudelaire had a century earlier—Camus criticized Hugo's "good convicts" and the "conventional imagery" to which they had given rise (OCC 4:159). Nevertheless, as critics have noted, both Hugo's 1832 preface to *Le Dernier Jour d'un condamné* and "Réflexions sur la guillotine" display the same verve and prescriptions.[12] *L'Étranger* and *Le Dernier Jour* also share several common denominators. Both novels feature unorthodox criminals who are guilty of a relatively unexplained *crime de sang*, experience capital justice with a certain bewilderment, and await the scaffold alone after rejecting the help of a religious representative.

Beyond these narrative intersections, a major overlap between the two works lies in their reliance on an intimate subjective realism.[13] Part I has showed that Hugo even goes so far as to create a form of hyperrealism for his novel-diary. In his own way, Camus also has Meursault's mind and body infuse the content and form of *L'Étranger*. The conjunction of at least three components that enforce subjectivity in *Le Dernier Jour* can also be traced in *L'Étranger*. First is the use of the "I" as both a dominant pronoun and a fundamental focal point shaping the narrative. In both novels, events are perceived through the exclusive lens of an increasingly isolated mind—even when it intermittently turns to what others think and say. With Camus as with Hugo, this close-up on subjectivity is not contradicted by the use of a tone of voice that is often clinical and objective: this very tone translates the protagonist's passive experiencing of lethal justice.[14] Second is the close connection of this subjectivity to the present, which reinforces a sense of lived experience. If the anchoring of Hugo's fictional diary in the present tense is one of the devices through which *Le Dernier Jour* immerses the reader in the capital experience, Camus's use of the *passé-composé* follows an analogous logic in *L'Étranger*, not one of perfect instantaneity but one that nonetheless abolishes temporal distance and has immediate anteriority encroach on the present. Third, as seen in the previous chapter, and by Meursault's own avowal (*OCC* 1:178), sensations suffuse *L'Étranger*, just as they permeate *Le Dernier Jour*. Besides, although the multiple forms of linguistic cutting that anticipate the condemned man's physical suffering on the day of his decapitation in Hugo's novel are not prominent in Camus's, they nevertheless surface at critical moments in *L'Étranger*, through rhythmic breaks, an intensified asyndetic syntax, and aposiopesis: "La cour est revenue. Très vite, on a lu aux jurés une série de questions. J'ai entendu 'coupable de meurtre' . . . 'préméditation' . . . 'circonstances atténuantes'" (The judges came back in. They read out a series of questions to the jury, very quickly. I could hear "guilty of murder" . . . "premeditation" . . . "extenuating circumstances"; 203). Marie Naudin also points out that Meursault's self-addressed reflections about his appeal recall the staccato rhythm of Hugo's intellectual autopsy of the condemned man.[15]

Because of the distinct narrative frameworks of the two novels—Meursault is presented as living a full life before his sentence, whereas the life of Hugo's protagonist is merely alluded to in an impressionistic fashion—the poetics of sensations do play out differently in *L'Étranger*: Meursault's sentencing appears to block his sensorial approach to the world. His life, processed through his body from the outset of the narrative, suddenly retracts in part, absorbed by a mind obsessed with mental calculations about how to avoid death. The "I" tends to turn inward and somewhat away from the body, thus reorienting the text's intimate subjective realism before the dénouement returns to the senses.

This first-person subjective realism, closely informed by the present and sensations that *Le Dernier Jour* and *L'Étranger* share, constitutes the first site of what Hugo and Camus appear to conceive as desirable, as opposed to deceitful, figurative language. Preparatory notes for *Le Premier Homme* argue that "D'un corps on ne peut parler que par métaphores" (One can only speak about a body through metaphors; *OCC* 4:982). Camus's fiction indicates that this is all the more applicable to a body that awaits execution. We have seen that animalization by way of metaphor affects both Meursault after his trial and the man that Tarrou's father seeks to sentence to death. Additionally, Meursault and Hugo's protagonists use figurative language when they experience (semi-)hallucinations, whether before their judges or prior to their beheading. Hugo's condemned man views himself as a puppet-like figure in the courtroom, "le centre auquel se rattachaient les fils qui faisaient se mouvoir toutes ces faces béantes et penchées" (the center from which the threads led off and that gave motion to all these gaping and tilted faces; II, 659), before seeing the faces of past criminals appear on the walls of his cell and imagining that he is in the presence of an incarnation of death, as seen in chapter 1. Metaphors likewise convey Meursault's self-admittedly distorted perception of reality before, during, and after his trial: he claims that, from within the prison, the same nameless and wave-like day "déferl[e]" (washes over [him]; OCC 1:187, 188); he is then under the impression that the jurors make up "une banquette de tramway et tous ces voyageurs anonymes épi[ent] le nouvel arrivant pour en apercevoir les ridicules" (a row of seats on a tram and all these anonymous passengers are scrutinizing the new arrival to spot his peculiarities; 189) and eventually states that the starry night sky covers his face shortly before his execution, as noted in chapter 5. All the *temps forts* of the condemned man's experience thus rely on imagistic language that allows for the representation of the bestialization, objectification, and estrangement from reality that affect him alternatively.

The "language replete with flesh and vivid images" (OCC 1:923) that Camus referred to in May 1944 thus also serves to represent the interiority of the individual who faces capital sentencing. In both Hugo and Camus, a certain disregard for the guilt of this individual comes through, unless, as for Camus, the individual in question is responsible for institutional lethal violence; the reader is invited to side with the condemned man's perspective whether he be a criminal murderer (Meursault), an individual who shed blood in an unknown context (Hugo's condemned man), or neither (the Hungarian political prisoner in *La Peste*). In other words, firsthand experience of state violence, however varied, seems to legitimize, and even necessitate, figuration as a way of triggering sympathetic identification. What could be called Camus's and Hugo's "experiential metaphors" expose critically what is usually unseen and unknown, namely the alienated perspective of the target of such violence.

A second locus in which Camus cultivates figurative language and rhetorical devices is the judicial world. In it, metaphors no longer act as a vessel designed to shine a light on the condemned man's experience. Rather, they form part of an imitative strategy designed to satirize a fraudulent use of words. Both Hugo and Camus portray the courtroom as a space of comedy, or rather tragicomedy, on several counts. Both underscore the ordinariness and ridiculousness of key actors in the trial. Hugo uses dark humor to contrast the judges' power of life and death over the condemned man with their "air satisfait, probablement de la joie d'avoir bientôt fini" (self-satisfied air, probably due to the joy of their work being soon finished; II, 660), for instance. A fleeting description presents the assessor as flirting with a lady placed behind him "par faveur," and the jurors as "bons bourgeois" who yawn and are "very sleepy" (660). The death sentence is thereby shown to emanate from individuals who display a mediocrity and frivolity that would otherwise be innocuous. This frail morality that underlies capital justice culminates with the bailiff declaring that it is convenient for him to write the minutes of two executions at the same time (XXIII, 686), as mentioned in chapter 1. Some critics have argued that Hugo's novel tends to steer clear of condemning the judiciary.[16] Yet similarly to *L'Étranger*, Hugo's fictional diary denounces the social comedy and ceremony that accompany lethal justice and heightens its cruelty and absurdity.[17] Both narratives also scathingly deride the judicial thoughtlessness and administrative pettiness that surround the scaffold.

To be sure, Camus pushes further the critical representation of this judicial theater. We have seen that *L'Étranger* revolves around a dramatic displacement of the object and actors of the trial: the crime and the guilty are not those one would expect on the basis of facts and due process. Through Meursault's eyes, the narrative also sheds light on the courtroom as a space of pure performance:

> Nous avons attendu, assis près d'une porte derrière laquelle on entendait des voix, des appels, des bruits de chaises et tout un remue-ménage qui m'a fait penser à ces fêtes de quartier où, après le concert, on range la salle pour pouvoir danser. . . . [L'un des journalistes] a serré la main du gendarme avec beaucoup de chaleur. J'ai remarqué à ce moment que tout le monde se rencontrait, s'interpellait et conversait, comme dans un club où l'on est heureux de se retrouver entre gens du même monde. . . . Mon avocat est arrivé, en robe, entouré de beaucoup d'autres confrères. Il est allé vers les journalistes, a serré des mains. Ils ont plaisanté, ri et ils

avaient l'air tout à fait à leur aise, jusqu'au moment où la sonnerie a retenti dans le prétoire. (*OCC* 1:188–90)

We waited, sitting next to a door behind which we could hear voices, names being called out, chairs being moved and a whole commotion that made me think of these neighborhood social events when, after the concert, the furniture is cleared away to make room for dancing.... [One of the journalists] shook the policeman's hand very warmly. At that point, I noticed that everyone was greeting everyone else, calling each other's names and chatting away as if in a club where people are happy to find themselves together amongst their peers.... My lawyer arrived, in his robe, surrounded by lots of other colleagues. He went over to the journalists, shook hands. They joked, laughed and seemed totally at ease, right until the moment when the bell rang in the courtroom.

By way of analogy, the courtroom becomes a concert hall or *salle des fêtes*. The individuals that occupy it belong to the same troupe, and they warmly interact as actors do—some of them dressed up ("en robe")—before the bell rings, signaling the start of their role-play. This art of performance emerges as early as Meursault's first meeting with the committing magistrate in a room adorned with curtains, not unlike a stage, and in which "un jeu" (a game/acting; *OCC* 1:177) seems to be taking place.

Later, this histrionic setup becomes more prominent. Meursault and the reader discover that make-believe is part and parcel of the judiciary's modus operandi. The protagonist himself picks up on the judge's simulation of courtesy and on his talent for acting: "Personne, en ces heures-là, n'était méchant avec moi. Tout était si naturel, si bien réglé et si sobrement joué que j'avais l'impression ridicule de 'faire partie de la famille.' ... Le juge me reconduisait à la porte de son cabinet en me frappant sur l'épaule et en me disant d'un air cordial: 'C'est fini pour aujourd'hui, monsieur l'Antéchrist'" (No one was unkind to me during these meetings. Everything was so natural, so well organized and so soberly acted out that I had the ridiculous impression that I was "part of the family." ... The judge would walk me back to the door of his office, slap me on the shoulder and say in a friendly voice: "That's it for today, Mr. Antichrist"; *OCC* 1:182). The accusatory vocative that unexpectedly concludes the exchange, the lexical field of pretense, and Meursault's awareness of his own naïveté stress the fact that inauthenticity characterizes the interaction between the law court and the defendant, as is the case at several other moments in the narrative, with the president of the court or his own lawyer (191, 203). The courtroom is not a place in which truth is sought and certified, then. Rather, it is the place in which truth proves highly pliable, to such an extent that it may stop existing: "Tout est vrai et rien n'est vrai!" (Everything is true and yet nothing is true!; 194). Within the judicial institution, verity becomes a function of the talent, or lack of talent, of its performers: they can be congratulated for their dramatic skills ("Magnifique, mon cher"; 202), suffer from stage fright as Meursault does, or make the audience laugh with or at them (194, 197, 201).

In this space of pure performance that sidelines the truth, Camus replicates judicial diction in order to denounce it. He does so *in* his novel, whereas Hugo condemned the judges' "doucereux verbiage" (saccharine verbiage; *OCH* 4:491) in the preface to *Le Dernier Jour*, that is to say outside of the fictional framework. *L'Étranger* dissects the rhetorical tricks and sociolect performed by courtroom professionals to discuss a defendant's personality and actions. The fact that Meursault's good-faith reporting filters their hyperbole, pompous phrasing, stock symbolism, and the gestures that complement them increases the critical distance to which this use of words and chest-thumping are subject. Senseless disproportion, for instance, characterizes the speech of Meursault's lawyer, who is described as "triomph[ant] bruyamment" (exult[ing] loudly) after hearing the concierge declare to the protagonist in Marengo that "c'était lui qui ... avait offert le café au lait" (he was the one who had offered ... some white coffee; *OCC* 1:194). The scene's absurdity then crescendoes as several actors in the trial resort to the same formulae ("Messieurs les jurys apprécieront") whose grotesque solemnity with regard to the topic at hand, namely the white coffee drunk by Meursault during the vigil, is reinforced by false markers of grandeur and gravity. They include the verb *tonner*, the future tense, and a pompous periphrasis referring to Meursault's mother: "Le procureur a tonné au-dessus de nos têtes et il a dit: 'Oui, messieurs les jurés apprécieront. Et ils concluront qu'un étranger pouvait proposer du café, mais qu'un fils devait le refuser devant le corps de celle qui lui avait donné le jour'" (The prosecutor shouted from over our heads and said: "Yes, the gentlemen of the jury will take note. And they will conclude that a stranger might offer a coffee, but that a son should refuse it when next to the corpse of the woman who brought him into this world"; 194). Symbolically, the prosecutor's rhetoric here misrepresents Meursault to such an extent that the substantive used to designate him in the novel's title ("étranger") ends up being applied to the concierge; a resounding misattribution.

The overkill of grandiloquence continues with a clichéd running metaphor of brightness and darkness in the prosecutor's plea against the defendant: "J'en ferai la preuve, Messieurs, et je la ferai doublement. Sous l'aveuglante clarté des faits d'abord et ensuite dans l'éclairage sombre que me fournira la psychologie de cette âme criminelle" (I shall prove it to you, gentlemen, and I shall do so in two ways. First in the blinding light of the facts, and then through the darkness that this criminal soul harbors; OCC 1:198–99). Free indirect speech (197) or the collision of indirect and direct speech in the same sentence establish a further distance between the cliché-ridden metaphors he wields and us, allowing for a more potent critique: "Il disait qu'il s'était penché sur [mon âme] et qu'il n'avait rien trouvé, messieurs les jurés" (He said that he had looked into [my soul] and had found nothing, gentlemen of the jury; 200).

At once shrewd and jocular, Camus's satire of judicial rhetoric also has serious accusatory implications. These linguistic pirouettes are shown to *cause* the radical distortion of reality during the trial and the inflection of due process—from the silencing of the witnesses to the *dialogue de sourds* on which it relies (OCC 1:195–97) to the confusion of people and crimes (178–79, 191, 197) and the replacement of the examination of the defendant's acts by that of his alleged personality (198). The prosecutor's speech climaxes with an unfounded accusation that feigns attention to causality yet contravenes it gravely: "J'en suis persuadé, messieurs. . . . Vous ne trouverez pas ma pensée trop audacieuse, si je dis que l'homme qui est assis sur ce banc est coupable aussi du meurtre que cette cour devra juger demain. Il doit être puni *en conséquence*" (I am convinced, gentlemen. . . . You will not deem my thought too rash if I say that the man sitting in this dock is also guilty of the murder that this court will have to judge tomorrow. He must be punished *accordingly*; 200; my emphasis). Such language of persuasion at all costs combines emphasis, litotes, and captatio to support a fallacious logic that reinvents Meursault's crime as a parricide and falsifies his identity, replacing it with that of another.

That the words of justice erase the defendant's identity is brought home by his feeling of exteriority and self-dispossession during the trial

("En quelque sorte, on avait l'air de traiter cette affaire en dehors de moi" [In a way, they seemed to be trying this case independently of me; OCC 1:198) as well as by a spectacular usurpation of his "je":

> À un moment donné, cependant, je l'ai écouté [mon avocat] parce qu'il disait: "Il est vrai que j'ai tué." Puis il a continué sur ce ton, disant "je" chaque fois qu'il parlait de moi. J'étais très étonné. Je me suis penché vers un gendarme et je lui ai demandé pourquoi. Il m'a dit de me taire et, après un moment, il a ajouté: "Tous les avocats font ça." Moi, j'ai pensé que c'était m'écarter encore de l'affaire, me réduire à zéro et, en un certain sens, se substituer à moi. (OCC 1:201)

> At one point, however, I listened to him [my lawyer] because he said: "It is true that I killed a man." Then he carried on like that, saying "I" every time he talked about me. I was very surprised. I leaned over to one of the policemen and asked him why he was doing that. He told me to be quiet and, after a while, he added: "All lawyers do that." *I* thought that this was another way of excluding me from proceedings, reducing me to nothing and, in a way, of taking my place.

Two "je"s compete in this passage: Meursault's and that of his counsel pretending to be him. Be it for his client's good, the lawyer silences him and violates his identity; indeed, "lawyers" in general do so, as the gendarme makes clear by noting that the technique is widespread.

In short, judicial rhetoric is portrayed as enabling falsification, the illogical, exclusion, and usurpation. It thereby fabricates "the stranger' and does so with fatal consequences. Hyperbole ultimately enables the prosecutor to ask for Meursault's death with "le cœur léger" (a light heart) by transforming the defendant into "rien que de monstrueux" (nothing but a monster; OCC 1:201). Judicial language here appears to go so far as to convince the very individual who utters it that his performance is not really one, that he has accessed the certainty of truth and is in the right. Meursault's lawyer is also shown to be convinced by his own rhetoric. "Very voluble" and satisfied with his speech for the defense, he guarantees to his client that the decision of the court will be favorable to him (203). Shortly thereafter, the statement that concludes the trial again hints at formal pyrotechnics and dubious procuration: "Le président m'a dit *dans une forme bizarre* que j'aurais la tête tranchée sur une place publique *au nom du peuple français*" (The presiding judge told me *in a peculiar way* that my head would be cut off in a public square *in the name of the French people*; 203; my emphasis).

Hugo and, more visibly even, Camus therefore tap into figurative language and a wealth of rhetorical devices that do not contradict their indictment of the metaphors to which society turns in adopting and implementing the death penalty. Theirs is an imagistic and rhetorical discourse designed either to supplement common language with a view to conveying fully the condemned man's experience or, conversely, to point to the travesty of justice for which certain manipulations of words allow. Symbolically, both writers sometimes depict those who twist reality through language to arrive at a death sentence through the same incriminating metaphors. Tarrou's father and the judges of *Le Dernier Jour* are associated with red and black, a chromatism that turns them into devilish or bloodstained figures, "chargés de haillons ensanglantés" (II, 659). But if language bears at least part of the responsibility for state-imposed death, what of the authors themselves, arguably the most zealous manipulators of language?

MIRROR MOMENTS: WRITER, ART, AND STATE
KILLING IN HUGO, BAUDELAIRE, AND CAMUS

The works by Hugo, Baudelaire, and Camus under examination all refer to the act of wording lethal justice by staging scenes and poetic moments that feature the figure of the artist or the writer. They provide information about how the three authors understand and problematize the stakes and risks of their "capital writings."

We have seen that Hugo makes references to himself and his profession in *Le Dernier Jour d'un condamné*. He lends some of his features to the protagonist and repeatedly thematizes writing—through an original paratext that includes the facsimile of a song, references to the condemned man's penning his experience and to the materiality of this enterprise, and his interrogations on a posthumous readership. The author's relationship to his abolitionist work in these self-referential instances is one of relative confidence in the potential of artistic expression to relay both pain and experience effectively. Additionally, *Le Dernier Jour* as a whole symbolically compensates for the blank section of the diary in which the condemned man's personal "histoire" is missing (chapter XLVII). Albeit with sinister irony, the novel redeems this silence by rendering his ultimate and most confidential story—that of his mental alteration in the face of death.

Hugo's postfactum preface also features a telling anecdote about what prompted the writing of his novel. He claims to have wanted to wash away the drop of blood that he, like all members of society, feels dripping on his forehead in the presence of the scaffold. *Le Dernier Jour*, he concludes, allowed for this figurative cleaning (481). Although he is quick to add that "se laver les mains est bien, empêcher le sang de couler serait mieux" (washing one's hands is a good thing, preventing bloodletting would be better), his work effectively satisfies the imperative to "donner mal aux nerfs aux femmes des procureurs du roi" (pinch the nerves of the wives of the king's prosecutors; 486) that he presents as a means of bringing about abolition. The novel is therefore implicitly recognized as a salutary vehicle that prevents, or is about to prevent, the shedding of blood. A certain trust in literature, and the abolitionist mission it sets for itself, thereby pierces through *Le Dernier Jour*, and even morphs into imperious satisfaction in 1832: "À l'époque où ce livre fut publié, l'auteur ne jugea pas à propos de dire dès lors toute sa pensée. Il aima mieux qu'elle fût comprise et voir si elle le serait. Elle l'a été" (At the time when this book was published, the author did not deem it necessary to express his opinions in their entirety. He preferred to let them be understood and to see whether they would be. They were indeed; *OCH* 4:479–80).

The same underlying contentment and trust in the transcendent power of art do not characterize Camus's fiction and Baudelaire's poetry. While Hugo and Camus share the same profound abolitionist conviction, the latter does not believe in the former's utilitarian vision of art. He writes plainly in *L'Homme révolté*, "'Art for the sake of progress' is a commonplace that pervaded the whole century and that Hugo took up without succeeding in making it convincing" (*OCC* 3:278–79). Camus also rebukes Maistre, Baudelaire's supposed philosophical point of reference. A section of "La Révolte historique" titled "La Prophétie bourgeoise" draws a parallel between Marx and the theocrat based on their shared "fatalism," justification of "the established order," and focus on "political realism, discipline, force" (225). The analogy is deeply critical: it underscores a common homicidal messianism, with Maistre calling for the complete "immol[ation]" of the earth (225) and Marx relying on a nonreligious version of "the historical sense of totality that Christianity has invented" and that has threatened to kill Europe, in Camus's eyes (226). *L'Homme révolté* does not spare the figure of the

Poetic Accountability | 185

dandy either, and presents Baudelaire as the "poet of crime" (105), in constant need of an audience and of performing (104–5).

Camus's "Réflexions sur la guillotine" return to Baudelaire's favored reactionary figure. They comment on Maistre's praise of the executioner. Camus cites the testimony of an assistant executioner before using it to gloss the *Soirées de Saint-Pétersbourg* with scathing irony:

> The new executioner is a guillotine fanatic. He sometimes spends days on end at home sitting on a chair, all ready to go, with his hat and coat on, waiting to be called in by the Ministry.
> Yes, here is the man about whom Joseph de Maistre said that, for him to exist, there had to be a special decree from divine power and that, without him, "order gives way to chaos, thrones collapse and society disappears." Here is the man through whom society rids itself of the guilty for good, since the executioner signs the prison release and a free man is then handed over to his discretion. (OCC 4:142)

Camus radically demystifies Maistre's figuration of the executioner. No longer the heroic and god-ordained guarantor of social order on earth, he is represented as both pitiful and dangerous—mentally disabled, used as a recipient of social waste, and endowed with the exorbitant power to dispose of a fellow man's freedom. Although Baudelaire does not faithfully abide by Maistre's theories, as seen in part II, the mystical potential for violence found in the counter-Revolutionary thinker's theory does fascinates him, however much of an illusion he shows it to be. Camus, for his part, conceives of violence pragmatically and sees no possible opportunity for sacredness or desirable aristocratic distinction in execution or sacrificial acts.

Nevertheless, in his notebooks, Camus picks up on a few of Baudelaire's aphorisms to which he appears to be sensitive (OCC 2:881, 942). They highlight the weakness and instability inherent in the individual: man's changes of heart, passions, and struggle to maintain fortitude. The *Carnets* also reproduce a quotation from Maistre on human wantonness that one would expect to find in *Baudelaire's* notes: "J. de Maistre: I do not know what the soul of the rascal is, but I believe that I know what the soul of a gentleman is, and that sends shivers down one's spine" (OCC 4:1093). Camus comes to an analogous conclusion: "I know like everyone else does that an intellectual is a dangerous animal to whom treason comes easily" (OCC 2:425). Baudelaire and Camus appear to agree through the figure of Maistre here: however morally, socially, or intellectually sophisticated man is, he is not to be trusted.

A possible cause for this, and an additional point of convergence between the two authors, lies in man's complexity of character. Part II has shown it to pervade Baudelaire's poetry centered on lethal violence, whose actors are frequently portrayed as both victims and executioners. Camus's fiction also morally oscillates when it comes to violence: Meursault the harmless clerk commits murder, Tarrou temporarily and passively condones an execution in Hungary, and Henri Cormery is initially supportive of a beheading, before it makes him sick to his stomach. "Réflexions sur la guillotine" likewise argue that the death penalty cannot be dissuasive precisely because human nature is neither "stable" nor "serene" (OCC 4:137–38). Duality, the precise form of moral instability underlined by Baudelaire, is prominent in Camus's postwar writings in particular: "For four years, at home, we witnessed the reasoned enforcement of this hatred. Men like you and me, who in the morning would pat children in the metro, at night would morph into meticulous executioners. They would become the state employees of hatred and torture" (424). Camus meditates the moral reversibility of the man on the street in its worst possible context, one in which it fully developed under historico-political circumstances that gave free rein to murder. Mutatis mutandis, Baudelaire, for his part, refers to Marat and Robespierre during the Reign of Terror, as we saw in chapter 3.

One difference between the nineteenth-century poet and the twentieth-century novelist lies in the fact that the former consistently affirms the coexistence of victim and executioner within the self, whereas after the Second World War, and more particularly after the Épuration that Camus supported before siding with the condemned, not unlike some of his characters, the Nobel laureate comes to a different conclusion:

> I am less and less inclined to believe that man is innocent. Only I still have this gut reaction that makes me stand up against punishment. After the Liberation, I attended one of the trials of the *Épuration*. The defendant was guilty in my opinion. I left the trial before it ended however, because *I was on his side* and I never again attended one of these trials. In any guilty man, there is an innocent streak. This is what makes any absolute sentencing totally unacceptable. People don't take pain sufficiently into consideration.

Man is not innocent *and* he is not guilty. How to get out of that one?[18]

What coexists in man, Camus argues at the end of the 1940s, is the *absence* of complete innocence and the *absence* of complete guilt, rather than alternating innocence and guilt in their acute forms. He thereby arrives at a picture of mankind that is at once darker and brighter than Baudelaire's. Together, the war, agnosticism, and humanism lead the novelist to distance himself from a Christian imaginary constructed—contrastively—around a figure that incarnates moral purity, but they also lead him to consider pain as mitigating human guilt and to abstain from passing a definitive negative moral judgment on the accused. The works of fiction examined in the previous chapter echo this positioning.

These nuances regarding the understanding and representation of man's moral nature in Baudelaire's and Camus's works shouldn't conceal their shared acknowledgment of man's fundamental violence. Chapter 3 contrasted Hugo's forward-looking and optimistic view of mankind with Baudelaire's insistence on humanity's taste for destruction. Like Baudelaire, Camus does not mask man's brutality. As noted previously, his fiction repeatedly features killing. "Réflexions sur la guillotine" drives home, and indeed generalizes, this homicidal inclination, arguing that "behind the most peaceful and the most familiar faces lurks the impulse to torture and kill" (*OCC* 4:142) and that "murder is in human nature" (143). In 1942, Camus went so far as to see this potentially ubiquitous act as "exhausting" life both in the victim *and* the murderer and even noted that this might explain why society wishes to put the latter to death (*OCC* 2:949).

> If it is true that crime exhausts the ability to live in a man (see above . . .). It is in that respect that Cain's crime (and not Adam's which, in comparison, comes across as a venial sin) has exhausted our strength and our love of life. Insofar as we are part of his nature and his damnation, we suffer from this strange void and this melancholy feeling of inadequacy that follows excessive effusion and exhausting actions. Cain has used up all the possibilities of actual life for us. That is what hell is. But we can clearly see that it is on earth. (*OCC* 2:971–72)

In this reframing of Christian mythology, the protagonist is Adam and Eve's fratricidal son, not his parents; man's original sin is lethal violence, not disobedience or access to the knowledge of good and evil; and damnation takes a new form, namely the suspension of the love of life. The state that ensues from this disinterest is defined as hell, which Camus relocates on earth.

Such a representation of murder as devouring all life, which the twentieth-century writer initially formulates in metaphysical and existential terms, gains new currency both at the end of the Second World War and during the Algerian War of Independence. These two moments in contemporary history compel him to describe collective, organized violence as dangerously contagious. In "Défense de l'intelligence," the speech he delivered at the Mutualité in March 1945, Camus mentioned the mutability of decent-looking men into murderers of children in the context of Nazism and Collaborationism. He also remarked that "The hatred of the victims came in response to the hatred of the executioners" (OCC 2:424) after the conflict, as shown by the recourse to lynchings. Likewise, on May 10, 1947, his article "La Contagion" (published in Combat) expressed concern at the signs of racism and antisemitism found in the French press and society at large in the context of the Malagasy uprisings of March 1947. It also condemned the collective repression perpetrated by the French state in Algeria following the Sétif massacres of May 1945. France, he argued, was embracing the same denial of equality and the terror against which part of the country had fought when the Nazis occupied its territory. Highlighting the same threat of contagion, the 1954 article "Terrorisme et amnistie" and the foreword to Chroniques algériennes (1958) respectively denounced the "surenchère dégoûtante entre les crimes" (disgusting way in which crimes outcompete each other; OCC 3:934) of anticolonial violence and repression in various colonized territories, and diagnosed the justification of both the "terrorism" of the Front de Libération Nationale in Algeria and that of the counterterrorism of the French state as a "casuistique du sang" (OCC 4:300). Camus's consistent critique of human violence as infectious and easily expansive anticipates Girard's reflections on mimetic violence and sacrificial malfunction. Indeed, Denis Salas has argued that Girard's thought on violence finds an antecedent in Camus's postwar diagnoses. Following this plausible argument, when I had recourse to Girard's concepts of "sacrificial crisis" and "essential violence" to shed light on Les Fleurs du mal in chapter 4, I turned to Camus's thought in order to qualify Baudelaire's figuration of violence.

Although the overlap between Baudelaire's and Camus's views on pandemic violence and our intrinsically homicidal human nature is striking, the writers come to differing conclusions. The poet seems to see few chances to escape from this brutality—and his poetic imaginary of capital punishment, with "le bourreau qui jouit" and "le martyr qui sanglote," illustrates this view. By contrast, the novelist calls for resistance to our violent inclinations and for solidarity. He insists on the possibility that instinctive reactions such as disgust may counter our drive to kill or to witness killing, and on the need for a "reconfiguring of our political mentality" (*OCC* 2:425).

These diverging conclusions aside, Baudelaire and Camus's common vision of human interiority and shared appraisal of the nature of lethal violence in the polis lead one to wonder if the writers conceived similarly of their own potential participation in such violence. Both seem willing to explore it reflexively and without complacency. As noted above, Camus's criticizes the intellectual as a dangerous animal (*OCC* 2:425), and his Nobel Prize speech interrogates the engagement (in the English sense) of art and the artist with the most sinister realities of his time, while Baudelaire's "Au lecteur" (*OCB* 1:5–6) and turn to Agrippa d'Aubigné's *Tragiques* in the apologetic epigraph to the first edition of *Les Fleurs* advocate the need to provide a no-holds-barred picture of man's flawed nature, including the poet's.

L'Étranger and *La Peste* feature a few explicit depictions of the I-writer, either through self-portraits or through the thematization of literary writing. When Meursault is in the courtroom, he catches sight of a journalist that turns out to be his mirror image:

> L'un d'entre eux, beaucoup plus jeune, habillé en flanelle grise avec une cravate bleue, avait laissé son stylo devant lui et me regardait. Dans son visage un peu asymétrique, je ne voyais que ses deux yeux, très clairs, qui m'examinaient attentivement, sans rien exprimer qui fût définissable. Et j'ai eu l'impression bizarre d'être regardé par moi-même. (*OCC* 1:190)

> One of them, much younger, dressed in grey flannel with a blue tie, had left his pen lying in front of him and was looking at me. In his slightly asymmetrical face, all I could see were his two eyes, which were very light in color, examining me intently, without expressing anything clearly discernible. And I got the bizarre impression of being watched by myself.

With his physical appearance, interest in judicial matters, and attentive yet discreet presence in the courtroom, this fictional journalist is not just

Meursault's mirror image but also Camus's. He too was a journalist reporting on trials (*OCC* 1:1246–47, 1253). That this face-to-face moment occurs in one of the novel's rare scenes of self-recognition (the second one, after the episode during which Meursault sees himself in his "gamelle" with perplexity and eventually identifies his own voice) makes it all the more noteworthy. Albeit "bizarre," this specular moment comes across as promising: viewing himself in the writer, the condemned man symbolically establishes a closeness with this figure—all the more so as Camus's avatar quietly stands out against a background in which other journalists candidly confess their need to write sensationalistic pieces and cover disparate court cases in one go (189–90).

Yet if the condemned man's symbolic communion with the author is presented as possible at the beginning of the trial, its conclusion suspends this complicity. Very shortly before the pronouncement of the verdict, the writer's avatar looks away from the condemned man, without the narrative specifying what may motivate this new body language—indifference, journalistic interest in the court's decision exclusively, or an identification so profound with the defendant that this moment proves unbearable to the witness, as is the case in *La Peste* and in Camus's own experience, if we are to believe his correspondence.

> Nous étions là, tous, à attendre. Et ce qu'ensemble nous attendions ne concernait que moi. . . . J'ai rencontré le regard du journaliste à la veste grise. . . . Puis j'ai entendu une voix sourde lire quelque chose dans la salle. Quand la sonnerie a encore retenti, que la porte du box s'est ouverte, c'est le silence de la salle qui est monté vers moi, le silence, et cette singulière sensation que j'ai eue lorsque j'ai constaté que le jeune journaliste avait détourné ses yeux. (*OCC* 1:202–3)

> We were all there, waiting. And what we were waiting for together was of interest only to me. . . . My gaze crossed that of the journalist in the grey jacket. . . . Then I heard a muffled voice read something out in the courtroom. When the bell rang again, and when the gate of the dock opened, what rose up toward me was the silence of the courtroom, the silence and that strange sensation I had when I noticed that the young journalist had turned his gaze away from me.

Through this unexplained looking away, the figure of the previously attentive writer ultimately shows itself to be unresponsive to the condemned man's utter exclusion from society. The strangeness of "the stranger," which had been somewhat reduced by his sameness with the journalist, returns. Fatally so.

Agnès Spiquel has compared this self-portrait in *L'Étranger* with a passage from *Le Dernier Jour* in which Hugo seems to discreetly represent himself as a young journalist:[19]

> Un jeune homme, près de la fenêtre, qui écrivait, avec un crayon, sur un portefeuille, a demandé à un des guichetiers ce qu'on faisait là.
> —La toilette du condamné, a répondu l'autre.
> J'ai compris que cela serait demain dans le journal. (XLVIII, 707)

> By the window, a young man who was writing in a pocketbook with a pencil asked one of the clerks what was happening.
> "The condemned man is being got ready," replied the other.
> I assumed that that would be in tomorrow's newspaper.

The parallel is indeed striking; all the more so as both Hugo and Camus had closely observed the judicial world prior to writing their novels. Spiquel remarks that both authors stress the contradiction, if not the "imposture," of their use of a first-person pronoun to capture an experience eventually shown to be that of absolute solitude.[20] While this is true, a distinction also sets the two scenes apart. In Hugo's text, the journalist is presented as actively investigating the way in which the condemned man is treated. He inquires about his "toilette" and then successfully fulfills his role as a relay, be it for voyeuristic ends. Once again, the faith that Hugo's early novel allusively places in writing is absent from Camus's narrative. Besides, in *L'Étranger*, the "histoire du Tchécoslovaque" (*OCC* 1:187) implicitly furthers the distrust for the printed word crystallized by the young journalist's failure to maintain visual contact with Meursault. This anecdote that the protagonist discovers on the old scrap of a press article in his cell pertains to a sordid *fait divers*, on which Camus's own play *Le Malentendu* is based.[21] At the metafictional level, *L'Étranger* therefore suggests that literature, and not just base journalism, may use violence as its *fonds de commerce*—the Czech's story being a real one, reported in *L'Écho d'Alger* and *La Dépêche algérienne* in early January 1935. The critical nature of this self-reference recalls the self-reflexive moments through which Baudelaire points to his own use of lethal violence for the sake of poetic production.

Both Camus's and Baudelaire's works further critique the relation of their own written words to capital crime and punishment by underlining another, opposite tendency of literature—and, more broadly, of art: that which consists in blocking out reality from creation. *La Peste* examines this occlusion through the character of Joseph Grand, a late and meaningful addition to Camus's first version of the novel (*OCC* 2:1185). Grand, whose last name sounds antiphrastic in light of his unassuming character and seeming lack of literary talent but is in fact deserved given his capacity to act with courage and solidarity, struggles with the opening sentence of the literary work he dreams of publishing:

> —Ne regardez pas, dit Grand. C'est ma première phrase. Elle me donne du mal, beaucoup de mal.
> Lui aussi contemplait toutes ces feuilles et sa main parut invinciblement attirée par l'une d'elles qu'il éleva en transparence devant l'ampoule électrique sans abat-jour. La feuille tremblait dans sa main. Rieux remarqua que le front de l'employé était moite.
> —Asseyez-vous, dit-il, et lisez-la-moi.
> L'autre le regarda et sourit avec une sorte de gratitude.
> —Oui, dit-il, je crois que j'en ai envie.
> Il attendit un peu, regardant toujours la feuille, puis s'assit. Rieux écoutait en même temps une sorte de bourdonnement confus qui, dans la ville, semblait répondre aux sifflements du fléau. Il avait, à ce moment précis, une perception extraordinairement aiguë de cette ville qui s'étendait à ses pieds, du monde clos qu'elle formait et des terribles hurlements qu'elle étouffait dans la nuit. La voix de Grand s'éleva sourdement: "Par une belle matinée du mois de mai, une élégante amazone parcourait, sur une superbe jument alezane, les allées fleuries du Bois de Boulogne." Le silence revint et, avec lui, l'indistincte rumeur de la ville en souffrance. (*OCC* 2:104–5)

"Don't look, said Grand. It's my first sentence. I am struggling with it, a lot."

He too was looking at all these sheets of paper and his hand seemed irresistibly drawn to one of them; he picked it up and held it in front of the shadeless light bulb to let the light shine through. The sheet was shaking in his hand. Rieux noticed that the forehead of the municipal clerk was moist with sweat.

"Sit down," he said, "and read it to me."

Grand looked at him and smiled with a sort of gratitude. "Yes," he said, "I think I feel like I need to."

He waited for a while, still looking at the sheet, then sat down. At the same time, Rieux was listening to a sort of indistinct buzzing from the city that seemed to be in reaction to the hissing of the plague. At that precise moment, he had an extraordinarily acute perception of this city spread out below, of the confined world it formed and of the terrible howling it stifled in the night. Grand's dull voice rose up: "On a fine morning in the month of May, an elegant Amazon/horsewoman was riding a superb chestnut mare through the flowery avenues of the Bois de Boulogne." The silence returned and, with it, the confused rumbling of a city that was suffering.

Derision mixed with pathos dominates this passage in which the nervous writer strives to find a verbal form liable to give "perfect" shape to the subject he has chosen, namely a horseback-riding Amazon—at once mythical and, in the context of the Bois de Boulogne, somewhat kitsch. The temporality, locus, character, and aesthetics of Grand's text seem at odds with the morbid reality of the plague that overwhelms Oran; in addition, while the moment that precedes Grand reading his first sentence is associated with an increasingly acute audibility of the city's ordeal ("écoutait," "bourdonnement," "sifflements," "perception ... aiguë," "terribles hurlements"), and a metaphorical visibility of this reality ("qui s'étendait à ses pieds"), his embryonic literary work erases this perception of the pain of others. Reality returns only after the pause that concludes the reading. This symbolic narrative segment encapsulates literature's capacity to ignore, and indeed silence, the outside world, even in its most violent manifestations.

A similar claim underlies the structure of "Un voyage à Cythère," one of Baudelaire's poems that features the death penalty most prominently. The first stanzas draw a stark opposition between the pleasant artistic representations that have traditionally portrayed the Greek island of Kythira, the birthplace of Aphrodite, and the somber reality of this site:

> Quelle est cette île triste et noire?—C'est Cythère,
> Nous dit-on, un pays fameux dans les chansons,
> Eldorado banal de tous les vieux garçons.
> Regardez, après tout, c'est une pauvre terre.
>
> —Île des doux secrets et des fêtes du cœur!
> De l'antique Vénus le superbe fantôme
> Au-dessus de tes mers plane comme un arôme
> Et charge les esprits d'amour et de langueur.
>
> Belle île aux myrtes verts, pleine de fleurs écloses,
> Vénérée à jamais par toute nation,
> Où les soupirs des cœurs en adoration
> Roulent comme l'encens sur un jardin de roses
>
> Ou le roucoulement éternel d'un ramier!
> —Cythère n'était plus qu'un terrain des plus maigres,
> Un désert rocailleux troublé par des cris aigres.
> J'entrevoyais pourtant un objet singulier!
>
> Ce n'était pas un temple aux ombres bocagères,
> Où la jeune prêtresse, amoureuse des fleurs,
> Allait, le corps brûlé de secrètes chaleurs,
> Entrebâillant sa robe aux brises passagères. (*OCB* 1:118)

> What is this black, gloomy island?—It is Cythera,
> They said, a land famous in songs,
> The banal Eldorado of all old bachelors.
> Look: after all, it's not much of a place.
>
> —Isle of sweet secrets and joys of the heart!
> The proud ghost of the Venus of antiquity
> Floats like a perfume above your seas,
> Filling minds with love and languor.
>
> Fair isle of green myrtles, covered in full-blown flowers,
> Ever venerated by all peoples,

Where the sighs of adoring hearts
Waft like incense over a rose garden
Or the eternal cooing of a dove!
—Cythera was now nothing but the most meager of lands,
A rocky desert disturbed by sharp cries.
I could half make out, however, a remarkable object!

It was not a temple set in bosky shades,
Where the young priestess, in love with the flowers,
Went forth, her body burning with secret heats,
Half-opening her robe to the passing breezes.[22]

From the opening line of the first cited stanza, a web of antitheses prevails. Hyphens punctuate a back-and-forth movement between the artistic idealization of the island and its deadly actuality. The repeated juxtaposition of dramatically incompatible figurations of Kythira shows the idyll with which it is associated to be mere fiction. That Baudelaire's poem draws his inspiration from Nerval's August 1844 publication of extracts from his future *Voyage en Orient* on the Greek island only highlights the play of contrasts at the heart of "Un voyage à Cythère" (*OCB* 1:1069–70): Nerval's text too stresses the asymmetry of two locations with irony, pitching the island's mythical or pastoral representation against its new, nineteenth-century reality, affected by British imperialism that Nerval sought to denounce by writing about a hanging.[23]

Baudelaire's poem quickly attributes the responsibility for the misrepresentation of Kythira to "songs," that is to say to a certain popular poetry. Painting also implicitly comes across as the culprit. The gallant aesthetics of Watteau's well-known 1717 *Pèlerinage à l'île de Cythère* is perceptible in the second and third stanzas above. The clichéd and anachronistic image of the "amazone" in a flowery park at the beginning of Grand's novel, whose first sentence he vainly refashions while capital sentences figuratively surround him, recalls the critique of art that underlies several of Baudelaire's stanzas. In the poem's first movement, art proves to be based on "banal" if appealing commonplaces (an idyllic island, Venus, an Edenic rose garden, a dove, a thinly clothed and exoticized young woman) as much as it is oblivious to the worst forms of violence: the suspense that builds up as the reader discovers the island through the increasingly disillusioned gaze of the speaker, who is embarked on a boat approaching Kythira, reaches a first climax when the "je" reveals the "objet singulier" he comes to make out in the middle of this desolate landscape. A hanged man on a gibbet, assailed by necrophagous animals that mutilate the victim's genitals, appears before his eyes, and before ours.

This dramatic revelation presaged by Kythira's gloomy geography, which poetry and painting are presented as concealing at the beginning of the poem, precedes a further surprise at the end of it:

> Habitant de Cythère, enfant d'un ciel si beau,
> Silencieusement tu souffrais ces insultes
> En expiation de tes infâmes cultes
> Et des péchés qui t'ont interdit le tombeau.
>
> Ridicule pendu, tes douleurs sont les miennes!
> Je sentis, à l'aspect de tes membres flottants,
> Comme un vomissement, remonter vers mes dents
> Le long fleuve de fiel des douleurs anciennes;
>
> Devant toi, pauvre diable au souvenir si cher,
> J'ai senti tous les becs et toutes les mâchoires
> Des corbeaux lancinants et des panthères noires
> Qui jadis aimaient tant à triturer ma chair. (*OCB* 1:119)

> Native of Cythera, born under such a beautiful sky,
> You were silently suffering these insults
> As an expiation of your infamous religious practices
> And of the sins which denied you burial.
>
> Laughable hanged man, your sufferings are my own!
> As I looked on your formless limbs, I felt
> Rising towards my teeth like vomit,
> The long river of gall of ancient sufferings.
>
> Looking at you, poor wretch whose memory is so dear,
> I felt all the beaks and all the jaws
> Of the tearing crows and the black panthers
> Who once so loved to pulverize my flesh.[24]

The final identification of the lyric "I" with the disfigured corpse contests the poem's first movement according to which art stands at an unbridgeable distance from reality. As in some of Camus's narratives, the radical identification of the witness with the executed victim is symbolically conveyed through the former's nausea. This siding of the poem's speaker with a sufferer who is simultaneously subject to humiliation and sacrifice—although in this case, sacrifice goes wrong again with the child's presumably sexual sins being subjected to a parody of expiation—recalls the core analogy and conclusion of other *Fleurs du mal* such as "L'Albatros" and "Le Cygne." It appears to restore art's solidarity with those subjected to violence.

However, the poem's ending also features the resurgence of two (related) causes for suspicion mentioned above, namely art's production of clichés contributing to undesirable mystification and its exclusion of outside reality. The three stanzas (stanzas 8 to 10) that depict the animals eating the hanged corpse in the middle of the poem tap into, indeed revel in imagery that aestheticizes the abject. This of course constitutes Baudelaire's trademark in *Les Fleurs*, as exemplified by "Une charogne," whose abjection "Un voyage à Cythère" actually surpasses with its "pourriture" (rottenness), "yeux ... trous" (eyes [as] holes), "ventre effondré" (collapsed paunch), "intestins ... coul[ant] sur les cuisses" (guts ... spilling over the thighs). The clichés of the poetic idyll that the beginning of the poem questioned therefore merely find themselves replaced by clichés of abjection that secure the reader's attraction-repulsion. Reality does not cease to be mystified: it is mystified anew, through graphic images whose caricatural ("ridicule") character echoes—and simply inverts—the idealized caricature denounced in the "chansons."

As for the relation to the "real" world that the poem seems to introduce by having the speaker eventually see himself in the hanged man, it is in fact not one in which the self considers or relates to the other but rather one in which the self considers himself *through* the other.

> —Le ciel était charmant, la mer était unie;
> Pour moi tout était noir et sanglant désormais,
> Hélas! et j'avais, comme en un suaire épais,
> Le cœur enseveli dans cette allégorie. (*OCB* 1:119)

> —The sky was delightful, the sea was smooth;
> For me now everything was black and bloody,
> Alas! and I had, as if in a thick shroud,
> My heart buried in this allegory.[25]

The other, and reality, remain ignored, as the egocentric ("Pour moi") gesture that repaints the blue sky and sea ("Le ciel était charmant, la mer était unie") in black and red indicates. The "allegory" through which the speaker sees and seals the spectacle he has witnessed is one that exclusively focuses on self-consideration ("je n'ai trouvé ... qu'"). Moving away from the actual gibbet to focus on its purely "symbolic" value and pray for self-reconciliation, the last stanza makes this clear:

> Dans ton île, ô Vénus! je n'ai trouvé debout
> Qu'un gibet symbolique où pendait mon image ...
> —Ah! Seigneur! donnez-moi la force et le courage
> De contempler mon cœur et mon corps sans dégoût! (*OCB* 1:119)
>
> In your island, o Venus! I found nothing standing
> But a symbolic gibbet where my own image hung.
> —O Lord! give me the strength and the courage
> To look on my heart and my body without disgust![26]

Camus's works find a distinctly different way out of the suspicion that weighs over art. While Baudelaire's speaker sees himself in the condemned man, Camus has the condemned man see himself in the avatar of the writer, as noted with *L'Étranger*. There also seems to be (literary) room for the subject of violence in *La Peste*. Grand eventually edits his sentence that silenced the agony of the plague-stricken city (*OCC* 2:105). He does so drastically, deleting all adjectives (*OCC* 2:246) from his prose. In the reading scene with Rieux examined above, this sentence reads, "Par une belle matinée du mois de mai, une élégante amazone parcourait, sur une superbe jument alezane, les allées fleuries du Bois de Boulogne." The removal of the qualifiers, all of which are highly laudatory, allows the syntagm to take on an entirely new meaning: "Par une matinée du mois de mai, une amazone parcourait, sur une jument, les allées du Bois de Boulogne." Sans hyperbolic embellishment, the symbol of the Amazon, a warring figure, comes through clearly, and the text reestablishes contact with the outside world. She becomes a potential analogue for what surrounds Grand and Rieux, namely the epidemic-as-war, and more specifically the epidemic-as-Second-World-War. That a fierce and nonhuman warrior is freely roaming one of the largest parks in Paris serves to figure the Occupation. An allegory of Grand's design therefore emerges within Camus's own allegorical novel. While Baudelaire's use of this trope in "Voyage à Cythère" serves to illuminate the speaking subject's experience exclusively, Camus, through Grand, shows that art can be edited and reshaped into representing a violence liable to affect a collectivity.[27]

Despite starkly dissimilar uses of allegory in their "capital writings," Baudelaire and Camus ultimately converge in underscoring the way lethal punishment and art feed off each other. The death penalty relies heavily on representation—as is visible in *L'Étranger, Le Premier Homme*, "Au lecteur," "Un voyage à Cythère," "Le voyage"—while creation often seeks to equal or surpass the intensity of this institutional violence and its imaginary. Earlier in this chapter and in chapter 4, I pointed to the ways in which Baudelaire and Camus signal the responsibility that their art may bear in relation to state killing and its imaginary: Baudelaire repeatedly flags his own use of their aesthetic potential and Camus alerts the reader to the fact that his own raw material, the word, and more specifically discursive stylization in particular contexts, are part and parcel of capital punishment.

There is more. Baudelaire and Camus occasionally explore the other side of this fraught relationship between figuration and the death penalty. In addition to reflecting on the extent to which artistic representation may take advantage of, shape, or plainly generate a political reality and its imaginary, their works occasionally probe the way this institution may impede art. In Baudelaire's case, this critical reflection does not emerge as clearly in his verse poetry as it does in his prose poems, particularly in "Une mort héroïque."

Two comparable symbolic moments testify to the way capital punishment—albeit in a figurative form—may strike back at creation in both this prose poem and *La Peste*. Both instances are self-referential. In "Une mort héroïque," the use of capitalization makes manifest the confrontation of state killing and art: that of "le Prince," "Son Altesse" (His Highness), and that of an allegorized "Art," shown to be subject to a peculiar "Martyre" (*OCB* 1:319, 321, 322). Fancioulle, a beloved jester who has attempted a coup against his sovereign, performs a pantomime on stage in front of the prince. The ruler, himself keen on the arts, is rumored to be inclined to pardon him and his accomplices because of the very organization of this show. As if pressed to outdo himself by the extreme fear that follows the unmasking of his high treason, Fancioulle performs in an unprecedentedly sublime manner. Yet following an order from the prince, a whistle is blown in the theater and the strident noise causes the performer to collapse on stage. He is thus killed in the middle of his artistic apotheosis. Critics have examined this poem closely and extensively, so my aim here is not to repeat the exercise or offer a drastic alternative to their analyses but rather to look more closely at the particular interface of art and capital sentencing in the poem and to compare it with an analogous scene in Camus's novel.[28]

Not only is Baudelaire's text interspersed with a fairly vast lexical field referring to the death penalty—"condamnés," "un homme condamné à mort," "expérience ... d'un intérêt capital," "supplices," "bourreau," "coupables." It also mobilizes, and indeed relies on, key structural components of lethal justice: a capital crime, a sovereign authority (the prince) who represents the state as a whole ("petit État") and confronts the author of this crime, the possibility of a pardon by this head of state, a setting and spatiotemporal configuration making the passing of judgment possible (the public venue, the face-to-face encounter between the sovereign and an audience-jury on the one hand and the criminal on the other), a sequence during which the subject of this judgment is weighed by an assembly (Fancioulle's performance), a verdict (the shrill whistling which the reader understands has been ordered by the prince and which is presented as having played the role of "le bourreau"), and, following it, the brutal death of the accused. Capital punishment therefore pervades the poem via an implicit running analogy. Indeed, it is *doubly* present, for more explicit references to the death penalty feature before and after Fancioulle's performance. Before the court and the reader "suddenly" ("tout à coup") find out about the show that Fancioulle has been invited to give, he and his accomplices are presented as "voués à une mort certaine," and, after his death, they too are "effacés de la vie" (wiped away from life; *OCB* 1:323). The jester-artist therefore finds himself caught between two death penalties, the first literal and expected, and the second (semi-)figurative and unexpected.

How does this double capital punishment affect the jester's art? First, it results in a "parfaite idéalisation" (*OCB* 1:321) whereby, as Sanyal notes, Fancioulle gets the upper hand over state power through aesthetics, whereas he had failed to do so through political conspiration.[29] He achieves aesthetic success precisely thanks to the "comique absolu" of pantomime praised in "De l'essence du rire" and discussed in chapter 4.[30] Yet political (capital) power returns to crush the performer. Although the narrator claims to be unsure of the sovereign's responsibility in the jester's death and goes so far as to suggest that the killing is unintentional, these considerations sound highly rhetorical. Irony conspicuously prevails through the italicization of both the phrase "une expérience physiologique d'un intérêt *capital*" (320), used to designate and anticipate the prince toying with his buffoon to death, and that of the poem's last word "*faveur*" (323), referring to the performer's unfortunate fate.

That the prince is portrayed as akin to the artist in many respects ("amoureux des beaux-arts," "véritable artiste lui-même," pale with envy when witnessing Fancioulle's transcendent performance, and apparently well-versed in the techniques that may sublimate art) is not incompatible with his responsibility in the killing. It is precisely *because* the sovereign is endowed with acute artistic sensibility that he can predict, as the reader is retrospectively led to deduce, that an abrupt rupture of artistic illusion through a mere shrill whistle will annihilate the artist. The annihilation of illusion is so brutal that it affects real life, beyond the space of representation.[31] As opposed to the artist's *failed* attempt to promote political liberalism ("idée de patrie et de liberté"; *OCB* 1:319) through plotting at the outset of the poem, the power that political order has over art, and which is embodied by the literal and the figurative forms taken by the death penalty in the poem, is ultimately irresistible. This is conveyed through suggestion and ellipsis but nevertheless comes across as indubitable. Political sovereignty definitively suppresses performance, performer, and "le mystère de la vie" after having sporadically magnified them. As in "Le Confiteor de l'artiste," the artist, if he challenges this power and the ultimate institution that incarnates it, namely the death penalty, finds himself "finalement vaincu" (ultimately defeated).

"Une mort héroïque" conspicuously recycles and redistributes the actors and decisive images that conclude "Au lecteur" in Les Fleurs du mal, and this intertextual play both reinforces and nuances somewhat the victory of capital political power over art, nevertheless. On the one hand, it strengthens the figuration of defeat and the sense that the prince effortlessly, even pleasurably, sides with the violence of the scaffold. In the third paragraph of the prose poem, the narrator reveals that the ruler's only enemy is the same allegorized "Ennui" presented as a powerful—albeit distressed, for tearful—figure at the end of the prefatory poem of Les Fleurs du mal. The scaffolds of which this figure dreams in Les Fleurs are implicit yet central in "Une mort héroïque," the crucial difference being that the sovereign who dreads boredom above all in "Une mort héroïque" no longer conjures up state killing through the imagination (i.e., poetry) as "l'Ennui" did in "Au lecteur" via the archetypal incarnation of the Oriental despot who "rêve d'échafauds en fumant son houka" (dreams of scaffolds while puffing his hookah; *OCB* 1:6). Instead, the prince—the Western despot—*actualizes* spectacular execution through the liquidation of the very being who produces images.

On the other hand, the figure of the artist itself is associated with despotism, namely that of revolutionary "ideas," at the beginning of the poem, and one factor mitigates the sacrificing of art and its failed attempt to destabilize politics by the end of the prose poem: the "monstre" of "Au lecteur," boredom, reemerges in the form of an "épithète" used by the "severe historian" to qualify the prince in "Une mort héroïque," and this monstrous ennui from "Au lecteur" presented by the narrator as motivating the sovereign's actions in "Une mort héroïque" covertly *remains* at the end of the allegorical narrative. The ruler fails to replace the extraordinary artist he has executed, and thus implicitly falls prey to the ultimate "tyran" that boredom is said to be in the third paragraph. The executioner is therefore victim again—especially as his traits are those found in Baudelaire's self-portraits elsewhere and as the poem triply refracts the figure of the artist into that of the prince, the jester, and the narrator—although he certainly isn't the first, or the only, casualty in this story. Capital political power and political vocabulary are trumped by an existential angst that only art can alleviate, however exposed to political destruction this art may be.

The poem ultimately combines the fantasy of distinction through capital punishment seen in chapter 3—since Fancioulle does temporarily achieve some form of "heroism" on the symbolic scaffold of the stage—*and* the configuration of failed sacrifice examined in chapter 4.[32] The distinction of the subject (here, the artist) through capital punishment is at once short-lived, given his execution, and long-lasting, given his irreplaceability.

La Peste features an episode that raises the same question of the intersection of (figurative) capital punishment and art but posits less ambiguously the failure of the latter under the irresistible pressure of the former. Cottard and Tarrou attend a performance at the Opéra municipal in which the plague, that is to say a sort of historical capital punishment, gradually creeps in:

> Pendant tout le premier acte, Orphée se plaignit avec facilité, quelques femmes en tuniques commentèrent avec grâce son malheur, et l'amour fut chanté en ariettes. La salle réagit avec une chaleur discrète. C'est à peine si on remarqua qu'Orphée

introduisait, dans son air du deuxième acte, des tremblements qui n'y figuraient pas, et demandait avec un léger excès de pathétique, au maître des Enfers, de se laisser toucher par ses pleurs. Certains gestes saccadés qui lui échappèrent apparurent aux plus avisés comme un effet de stylisation qui ajoutait encore à l'interprétation du chanteur.

Il fallut le grand duo d'Orphée et d'Eurydice au troisième acte (c'était le moment où Eurydice échappait à son amant) pour qu'une certaine surprise courût dans la salle. Et comme si le chanteur n'avait attendu que ce mouvement du public, ou, plus certainement encore, comme si la rumeur venue du parterre l'avait confirmé dans ce qu'il ressentait, il choisit ce moment pour avancer vers la rampe d'une façon grotesque, bras et jambes écartés dans son costume à l'antique, et pour s'écrouler au milieu des bergeries du décor qui n'avaient jamais cessé d'être anachroniques mais qui, aux yeux des spectateurs, le devinrent pour la première fois, et de terrible façon.... Peu à peu, le mouvement se précipita, le chuchotement devint exclamation et la foule afflua vers les sorties et s'y pressa, pour finir par s'y bousculer en criant. Cottard et Tarrou, qui s'étaient seulement levés, restaient seuls en face d'une des images de ce qui était leur vie d'alors: la peste sur la scène sous l'aspect d'un histrion désarticulé et, dans la salle, tout un luxe devenu inutile, sous la forme d'éventails oubliés et de dentelles traînant sur le rouge des fauteuils. (OCC 2:171)

Throughout the first act, Orpheus lamented with ease, a few tunic-clad women gracefully commented on his plight, and love was sung through ariette. The audience responded with subdued appreciation. It was hardly noticed that in his song during the second act Orpheus introduced tremolos that were not in the score, and asked the Lord of the Underworld to be moved by his tears with slightly excessive pathos. Some jerky movements he failed to control appeared to the connoisseurs in the audience as stylized affectation that enriched the singer's performance.

It wasn't until Orpheus and Eurydice's big duet in the third act (that was the moment when Eurydice was lost to her lover) that a certain sense of surprise spread through the audience. And as though the singer had been waiting for this response, or, more likely, as though the murmur emanating from the stalls had confirmed what he was feeling, he chose this moment to totter toward the footlights in a grotesque manner, his arms and legs wide apart in his antique robe and collapsed in the middle of the set's makeshift sheep-pen, which had never ceased to look anachronistic but which, in the eyes of the spectators, now came across as such for the first time, and horribly so. . . . Gradually, the reaction increased, whispers turned into exclamations, and the crowd rushed toward the exits and pressed against them before stampeding out to loud cries. Cottard and Tarrou, who had merely risen from their seats, stood alone, opposite an image of what their life was in those days: the plague on stage in the guise of a disarticulated histrio and, in the stalls, a whole array of luxurious items that were now useless, forgotten fans and lace shawls lying around the red theater seats.

Here too, art is killed by an authoritarian (indeed, totalitarian) political order, if one takes the allegorical meaning of the plague into account. And again, this killing happens after art has been magnified by this domineering order, but this time in a caricatural and artistically unsatisfactory way. This scene prefigures the critique of unimpressive and anachronistic art found in the subsequent passage that presents Grand's writing as clichéd. The obsolescence that the narrator describes as inherent in operatic aesthetics ("ariettes," "bergeries du décor qui n'avaient jamais cessé d'être anachroniques") is amplified and, for the spectators of the performance, suddenly made visible by the deadly crescendo that the epidemic introduces on stage.

Art, and more specifically, through Orpheus's figure, music and poetry, is subject to destruction in multiple ways. The main performance becomes that of this destruction itself, and not the opera. The suspension of artistic illusion is gradual and derisive here, whereas it was sudden and sublime in Baudelaire. Physically, the performer undergoes a metamorphosis that begins with "tremblements" and ends with his dropping dead on stage, seemingly dismembered ("bras et jambes écartés," "histrion désarticulé"). Aesthetically, the symptoms of the plague result in slips in register within the performance (unwanted pathos and a dramatization initially misread as deliberate "stylization"), the mounting irony of the narrative voice, and increasingly grotesque descriptions. To-

Poetic Accountability | 205

gether, they further undercut the grandeur for which both the operatic genre and the tragic, mythical subject matter of Orpheus and Eurydice would appear to call. Ultimately, the growing anxiety of the audience that climaxes with a collective panic (from "surprise" to "rumeur" to "mouvement" and "bouscul[ade]") and the spectators rushing to exit the theater show the performance neither to be sustainable nor to fulfill its social function.

But the death of art is most prominently symbolized by the existential desolation that the plague brings about, when the disease eventually substitutes itself for the entire performance and leaves the protagonists alone, facing a lifeless image composed of a corpse and abandoned objects. The gradual move away from the initial close-up on the stage to take in the whole theater, as well as the gaze of the audience giving way to Cottard and Tarrou's observation of the scene as they remain standing, frame this mini-apocalypse most dramatically. So does the fact that the narrator introduces such a "récit"-within-the-chronicle as a conclusion to Tarrou's notes; a conclusion taken to "illustre[r] cette conscience singulière qui venait ... aux pestiférés" (illustrate this peculiar consciousness that came over ... the plague-stricken Oranians; OCC 2:170).

In both Baudelaire's vortical prose poem and Camus's tragi-sarcastic scene, the shadow of capital condemnation becomes literal death. Artistic tragedies merge with real-life ones. Figuratively, Fancioulle and the actor playing Orpheus interrogate the dangerous closeness of art with deadly politics and hint at the possibility of such politics taking over creation—even if, in Baudelaire's case, creation retains some power. Read as parables, the texts seem to expose the uncertain position in which the writers too place themselves, in between a distancing from and an absorption into the lethal political practice and imaginary to which they strive to give form.

* *
*

Camus places plain language at the heart of his reflection on the guillotine and, more broadly, on organized lethal violence. Yet his prose fiction reveals that, just like the bodily ethos on which his protagonists sometimes rely to reject the death penalty, this remedy is imperfect and unsystematic. Our temptation to be silent, to lie, or to fail to put into words the full horror of executions inflects it. These shortcomings are not denied but rather uncovered by Camus's narratives. In fact, both he and Hugo establish, in *L'Étranger* and *Le Dernier Jour d'un condamné*, that plain language does not suffice to counter the concealing metaphors with which society at large, and the legal and judicial powers in particular, perpetrate capital punishment. For the two novelists, this veiled discourse must be overcome by images and vivid tropes that they mobilize in two main contexts: the revelation of the condemned man's experience and the satire of judicial jargon. In resorting to these strategies of linguistic *monstratio*, Hugo and Camus delegitimize state killing through poetics. Yet Camus also problematizes his own art, and thereby recalls the reflections at play in some of Baudelaire's poems, whereas Hugo's fiction implies a more uncritical faith in the power of the written work to relay "capital experience." Despite the obvious differences that set them apart, Baudelaire and Camus share a common vision of man's violent nature and of the potential degeneration of sociopolitical violence. The violence featured in Baudelaire's verse could be deemed Camusian on account of the novelist's pre-Girardian emphasis on the pandemic nature of murder. Conversely, key moments in Camus's fiction echo the anxiety and mistrust for mankind perceptible in Baudelaire's writings. *L'Étranger*, *La Peste*, and *Le Premier Homme* display symbols and strategies of outright resistance to executions that seem at odds with the imaginary deployed in *Les Fleurs du mal* and *Le Spleen de Paris*. Both the novelist and the poet show some awareness of their possible symbolic complicity with lethal justice and its imaginary, however. They suggest that art may ignore the lethal state altogether, but also respond to this suspicion by staging moments when the literary realm reintegrates this deadly reality, either through the prism of self-exploration or through that of solidarity enabled by a particular kind of language. Sporadically, their works also identify how the killing state may encroach upon creation. When this eventuality is envisaged by way of parables, Baudelaire's verse leaves open the possibility that sovereign power may ultimately be both murderous and vulnerable without art. Camus's fiction, conversely, acknowledges that a homicidal state might turn art into a self-parody, atomize it, and leave man helpless.

Conclusion

Я думал в ту минуту, что весть о казни убьет тебя.

I thought that the news of the execution would kill you.

—Fyodor Dostoevsky, letter to his brother Mikhail following the writer's mock execution (December 22, 1849)

How do some major modern literary works respond to society's most violent legal institution, the death penalty? In what ways do they both shape and find themselves shaped by its imaginary in the country of the guillotine? What intersections of poetics and ethics come to light in this process?

Capital Letters has attempted to reflect on these questions by examining a trio of renowned French authors and uncovering the dialogue in which they engaged while representing state killing. Although they portray it in distinct ways and hold entirely or subtly different political views about lethal justice and the grounds for its (il)legitimacy, their prose and poetry converge in several respects. On the one hand, Hugo, Baudelaire, and Camus represent the death penalty as a practice that exceeds human solidarity and, sometimes, understanding. On the other, they show that it defies conventional literary representations and plays a significant role in their reflections on what the modalities and place of literature should be in post-Revolutionary French society.

Le Dernier Jour d'un condamné radically breaks away from a classical, Aristotelian mode of representation and replaces it with a "regime of expression" (Rancière) that exposes the experience of capital punishment from within. Hugo stages a crisis of communication that overlaps with this shift in regime. He effectively turns on its head the traditional spectacle of execution and replaces the viewer's perspective with that of its main actor. The condemned man's cry, literal and figurative, gives

207

the fiction its rhythm and consistency, against narrative, aesthetic, and linguistic conventions. *Le Dernier Jour* also investigates the reality of penal modernity through this innovative expressive regime. While head severance by guillotine was conceived as a replacement for the excruciating *supplices*, and was thus considered a major penal improvement bequeathed by the Enlightenment, Hugo's manipulation of language brings to the fore both the mental ordeal inflicted upon the condemned man anticipating his execution and the brutality of decapitation as a method of killing. The novel therefore exposes the double perpetration of violence inherent in, if not magnified by, the systematic use of the guillotine. It goes so far as to suggest that this produces a new form of torture. Indeed, the condemned man finds himself slowly but sensibly tortured in the original sense of the word, that is to say "distorted" into what Agamben, following Benjamin and Aristotle, names *zoē*, or "bare life": a carnal self devoid of political status. Poetic craft exposes this excruciating metamorphosis that culminates in absolute silence.

Baudelaire's aesthetics of violence, evil, and sacrifice appears to oppose spectacularly the abolitionist commitment to which Hugo gives an original expression in his early narrative. The modern poet's prose, verse, and unfinished projects feature a political and artistic enthusiasm for lethal justice and its imagery. Nevertheless, this double enthusiasm cannot be taken at face value. Baudelaire's prose in favor of capital punishment, a practice he redefines as sacrifice, should be understood within a larger polemic against both progress and the overtly didactic, utilitarian literature he takes Hugo to incarnate—especially, but not exclusively, toward the end of his life. The "poète maudit" uses the death penalty as a means of literary, social, and moral distinction. His praise of sacrifice partly leans on the ideas of the reactionary Maistre, champion of the virtues of bloodletting. Yet it does not rigorously follow Maistre's thought. Instead, the poet complicates, if not subverts, the theocratic thinker's typology of sacrifice. His celebration of a sacrificial death penalty conflates or inverts a number of figures, including the innocent and the criminal, and the human and the animal, in contrast with Maistre.

Moreover, *De l'essence du rire* and *Les Fleurs du mal* show that Baudelaire essentially turns the dark imagery that capital punishment offers into an aesthetic reservoir. It serves both to compete with such plastic and dramatic arts as caricature and pantomime, whose intensity Baudelaire envies, and to puncture the moralism and pharisaism of his age. The poet also further contests the Maistrean logic of sacrifice in key compositions that stage lethal violence and present it as far less galvanizing than the mystic justification of capital punishment seemingly present in Baudelaire's provocative prose pieces. In a number of "slaughter poems," sacrifice fails to fulfill its role as a controlled and beneficial homicidal mechanics providing society with social and spiritual stability and grandeur. Instead, whoever perpetrates execution soon becomes subject to it. Baudelaire disrupts, in fact overturns the redeeming and regulatory function of sacrifice identified respectively by Maistre and contemporary critic René Girard. While his capital imaginary is aesthetically productive, a "sacrificial crisis" in which violence proliferates simultaneously plagues it.

Camus's prose fiction at once prolongs and responds to the complex relationships between lethal punishment, ethical questioning, and the craft of writing perceptible in Hugo's and Baudelaire's works. The reactions and convictions elicited by the death penalty are so powerful in *L'Étranger*, *La Peste*, and *Le Premier Homme* that this institution, which appears to constitute a mere recurring motif in these plots, reveals itself both as a critical narrative pivot and as the foundation of an abolitionist myth and involuntary ethics. All three novels turn the refusal of capital punishment into a sort of initiatory rite through which the protagonists appear to attain maturity, sometimes after developing an unexpected and visceral ethos of resistance through their body. Although this central role of the corporeal and the novels' underlying imperative of what Hugo termed "inviolabilité de la vie humaine" (*OCH* 4:482) echo aspects of *Le Dernier Jour*, Camus's fiction concurrently avoids staging universal abolitionism. It narrates man's possible fascination, silence, or support in the face of state killing, acknowledges the human inclination to kill, and questions the possibility of making a work of art explicitly and unambiguously promote political—and moral—principles. Much like Baudelaire, surprisingly, Camus rejects a utilitarian view of literature and his fiction acknowledges a malaise mixing attraction and repulsion vis-à-vis lethal violence, suggesting that man can be both tempted and mesmerized by killing and profoundly troubled by the execution of others.

Camus's nuanced positioning and the involuntary, body-centered abolitionist ethics deployed in his novels continue the complex forms of engagement with the death penalty found in *Le Dernier Jour*'s covert, poetics-based abolitionism and in Baudelaire's supposed but in fact inoperative praise of sacrificial executions that his poetry further disavows. All three writers favor strategies of indirection, in the form of original modes of representation that maximize the symbolic possibilities of language, image, and narration, to critique lethal justice and its imaginary.

All three also come together in posing the crucial question of their own use of words, and that of the law, as death penalty stories are told. The relationship between expression and lethal justice is central to Camus's works, which set out to reject both the silence and the metaphors surrounding the scaffold and to replace them with "plain language"—an objective reminiscent of Hugo's critique of judicial rhetoric in his preface of 1832. For Camus, discourse on legal killing must come as close as possible to reality and, to do so, must strip itself of its transformative devices, metaphorical and euphemizing. This project verges on a linguistic utopia, and his narratives contradict it. Nevertheless, both his and Hugo's novels manage to craft devices that lay bare the weaknesses, arbitrariness, and unacceptability of human justice. Their fiction satirizes those who determine whether or not a man should live, point to the duplicitous language of lethal law and its representatives, and dissect the human distress and fascination before the guillotine. But the two writers and Baudelaire also pick apart their own poetic gestures and liability. Key "mirror moments" symbolically expose this reflection. They reveal that Baudelaire and Camus converge in suggesting that some degree of participation in the practice of violence, even if it remains purely rhetorical, may well be the price to pay for the literary representation of the death penalty.

Although some key distinctions set apart the writings of Hugo, Baudelaire, and Camus, unexpected points of convergence also link them. Ultimately, their works undo two crucial preconceptions: one penal, and the other literary. First, despite their differing political stances on lethal justice, with Hugo and Camus opposing the death penalty and Baudelaire provocatively claiming to support it, the three authors invalidate, explicitly or implicitly, the premises that legitimated the guillotine from the French Revolution until the abolition of capital punishment in 1981. The novel poetics they develop are distinct: Hugo employs a fictional diaristic writing that maximizes internal focalization and alternates between the clinical and the hallucinatory; Baudelaire sets up a hyperbolic and falsely bloodthirsty aesthetic; Camus alternatively abides by and moves away from transparency and the strict reporting of legal lethal violence. The first writer could be said to have poetics, and not argument, serve ethics, the second to have poetic excess tease out ethical concerns, and the third to expose such concerns through

Conclusion | 211

the concomitant implementation *and* destabilization of a poetic regimen of strict restraint. Beyond their diversity, the poetic choices of all three writers result in a pointed criticism of the enlightened philosophy and pragmatic arguments that led to the reconception and the preservation of capital punishment in the modern period. They associate lethal justice with dehumanization, the proliferation of violence, and revulsion, thereby questioning the supposed painlessness and immediacy of beheading and the guillotine's ability to maintain order in society—whether objectively, by excising "dangerous" individuals from it, or subjectively, by using lethal retribution to provoke a sense of safety or satisfaction among its members.

Second, this invalidation of the alleged virtues of head severance by guillotine emerges from texts that complicate the apparent divide between politically committed writing and strictly aesthetic literature. As they mobilize and interrogate the resources of language, these works open up a space contesting this reductive opposition established by Hugo and Baudelaire themselves in their most vehement exchanges and public poses—an opposition continued into the twentieth century by Sartre's definition of "engagement" as limited to prose and calling for a certain political prescriptiveness. In *Le Dernier Jour d'un condamné*, Hugo keeps overt militancy at bay: the novel relies on an activist poetics instead of the explicit abolitionist political discourse and edifying sentimentalism he mobilizes elsewhere. Also original is Baudelaire's stance on lethal violence, which, below the surface of voluble glorification and detachment from the Other's pain, is at least in part one of concern. The poet points to the impossibility of an actual "désengagement" and rejoicing in suffering by presenting homicidal brutality as a process in which all partake, both as perpetrators and as victims. Camus further undoes the neat partition of "engagement" and disengagement. His fiction actualizes the concept of "engagement involontaire" (*OCC* 4:1066) or "embarquement," which it defines as direct and supportive participation in sociopolitical realities that require intervention but without subjecting this solidarity to programmatic dogmatism. In their literary treatment of the death penalty, all three writers consequently go beyond the most commonly established models used to envisage the modern relationship between poetics and politics—aestheticist art and "littérature engagée."

Instead, they cultivate literary transgression to represent state killing. Hugo's fiction challenges decorum and verisimilitude to present, in blunt language, the improbable considerations of a prematurely dead man almost until the moment of his killing. Baudelaire's prose and verse test the boundaries of the aesthetically bearable and the author's own assertion that the realm of beauty is sovereign, impervious to moral considerations, and fecundated by all "voluptés," however brutal they may be. And Camus's novels at once reject and are caught within the limitations of language when it comes to wording legal killing. All the works at hand also strive to preserve a certain artistic autonomy even as they do not detach art from worldly politics.

A literature in extremis, which both represents the limit experience of state-sanctioned death and probes the limits of aesthetics and politics, could be said to emerge from the "capital works" of the three writers. In it, poetic expression and self-reflexivity impose themselves as particular modes of ethical discourse. They critique the inadequacy of state killing without using discourse and argument. Instead, they craft forms that both capture and expose this violence. In other words, the language that Hugo, Baudelaire, and Camus invent to represent state killing unsettles the aesthetic standards and theoretical frameworks that successively define literature's role throughout French modernity while at the same time contesting the politico-moral agenda, and the rhetoric, used by post-Revolutionary society to render the guillotine acceptable. In thus inking the scaffold, the authors make palpable the poetic dimension of ethics and the ethical dimension of language.

While the issue of literature's interface with ethics is age-old, through the fundamental moral question of the death penalty, these authors shed light on it in a way that is arguably more profound and disquieting than that found in the works of many of their peers. The ultimate trademark of the "capital writings" examined here may be their poetics of discomfort. By this phrase, I mean that all three writers have poetic work generate profound unease in the reader. It forces us to take on board the experience, violence, failures, and troubling mechanisms—judicial and human—that underlie state killing. In Hugo's novel, this discomfort stems from a poetics that renders the crushing of the subject in real time, in a manner that forecloses any distancing from lethal state violence. Purification, or mere relief, is consequently unattainable for the reader-voyeur. In Baudelaire, poetic strategies constantly destabilize the positions of the subject and object of violence and portray this violence as uncontainable. Poet and Other are caught within an ever-failing sacrificial ritual. Such markers as laughter and irony testify to this uncomfortable positioning. With Camus, discomfort lies in the awareness of a possible complicity with lethal violence, which, in its institutional form, is shown to rely largely on a language that his own writing seeks to denounce despite the fact that it must rely on the same material—words—to do so and in the physical disgust that execution may elicit in some individuals.

Critics have reflected on emotions as a means of ethical formation and on literature's ability to generate such emotions, with a marked preference for compassion.[1] Away from this affect that posits a distance between the suffering individual and the sympathetic one, the works under consideration frequently entrap the reader in their representations of state killing. Through their language and anthropological symbolism, these writings block the possibility of perception from afar and of a secure posture, whether exterior, conservative, or humanistic. They place the reader in what Camus's novel *La Chute* (The Fall; 1956) calls *le malconfort*: a medieval dungeon whose reduced dimensions prevent one from adopting a comfortable position, either standing or lying down.

Notes

INTRODUCTION

1. Speech to the Assemblée Constituante of September 15, 1848. Because of limited space, French citations that do not originate from literary texts or are not subject to close reading are provided in English only throughout the book. Translations are my own unless otherwise stated.

2. The "Frenchness" of the guillotine should be relativized, nonetheless: a German harpsichord maker constructed the machine, and it had ancestors in the Italian *mannaia*, the Scottish maiden, and the Halifax gibbet.

3. While there are many ways the state can kill, the phrase "state killing," notably used by Austin Sarat in his numerous significant publications on the death penalty in the United States, is often employed to refer to capital punishment in particular. See, for instance, his *When the State Kills*.

4. Julia Kristeva notes that calls for the reinstatement of capital punishment are still heard "in times of popular depression" (*Visions capitales*, 101) despite the abolition, and she argues that one of the political functions of the numerous artistic representations of the death penalty might be to quench this thirst for a "restoration" of state killing.

5. The use of lethal injection in the United States today provides another example of the reliance of state killing on figuration. It consists of three phases. The second, informally called the "cosmetic" one, brings about muscular paralysis designed to render the condemned prisoners' suffering imperceptible to the audience around them. On capital punishment in the United States, see work by David Garland, Stephen John Hartnett, Austin Sarat, and David Von Drehle, among others.

6. Numerous philosophers and critics have argued that literary texts have the ability to hone our moral and political imagination and that some can be considered works of moral philosophy. See, for instance, Iris Murdoch's *The Fire and the Sun* and *Existentialists and Mystics* and Martha Nussbaum's *Love's Knowledge* (125–67 and 195–219, in particular). Peter Brooks has specifically underlined the way Hugo's capital fiction compensates for possible failures of the moral imagination ("Death in the First Person," 543–44). In the social sciences, psychology, and the neurosciences, an increasing body of scholarship has reinforced this claim over the past two decades. See, for example, Jèmeljan Hakemulder, *The Moral Laboratory* and Keith Oatley, "Fiction."

7. For studies on the representation of the death penalty in other national contexts, and specifically in British and American literature and culture, see Wendy Lesser, David Guest, Kristin Boudreau, Mark Canuel, Paul Christian Jones, and John Cyril Barton.

8. Their research has tended to concentrate on one author only (Hugo), on a single school and era (Romanticism or, to a lesser extent, Realism), or on a particular genre (the novel, and, more rarely, drama).

9. The major studies on the Romantic-era death penalty in France, evoked in the forthcoming chapters, include Paul Savey-Casard's *Le Crime et la peine dans l'œuvre de Victor Hugo*, Elizabeth Riley's "La Voix qui sort de l'ombre," Christine Marcandier-Colard's *Crimes de sang et scènes capitales*, Laura J. Poulosky's *Severed Heads and Martyred Souls*, Sonja Martin Hamilton's "La Plume et le couperet," and Loïc Guyon's *Les Martyrs de la veuve*.

10. Among them, Daniel Arasse's seminal essay *La Guillotine et l'imaginaire de la Terreur*, Daniel Gerould's *Guillotine*, and Patrick Wald Lasowski's *Les Échafauds du romanesque*, as well as his less academic *Guillotinez-moi!*

11. The most significant contributions of this kind are Paul Savey-Casard's *La Peine de mort*, Paul-Henri Stahl's *Histoire de la décapitation*, Linda Orr's *Headless History*, Régis Bertrand and Anne Carol's edited volume *L'Exécution capitale*, and Regina Janes's *Losing Our Heads*.

12. Exceptions were made in times of war, when the death penalty could be carried out by firing squads.

13. Beccaria, *On Crimes and Punishments*, 66.

14. Morellet freely rearranges Beccaria's argument in his translation.

15. Badinter, *L'Abolition de la peine de mort*, 69.

16. For an extensive investigation of the guillotine during the French Revolution, see Arasse, *La Guillotine et l'imaginaire de la Terreur*, 17–42.

17. See Article 13 of the *Code pénal* of 1810.

18. Farcy, "La Peine de mort: Pratique judiciaire et débats."

19. Arasse, *La Guillotine et l'imaginaire de la Terreur*, 95–98.

20. If one includes civil war deaths in addition to the judicial terror, the number of casualties amounts to between 250,000 and 400,000. On the Terror, see, for instance, Greer, *The Incidence of the Terror*; Jones, *The Longman Companion to the French Revolution*.

21. See Wald Lasowski, *Les Échafauds du romanesque*, 30; Farcy, "La Peine de mort en France: Deux siècles pour une abolition"; Aubusson de Cavarlay, Huré, and Pottier, "Les Statistiques criminelles de 1831 à 1981," 182–83.

22. This is true not only from philosophical and legal standpoints, but also from a scientific perspective. Phrenology, pioneered by Franz Joseph Gall (1758–1828), criminal anthropology, invented and promoted by Cesare Lombroso (1835–1909), as well as anthropometry and craniometry, which such French figures as Alphonse Bertillon and Georges Vacher de Lapouge respectively supported, claimed to contribute to the understanding of criminality.

23. In the 1850s, Hugo famously summarized his shifting political orientations as follows: "1818.—Royaliste. / 1824.—Royaliste libéral. / 1827.—Libéral. / 1828.—Libéral-socialiste. / 1830.—Libéral-socialiste-démocrate. / 1849.—Libéral-socialiste-démocrate-républicain" (OCH 9:1019–20).

24. See "Théophile Gautier" (OCB 2:113) and "Notes nouvelles sur Edgar Poe" (OCB 2:333), two essays in which Baudelaire condemns the "heresy" of "morality" in poetry by taking up Poe's criticism of didacticism in his *Poetic Principle*.

25. Barthes, *Le Degré zéro de l'écriture*, 108.

26. Baudelaire, *JIB*, 301.

27. "The theater of the guillotine culminates in an instant of invisibility" (Arasse, *La Guillotine et l'imaginaire de la Terreur*, 49).

28. Valéry, "Enseignement de la poétique," in *Variété V*, 291.

29. Ricœur, "Éthique et morale," 260.

PART I

1. See chapters 6, 21, and 22 of Adèle Hugo's *Victor Hugo raconté par un témoin de sa vie*.

2. See the 1832 preface to *Le Dernier Jour d'un condamné*. Chapter XXVIII of the novel also refers to the greasing of the guillotine.

3. Several edited volumes have provided an overview of Hugo's substantial textual production pertaining to capital punishment. Among them are Raymond Jean's *Écrits de Victor Hugo sur la peine de mort*, Jérôme Picon and Isabel Violante's *Victor Hugo contre la peine de mort*, and Paul F. Smets's shorter *Le Combat pour l'abolition de la peine de mort*. The landmark study analyzing this production in its entirety remains Paul Savey-Casard's *Le Crime et la peine dans l'œuvre de Victor Hugo*. See also the opening section of Stéphanie Boulard's *Rouge Hugo*, which focuses on the writer's obsession with and aesthetics of "Dame guillotine" (21–93). On the broader question of Hugo as "lawgiver," see part VII of Roger Pearson's *Unacknowledged Legislators*.

4. More than thirty years before the publication of the eponymous novel, Hugo uses the term "misérables" in the preface of *Le Dernier Jour d'un condamné*. According to Benoît Chabert, of the 1,775 people who were sentenced to death in France between 1833 and 1880, only 38 benefited from higher education, whereas 812 were illiterate, and 925 knew how to read and write but had not had access to an education ("Sur la peine de mort en France," 173).

5. Chevalier, *Classes laborieuses et classes dangereuses*, 314–15; Gohin, "Les Réalités du crime et de la justice pour Victor Hugo avant 1829," xviii.

6. For Monestier (*Peines de mort*, 216) and Lascoumes ("Révolution ou réforme juridique?," 65), there are thirty-nine crimes punishable by death in the

1810 *Code pénal*. For Chabert, there are thirty-six ("Sur la peine de mort en France," 169). Depending on how one considers what constitutes a distinct capital crime or what is simply a variant of another, the number may therefore vary. About the harshness of the 1810 *Code pénal* and its move away from the idea of human perfectibility promoted in 1791, see Lascoumes (68–69).

7. Among the capital cases defined by the 1810 *Code pénal*, one also finds a number of nonlethal crimes: illegal arrests executed by an individual wearing a fake officer's uniform; tampering with a witness of a capital crime; certain offenses committed against property, private or public, such as theft with five aggravating circumstances; certain cases of arson. See Chabert, "Sur la peine de mort en France," 169.

8. See, for instance, Guizot's *De la peine de mort en matière politique* (1822), Jean-Baptiste Salaville's *De la peine de mort et du système pénal dans ses rapports avec la morale et la politique* (1826), Lucas's *Du système pénal et du système répressif en général et de la peine de mort en particulier* (1827), and Ballanche's "Abolition de la peine de mort et de toute loi répressive" (1834). For a thorough study of the debate on capital punishment during the Second Restoration, see Martin Hamilton, "La Plume et le couperet," 12–95.

9. The law allowing for the consideration of extenuating circumstances, the elimination of nine capital cases, and of the most brutal bodily punishments was not adopted until April 1832.

10. Gohin, "Les Réalités du crime et de la justice," xviii. Du Camp asserts that a total of 554 death sentences were pronounced between 1826 and 1830, leading to 360 effective executions ("La Guillotine," 394). In *Peines de mort*, Monestier writes that 4,520 people were guillotined between 1811 and 1825, and 1029 between 1826 and 1850—a decrease for which the adoption of extenuating circumstances in 1832 partly accounts.

11. See Farcy, "La Peine de mort: Pratique judiciaire et débats."

12. See Biré, *Victor Hugo avant 1830*, 473–74; Nisard (?), review published in *Journal des Débats*, February 26, 1829; the 1963 edition *Le Dernier Jour d'un condamné* presented by Guillemin, 205; Vallois, "Écrire ou décrire," 92.

13. See Jules Lefèvre-Deumier's *Un poète romantique contre la peine de mort* in Guyon's online critical edition.

14. Vidocq, *Mémoires de Vidocq*; Anicet Bourgeois and Victor Ducange, *Sept heures*.

15. See, respectively, the ode "Contre la peine de mort" (Against the Death Penalty; 1830), *La Maréchale d'Ancre* (1831), and "Histoire d'Hélène Gillet" (1832).

16. See for example, Benjamin Antier, Alexis Decomberousse, and J.-S. Raffard-Brienne's melodrama *L'Abolition de la peine de mort*, Anne Bignan's novel *L'Échafaud*, or Charles Rabou's fantastic tale "Le Ministère public," all published in the collective volume *Contes bruns* in 1832.

17. A proposition supported by the famous abolitionist figure Victor Destutt de Tracy. See Bowman, "The Intertextuality of Victor Hugo's *Le Dernier Jour d'un condamné*," 37–38.

18. The 1832 preface can legitimately be said to constitute a separate work in and of itself. It is a direct address from the writer to the reader and came out

in a different historico-political context—after the events of July 1830 and after December 1830, when four ex-ministers of Charles X accused of high treason were sentenced not to death but to exile. Their accusal had led the Chambre des députés to support the abolition of capital punishment for political crimes only; this measure was actually adopted only in 1848. Hugo denounces an abolition intended for these "happy few" in his preface of 1832. Shortly thereafter, nine capital cases were also removed from the *Code pénal* (law of April 28, 1832); so were the mutilation of the parricide's hand and the use of branding and iron collars. In addition, extenuating circumstances were generalized. Along with other critics, including Flaubert (*Correspondance*, 204), Massin (in *OCH* 3:606, 4:473), Brombert ("Le Condamné de Hugo," 75), Roman ("*Le Dernier Jour d'un condamné*," 35), Rosa ("Commentaire du *Dernier Jour d'un condamné*," 268), and Martin Hamilton ("La Plume et le couperet," 174), I would argue that the preface of 1832 is a text in itself, to be considered either as separate from the condemned man's journal or as shedding a different light on it.

19. Part I mainly focuses on the narrative as it was available to readers when the book first came out in 1829. For an examination of the book's multiple para- or pre-texts, see Grossman's insightful *The Early Novels of Victor Hugo*, 111–58, and Halsall, "*Le Dernier Jour d'un condamné à mort* [sic]," 408–34.

CHAPTER I

1. For a survey of the various forms of late eighteenth- and early-nineteenth century abolitionist thought, see, for instance, Bowman, "The Intertextuality of Victor Hugo's *Le Dernier Jour d'un condamné*," 28–30.

2. Bowman also argues that Hugo is quite indifferent to another consideration that interests Beccaria and others, namely that man cannot alienate his right to life in a social contract ("The Intertextuality of Victor Hugo's *Le Dernier Jour d'un condamné*," 30). Chapter 2 nuances this claim.

3. Badinter, "Je vote l'abolition de la peine de mort," 56. It is noteworthy that a laudatory review by Duvergier from February 7, 1829, published in the *Gazette des Tribunaux* made the very same point. Several other readers have analyzed the book's imagistic—but also poetic—power that this chapter seeks to investigate further. They include Victor Brombert, Jean Rousset, Lucien Dällenbach, Guy Rosa, Delphine Gleizes, and Myriam Roman, in particular.

Like Badinter, Guizot and Broglie had underlined the necessity to rely on emotion as well as reason to critique capital punishment (Bowman, "The Intertextuality of Victor Hugo's *Le Dernier Jour d'un condamné*," 41–42).

4. Hugo's praise was published in a review for *Le Réveil* on February 19, 1823.

5. For an examination of the central role played by the literary representations of capital punishment in the "querelle des Classiques et des Modernes" and the innovativeness of the Romantic works that dealt with the death penalty, including but not limited to *Le Dernier Jour*, see Guyon, *Martyrs de la veuve*, 81–124. The analysis proposed in this chapter complements his. On French Romantic aesthetics in its relation to bloody and capital scenes, see Marcandier-Colard, *Crimes de sang et scènes capitales*, 277, 279. Politically speaking,

Hugo claims to have been "liberal-royalist" in 1824, "liberal" in 1827, and "socialist-liberal" in 1828 (*OCH* 9:1019–20).

6. Gohin, "Les Réalités du crime et de la justice," iv–v.

7. About the anticlassical character of *Han*, see, for instance, Nodier's review in *La Quotidienne*, March 12, 1823. About the influence of the *genre frénétique*, the *roman noir*, and British and German fiction on Hugo's *Han d'Islande*, see Massin, in *OCH* 2:58–59.

8. It is no coincidence that the first epigraph of chapter XLVIII is an excerpt from "Parisina," one of the poems in Lefèvre-Deumier's *Le Parricide*.

9. See Nisard (?), review of *Le Dernier Jour d'un condamné*, for instance.

10. See, for example, Corre, "À propos de la peine de mort et du livre du Professeur Lacassagne, *Peine de mort et criminalité*," 231, 238. See also Farcy, "La Peine de mort: Pratique judiciaire et débats."

11. Rousset ("*Le Dernier Jour d'un condamné* ou l'invention d'un genre littéraire," 40–41) also points to these passages that I call "moments of interpellation."

12. See Massin, in *OCH* 3:611–13. Hugo interestingly expanded on the biographical traits he shared with his character when revising his text.

13. Dostoevsky underlines this very point in his preface to *A Gentle Creature*, 216.

14. Rousset, "*Le Dernier Jour d'un condamné*," 42.

15. "*Le Dernier Jour d'un condamné*, roman; par M. Victor Hugo," *Le Globe*, February 4, 1829.

16. *Giornale, incominciato li 25 Novembre dell'anno 1821 da Luc'Antonio Viterbi, condannato alla pena di morte*, published in its entirety by Robert Benson in 1825 as *Sketches of Corsica; Or, A Journal Written during a Visit to That Island in 1823*, then taken up in the *London Magazine*, before a passage translated into French came out in the *Revue Britannique* in May 1826.

17. "Angleterre: Dernières sensations d'un homme condamné à mort," *Le Globe*, January 3, 1828.

18. Hugo visited Bicêtre with David d'Angers in October 1827, and again in October 1828. They also went to the jail of the Conciergerie in 1827. In addition, Hugo relied on reports from the *Gazette des Tribunaux* and on Vidocq's evocations of the convict's carceral life and argot (Charlier, "Comment fut écrit *Le Dernier Jour d'un condamné?*," 345). The review of *Le Dernier Jour* published in *Le Globe* on February 4, 1829, criticized this quest for the picturesque.

19. Dostoevsky, preface to "A Gentle Creature," 216. Rousset ("*Le Dernier Jour d'un condamné*," 35) and Brombert (*Victor Hugo and the Visionary Novel*, 29, 248) briefly mention this Dostoevskian connection as well.

20. On *Le Dernier Jour d'un condamné* as a *nouveau roman*, see also Lowe-Dupas ("Innommable guillotine," 343), following in France Vernier's footsteps, and Guyon (*Les Martyrs de la veuve*, 115–20). In one of the best studies of *Le Dernier Jour* ever published, Lucien Dällenbach has argued that the book could have been written by Butor or Robbe-Grillet in the 1950s ("Le Vide plein," 52).

21. See Bozon, *L'Expression du moi*, 18. For the criticism leveled against *Le Dernier Jour* by Hugo's contemporaries, see, for instance, the review by Nisard (?), who suggested that every breach of fiction and classical representa-

Notes to Chapter 1 | 221

tion discussed here be remedied by a more conventional rewriting of the novel. The review of *Le Dernier Jour* published in *Le Globe* on February 4, 1829 also deplores the reader's absence of knowledge regarding the protagonist's past and identity.

22. Hugo points to two potential eighteenth-century predecessors, Xavier de Maistre and Laurence Sterne, only to signal the originality of his work with more emphasis. Maistre's *A Journey around My Room* and Sterne's *A Sentimental Journey through France and Italy* differ from *Le Dernier Jour* in that they mainly resort to retrospection, include an addressee, and are often humorous and playful in substance and tone.

23. Rancière, *Mute Speech*, 50.

24. See the speaker's unambiguous judgment: "Les forçats, les patients sont du ressort de son éloquence. Il les confesse et les assiste, parce qu'il a sa place à faire" (Those doing hard labor, the patients come under the remit of his eloquence. He confesses and assists them because he must climb the ladder; 693).

25. See also II, 659.

26. Meschonnic ("Vers le roman-poème," vii–viii, xii), Brombert, and Rosa ("Commentaires du *Dernier Jour*," 250) have also pointed to the condemned man's *cris*, which I connect to an extensive poetic strategy here.

27. Rancière, *Mute Speech*, 50.

28. Rancière, *Mute Speech*, 42.

29. Charlier's study of the evolution of the manuscript of *Le Dernier Jour* indicates that Hugo avidly sought to heighten the imagistic quality of his work.

30. Meschonnic points out that "the attention that Hugo pays to the powers of language is the basis for his word plays" ("Vers le roman-poème," viii). Guyon notes that the image of the head saturates the novel, with thirty-eight utterances (*Martyrs de la veuve*, 101).

31. Meschonnic rightly called *Le Dernier Jour* a proto-"roman-poème." For a detailed examination of the alliterations, echoes, and sound plays that make up what Meschonnic calls the novel's chiseled and powerful "phrasé," see the section entitled "La Prosodie" in "Vers le roman-poème" (xi–xiii).

32. Yvette Parent has shown that a few of the terms that Hugo presents as *argotiques* are in fact *poissards* (another form of popular dialect) and that a small number of his words does not appear in argot dictionaries ("L'emploi de l'argot"). On the reinvention of argot in Hugo's fiction, see also Boulard, *Rouge Hugo*, 319–20.

33. The *condamné* himself is able to play with this disincarnate speech sporadically: he uses a "dead" language, Latin, to impress the prison concierge, who does not understand it but perceives its prestige. As a consequence, he allows the convict to go on weekly walks inside the jail (V, 663).

34. The idiomatic phrase "langue de bois" prolongs the analogy between vegetation and language that Hugo sketches through the metaphor of the grafted tongue—thereby harking back to a long-standing ambition to enrich the French language, as exemplified by du Bellay's *Défense et illustration de la langue française* (1549). Thus in *Le Dernier Jour*, one finds, on the one hand, the hideous but living graft of the argot and, on the other, the *bois mort* of "la langue générale" as it is used by officials.

35. For a survey of hallucinations and the guillotine in Hugo's works other than *Le Dernier Jour*, see Boulard, *Rouge Hugo*, 38–44.

36. For an overview of the crimes and executions of these figures, see Gohin's "Les Réalités du crime et de la justice" (iv–ix, xii–xiii).

37. Meschonnic, "Vers le roman-poème," ix.

38. Flaubert, letter to Louise Colet, December 9, 1852, *Correspondance*, 204.

CHAPTER 2

1. Foucault, *Discipline and Punish*, 16–17. Although Foucault's diagnosis concerns punishment at large, the first part of his book addresses the particular issue of the death penalty. I use it to summarize the progressive redefinition of penalty in the modern period and do not purport to discuss Foucault's larger demonstration regarding the development of insidious modes of disciplining and the modern rise of surveillance.

2. The preface of 1832 denounces the way in which, from this year onward, France carried out its executions surreptitiously, at dawn and far from the center of Paris, by the barrière Saint-Jacques (*OCH* 4:491). When *Le Dernier Jour* came out in 1829, the guillotine was still used on the place de Grève.

3. Foucault, *The History of Sexuality, Volume 1*, 138.

4. The opening of the 1832 preface remarkably goes as far as to suppress the one element that makes Hugo's character suspicious, his guilt, by calling attention to the book's focus on "les accusés" (the accused), and not "les condamnés" (the condemned; *OCH* 4:480).

5. Foucault, *Discipline and Punish*, 18. Regarding this *qualification* of the individual, Foucault argues that the misinterpretation of article 64 of the 1810 *Code pénal* stipulating that it is impossible to condemn lawbreakers who were declared insane illustrates, early on in the nineteenth century, the use of personal data to inflect a legal judgment. Law courts did not rule that there were no grounds for prosecution regarding these criminals but instead settled either for acquittal or the consideration of extenuating circumstances. About the growing interest in moral characterization, Lascoumes also notes that the 1810 *Code pénal* is highly "individualizing" ("Révolution ou réforme juridique?" 68).

6. See Renneville, *Le Langage des crânes*, 70.

7. Brombert has also identified the recurring parallels that conjoin these two poles of the social ladder, one subaltern and the other sovereign ("Le Condamné de Hugo," 76–77, 79–80).

8. Agamben, *Homo Sacer*, 73.

9. Agamben, *Homo Sacer*, 18, 183.

10. Nevertheless, like the condemned man, the *homo sacer* is to be killed within a framework strictly prescribed by the law. Given the ban on his sacrifice, he does not escape legal prescription. Regarding the fact that the condemned man is to be killed in a prescribed context, see *Le Dernier Jour d'un condamné*, XXV, 690.

11. See Rousseau, "The Right of Life and Death" in *The Social Contract*. Although, like Montesquieu and Beccaria, Rousseau notes that "frequent punishments are always a sign of weakness or remission on the part of the gov-

ernment," and that "the State has no right to put to death, even for the sake of making an example, any one whom it can leave alive without danger," these remarks are preceded by considerations on what the philosopher views as the end of the social contract, namely "the preservation of the contracting parties," an end that allows the state to terminate life (*The Social Contract*, 208–9).

12. Beccaria, *On Crimes and Punishments*, 66.

13. Quoted in Badinter, *L'Abolition de la peine de mort*, 46–47.

14. Martin Hamilton also identifies these moments as revealing of the protagonist's untimely death ("La Plume et le couperet," 181).

15. Foucault, *Discipline and Punish*, 11.

16. Benjamin mentions "das bloße Leben" in "Destiny and Character" and in "The Critique of Violence." Agamben's essay engages in a direct dialogue with Foucault, and more particularly with the thesis according to which a key characteristic of modern politics is "the inclusion of *zoē* in the *polis*" (*Homo Sacer*, 9). Agamben revises it by suggesting that, in fact, "together with the process by which the exception everywhere becomes the rule, the realm of bare life—which is originally situated at the margins of the political order—gradually begins to coincide with the political realm, and exclusion and inclusion, outside and inside, *bios* and *zoē*, right and fact, enter a zone of irreducible indistinction" (9).

17. Dällenbach has also noted that the book acts on our nerves through a "rush of affects" that nevertheless blocks a standard identificatory reading ("Le Vide plein," 52).

18. Review of *Le Dernier Jour d'un condamné* in *Journal des Débats*, February 26, 1829.

19. Review of *Le Dernier Jour d'un condamné* in *La Quotidienne*, February 3, 1829.

20. The phrase is Arasse's in *La Guillotine et l'imaginaire de la Terreur*, 49.

21. Hugo's concern with the moral torture inherent in modern capital punishment finds a striking echo in more recent testimonies. See Fernand Meyssonnier, assistant executioner in Algeria in the 1940s and 1950s, in Bessette, "L'Exécution," 26.

22. The preface of 1832 calls for a time when "the gentle law of Christ will enter the [Penal] Code at last and shine through it." Derrida calls this paratext "logico-teleological." Regarding materialism and empiricism in *Le Dernier Jour*, Martin Hamilton notes that the depiction of moral suffering in the novel depends on that of pathologies ("La Plume et le couperet," 186).

23. Hugo also suggests that, while capital punishment exalts horror, it impedes all repentance and, consequently, any salvation, for only death obsesses the condemned man (XXXIV, 698).

24. This is not to say that the French Church supported capital punishment unilaterally. In 1825, Charles X associated it with an expansion of capital cases by passing the "law on sacrilege," but such Christian associations as the Société de la morale chrétienne actively promoted the abolition. In 1836 and 1837, Lamartine delivered speeches against the death penalty before this society, which also organized essay competitions on the issue in 1826 and 1836.

25. Although modern law based the legitimacy of mechanized decapitation on painlessness, a number of scientists, including Samuel Thomas von Söm-

mering, Jean-Joseph Sue, the Swiss physiologist Albrecht von Haller, Weicard, Oelsner, and Leveling, questioned this thesis. Reservations were also expressed in an anonymous *Notice historique et physiologique sur les supplices de la guillotine* from 1830 and in literary works and newspaper articles discussing the fact that certain limbs or the head seem to show signs of life after their severance (the most famous example being Charlotte Corday). See also Carol, "La Question de la douleur," 73–75; Millingen, "Decapitation"; Jordanova, "Medical Mediations."

26. Louis, "Avis motivé sur le mode de la décollation," 39:686; my emphasis.

27. Monestier, *Peines de mort*, 212, 211. The parliamentary archives simply summarize Guillotin's intervention as follows: "M. Guillotin reads out a report on the Penal Code. He establishes that in principle the law must be the same, when it punishes as when it protects" (Guillotin, "M. Guillotin lit un travail sur le Code pénal," 10:346).

28. A long passage from Louis's "Avis motivé sur le mode de décollation" (March 1792) was reproduced in Bourg Saint-Edme's *Dictionnaire de la pénalité* (4:161–63) in 1828, the year Hugo wrote *Le Dernier Jour*.

29. Several critics have commented on these devices. See Lowe-Dupas, "Innommable guillotine," 343–45; Guyon, *Les Martyrs de la veuve*, 92–95, 120; Martin Hamilton, "La Plume et le couperet," 187–88.

30. Guyon also underlines this use of synecdoche in *Les Martyrs de la veuve*, 100.

31. Without pointing to this particular passage, Boulard also contends that linguistics is one of the means by which Hugo attacks the guillotine (*Rouge Hugo*, 14).

32. In his preface of 1832, Hugo himself comments on the way his novel plainly puts on display the question of capital punishment (*OCH* 4:480).

33. Foucault, "The Order of Discourse," 52.

34. Foucault, "The Order of Discourse," 66.

35. Badinter, *L'Abolition de la peine de mort*, 63.

36. On February 19, 1829, a negative review of Hugo's book published in *La Gazette de France* vehemently condemned the novel's denunciation of the moral torture that formed part of capital punishment by decapitation.

37. Scarry, *The Body in Pain*, 30, 31, 38.

38. Scarry, *The Body in Pain*, 28.

39. Scarry, *The Body in Pain*, 29.

40. "The same bare life that in the *ancien régime* was politically neutral and belonged to God as creaturely life and in the classical world was (at least apparently) clearly distinguished as *zoē* from political life (*bios*) now fully enters into the structure of the state and even becomes the earthly foundation of the state's legitimacy and sovereignty" (Agamben, *Homo Sacer*, 127).

41. Agamben, *Homo Sacer*, 128.

42. Agamben, *Homo Sacer*, 183–84; my emphasis.

43. Foucault, *Discipline and Punish*, 14.

44. Foucault, *Discipline and Punish*, 9.

45. Foucault, *Discipline and Punish*, 9.

46. Foucault, *Discipline and Punish*, 12.

47. Some critics have tended to overlook the importance of *Le Dernier Jour d'un condamné* independently of its 1832 preface. See Halsall, *Victor Hugo et l'art de convaincre*, 408. In the first volume of his seminar on the death penalty, Derrida mentions *Le Dernier Jour* in passing, insisting on the preface (*Séminaire: La Peine de mort*, 154–55). Yet the components of Hugo's abolitionism he identifies and praises in this later paratext are already present in the main body of the novel. Despite his overarching thesis on the indissociability of literature (of the work done by poetics, then) and the "contestation" of capital punishment (59), Derrida focuses on explicit argumentation and philosophy. Even when it comes to the preface only, he concedes that Hugo's writing and "poetics" should be analyzed in and of themselves (291).

48. Review published in *La Gazette de France* on February 19, 1829, and Hugo, *Écrits sur la peine de mort*, 189.

49. See, in particular, the first "vision" of the scaffold that occurs in *Les Misérables* (*OCH* 2:64), or the beginning of "Cependant le soleil se lève" in *Quatrevingt-Treize* (*OCH* 15:505).

50. Hugo also defends this idea in the previously cited article he published on *Le Parricide* in *Le Réveil* on February 19, 1823, and in the preface to the *Nouvelles odes* from March 1824 (*OCH* 2:472).

PART II

1. Three critics in particular have examined Baudelairean violence thoroughly, sometimes pointing to aspects of the poet's "capital imaginaire." Jérôme Thélot has shown that Baudelairean poetry is aware of the fact that it is rooted in violence (*Baudelaire*, 495). He has demonstrated that it both perpetrates and illuminates this violence and that it opens up the possibility of sympathy. Debarati Sanyal has called into question the representation and consecration of Baudelaire as a "traumatophile," and instead proposes considering his "myriad structures of 'victime' and of 'bourreau'" and complex use of "[textual] violence, counterviolence, and irony" (*The Violence of Modernity*, 30, 12). Pierre Pachet has investigated the issue of capital punishment more carefully than any other critic through the notion of distinction. He has connected Baudelaire's thought on the death penalty, suicide, and solitude to what underlies sacrifice, namely "the impossibility of a contractual interhuman relation" (*Le Premier venu: Baudelaire*, 161).

2. This introduction provides a brief overview of the capital imaginary in Baudelaire's life and works. For a more detailed reconstitution and chronology, see Morisi, "Baudelaire's Death Penalty."

3. Barral, "L'Hôtel des colonnes à Mont-Saint-Jean," 17.

4. Quoted in Crépet and Crépet, *Charles Baudelaire*, 110, 130.

5. See, for instance, Barral, *Cinq journées avec Ch. Baudelaire*, 25; *OCB* 1:184, 668, 685; *CB* 1:303; *CB* 2:142; and Morisi, "Baudelaire's Death Penalty," 143–47.

6. In the section of the 1954 Pléiade edition dedicated to *Mon cœur mis à nu*, Y.-G. Le Dantec seems to have mistakenly grouped together in a single paragraph the passage beginning with "Un condamné à mort," the section of folio

12 stating "La peine de mort est le résultat d'une idée mystique," another on torture and cruelty (*OCB* 1:683; folio 12), and "L'envers de Claude Gueux" (*OCB* 1:598; folio 24). "L'envers de Claude Gueux" and "Un condamné à mort" do not belong to *Mon cœur mis à nu*. Several editions have also added the title "Dandies" to folios 24 and 25, but it seems that this word never appeared in the original folios.

7. Sanyal has shown how this prose poem blurs, if not collapses, the contrast between executioner and victim—just as it undermines the demarcation between despotism and resistance, the political and the aesthetic, agency and passivity, complicity and innocence. It therefore echoes a number of poems from *Les Fleurs du mal* discussed in what follows (*The Violence of Modernity*, 65).

CHAPTER 3

1. About the law of 1832, see Monestier, *Peines de mort*, 223.

2. In 1870, the *décret Crémieux* was to stipulate that only one executioner would work in the *métropole* and that the guillotine would no longer be placed on a scaffold. Another evolution testifying to the desacralization and the de-spectacularization of executions is the resort to faster, portable guillotines, called "accélératrices" (Monestier, *Peines de mort*, 224).

3. See especially Léon Cellier's extensive study *Baudelaire et Hugo*. More recently, André Guyaux's "Baudelaire et Victor Hugo" and Giovanni Dotoli's *Baudelaire-Hugo* have traced the story of this relationship.

4. Cellier, *Baudelaire et Hugo*, 169.

5. Valéry, *Variété II*, 233, and letter from Valéry to Paul Souday, 1923, *Œuvres* 1:1715.

6. Crépet and Crépet, *Charles Baudelaire*, 85–86. See also *OCB* 2:1563–64.

7. Pachet, *Le Premier Venu: Essai sur la politique baudelairienne*, 86.

8. See, for instance, George Sand's novels and Eugène Sue's *romans-feuilletons*, which periodicals such as *Le Globe* and *La Réforme* tended to promote. The following section examines Hugo's particular case.

9. Poe, *Essays and Reviews*, 13.

10. Thélot dates a passage from the poet's prose projects in folio 24 (on voluptuousness and conversion) to 1859 ("La Conversion baudelairienne," 120). Baudelaire's remarks on *Claude Gueux* and on the condemned man going back to the executioner after he has been freed by the people are therefore likely to date from 1859 too.

11. On Baudelaire's reactionary suspicion toward equality, universal suffrage, and the belief in progress, see, for instance, Compagnon, *Les Antimodernes*, 31–33, 57–58.

12. See also folio 14 of *Mon cœur mis à nu*, *OCB* 1:684–85.

13. Derrida, *Séminaire: La peine de mort*, 170.

14. Balzac, *Le Curé de village*, 591.

15. Pachet, *Le Premier Venu: Baudelaire*, 84.

16. Sanson, *Memoirs of the Sansons*, 285–86.

17. Poe, *The Brevities*, 322–23. Claude Pichois notes that the terms that define the project of which Poe dreamed and that Baudelaire executed are taken

up in Maître Chaix d'Est-Ange's defense speech during Baudelaire's trial (*OCB* 1:1491). The argument made in this speech recalls the preemptive epigraph to the first edition of *Les Fleurs du mal* excerpted from d'Aubigné's *Tragiques*. The defensive aim of both texts differs markedly from the offensiveness of *Mon cœur mis à nu*, however.

18. Baudelaire, *Selected Letters of Charles Baudelaire*, 166; translation modified.

19. *CB* 2:305. On January 13, 1863, Hetzel committed to publishing *Mon cœur mis à nu* (*OCB* 1:1468), a project that did not come to fruition: the text first appeared in Eugène Crépet's edition of Baudelaire's *Œuvres posthumes* in 1887.

20. Baudelaire, *The Letters of Charles Baudelaire to His Mother*, 216.

21. I agree with Guyaux ("Baudelaire et Victor Hugo," 144, 147) that Cellier's optimistic view regarding the way Baudelaire considered Hugo—with increased benevolence, supposedly—should be qualified in light of the later Baudelaire's hostile comments about his peer.

22. As opposed to *Le Dernier Jour d'un condamné*, *Claude Gueux* does not concern itself exclusively with the death penalty. Rather, it emphasizes the need to reform unsuitable laws and judiciary institutions that criminalize misery. For a comparison of the two works, see, for example, Lewis, "The Making of a Condamné."

23. See Baudelaire's letter to his mother, December 5, 1837 (*CB* 1:48).

24. "Notes nouvelles sur Edgar Poe" (*OCB* 2:333) and "Théophile Gautier" (*OCB* 2:113); my emphasis. The passage from "Théophile Gautier" (1859) in which Baudelaire recycles his remarks from "Notes nouvelles sur Edgar Poe" (1857) replaces "défaillance" with "déchéance," thereby moving toward a more damning view of morality in art.

25. So derisive that Baudelaire dampens his considerations later on.

26. The same point is made in Baudelaire's letter to Armand Fraisse, February 18, 1860 (*CB* 1:675).

27. See also "Notes nouvelles sur Edgar Poe" (1857), *OCB* 2:337.

28. Baudelaire, *Selected Letters of Charles Baudelaire*, 134.

29. Pichois, *Lettres à Baudelaire*, 187–88.

30. Hugo, letter to Baudelaire, October 18, 1859 (Pichois, *Lettres à Baudelaire*, 189). See also Hugo's letters to Antonio-Maria Padilla, minister of the Republic of Colombia, October 12, 1863 (*OCH* 12:1229), and to the members of the Central Italian Committee for the Abolition of the Death Penalty, February 4, 1865 (*OCH* 12:897).

31. Hugo, *Écrits sur la peine de mort*, 189.

32. On the right to life and Hugo's emphasis on the inviolability of human life, see Derrida, *Séminaire: La peine de mort*, 150, 152, 153, 164, 170; on the right to death, see 164 and in particular 171.

33. Hovasse, "Les Signes de Hugo," 374.

34. In his *Confessions*, Rousseau does not attribute the anecdote of a "great princess" exclaiming about starving peasants "qu'ils mangent de la brioche" to Marie-Antoinette, but the phrase is commonly—albeit mistakenly—associated with her.

35. See the fine reading proposed by Oehler, *Le Spleen contre l'oubli*, 323, 329, 331, 332–33.

36. For an insightful analysis of Baudelaire's disagreement with Hugo on this question and that of original sin in the review of *Les Misérables*, see the fifth chapter of Rosemary Lloyd's *Baudelaire's Literary Criticism*, and in particular 185–87.

37. Letter of April 14, 1864.

38. The fact that Renan's *Histoire des origines du christianisme* supported the then-controversial idea that Jesus was to be considered as a physical human being highlights this contrast between the spiritual (Christ) and the scientific (Renan).

39. An impossible task, if one is to believe the conclusion of Baudelaire's review of *Les Misérables* (*OCB* 2:224).

40. "On dit qu'il faut couler les exécrables choses / Dans le puits de l'oubli et au sépulchre encloses, / Et que par les escrits le mal ressuscité / Infectera les mœurs de la postérité; / Mais le vice n'a point pour mère la science, / Et la vertu n'est pas fille de l'ignorance" (It is said that atrocious things must be drowned / In the well of oblivion and in the sepulcher be enclosed, / And that through texts evil resuscitated / Shall infect the mores of posterity; / But vice is not born of science, / And virtue is not the daughter of ignorance; *OCB* 1:807).

41. A similar, vehement rejection of optimistic and consoling literature appears in Baudelaire's draft response to Jules Janin, the despised author of *Les Petits Bonheurs* and *La Religieuse de Toulouse* (1850)—a book "À TUER" (TO BE KILLED), in the poet's words (*OCB* 2:50). Not the Janin of *L'Âne mort et la femme guillotine*, which sought to parody Hugo's *Le Dernier Jour*, then, but the Janin who did not appreciate Heine and whom Baudelaire took to be critical of sinister and ironic poetry (*OCB* 2:233–34).

42. On October 20, 1848, an article by Baudelaire portrayed the people of Paris as viewing the abolition of the death penalty for political crimes as a way of compensating for the government's inability to curb joblessness (*OCB* 2:1061). For a thorough examination of Baudelaire's political critique of his era, and particularly of June 1848 and its aftermath, see the fifth and sixth chapters of Oehler's *Le Spleen contre l'oubli*.

43. Fondane, *Baudelaire et l'expérience du gouffre*, 159.

44. The poem was later inserted in *Les Quatre Vents de l'esprit*.

45. Thélot, *Baudelaire*, 50.

46. Blin, *Le Sadisme de Baudelaire*, 20–21. Of Sade's works (*OCB* 1:595; 2:39, 68), Baudelaire knew at least *Justine, ou les malheurs de la vertu* (letter to Poulet-Malassis, October 1, 1865; *CB* 2:532).

47. Sade evokes capital punishment in *La Philosophie dans le boudoir* through the voice of one of his *libertins*, who posits an opposition between murder committed by individuals and the abstract perpetration of murder through the law (505). On August 2, 1793, as the president of the section des Picques, he refused to organize the vote of measures serving the Terror (letter to Gaufridy, August 3, 1793; Bourdin, *Correspondance inédite du marquis de Sade*, 342). Two years later, he told the same interlocutor that the spectacle of the guillotine

hurt him more than his stay in the Bastille (letter, January 21, 1795; Bourdin, 365).

48. Baudelaire remembers this title as *Lettres et mélanges*.

49. See the first, ninth, and seventh "entretiens" of the *Soirées*, respectively (*Œuvres*, 470–71, 651, 714, 661).

50. Baudelaire, *Selected Poems*, 142.

51. Baudelaire, *Selected Poems*, 142.

52. Maistre, *St Petersburg Dialogues*, 217–18.

53. Maistre, *Œuvres*, 812; Maistre, *St Petersburg Dialogues*, 358; translation modified.

54. This theory is contrasted with that of René Girard in what follows.

55. See Maistre's "Discours à Mme La Marquise de Costa sur la vie et la mort de son fils Alexis-Louis-Eugène de Costa": "Rather, let us suffer, suffer with thoughtful resignation. If we can unite our reason to eternal reason, instead of being only *patients*, we will at least be *victims*" (*Discourse for Madam La Marquise de Costa on the Life and Death of Her Son*, 274).

56. I return to this concept of reversibility in chapter 4.

57. Daniel Vouga has tended to defend this thesis in *Baudelaire et Joseph de Maistre*. So has Compagnon in *Les Antimodernes*, 118, 119, 146.

58. Maistre, *Œuvres*, "Des sacrifices humains," *Éclaircissement*, 817.

59. Maistre, *Œuvres*, "Des sacrifices en général," *Éclaircissement*, 812–13.

60. Maistre, *Œuvres*, *Éclaircissement*, 833.

61. See the third chapter of *Éclaircissement sur les sacrifices*, entitled "Théorie chrétienne des sacrifices," *Œuvres*, 833.

62. Maistre, *Œuvres*, 706; Maistre, *St Petersburg Dialogues*, 264; translation modified.

63. Blin, *Le Sadisme de Baudelaire*, 188.

64. Maistre himself reflects on this semantic duality in *Éclaircissement* (*Œuvres*, 816).

CHAPTER 4

1. Louis Goudall, "Revue littéraire," *Le Figaro*, November 4, 1855; Guyaux, *Baudelaire*, 147.

2. Baudelaire, "Projet de préface" for the second edition of *Les Fleurs du mal*.

3. "Boucherie," in Larousse, *Grand Dictionnaire universel du XIXe siècle*, 1053.

4. Baudelaire, *Selected Poems*, 29–30.

5. Baudelaire, *The Flowers of Evil*, 143; translation modified in l. 1, 5–8.

6. "Boucherie," in Larousse, *Grand Dictionnaire universel du XIXe siècle*, 1053.

7. Baudelaire, *The Flowers of Evil*, 155, 157.

8. Baudelaire, *Selected Poems*, 68.

9. For Pichois, "À une Madone" and "L'Héautontimorouménos" belong to the same class of poems, namely the "vengeance-poem" (*OCB* 1:985). This categorization seems relevant in view of the deliberate harming of others that they

feature. However, we will see that, upon closer examination, the existence of two distinct agents required by vengeance fades away in these poems.

10. Baudelaire himself notes that violence is the "distinctive sign" of the absolute comic (*OCB* 2:538). On Baudelaire's interest in color in general, and red in particular, see also the well-known section "De la couleur" in *Salon de 1846* (*OCB* 2:423, 426) and "La Fanfarlo" (*OCB* 1:577).

11. On Delacroix, see *Salon de 1846* (*OCB* 2:431–32), "L'Œuvre et la vie de Delacroix" (*OCB* 2:760), and the well-known stanza of "Les Phares" dedicated to the painter's use of color to represent human torment. Interestingly, Baudelaire describes him as capable of "tearing out the guts" of his subject (*OCB* 2:432). The painter is also a butcher of sorts, then. Goya's brutal imagination features in "Les Phares" as well.

12. Baudelaire, *The Flowers of Evil*, 157.

13. Baudelaire, *The Flowers of Evil*, 229, 231.

14. Drawing an opposition between politics and spiritual, moral, and perhaps anthropological beliefs, Baudelaire adds that he does "have a few convictions, in a more elevated sense" (*OCB* 1:680). The references to the 1848 Revolution in *Mon cœur mis à nu* and Baudelaire's agitation at the time qualify the claim that he had no political convictions, but he famously declared himself "physically depoliticized" (*CB* 1:188) in 1852. A posteriori, he also provocatively attributed his actions in 1848 to a mere "taste for destruction" and "literary intoxication" (*OCB* 1:679). For a summary of the poet's iconoclastic political trajectory, see Clark, *Image of the People*, 68.

15. Edward Kaplan makes a similar point, highlighting the "screen of ethical ambiguity" in Baudelaire's most sinister and provocative writings ("Baudelairean Ethics," 89).

16. The proximity of the terms *boucher* and *bourreau* is striking: beyond their phonemic and graphemic similarities, *bourreau* has the same second meaning as *boucher*, according to Larousse. By extension, it refers to a "murderer," a "cruel individual" (Larousse, *Grand Dictionnaire universel du XIXe siècle*, 1137).

17. Baudelaire, *The Flowers of Evil*, 157.

18. Wilcocks, "Towards a Re-examination of *L'Héautontimorouménos*," 567, 569.

19. Sanyal, *The Violence of Modernity*, 31–33.

20. Sanyal, *The Violence of Modernity*, 34. In "Les Foules," Baudelaire famously wrote, "Le poète jouit de cet incomparable privilège, qu'il peut être à sa guise lui-même et autrui" (The poet enjoys the incomparable privilege of being able to be both himself and another, as he pleases; *OCB* 1:291). In the context of lethal violence, the privilege appears to turn into a curse.

21. Sanyal, *The Violence of Modernity*, 36.

22. Baudelaire, *The Flowers of Evil*, 157; translation modified. On the passivity of the allegorized and depersonalized self in the last stanzas of the poem, see Starobinski, *La Mélancolie au miroir*, 35.

23. Baudelaire and Malassis discuss the possible spellings of the French retranscription of "heautontimoroumenos" in the poem's proofs from 1857 (*OCB* 1:987). Maistre also uses the term in *Les Soirées de Saint-Pétersbourg* (*Œuvres*, 539), acknowledging Terence as a source.

24. Terence, *L'Héautontimorouménos*, 27; l. 147–48.

25. "The righteous one, in suffering voluntarily, makes amends not only for himself, but for the guilty one by way of reversibility," according to the "Huitième entretien" of *Les Soirées de Saint-Pétersbourg* (Maistre, *Œuvres*, 693). The concept of reversibility is central to Maistre's reflection, since it enables him to answer a crucial question regarding divine justice: Why do innocent people suffer?

26. On nonredemption, or a-redemption, in *Les Fleurs du mal*, see "L'Irrémédiable" and Acquisto's study of Baudelaire's "poetics of the unredeemable" in *The Fall Out of Redemption*, in particular chapters 1 and 2, 19–98.

27. Baudelaire, *Selected Poems*, 117; translation modified in l. 5.

28. Baudelaire, *Selected Poems*, 145.

29. The mating is literal, since the imagery of sexual consummation runs through the text.

30. This poem about the imbrication of killer and victim and about a murder that is also suicidal is not an isolated instance. See also "Le Vampire," a pendant to "À une Madone" in which the murderer is the woman.

31. Baudelaire, *Selected Poems*, 66; translation modified in l. 1.

32. Baudelaire, *The Flowers of Evil*, 231; translation modified in l. 7.

33. Baudelaire, *The Flowers of Evil*, 233; translation modified in l. 5.

34. Baudelaire, *The Flowers of Evil*, 233.

35. Similarly, Pachet highlights the indistinction that characterizes focalization and subjectivity in *Spleen de Paris* ("Baudelaire et le sacrifice," 446).

36. This flexible status of the victim and the perpetrator of violence is famously evoked in *Mon cœur mis à nu*: "alternativement victime et bourreau" (alternately victim and executioner; *OCB* 1:676).

37. Corroborating this reading, Pachet has also contended that plainly opposing Hugo's humanism to Baudelaire's sadism would be erroneous, whether it comes to crime, its repression, or death sentences, with whose depiction Hugo remains fascinated (*Le Premier venu: Baudelaire*, 105–6).

38. Toal, *The Entrapments of Form*, 19–26, 32–36 in particular.

39. Girard, *La Violence et le sacré*, 49.

40. Girard, *La Violence et le sacré*, 50, 63–104. Girard defines the sacrificial crisis as follows: "The *sacrificial crisis*, that is to say the disappearance of sacrifice, is the disappearance of the difference between impure violence and purifying violence. When this difference is lost, purification is no longer possible, and impure, contagious violence, that is to say reciprocal violence, spreads throughout the community" (77). In his seminal article entitled "Baudelaire et le sacrifice," Pachet has also argued that Baudelaire "surpasses" Maistre (443), but without focusing on Baudelairean poetry.

41. Girard, *La Violence et le sacré*, 18.

42. Girard, *La Violence et le sacré*, 64.

43. Girard, *La Violence et le sacré*, 77–78, inter alia.

44. Bernard Degout has argued that Hugo's position regarding the executioner in *Han d'Islande* opposes Maistre's not only because of the novelist's abolitionism *de principe* and belief in Christian charity but also because of the executioner's failure to contain or to halt violence ("De Joseph de Maistre à Victor Hugo," 649).

232 | Notes to Part III and Chapter 5

45. Oehler rightly applies Levinas's polysemous aphorism "Autrui me regarde" (The Other looks at/concerns me) to Baudelaire ("Baudelaire's Politics," 25). Thélot also underscores the role played by, and the conflict that originates in, the Other's weakness in Baudelaire's oeuvre and art ("La Conversion baudelairienne," 129).
46. Sanyal, *The Violence of Modernity*, 107.
47. For a reading of this poem, in which Thélot locates a "violence fondatrice" that also draws on Girard, see *Baudelaire*, 399–411.
48. Baudelaire, *Selected Poems*, 66.
49. Baudelaire, *The Flowers of Evil*, 155, 157.

PART III

1. All of Camus's writings on the subject, including previously unpublished documents that shed light on his defense of condemned men during the Algerian War of Independence, are collected in Morisi, *Albert Camus contre la peine de mort*. For a synthetic reconstitution of Camus's abolitionism based on these various writings, see Morisi, *Albert Camus: Le souci des autres*, 65–90, and Morisi, "To Kill a Human Being." For a survey of the multiform presence of death sentences in his works and thought, see also Baciu, *Albert Camus et la condamnation à mort*. His reflections on the killing state are examined in Salas, *Albert Camus: La juste révolte*. In "Le Partage de la souffrance" and "Camus et le droit de mort de l'État," Philippe Vanney offers a very insightful analysis of Camus's critique of the right of the state to kill in "Réflexions sur la guillotine."
2. Camus, "Le Siècle de la peur" and "Sauver les corps" (1946), in CC 612–16. See also the beginning of *L'Homme révolté*, in OCC 3:66.
3. The Germans executed Camus's friend René Leynaud, a fellow member of the "Combat" group, on June 13, 1944.
4. See also the editorials published in *Combat* from August 22 to November 2, 1944.
5. I trace these progressive roots of European penal philosophy in "European Visions in Albert Camus's Abolitionism."
6. First reply to Vigerie's critique of "Ni Victimes ni bourreaux" titled "Arrachez la victime aux bourreaux," in *Œuvres complètes*.

CHAPTER 5

1. Camus's notes from 1953 suggest that, had he been able to complete this work, it may have been three times as long as it is today (OCC 4:1176).
2. Camus's biography and his notes for *Le Premier Homme* confirm the novel's autobiographical basis (OCC 4:926, 940).
3. Camus noted that the "meaning" of his novel emerges "precisely" from "the parallelism of [its] two parts" (OCC 2:951).
4. Camus wrote in 1954, in the draft of a reply to Rolf Hädrich, who wished to adapt *L'Étranger* for the stage: "The frontal attack here doesn't target moral-

ity but *the world of the trial* that is bourgeois as much as Nazi and Communist, and which, in a word, is today's cancer" (*OCC* 1:1269; my emphasis).

5. Jacqueline Lévi-Valensi and other critics have noted that Meursault himself initially does not feel guilty and fails to regret his crime ("L'Étranger: Un 'meurtrier innocent'?," 85–86).

6. In the novel's tentative outline, Camus also repeatedly nicknames his characters "les condamnés à mort" (the men condemned to death; *OCC* 2:249–50).

7. In some passages of Camus's manuscript, Catherine's first name is changed to Lucie.

8. Catherine Cormery's difficulty in communicating is not isolated in the novel. On the whole, Jacques's family, including his father, uncle, and grandmother, are either quiet or use approximative language. Edward J. Hughes has rightly highlighted the "hymn of praise to inarticulateness and animal physicality" (*Albert Camus*, 14) that underlies the novel's characterization. See also "Les Taiseux" in Morisi, *Albert Camus: Le souci des autres*, 119–44. In the passage under consideration, however, the limits of this praise become apparent.

9. "La société des vivants craignait à longueur de journée d'être obligée de céder la place à la société des morts" (Day in and day out, the society of the living feared that it would have to give way to the society of the dead; *OCC* 2:153).

10. Weyembergh, *Albert Camus ou la mémoire des origines*, 13.

11. Davis, "Violence and Ethics in Camus," 109, 115. See also Davis, "Camus, Encounters, Reading" and "The Cost of Being Ethical."

12. Like Gaëtan Picon ("Remarques sur *La Peste* d'Albert Camus") before him, Roger Quilliot draws a parallel between this *pensée* and *La Peste* ("Un exemple d'influence pascalienne," 123). Lévi-Valensi underscores the same analogy (*Jacqueline Lévi-Valensi présente* La Peste *d'Albert Camus*, 39). Camus's admiration for Pascal is well-known; see *OCC* 4:640, 646, 1236.

13. The metaphors used to narrate the scene in which Meursault kills the Arab turn the protagonist into the victim of the sun. As for the murder and mutilation of the soldier in Morocco, while Henri Cormery condemns them vehemently, Mr. Levesque, the schoolteacher who is with him, begs to differ.

14. On the possibility of interrupting violence when it is perpetrated by an individual in Camus's fiction, see Blanchot's reading of Kaliayev's inability to throw the bomb at the Grand Duke when he sees the faces of his nephew and niece in *Les Justes* ("Tu peux tuer cet Homme," 1068–69).

15. The religiosity inherent in the notion of epiphany is also found in the biblical echoes of the novel's title, although Camus draws on a wide variety of sources, including scientific, historical, and literary (Artaud, Defoe, etc.) texts. See Lévi-Valensi, *Jacqueline Lévi-Valensi présente* La Peste *d'Albert Camus*, 38.

16. This "confession" is a belated addendum to the typescript and replaces a brief and somewhat stereotypical scene of Alpine retreat in which Tarrou reflects on the "lies" and "futility" (*OCC* 2:1196) of his life.

17. In the second half of *L'Étranger*, the magistrates are also reduced to red and dark patches of color that turn the courtroom into a hellish space (*OCC* 1:190).

18. See Quilliot, *La Mer et les prisons*, 169. A non-negligible autobiographical background informs several passages of the "Confession d'un pestiféré."

For instance, although Camus briefly supported the Communist Party in his youth, he subsequently denounced the crimes committed in the name of its ideology, thereby opposing a large part of his era's leftist intelligentsia, including Sartre and Beauvoir. The publication of *L'Homme révolté* in 1951 sealed this antagonism. Furthermore, like Tarrou, Camus witnessed a number of trials as a journalist; those of Hodent and Pétain, for example.

19. *Les Justes* (1949) examines this thorny concept. Earlier texts explore the question of responsibility and extreme violence as well. See for instance "La Crise de l'homme" (*OCC* 2:744) and "Nous autres meurtriers" (*OCC* 2:686–87), which anticipate Tarrou's confession in several respects. For a study of the points of contact between *La Peste* and *Ni victimes ni bourreaux*, see Jeanyves Guérin's "Jalons pour une lecture politique de *La Peste*." Lévi-Valensi also proposes a useful census of the main overlaps between *Combat* and *La Peste* (*Jacqueline Lévi-Valensi présente* La Peste *d'Albert Camus*, 164–68).

20. Dismissing critics such as Claude Roy and Barthes, who objected to the lack of realism in *La Peste*, and going further than Camus himself, Quilliot has suggested that the plague, which stands for a multiplicity of evils, appears in many of Camus's works, including *Noces*, *Caligula*, *L'Étranger*, and *Le Malentendu* (*La Mer et les prisons*, 170).

21. Camus develops further this political reflection on lethal violence in other fictional and non-fictional works, including *Les Justes* and "Réponse à Emmanuel d'Astier de la Vigerie." See Morisi, "Staging the Limit."

22. At the metafictional level, judicial records confirm that this narrative is (re)invented: no Pirette was ever executed in Algiers. The beheading that Camus's father witnessed must have been that of Juan Vidal, also known as "Figarette." It took place on May 24, 1910. "Pirette" is the name of a town where another capital crime was committed, on November 27, 1913. It also led to an execution, but in Tizi-Ouzou, on January 29, 1914, that is to say *after* the death of Camus's father/Henri Cormery (*L'Express du midi*, "Exécutions capitales," May 25, 1910).

23. The mother, the uncle, and the grandmother refer to it in turn. Moreover, a "ressasse[ment]" (rehash[ing]) of the narrative occurs in Jacques's mind.

24. Blanchot, "Le Roman de l'étranger," 248, 252. Camus disagreed. He argued that there was no rupture in his character, and that, at the end of his novel, Meursault "merely" keeps "answering the questions" he is asked (*OCC* 2:950). While the protagonist indeed applies himself to responding to the events and discourses with which he is confronted throughout, his sudden readiness to be executed does contrast with his persistent hope to escape capital punishment after the sentence is pronounced (*OCC* 1:204, 207).

25. Sartre, "Explication de *L'Étranger*," 93, 95, 97, 98. Although Sartre concedes that *L'Étranger* isn't a *roman à thèse* (97) and that there is some gratuitousness to it (98), he nonetheless asserts that "*Le Mythe de Sisyphe* has given us the exact commentary" (93) of the novel, and that this essay "is going to teach us the way in which our author's novel is to be read" (97).

26. Sartre, "Explication de *L'Étranger*," 101.

27. And like Hugo, Camus seems to have been influenced by a newspaper report on the experience of an actual condemned man (*OCC* 1:1453).

28. Likewise, Camus's notebooks from 1944 read, "We mustn't sentence to death since we have been turned into men condemned by death [des condamnés de mort (sic)]" (OCC 2:1019).

29. Golgotha is symbolically connected with decapitation, the punishment that awaits Meursault. It is the "place of the skull" in Aramaic.

30. *La Bible: Nouveau Testament*, 333–34; my emphasis.

31. While this intertext is covert in the novel, Camus makes Meursault's Christ-like character explicit in the preface to the American edition of *L'Étranger* (OCC 1:216). On the resemblance between Meursault and Jesus Christ, see also Auroy, "Jésus-Christ," 441.

32. *La Chute* (The Fall) arguably picks up on this reversal: Clamence the thief and false prophet briefly fantasizes about his possible decapitation and the paradoxical apotheosis that this would allow him to enjoy postmortem, if his severed head were "lifted" above the people.

33. Bespaloff, "Le Monde du condamné à mort," 3–6.

34. See Girard, "Camus's Stranger Retried," 522, as well as Blanchot, "Le Roman de l'étranger," 250, 251.

35. See the narrator's well-known comment on Grand, OCC 2: 128.

36. Bespaloff, "Le Monde du condamné à mort," 16, 13.

37. See Camus, OCC 1:215; Blanchot, "Le Roman de l'étranger," 249; Bespaloff, "Le Monde du condamné à mort," 2.

38. This lack of imagination, which Camus also calls the danger of "abstraction," comes to authorize capital punishment, the perpetration of mass murder, and the flourishing of homicidal ideologies, in his view. See his 1944 article "Tout ne S'arrange pas" (OCC 1:922), his editorial from November 2, 1944 (CC 302), passages from "Sauver les corps" (CC 613) and "L'Incroyant et les chrétiens" (OCC 2:506), and the reference to the "imagination" made in a collective letter sent to the president of the Greek Republic in 1951 to ask for the pardon of thousands of condemned men and women (including former *résistants*) waiting to be liberated or executed after the Greek Civil War (Morisi, *Albert Camus contre la peine de mort*, 137–39).

39. Camus, *Correspondance: 1932–1960*, 141.

40. "Réflexions sur la guillotine" insists that all crimes should not be equated, but the essay also argues that "Supreme justice . . . is no less repulsive than the crime" (OCC 4:128) and defines the death penalty as the most premeditated of murders.

41. Here, one may think of the rewriting of the Cartesian *cogito* in *L'Homme révolté* (OCC 3:79).

42. Camus, *Correspondance: 1932–1960*, 141.

43. See, for instance, Frantz Favre, "Camus et Nietzsche: Philosophie et existence," 73, 74.

44. In 1957, Camus clarifies this importance and use of compassion in the context of capital justice: "Of course, compassion can only be the feeling of a common suffering here, and not some frivolous indulgence that would pay no attention to the sufferings and the rights of the victim. It doesn't exclude punishment, but it suspends the ultimate sentence" (OCC 4:156).

45. See also the conclusion of "Réflexions sur la guillotine" (OCC 4:167).

46. Lévinas, *Éthique et infini*, 92.
47. A passage from "Réflexions sur la guillotine" specifies, about the Pirette anecdote, "On the day of the execution, around my father, there must have been a large enough number of criminals who, unlike him, did not throw up" (*OCC* 4:137).
48. On this mode of engagement promoted by Sartre in *Qu'est-ce que la littérature,* see, for instance, Benoît Denis, *Littérature et engagement, de Pascal à Sartre,* 270.
49. While Kant's and Camus's views on the death penalty are diametrically opposed, Vanney and Salas note that, in "Réflexions sur la guillotine," the writer puts forth a moral imperative, much like the philosopher. Like Kant, he also defines (but, for his part, condemns) capital punishment as a *lex talionis*. Vanney, "Le partage de la souffrance," 103; Salas, *Albert Camus: La juste révolte,* 47.

CHAPTER 6

1. This rhetoric includes "formules stéréotypées" (stereotypical formulae), "ruses du langage" (tricks of language), and "phrases cérémonieuses" (ceremonious sentences) for Camus (*OCC* 4:128–29).
2. Using a similar vocabulary, Hugo's 1832 preface exhorted the "gens du roi" (the king's people) to "ne ... plus nous demander des têtes ... en nous adjurant d'une voix caressante *au nom de la société*" (not to ask us for beheadings ... imploring us with a caressing voice *in the name of society*; OCH 4:491; my emphasis).
3. On the euphemization of silence in Camus's œuvre, see Hiroshi Mino, *Le Silence dans l'œuvre d'Albert Camus.*
4. Monestier, *Peines de mort,* 227–28.
5. In November and December 1946, the article "Nous autres meurtriers" (*Franchise,* n°3), reminiscent of two lectures Camus gave in the United States earlier that year ("La Crise de l'homme" [The Crisis of Man] and "Sommes-nous des pessimistes?" [Are we pessimists?]) insisted, "The words of hope are courage, clear speech, and friendship" (*OCC* 2:686).
6. Barthes famously referred to Camus's "blank ... amodal ... neutral writing" more generally (*Le Degré zéro de l'écriture,* 108–9).
7. The père Paneloux delivers two sermons that both tap into a pompous and moralizing rhetoric, although they differ from each other in other ways.
8. This disclosure of pure violence is found in *Le Dernier Jour d'un condamné* as well, although Hugo doesn't only or mainly rely on a clinical style, as we have seen.
9. Camus himself taps into this imaginary in *Le Mythe de Sisyphe* when referring to the "divine disponibilité" of the man awaiting his execution, but all his works of fiction rebuff such romanticization.
10. Davis has underscored a disconnect between the theory and the practice of linguistic transparency in Camus's works and has shown their force to emerge precisely from moments when "meaning is made unstable" and "resists easy conceptualization" ("Violence and Ethics in Camus," 114).

11. On the question of witnessing in *La Peste*, see the fourth chapter of Felman and Laub, *Testimony: Crises of Witnessing in Literature, Psychoanalysis, and History*, 93–119, and Jennifer Cooke's critical response to Felman in "Writing Plague: Transforming Narrative, Witnessing, and History," 21–42.

12. See Naudin, "Hugo et Camus face à la peine capitale," 265, and Vanney, "Le Partage de la souffrance," 98.

13. This intimate subjective realism distinguishes itself from the subjective realism found in such writers as Flaubert and Stendhal by virtue of the fact that it is dependent on a first-person narrator who is the novel's protagonist.

14. Barthes, *Le Degré zéro de l'écriture*, 108.

15. Naudin, "Hugo et Camus face à la peine capitale," 265–66.

16. Bowman, "The Intertextuality of Victor Hugo's *Le Dernier Jour d'un condamné*," 38, 41.

17. Beccaria notices this too. *On Crimes and Punishments*, 70.

18. Letter from January 21, 1948, in Camus and Grenier, *Correspondance: 1932–1960*, 141.

19. Spiquel, "*L'Étranger* et *Le Dernier Jour*," 116.

20. Spiquel, "*L'Étranger* et *Le Dernier Jour*," 117.

21. Camus sketched the play in 1939, completed and published its first version in 1943, published it in 1943, and produced a definitive version in 1958.

22. Baudelaire, *Selected Poems*, 118–9.

23. Even if this criticism wasn't apparent to some of his contemporaries. For a summary of the Greek political context that inspired Nerval's publication and the dispute it brought about between Nerval and Champfleury, see Richard D. E. Burton, *Baudelaire and the Second Republic: Writing and Revolution*, 311–12. Burton also proposes a political reading of this poem centered on the context of 1849–51 and "the castration of the Second Republic" (315–19). For a comparative examination of Nerval's and Baudelaire's texts, see the eighth chapter of John E. Jackson, *Baudelaire sans fin, essai sur* Les Fleurs du mal.

24. Baudelaire, *Selected Poems*, 119–21.

25. Baudelaire, *Selected Poems*, 119–21.

26. Baudelaire, *Selected Poems*, 119–21.

27. Baudelaire also uses allegory to project the self onto the outside world in "Le Cygne": "Tout pour moi devient allégorie" (Everything to me becomes an allegory; *OCB* 1:86).

28. Sanyal's analysis is especially rich. It highlights the proximity of the two protagonists, the "sabotage of aesthetic sovereignty and autonomy" (*The Violence of Modernity*, 75), and a conspiratorial poetics staged in the context of a Second Empire in which absolute authority somehow ends up being preserved (65–79). On this prose poem, see also, among others, Starobinski, "Sur quelques répondants allégoriques du poète"; Virginia Swain, "The Legitimation Crisis: Event and Meaning in 'Le Vieux Saltimbanque' and 'Une Mort héroïque'"; Thélot, *Baudelaire*, 142–44; and Patrick Labarthe, *Baudelaire et la tradition de l'allégorie*, 544–47.

29. Sanyal, *The Violence of Modernity*, 68–69.

30. Sanyal interestingly views the narrator of the poem as incarnating the "comique significatif" that Baudelaire distinguishes from the "comique absolu" (*The Violence of Modernity*, 73).

31. Starobinski attributes Fancioulle's death following the strident blowing of the whistle to his being "désavoué dans son orgueil d'artiste" (disavowed in his pride as an artist; *La Mélancolie au miroir*, 408).

32. Thélot also talks about the prince as a "sacrificator fascinated by his victim" and rightly reads the representation of the (murderous) preservation of political order as a boring and tragic "buffoonery" unmasked by the narrator-poet (*Baudelaire*, 144). Labarthe likewise argues that this narrative allegory presents "a 'sacrificial' conception of art" (*Baudelaire et la tradition de l'allégorie*, 110).

CONCLUSION

1. See, for instance, Nussbaum, *Love's Knowledge*; *Cultivating Humanity*; *Upheavals of Thought*; Suzanne Keen, *Empathy and the Novel*.

Works Cited

I. PRIMARY SOURCES

Balzac, Honoré de. *Le Curé de village*. In *La Comédie humaine*, edited by Marcel Bouteron, vol. 8, 536–769. Paris: Gallimard, 1949.
Baudelaire, Charles. *Correspondance*. Edited by Claude Pichois and Jean Ziegler. 2 vols. Paris: Gallimard, 1973.
———. *The Flowers of Evil*. Translated with notes by James McGowan. Oxford: Oxford University Press, 1993.
———. *Journaux intimes. Fusées. Mon cœur mis à nu. Carnet*. Edited by Jacques Crépet and Georges Blin. Paris: José Corti, 1949.
———. *The Letters of Charles Baudelaire to His Mother*. London: Rodker, 1928.
———. *Œuvres complètes*. Edited by Claude Pichois. 2 vols. Paris: Gallimard, 1975.
———. *Œuvres posthumes et correspondances inédites*. Edited by Eugène Crépet. Paris: Quantin, 1887.
———. *Selected Letters of Charles Baudelaire: The Conquest of Solitude*. Translated and edited by Rosemary Lloyd. London: Weidenfeld and Nicolson, 1986.
———. *Selected Poems*. Translated by Carol Clark. London: Penguin, 1995.
Benson, Robert. *Sketches of Corsica; Or, A Journal Written during a Visit to That Island in 1823*. London: Longman, Hurst, Rees, Orme, Brown, and Green, 1825.
Bourdin, Paul, ed. *Correspondance inédite du marquis de Sade, de ses proches et de ses familiers*. Paris: Librairie de France, 1929.
Bourgeois, Anicet, and Victor Ducange. *Sept heures, ou Charlotte Corday, drame en trois actes et six tableaux*. Paris: Bezou, 1829.

Camus, Albert. *Camus à Combat: Éditoriaux et articles d'Albert Camus 1944–1947*. Edited by Jacqueline Lévi-Valensi. Paris: Gallimard, 2002.

———. *Œuvres complètes*. Edited by Jacqueline Lévi-Valensi, André Abbou, Zedjiga Abdelkrim, Marie-Louise Audin, Raymond Gay-Crosier, Samantha Novello, Pierre-Louis Rey, Philippe Vanney, David H. Walker, and Maurice Weyembergh. 4 vols. Paris: Gallimard, 2006–8.

Camus, Albert, and Jean Grenier. *Correspondance 1932–1960*. Paris: Gallimard, 1981.

Dostoevsky, Fyodor. *Complete Letters*. Trans. by David Lowe and Ronald Meyer. Vol. 1. Ann Harbor: Ardis, 1988.

———. "A Gentle Creature: A Fantastic Story." In *The Best Short Stories of Fyodor Dostoevsky*, translated by David Magarshack, 215–62. New York: Modern Library, 2001.

Flaubert, Gustave. *Correspondance*. Edited by Jean Bruneau. Vol. 2. Paris: Gallimard, 1980.

Hugo, Victor. *Le Dernier Jour d'un condamné*. 3rd edition preceded by "Une Comédie à propos d'une tragédie." Paris: Charles Gosselin and H. Bossange, 1829.

———. *Le Dernier Jour d'un condamné*. 5th edition with a frontispiece by Célestin Nanteuil and a lithography after L. Boulanger by Ch.–. Paris: Renduel, 1832.

———. *Le Dernier Jour d'un condamné*. Presented by Henri Guillemin. Paris: Du Seuil, 1963.

———. *Écrits sur la peine de mort*. Presented by Raymond Jean. Paris: Actes sud, 1985.

———. *Œuvres complètes: Édition chronologique*. 18 vols. Edited by Jean Massin. Paris: Le Club français du Livre, 1967–70.

Janin, Jules. *L'Âne mort ou la femme guillotinée*. N.p.: n.p., 1829.

La Bible: Nouveau testament. Edited and translated by Jean Grosjean and Michel Léturmy, with Paul Gros. Paris: Gallimard, 1971.

Lamartine, Alphonse de. *Ode contre la peine de mort*. Paris: C. Gosselin, 1830.

Lefèvre-Deumier, Jules. *Jules Lefèvre-Deumier: Un poète romantique contre la peine de mort. Quatre poèmes*. Edited by Loïc Guyon. Liverpool: Liverpool University Press, 2005. https://www.liverpool.ac.uk/media/livacuk/modern-languages-and-cultures/liverpoolonline/peinedemort.pdf.

———. *Le Parricide, poëme suivi d'autres poésies*. Paris: Amyot, 1823.

Maistre, Joseph de. *Discourse for Madam La Marquise de Costa on the Life and Death of Her Son Eugene*. in *The Collected Works of Joseph de Maistre: Electronic Edition I. General Works*. Trans. Richard A. Lebrun. Montreal: McGill-Queen's University Press, 1993. http://pm.nlx.com/xtf/view?docId=maistre/maistre.03.xml;chunk.id=div.maistre.discourse.3;toc.depth=1;brand=default;query=de%20costa;query-prox=.

———. *Lettres et opuscules inédits*. Vol. 2. Paris: Vaton, 1861.

———. *Œuvres*. Edited by Pierre Glaudes. Paris: Robert Laffont, 2007.

———. *St Petersburg Dialogues or Conversations on the Temporal Government of Providence*. In *The Collected Works of Joseph de Maistre: Electronic Edition I. General Works*, translated by Richard A. Lebrun. Montreal: Mc-

Gill-Queen's University Press, 1993. http://pm.nlx.com/xtf/view?docId=-maistre/maistre.07.xml;chunk.id=div.maistre.soirees.1;toc.depth=1;toc.id=div.maistre.soirees.1;brand=default.
Nodier, Charles. "Histoire d'Hélène Gillet." *Revue de Paris* 35 (1832): 18–36.
———. *Smarra, ou les Démons de la Nuit, songes romantiques*, Paris: Ponthieu, 1821.
Poe, Edgar Allan. *The Brevities: Pinakidia, Marginalia, Fifty Suggestions and Other Works*. Edited by Burton R. Pollin. New York: Gordian Press, 1985.
———. *Essays and Reviews*. Edited by G. R. Thompson. New York: Library of America, 1984.Rousseau, Jean-Jacques. *The Social Contract and Discourses*. Translated by G. D. H. Cole. London: Everyman, 1993.
Sade, marquis de. *La Philosophie dans le boudoir*. In *Œuvres complètes du marquis de Sade*, edited by Annie Le Brun and Jean-Jacques Pauvert, vol. 3, 375–561. Paris: Pauvert, 1986.
Simonnin, Antoine, and Louis-Émile Vanderburch. *Le Doge et le dernier jour d'un condamné, ou Le canon d'alarme: Vaudeville en 3 tableaux*. Paris: Quoy, 1829.
Terence. *L'Héautontimorouménos*. Translated by J. Marouzeau. Paris: Les Belles Lettres, 1990.
Vidocq. *Mémoires de Vidocq, chef de la police de sûreté jusqu'en 1827*. Paris: Tenon, 1828.
Vigny, Alfred de. *La Maréchale d'Ancre*. Paris: C. Gosselin; Barba, 1831.
Voltaire. *Commentaire sur le livre* Des délits et des peines *par un avocat de province*. N.p.: n.p., 1766.

II. CRITICISM RELATED TO HUGO, BAUDELAIRE, AND CAMUS

1. Hugo

"Angleterre: Dernières sensations d'un homme condamné à mort." *Le Globe* (Paris), January 3, 1828.
Badinter, Robert. "Je vote l'abolition de la peine de mort." *L'Histoire* 261 (2002): 56–57.
———, ed. *L'Abolition de la peine de mort*. Paris: Dalloz, 2007.
———. Preface to *Choses vues à travers Hugo: Hommage à Guy Rosa*, edited by Claude Millet, Florence Naugrette, and Agnès Spiquel, 7–10. Valenciennes: Presses universitaires de Valenciennes, 2007.
Biré, Edmond. *Victor Hugo avant 1830*. Paris: Jules Gervais, 1883.
Boulard, Stéphanie. *Rouge Hugo*. Villeneuve d'Ascq: Presses universitaires du Septentrion, 2014.
Bowman, Frank Paul. "The Intertextuality of Victor Hugo's *Le Dernier Jour d'un condamné*." In *Alteratives*, edited by Warren Motte and Gerald Prince, 25–45. Lexington, Ky.: French Forum, 1993.
Bozon, Émilie. *L'Expression du moi dans* Le Dernier Jour d'un condamné *de Victor Hugo*. Paris: Le Manuscrit, 2002.

Brombert, Victor. "Le Condamné de Hugo: 'Comme pour le roi.'" In *Hugo et l'Histoire*, edited by Léon-François Hoffmann and Suzanne Nash, 73–83. Paris: Presses de l'Université de Paris-Sorbonne, 2005.

———. *The Romantic Prison: The French Tradition*. Princeton, N.J.: Princeton University Press, 1978.

———. *Victor Hugo and the Visionary Novel*. Cambridge, Mass.: Harvard University Press, 1984.

Brooks, Peter. "Death in the First Person." *South Atlantic Quarterly* 107.3 (2008): 531–46.

Chabert, Benoît. "Sur la peine de mort en France de la Restauration au début de la IIIe République." In *Victor Hugo contre la peine de mort*, edited by Jérôme Picon and Isabel Violante, 169–73. Paris: Textuel, 2001.

Charlier, Gustave. "Comment fut écrit *Le Dernier Jour d'un condamné?*" *Revue d'Histoire Littéraire de la France* 22 (1915): 321–60.

Dällenbach, Lucien. "Le Vide plein ou les révélations de l'homme sans tête." In *Hugo dans les marges*, edited by Lucien Dällenbach and Laurent Jenny, 51–90. Geneva: Éditions Zoë, 1985.

Degout, Bernard. "De Joseph de Maistre à Victor Hugo: L'Époque de *Han d'Islande* (1823)." In *Joseph de Maistre*, 648–52. Lausanne: L'Âge d'Homme, 2005.

"*Le Dernier Jour d'un condamné*, roman; par M. Victor Hugo." *Le Globe* (Paris), February 4, 1829.

Duvergier, J. B. "De la peine de mort à l'occasion d'un écrit de M. Victor Hugo." *Gazette des Tribunaux: Journal de Jurisprudence et des Débats Judiciaires*, February 7, 1829.

Gleizes, Delphine. "L'Acte et la parole: Les stratégies de Victor Hugo contre la peine de mort." In *Victor Hugo contre la peine de mort*, edited by Jérôme Picon and Isabel Violante, 15–41. Paris: Textuel, 2001.

Gohin, Yves. "Les Réalités du crime et de la justice pour Victor Hugo avant 1829." In *Victor Hugo: Œuvres complètes*, edited by Jean Massin, vol. 3, i–xxvi. Paris: Le Club français du Livre, 1967.

Grossman, Kathryn M. *The Early Novels of Victor Hugo: Towards a Poetics of Harmony*. Geneva: Droz, 1986.

Halsall, Albert W. "*Le Dernier Jour d'un condamné à mort* [sic]: Récit exemplaire hugolien." In *Victor Hugo et l'art de convaincre: Le récit hugolien; rhétorique, argumentation, persuasion*. Montreal: Éditions Balzac, 1995.

[Hugo, Adèle]. *Victor Hugo raconté par un témoin de sa vie*. Paris: Lacroix, 1863.

Janin, Jules. Review of *Le Dernier Jour d'un condamné*. *La Quotidienne* (Paris), February 3, 1829.

Jean, Raymond. *Écrits de Victor Hugo sur la peine de mort*. Maussane-les-Alpilles: Actes Sud, 1979.

Lewis, Briana. "The Making of a Condamné: State Power and the Ritual of Trial in *Le Dernier Jour d'un Condamné* and *Claude Gueux*." *Romanic Review* 102 (2011): 183–99.

Lowe-Dupas, Hélène. "Innommable guillotine: La peine de mort dans *Le Dernier Jour d'un condamné* et *Histoire d'Hélène Gillet*." *Nineteenth-Century French Studies* 23 (1995): 341–48.

Meschonnic, Henri. "Vers le roman-poème: Les romans de Hugo avant *Les Misérables*." In *Victor Hugo: Œuvres complètes*, edited by Jean Massin, vol. 3, i–xx. Paris: Le Club français du Livre, 1967.
Naudin, Marie. "Hugo et Camus face à la peine capitale." *Revue d'Histoire Littéraire de la France* 2 (March–April 1972): 264–73.
[Nisard, Charles?] Review of *Le Dernier Jour d'un condamné*. *Le Journal des Débats* (Paris), February 26, 1829.
Nodier, Charles. Review of *Han d'Islande*. *La Quotidienne* (Paris), March 12, 1823.
Parent, Yvette. "L'Emploi de l'argot dans *Le Dernier Jour d'un condamné*." Groupe Hugo. Université Paris 7. February 8, 2003. http://groupugo.div.jussieu.fr/Groupugo/03-02-08Parent.htm.
Pearson, Roger. *Unacknowledged Legislators: The Poet as Lawgiver in Post-Revolutionary France*. Oxford: Oxford University Press, 2016.
Picon, Jérôme, and Isabel Violante, eds. *Victor Hugo contre la peine de mort*. Paris: Textuel, 2001.
Review of *Le Dernier Jour d'un condamné*. *La Gazette de France*, February 19, 1829.
Riley, Elizabeth Rose. "La Voix qui sort de l'ombre: Victor Hugo's *Le Dernier Jour d'un condamné*." Ph.D. diss., University of California, Davis, 1997.
Roman, Myriam. "*Le Dernier Jour d'un condamné*: Le style contre la rhétorique." In *Victor Hugo et la langue*, edited by Florence Naugrette and Guy Rosa, 35–50. Rosny-sous-bois: Bréal, 2005.
Rosa, Guy. "Commentaires du *Dernier Jour d'un condamné*." In *Le Dernier Jour d'un condamné suivi de Claude Gueux et de l'affaire Tapner*, edited by Guy Rosa, 247–81. Paris: Librairie générale française, 1989.
Rousset, Jean. "*Le Dernier Jour d'un condamné* ou l'invention d'un genre littéraire." In *Hugo dans les marges*, edited by Lucien Dällenbach and Laurent Jenny, 35–50. Geneva: Éditions Zoë, 1985.
Savey-Casard, Paul. *Le Crime et la peine dans l'œuvre de Victor Hugo*. Paris: PUF, 1956.
Smets, Paul F. *Le Combat pour l'abolition de la peine de mort: Hugo, Koestler, Camus, d'autres. Textes, pré-textes et paratextes*. Brussels: Académie royale de Belgique, classe des lettres, 2003.
Vallois, Marie-Claire. "Écrire ou décrire: L'impossible histoire du 'sujet' dans *Le Dernier Jour d'un condamné* de Victor Hugo." *Romantisme* 48 (1985): 91–104.
Vernier, France. "Cela 'fait mal et ne touche pas.'" *La Pensée* 245 (May–June 1985): 41–58.

2. Baudelaire

Acquisto, Joseph. *The Fall Out of Redemption: Writing and Thinking beyond Salvation in Baudelaire, Cioran, Fondane, Agamben, and Nancy*. New York: Bloomsbury, 2015.
Barral, Georges. *Cinq journées avec Ch. Baudelaire*. Edited by Maurice Kunel. Liège: Vigie 30, 1932.

———. "L'Hôtel des colonnes à Mont-Saint-Jean." *Revue des Curiosités Révolutionnaires 1911–1912*. Vol. 2 (1912): 15–18.
Blin, Georges. *Le Sadisme de Baudelaire*. Paris: José Corti, 1948.
Burton, Richard D. E. *Baudelaire and the Second Republic: Writing and Revolution*. Oxford: Oxford University Press, 1991.
Cellier, Léon. *Baudelaire et Hugo*. Paris: José Corti, 1970.
Compagnon, Antoine. *Les Antimodernes, de Joseph de Maistre à Roland Barthes*. Paris: Gallimard, 2005.
Crépet, Eugène, and Jacques Crépet. *Charles Baudelaire: Étude biographique*. Paris: Messein, 1928.
Dotoli, Giovanni. *Baudelaire-Hugo: Rencontres, ruptures, fragments, abîmes*. Cultura Straniera 123. Fasano: Schena Editore; Paris: Presses de l'Université de Paris-Sorbonne, 2003.
Fondane, Benjamin. *Baudelaire et l'expérience du gouffre*. Paris: Seghers, 1972.
Guyaux, André. "Baudelaire et Victor Hugo." In *Georges Sand et son temps I: Hommage à Annarose Poli*, edited by Elio Mosele, 143–56. Geneva: Slatkine, 1993.
———, ed. *Baudelaire: Un demi-siècle de lectures des* Fleurs du mal *(1855–1905)*. Paris: Presses de l'Université Paris-Sorbonne, 2007.
Hovasse, Jean-Marc. "Les Signes de Hugo au cygne de Baudelaire." In *Choses vues à travers Hugo: Hommage à Guy Rosa*, edited by Claude Millet, Florence Naugrette, and Agnès Spiquel, 367–76. Valenciennes: Presses universitaires de Valenciennes, 2008.
Jackson, John E. *Baudelaire sans fin, essai sur* Les Fleurs du mal. Paris: Corti, 2005.
Kaplan, Edward. "Baudelairean Ethics." In *The Cambridge Companion to Baudelaire*, edited by Rosemary Lloyd, 87–100. Cambridge, U.K.: Cambridge University Press, 2005.
Labarthe, Patrick. *Baudelaire et la tradition de l'allégorie*. Genève: Droz, 2015.
Larousse, Pierre. *Grand Dictionnaire universel du XIXe siècle*. Vol. 2. Paris: Administration du grand dictionnaire universel, 1867.
Lloyd, Rosemary. *Baudelaire's Literary Criticism*. Cambridge, U.K.: Cambridge University Press, 1981.
Morisi, Ève. "Baudelaire's Death Penalty: Mapping an *Imaginaire*." *Dix-Neuf* 22 (2018): 130–52.
Oehler, Dolf. "Baudelaire's Politics." In *The Cambridge Companion to Baudelaire*, edited by Rosemary Lloyd, 14–30. Cambridge, U.K.: Cambridge University Press, 2005.
———. *Le Spleen contre l'oubli, juin 1848: Baudelaire, Flaubert, Heine, Herzen*. Translated by Guy Petitdemange. Paris: Payot, 1996.
Pachet, Pierre. "Baudelaire et le sacrifice." *Poétique: Revue de Théorie et d'Analyse Littéraires* 20 (1974): 437–51.
———. *Le Premier Venu: Baudelaire. Solitude et complot*. Paris: Denoël, 2009.
———. *Le Premier Venu: Essai sur la politique baudelairienne*. Paris: Denoël, 1976.
Pichois, Claude, ed. *Lettres à Baudelaire*. Études baudelairiennes IV–V. Neuchâtel: La Baconnière, 1973.

Sanyal, Debarati. *The Violence of Modernity: Baudelaire, Irony, and the Politics of Form.* Baltimore, Md.: Johns Hopkins University Press, 2006.
Starobinski, Jean. *La Mélancolie au miroir: Trois lectures de Baudelaire.* Paris: Julliard, 1989.
———. "Sur quelques répondants allégoriques du poète." *Revue d'Histoire littéraire de la France* 67.2 (April–June 1967): 178–88.
Swain, Virginia. "The Legitimation Crisis: Event and Meaning in 'Le Vieux Saltimbanque' and 'Une Mort héroïque.'" *Romanic Review* 73.4 (1982): 452–62.
Thélot, Jérôme. *Baudelaire: Violence et poésie.* Paris: Gallimard, 1993.
———. "La Conversion baudelairienne." *L'Année baudelaire* 5 (1999): 119–42.
Toal, Catherine. *The Entrapments of Form: Cruelty and Modern Literature.* New York: Fordham University Press, 2016.
Valéry, Paul. *Œuvres.* Edited by Jean Hytier. 2 vols. Paris: Gallimard, 1957–60.
Vouga, Daniel. *Baudelaire et Joseph de Maistre.* Paris: José Corti, 1957.
Wilcocks, Robert. "Towards a Re-examination of *L'Héautontimorouménos.*" *French Review* 48.3 (1975): 566–79.

3. Camus

Auroy, Carole. "Jésus-Christ." In *Dictionnaire Albert Camus*, edited by Jean Yves Guérin, 441. Paris: Robert Laffont, 2009.
Baciu, Virginia. *Albert Camus et la condamnation à mort.* Bucharest: Junimea, 1998.
Bespaloff, Rachel. "Le Monde du condamné à mort." *Esprit* 163 (1950): 1–26.
Blanchot, Maurice. "Le Roman de l'étranger." In *Faux pas*, 248–53. Paris: Gallimard, 1943.
———. "Tu peux tuer cet Homme (III)." *Nouvelle Nouvelle Revue Française* 18 (June 1954): 1059–69.
Cooke, Jennifer. "Writing Plague: Transforming Narrative, Witnessing, and History." In *The Tapestry of Health, Illness and Disease*, edited by Vera Kalitzkus and Peter L. Twohig, 21–42. Amsterdam: Rodopi, 2009.
Davis, Colin. "Camus, Encounters, Reading." In *Ethical Issues in Twentieth-Century French Fiction: Killing the Other*, 64–85. Houndmills, U.K.: Macmillan, 2000.
———. "The Cost of Being Ethical: Fiction, Violence and Altericide." *Common Knowledge* 9 (2003): 241–53.
———. "Violence and Ethics in Camus." In *The Cambridge Companion to Camus*, edited by Edward J. Hughes, 106–17. Cambridge, U.K.: Cambridge University Press, 2007.
"Exécutions capitales." *L'Express du midi* (Toulouse), May 25, 1910.
Favre, Frantz. "Camus et Nietzsche: Philosophie et existence." In *Albert Camus 9: La Pensée de Camus*, edited by Raymond Gay-Crosier and Brian T. Fitch, 65–94. Paris: Lettres modernes, 1979.
Felman, Soshana, and Dori Laub, eds. *Testimony: Crises of Witnessing in Literature, Psychoanalysis, and History.* New York: Routledge, 1992.
Girard, René. "Camus's Stranger Retried." *PMLA* 79 (December 1964): 519–33.

Guérin, Jeanyves. "Jalons pour une lecture politique de *La Peste*." *La Peste d'Albert Camus: Études réunies par Jacqueline Lévi-Valensi. Roman 20–50*, Revue d'Étude du Roman du XXe Siècle 2 (December 1986): 7–25.
Hughes, Edward J. *Albert Camus: Le Premier Homme, La Peste*. Glasgow: University of Glasgow French and German Publications, 1995.
Lévi-Valensi, Jacqueline. "L'Étranger: Un 'meurtrier innocent'?" In *Romans et crimes: Dostoïevski, Faulkner, Camus, Benet*, edited by Jean Bessière, 79–121. Paris: Honoré Champion, 1998.
———. *Jacqueline Lévi-Valensi présente* La Peste *d'Albert Camus*. Paris: Gallimard, 1991.
Mino, Hiroshi. *Le Silence dans l'œuvre d'Albert Camus*. Paris, Corti: 1987.
Morisi, Ève, ed. *Albert Camus contre la peine de mort*. Paris: Gallimard, 2011.
———. *Albert Camus: Le souci des autres*. Paris: Classiques Garnier, 2013.
———. "European Visions in Albert Camus's Abolitionism." In *Visions of Europe: Interdisciplinary Contributions to Contemporary Cultural Debates*, edited by Anke S. Biendarra and Gail K. Hart, 121–37. Berlin: Peter Lang, 2014.
———. "Staging the Limit: Albert Camus's Just Assassins and the Il/legitimacy of Terrorism." In *Literature and Terrorism*, edited by Peter Herman. 263–82. Cambridge, U.K.: Cambridge University Press, 2018.
———. "To Kill a Human Being: Camus and Capital Punishment." In "A Centennial Celebration of Albert Camus," edited by Robert Zaretsky. Special issue of *South Central Review* 31.3 (Fall 2014): 43–63.
Naudin, Marie. "Hugo et Camus face à la peine capitale." *Revue d'Histoire Littéraire de la France* 62 (March–April 1972): 264–73.
Picon, Gaëtan. "Remarques sur *La Peste* d'Albert Camus." *Fontaine* 61 (September 1947): 453–60.
Quilliot, Roger. *La Mer et les prisons*. Paris: Gallimard, 1970.
———. "Un exemple d'influence pascalienne au XXe siècle: L'œuvre d'Albert Camus." In *Les Pensées de Pascal ont trois cents ans*, 119–33. Clermont-Ferrand: G. de Bussac, 1971.
Roy, Claude. "Sur l'espèce humaine." *Europe* 22 (October 1947): 99–101.
Salas, Denis. *Albert Camus: La juste révolte*. Paris: Michalon, 2002.
Sartre, Jean-Paul. "Explication de *L'Étranger*." In *Situations, I: Essais critiques*, 92–112. Paris: Gallimard, 1947.
Smets, Paul-F. *Le Combat pour l'abolition de la peine de mort: Hugo, Koestler, Camus, d'autres. Textes, pré-textes et paratextes*. Brussels: Académie royale de Belgique, classe des lettres, 2003.
Spiquel, Agnès. "*L'Étranger et Le Dernier Jour d'un condamné*." *Revue des Lettres Modernes. Albert Camus* 16 (1995): 109–21.
Takatsuka, Hiroyuki. "De la correction des *Carnets* au *Premier Homme*." In *Camus l'artiste*, edited by Sophie Bastien, Anne Prouteau, and Agnès Spiquel. 197–209. Rennes: Presses Universitaires de Rennes, 2015.
Vanney, Philippe. "Camus et le droit de mort de l'état." *Bulletin d'études françaises de l'Université de Dokkyo* 34 (March 2003): 49–73.

———. "Le Partage de la souffrance: Camus et le débat traditionnel sur la peine de mort." *Bulletin d'études françaises de l'Université de Dokkyo* 32 (March 2001): 95–120.
Weyembergh, Maurice. *Albert Camus ou la mémoire des origines*. Brussels: De Bœck et Larcier, 1998.

III. PUBLICATIONS ON CAPITAL PUNISHMENT FROM THE EIGHTEENTH CENTURY TO TODAY

Arasse, Daniel. *La Guillotine et l'imaginaire de la Terreur*. Paris: Champs Flammarion, 1987.
Aubusson de Cavarlay, Bruno, Marie-Sylvie Huré, and Marie-Lys Pottié. "Les Statistiques criminelles de 1831 à 1981." *Déviance et Contrôle Social* 5 (1989): 182–83.
Badinter, Robert. *L'Abolition de la peine de mort*. Paris: Dalloz, 2007.
———. "Je vote l'abolition de la peine de mort." *L'Histoire* 261 (2002): 56–57.
Ballanche, Pierre. "Abolition de la peine de mort et de toute loi répressive." *La France Littéraire* 12 (April 1834): 273–97.
Barton, John Cyril. *Literary Executions: Capital Punishment and American Culture, 1820–1925*. Baltimore, Md.: Johns Hopkins University Press, 2014.
Beccaria, Cesare. *Dei delitti e delle pene*. Edited by Franco Venturi. Turin: Einaudi, 2007.
———. *On Crimes and Punishments, and Other Writings*. Edited by Richard Bellamy. Translated by Richard Davies with Virginia Cox and Richard Bellamy. Cambridge, U.K.: Cambridge University Press, 1995.
Bertrand, Régis, and Anne Carol, eds. *L'Exécution capitale: Une mort donnée en spectacle XVIe–XXe siècle*. Aix-en-Provence: Publications de l'Université de Provence, 2003.
Bessette, Jean-Michel. "L'Exécution: Gestes techniques et rapports humains." In *L'Exécution capitale: Une mort donnée en spectacle XVIe–XXe siècle*, edited by Régis Bertrand and Anne Carol, 25–32. Aix-en-Provence: Publications de l'Université de Provence, 2003.
Boudreau, Kristin. *The Spectacle of Death: Populist Literary Responses to American Capital Cases*. Amherst, N.Y.: Prometheus Books, 2006.
Bourg Saint-Edme, Théodore. *Dictionnaire de la pénalité dans toutes les parties du monde connu*. Vol. 4. Paris: Rousselon, 1828.
Canuel, Mark. *The Shadow of Death: Literature, Romanticism and the Subject of Punishment*. Princeton, N.J.: Princeton University Press, 2007.
Carol, Anne. "La Question de la douleur et les expériences médicales sur les suppliciés au XIXe siècle." In *L'Exécution capitale: Une mort donnée en spectacle XVIe–XXe siècle*, edited by Régis Bertrand and Anne Carol, 71–81. Aix-en-Provence: Publications de l'Université de Provence, 2003.
Chevalier, Louis. *Classes laborieuses et classes dangereuses à Paris pendant la première moitié du XIXe siècle*. Paris: Plon, 1958.
Corre, A. "À propos de la peine de mort et du livre du Professeur Lacassagne, Peine de mort et criminalité." In *Archives d'anthropologie criminelle de mé-*

decine légale et de psychologie normale et pathologique, vol. 23, 230–41. Lyon: A. Rey, 1908.
Derrida, Jacques. *Séminaire: La peine de mort*. Volume 1: *1999–2000*. Edited by Geoffrey Bennington, Marc Crépon, and Thomas Dutoit. Paris: Galilée, 2012.
Du Camp, Maxime. "La Guillotine." In *Paris, ses organes, ses fonctions et sa vie dans la seconde moitié du dix-neuvième siècle*, vol. 3, 331–403. Paris: Hachette, 1972.
Farcy, Jean-Claude. "La Peine de mort en France: Deux siècles pour une abolition (1791–1981)." *Criminocorpus*, October 8, 2006. https://criminocorpus.org/musee/16534/.
———. "La Peine de mort: Pratique judiciaire et débats." *Criminocorpus*, April 13, 2010. http://criminocorpus.revues.org/129.
Garland, David. *America's Death Penalty: Between Past and Present*. New York: New York University Press, 2011.
———. *Peculiar Institution: America's Death Penalty in an Age of Abolition*. Cambridge, Mass.: Belknap Press of Harvard University Press, 2010.
Gerould, Daniel. *Guillotine: Its Legend and Lore*. New York: Blast Books, 1992.
Girard, René. *La Violence et le sacré*. Paris: Hachette Littératures, 2006.
Greer, Donald. *The Incidence of the Terror during the French Revolution: A Statistical Interpretation*. Gloucester, Mass.: P. Smith, 1966.
Guest, David. *Sentenced to Death: The American Novel and Capital Punishment*. Jackson: University Press of Mississippi, 1997.
Guillotin, Joseph Ignace. "M. Guillotin lit un travail sur le Code pénal." In *Archives parlementaires*, vol. 10, 346. Paris: Librairie administrative Paul Dupont, 1878.
Guizot, François. *De la peine de mort en matière politique*. Paris: Béchet, 1822.
Guyon, Loïc. *Les Martyrs de la veuve: Romantisme et peine de mort*. Oxford: Peter Lang, 2010.
Hartnett, Stephen John. *Executing Democracy: Capital Punishment and the Making of America, 1683–1807 and 1835–1843*. 2 vols. East Lansing: Michigan State University Press, 2010–12.
Janes, Regina. *Losing Our Heads: Beheadings in Literature and Culture*. New York: New York University Press, 2005.
Jones, Colin. *The Longman Companion to the French Revolution*. London: Longman, 1988.
Jones, Paul Christian. *Against the Gallows: Antebellum American Writers and the Movement to Abolish Capital Punishment*. Iowa City: University of Iowa Press, 2011.
Jordanova, Ludmilla. "Medical Mediations: Mind, Body, and the Guillotine." *History Workshop Journal* 28 (1989): 39–52.
Kristeva, Julia. *Visions capitales: Arts et rituels de la décapitation*. Paris: Fayard and La Martinière, 2013.
Lacassagne, Alexandre. *Peine de mort et criminalité, l'accroissement de la criminalité et l'application de la peine capitale*. Paris: A. Maloine, 1908.
Lascoumes, Pierre. "Révolution ou réforme juridique? Les codes pénaux français de 1791 à 1810." In *Révolution et justice pénale en Europe:*

Modèles français et traditions nationales (1780–1830), edited by Xavier Rousseaux, Marie-Sylvie Dupont-Bouchat, and Claude Vael, 61–69. Paris: L'Harmattan, 1999.
Lesser, Wendy. *Pictures at an Execution: An Inquiry into the Subject of Murder*. Cambridge, Mass.: Harvard University Press, 1994.
Louis, Antoine. "Avis motivé sur le mode de la décollation" (March 14, 1792). In *Archives parlementaires*, vol. 39, 686. Paris: Librairie administrative Paul Dupont, 1892.
Lucas, Charles. *Du système pénal et du système répressif en général et de la peine de mort en particulier*. Paris: Béchet, 1827.
Marcandier-Colard, Christine. *Crimes de sang et scènes capitales: Essai sur l'esthétique romantique de la violence*. Paris: PUF, 1998.
Martin Hamilton, Sonja. "La Plume et le couperet: Enjeux politiques et littéraires de la peine de mort autour de 1830." Ph.D. diss., Johns Hopkins University, 2003.
Millingen, J. G. "Decapitation." In *Curiosities of Medical Experience*, 516–17. London: Richard Bentley, 1839.
Monestier, Martin. *Peines de mort: Histoire et techniques des exécutions capitales des origines à nos jours*. Paris: Cherche Midi, 1994.
Notice historique et physiologique sur les supplices de la guillotine. Paris: Chez l'éditeur, 1830.
Orr, Linda. *Headless History: Nineteenth-Century French Historiography of the Revolution*. Ithaca, N.Y.: Cornell University Press, 1990.
Poulosky, Laura Jean. *Severed Heads and Martyred Souls: Crime and Capital Punishment in French Romantic Literature*. Oxford: Peter Lang, 2003.
Renneville, Marc. *Le Langage des crânes: Une histoire de la phrénologie*. Paris: Institut d'édition Sanofi-Synthélabo, 2000.
Salaville, Jean-Baptiste. *De la peine de mort et du système pénal dans ses rapports avec la morale et la politique*. Paris: Mme Huzard, 1826.
Sanson, Henri, ed. *Memoirs of the Sansons: From Private Notes and Documents (1688–1847)*. Vol. 2. London: Chatto and Windus, 1876.
Sarat, Austin, ed. *The Killing State: Capital Punishment in Law, Politics, and Culture*. Oxford: Oxford University Press, 2001.
———, ed. *Life without Parole: America's New Death Penalty?* New York: New York University Press, 2012.
———. *When the State Kills: Capital Punishment and the American Condition*. Princeton, N.J.: Princeton University Press, 2001.
Sarat, Austin, and Christian Boulanger, eds. *The Cultural Lives of Capital Punishment: Comparative Perspectives*. Stanford, Calif.: Stanford University Press, 2005.Sarat, Austin, and Jennifer L. Culbert, eds. *States of Violence: War, Capital Punishment, and Letting Die*. Cambridge, U.K.: Cambridge University Press, 2009.
Sarat, Austin, and Jürgen Martschukat, eds. *Is the Death Penalty Dying? European and American Perspectives*. New York: Cambridge University Press, 2011.
Sarat, Austin, and Charles J. Ogletree, eds. *From Lynch Mobs to the Killing State: Race and the Death Penalty in America*. New York: New York University, 2006.

———. *The Road to Abolition? The Future of Capital Punishment in the United States*. New York: New York University Press, 2009.
Savey-Casard, Paul. *La Peine de mort: Esquisse historique et juridique*. Geneva: Droz, 1968.
Stahl, Paul-Henry. *Histoire de la décapitation*. Paris: PUF, 1986.
Sue, Jean-Joseph. *Recherches physiologiques et expériences sur la vitalité, suivies d'une nouvelle édition de son Opinion sur le supplice de la guillotine ou sur la douleur qui survit à la décolation* [sic]. Paris: l'auteur, 1797.
Tarde, Gabriel. *La Philosophie pénale*. 2nd ed. Paris: Masson and Stock, 1891.
Von Drehle, David. *Among the Lowest of the Dead: Inside Death Row*. New York: Fawcett Crest, 1995.
Wald Lasowski, Patrick. *Les Échafauds du romanesque*. Lille: Presses universitaires de Lille, 1991.
———. *Guillotinez-moi! Précis de décapitation*. Paris: Le Promeneur, 2007.

IV. OTHER CRITICAL AND PHILOSOPHICAL STUDIES

Agamben, Giorgio. *Homo Sacer: Sovereign Power and Bare Life*. Translated by Daniel Heller-Roazen. Stanford, Calif.: Stanford University Press, 1998.
Barthes, Roland. *Le Degré zéro de l'écriture*. Paris: Du Seuil, 1953.
Clark, T. J. *Image of the People: Gustave Courbet and the Second French Republic 1848–1851*. Greenwich, Conn.: New York Graphic Society, 1973.
Denis, Benoît. *Littérature et engagement, de Pascal à Sartre*. Paris: Du Seuil, 2000.
Foucault, Michel. *Discipline and Punish: The Birth of the Prison*. Translated by Alan Sheridan. London: Penguin, 1991.
———. *The History of Sexuality, Volume 1: An Introduction*. Translated by Robert Hurley. New York: Pantheon Books, 1978.
———. "The Order of Discourse." Translated by Ian McLeod. In *Untying the Knot: A Post-Structuralist Reader*, edited by Robert Young. 51–78. Boston, Mass.: Routledge, 1981.
Hakemulder, Jèmeljan. *The Moral Laboratory: Experiments Examining the Effects of Reading Literature on Social Perception and Moral Self-Concept*. Utrecht Publications in General and Comparative Literature 34. Utrecht: John Benjamins, 2000.
Keen, Suzanne. *Empathy and the Novel*. Oxford: Oxford University Press, 2007.
Lévinas, Emmanuel. *Éthique et infini*. Paris: Fayard, 1982.
Menninghaus, Winfried. *Disgust: The Theory and History of a Strong Sensation*. Translated by Howard Eiland and Joel Golb. Albany: State University of New York Press, 2003.
Murdoch, Iris. *Existentialists and Mystics: Writings on Philosophy and Literature*. Edited by Peter Conradi. London: Chatto and Windus, 1997.
———. *The Fire and the Sun: Why Plato Banished the Artists*. Oxford: Oxford University Press, 1978.
Nussbaum, Martha. *Cultivating Humanity: A Classical Defense of Reform in Liberal Education*. Cambridge, Mass.: Harvard University Press, 1997.

———. *Hiding from Humanity: Disgust, Shame, and the Law.* Princeton, N.J.: Princeton University Press, 2004.
———. *Love's Knowledge: Essays on Philosophy and Literature.* New York: Oxford University Press, 1990.
———. *Upheavals of Thought: The Intelligence of Emotions.* Cambridge, U.K.: Cambridge University Press, 2003.
Oatley, Keith. "Fiction: Simulation of Social Worlds." *Trends in Cognitive Sciences* 20.8 (August 2016): 618–28.
Rancière, Jacques. *Mute Speech: Literature, Critical Theory and Politics.* Translated by James Swenson. New York: Columbia University Press, 2011.
Ricœur, Paul. "Éthique et morale." In *Lectures 1: Autour du politique,* 256–69. Paris: Du Seuil, 1992.
Sartre, Jean-Paul. *Qu'est-ce que la littérature?* Paris: Gallimard, 1948.
Scarry, Elaine. *The Body in Pain: The Making and Unmaking of the World.* New York: Oxford University Press, 1985.
Valéry, Paul. *Variété V.* Paris: Gallimard, 1944.

Index

abolition, 4–5, 7, 70, 76–78, 87, 91, 93, 126, 129, 131–33, 157–58, 183–84, 208–11, 225n47, 228n42, 231n44; abolitionist activism, 16–17, 132, 223n24; abolitionist argument, 15, 18, 21, 164, 175, 211; abolitionist plea, 18–19; abolitionist poetics, 12, 15–66, 209; and penal reform, 7, 73–74; provision of 1795, 7, 17, 66, 95. *See also* death penalty
Académie de chirurgie, 6, 45
aesthetics, 4, 9, 50, 67–68, 121, 122, 169, 193, 195, 197, 199–201, 204, 207–12, 226n7; aesthete, 89; aesthetic ideal, 124–26; aestheticist literature, 89–90, 94, 211; bloody aesthetics, 104–13, 210; capital aesthetics, 72, 133; transgressive aesthetics, 5–6
Agamben, Giorgio, 12, 51–54, 63–64, 208; *Homo sacer: Sovereign Power and Bare Life*, 51, 54, 63–64. *See also* bare life; *bios*; *homo sacer*
Alembert, Jean Le Rond d', 7

Algeria, 136, 144, 188; Algerian War of Independence, 6, 8, 130–31, 136, 160, 188, 232n1. *See also* colonialism; decolonization; Front de Libération Nationale (FLN)
allegory, 71, 105–6, 123–24, 135, 137, 147, 150, 168, 174, 197–99, 201–2, 204, 230n22
Ancelle, Narcisse, 83, 86
Ancien Régime, 17, 62, 224n40. *See also* French Revolution; monarchy
argument, 6, 65, 133, 147, 152, 159, 167, 210–12, 226n17; abolitionist argument, 15, 18, 21–22, 77–78, 132, 164, 175; retentionist argument, 58, 78
aristocracy, 24, 76–78, 93, 185
Aristotle, 38, 55, 207–8. *See also* Classicism; tragedy
art for art's sake, 6, 86–87, 101, 127
Asselineau, Charles, 93
Assemblée constituante, 16, 52, 215n1
Aubigné, Agrippa d', 93, 189, 226n17; *Les Tragiques*, 189, 226n17

253

Index

Aupick, Caroline, 80–81

Badinter, Robert, 15–16, 22
Ballanche, Pierre-Simon, 17, 21
Balzac, Honoré de, 5, 23, 78, 124
Barbey d'Aurevilly, Jules, 67
bare life, 53–54, 57, 63–66, 208.
  See also Agamben, Giorgio; body; *homo sacer*; *zoē*
Barrière Saint-Jacques, 73, 222n2
Barthes, Roland, 9, 145, 234n20, 236n6
Baudelaire, Charles, 3–13, 67–127, 134, 165–66, 175, 183–206, 207–13; biblical images in, 106–7; on butchery and slaughter, 71, 103–27, 209; and the comic, 108–10, 200; and dandyism, 9, 10, 78, 184–85; on evil, 90–98, 103, 121–22, 125, 208; on laughter, 71, 108–10, 113–15, 125, 212; praise of capital punishment, 3, 12, 68–84, 99–101, 104, 126, 208–9; on sacrifice, 12, 68–69; 73–101, 104, 115, 117, 121–22, 125–26, 197, 202, 208–9, 212, 225n1; on sadism, 71, 100, 107, 114, 117, 121; on the *sponte sua*, 68–69, 83–84, 78–79, 91, 97–100; trial of 1857, 68, 93, 226n17; and the victim-executioner duo, 71, 113–14, 121, 186, 202, 231n30. *See also* reversibility; torture; violence
—Works by: "L'École païenne," 94; *Edgar Allan Poe, sa vie et ses œuvres*, 78, 86; "De l'essence du rire et généralement du comique dans les arts plastiques," 12, 103, 105, 108, 115, 200, 208; "La Fanfarlo," 230n10; *Les Fleurs du mal*, 10, 12, 68, 70–72, 76, 86, 88–89, 93, 95–96, 103–27, 188, 189, 194–99, 201–2, 206, 208–13, 226n17: "L'Albatros," 116, 197, "L'Amour et le crâne," 71, "À Théodore de Banville," 117, "Au lecteur," 71, 121, 189, 199, 201–2, "À une Madone," 71, 107–8, 110–11, 117–18, 121, 123, "La Béatrice," 71, "Bénédiction," 116, "Brumes et pluies," 71, "Chant d'automne," 71, "Une charogne," 104–5, 120–21, 124, 197, "Le Cygne," 71, 88–89, 197, 237n27, "Danse Macabre," 71, "Duellum," 123, "La Fin de la journée," 71, "La Fontaine de sang," 116, 121, "L'Héautontimorouménos," 71, 95, 106–8, 111, 113–18, 121–24, "Les Litanies de Satan," 71, "Une martyre," 71, 111–12, 117–21, 123, "Les Métamorphoses du Vampire," 71, 115, "Les Petites Vieilles," 86, "Les Phares," 230n11, "Le Reniement de Saint Pierre," 71, "Les Sept Vieillards," 86, "Spleen LXXVI," 71, "Spleen LXXVIII," 71, "Le Tonneau de la haine," 105–7, 121, 124, "Le Vampire," 71, 115, 231n30, "Le Voyage," 71, 95–96, 117, 199, "Un Voyage à Cythère," 71, 194–99; *Fusées*, 71, 77, 79, 81, 100–101; "Liste de titres et canevas de romans et nouvelles," 68; *Mon cœur mis à nu*, 10, 68–70, 75–84, 92, 96–97, 99, 113, 165, 231n36; "Notes nouvelles sur Edgar Poe," 68, 90, 217n24, 227n24; *Pauvre Belgique!*, 68, 77–79, 81, 91–92, 93; *Salon de 1846*, 78–79, 125, 230nn10, 11; *Le Spleen de Paris*, 88–89, 201, 206, 231n35: "Le Confiteor de l'artiste," 201, "Le Gâteau," 88–89, "Une mort héroïque," 71, 199, 201–2; "Théophile Gautier," 85–86, 217n24, 227n24
Beccaria, Cesare, 7, 21–22, 52, 95, 237n17
beheading. *See* decapitation
Belle Époque, 8
Benjamin, Walter, 53–54, 124, 208
Bespaloff, Rachel, 157

Bible, 106–7, 155–56, 187–88, 233n15; New Testament, 107–6, 155–56; Old Testament, 106–7, 187–88. *See also* Christianity
bios, 63–64, 223n16. *See also* Agamben, Giorgio; body, condemned body; Foucault, Michel; *homo sacer*
Blanchot, Maurice, 78, 152
Blin, Georges, 95, 99
Bloch-Michel, Jean, 133
body, 17, 48–49, 54, 61, 63–64, 106, 143, 151, 157–64, 167, 175–77, 205, 209; body language, 32, 63, 68, 190; condemned body, 31, 46, 57–58, 64–65, 133, 159, 169; corpse, 42, 46, 61, 104–5, 108, 111–12, 117–19; dismemberment of, 7, 17, 60–61, 65, 71, 111, 122–24, 204; and head, 11, 57–58; sickness of, 3, 136, 142–44, 151–52, 159–64, 167, 169, 172, 186, 189, 196–97, 213; and soul, 45–46, 57–58, 65. *See also* bare life; *bios*; pain; torture; violence
bourgeoisie, 24, 75, 88–89, 125, 168, 178, 184, 232n4
Brasillach, Robert, 132
Brecht, Bertolt, 27
Brown, John, 16
Buloz, François, 75
butchery (*boucherie*), 39, 71, 103–26, 160. *See also* violence

Camus, Albert, 3–13, 16, 129–206, 207–13; on the Absurd, 4, 130, 152, 154, 180; on disgust and nausea, 3, 136, 142–44, 151–52, 159–64, 167, 169, 172, 186, 189, 213; and "engagement involuntaire," 163–64, 211; on Épuration, 131–32, 160, 186–87; on legitimized murder, 130–32; on memory, 139–44, 159; Nobel Prize, 163, 189; on physical justice, 157–64; on Revolt, 4, 130–31, 159–61; on solidarity, 11, 133–34, 149–50, 158–60, 163–64, 189, 192, 206–7, 211
—Works by: *Actuelles. Chroniques 1944–1948*: "La Contagion" (*Combat*), 188, "Défense de l'intelligence," 188, "L'Incroyant et les chrétiens," 235n38, "Un nouveau contrat social" ("Ni victimes ni bourreaux"), 132, "Réponse à Emmanuel d'Astier de la Vigerie," 234n21, "Sauver les corps" ("Ni victimes ni bourreaux"), 232n2, 235n38, "Le Siècle de la peur" ("Ni victimes ni bourreaux"), 232n2; *Actuelles III. Chroniques algériennes 1939–1958*: Foreword, 188; *Caligula*, 234n20; *Carnets*, 135, 144–45, 165, 185–86; *La Chute*, 213, 235n32; "Le Dernier Jour d'un mort-né," 10, 129; "Discours de Suède," 189; *L'Envers et l'endroit*, 129–30, 144–45; *L'Étranger*, 10–11, 13, 135, 136–37, 142–48, 151–59, 162, 164, 165, 167–69, 171–72, 175–83, 186, 189–92, 198–99, 205–6, 209; *L'Homme révolté*, 10, 131, 147, 167–68, 184–85, 233n18, 235n41; *Les Justes*, 131, 169–72, 234n19; *Le Malentendu*, 145, 191–92, 234n20; "Métaphysique chrétienne et néoplatonisme," 146; *La Mort heureuse*, 135; *Le Mythe de Sisyphe*, 130, 152, 236n9; *Noces*, 234n20; "Nous autres meurtriers," 234n19, 236n5; *La Peste*, 10–11, 13, 131, 135–39, 143–52, 156–64, 168–69, 172–75, 177, 189–90, 192–93, 198–99, 202–6, 209; *Le Premier Homme*, 6, 10–11, 13, 135–36, 139–48, 151–52, 158–64, 168–69, 172, 176–77, 199, 206, 209; *Réflexions sur la peine capitale*, 133: "Réflexions sur la guillotine," 10, 13, 133–34, 144–45, 154, 160, 164, 165–67,

169, 175, 185–87, 232n1, 236n47; "Terrorisme et amnistie," 188; "Tout ne s'arrange pas," 235n38
capital punishment. *See* death penalty
Cellier, Léon, 74, 227n21
Chambre des députés, 17, 18–19
characterization, 11, 13, 22, 23–27, 29, 31, 45, 48–49, 89, 135, 145, 147–57, 161, 163–64, 168–69, 171, 174, 186, 192, 233nn6, 8; antihero, 89, 157–58, 164, 185; erasure of, 46–54; hero, 24, 78, 84, 98, 152, 157–58, 169, 202; of the nineteenth-century criminal, 24, 46–48, 50; use of caricature, 88, 108–10, 124
Charles X, 17, 218n18, 223n24
Chateaubriand, François-René de, 5, 21, 23
Christianity, 8, 21, 57–58, 90, 98–99, 133–34, 137, 146, 154, 184, 187–88, 231n44; Christ, 21, 78, 91, 98, 107, 117, 155–57, 197, 223n22; Fall, 90, 93, 97; Last Judgment, 90; original sin, 77, 92–93, 97, 187–88; redemption, 78, 94, 98–99, 115–16, 156, 209; saint, 98–99, 100, 157; salvation, 8, 97–98, 125–26, 223n23. *See also* Bible; reversibility; sacrifice
Classicism, 22–27, 44, 54, 115, 207, 220n21, 224n40. *See also* Aristotle; tragedy
Collaborationism, 131–32, 188. *See also* Occupation of France; Pétain, Philippe; World War II
colonialism, 6, 130–31, 136, 144, 188. *See also* Algeria; decolonization
comic, 108–110, 200. *See also* Baudelaire, Charles, on laughter
communication, 31–38, 40, 44, 140–42, 168, 207. *See also* language; metaphor, of deafness
Communism, 9, 232n4, 233n18
Constant, Benjamin, 17
Corday, Charlotte, 18, 223n25

coup d'état of 1851, 6, 76
Crémieux decree, 4, 226n2
crime, 3–4, 47–48, 50, 70, 74, 87, 98, 137–38, 142, 145–47, 151, 178, 181, 185, 187–88, 231n37, 233n18, 235n40; capital crime, 7, 10, 17, 18–19, 73, 104, 133, 136–37, 192, 200; crime of passion, 10, 15, 175, 131, 133; criminal nature of man, 90–94; criminology, 24, 50, 133, 217n22; political crime, 10, 16, 218n18, 228n42
criminal, 16–18, 42, 61, 74–75, 78–79, 84, 91, 155, 175, 177, 200, 208, 236n47; exclusion of, 17, 51–54, 61, 159, 164, 190–91; martyrdom of, 69, 97–100; monstrosity of, 46–48, 54; nineteenth-century stereotype of, 24, 46–48, 50; solidarity with, 11, 43–44, 148–50, 160, 163. *See also* homo sacer
cruelty, 19, 33, 56, 89, 108, 110, 117, 119, 159, 230n16; cruel modes of punishment, 7, 65, 178. *See also* torture; violence

Davis, Colin, 145, 236n10
death penalty: death sentence, 8, 16–17, 23–28, 31–34, 41, 43–44, 46, 52–53, 57, 59–60, 63–64, 67–68, 79, 84, 129–30, 132, 136–38, 142, 147–49, 152, 154, 158–59, 168, 176–78, 183, 186, 195, 200, 205, 215n4, 218n18, 231n37, 235n44; and divine justice, 8–9, 133–34; and the Enlightenment, 7; extenuating circumstances for, 66, 73, 176, 218nn9, 10, 18, 222n5; human agency in the administering of, 8–9; legitimation of; 7–8, 46, 52, 58, 68, 74–75, 84, 104, 130–32, 147, 150, 158, 160, 167, 206–7, 210; modern definition of, 6–7, 62, 222n1; as a rite of passage, 156, 209; and sacrifice, 12, 51–52, 67–69; 73–101, 104,

115, 117, 121–22, 125–26, 185, 197, 202, 208–9, 212; secrecy of, 4, 65. See also abolition; decapitation; execution; guillotine; spectacularity; witness
decadence, 76–77, 83, 91, 161
decapitation, 4, 6–8, 16, 27, 34, 36–39, 41–42, 46, 52, 56, 60–61, 68, 71, 76, 88, 103–4, 109, 112, 123, 139–44, 148–49, 151–53, 158, 162, 167–68, 177, 186, 208, 235nn29, 32; moment of, 11, 50, 53, 65; painlessness of, 58–59, 127, 211; post-decapitation, 57–58; swiftness of, 11, 45, 58–59; and torture, 55, 61–65, 176, 208, 223n21. See also death penalty; execution; guillotine; scaffold
decolonization, 6. See also Algeria; colonialism; Front de Libération Nationale (FLN)
Defoe, Daniel, 174, 233n15
Delacroix, Eugène, 110
democracy, 4, 77, 82–83, 92, 100–101
Derrida, Jacques, 78, 87, 223n22, 225n47
Descartes, René, 57
Devil. See Satan
dismemberment, 7, 17, 60–62, 65, 71, 111, 204, 218n18. See also body; parricide
Dostoevsky, Fyodor, 16, 29, 207, 220n13; "A Gentle Creature," 29; letter to his brother Mikhail (December 22, 1849), 207
dramatization, 68, 143–45, 147, 174, 204. See also narrative
Duval, Jeanne, 79

egalitarianism, 7, 76, 90, 99. See also humanitarianism; liberalism; progressivism
Enlightenment, 7, 12, 91, 95, 100, 208, 211. See also reform
enunciation, 10, 24; speaker, 27–28, 35–36, 40, 42, 49, 71, 89, 105, 107, 113–25, 195–98, 221n24. See also intersubjectivity
Épuration, 131–32, 160, 186. See also Liberation of France; Occupation of France; World War II
ethics, 4, 15, 18, 65, 123, 125, 133–34, 136, 150, 169, 209–13; definition of, 12; ethical discourse, 212; involuntary ethics, 157–64, 209; and poetics, 5–6, 12, 113, 174, 207, 210–12; of solidarity, 163; of violence, 113
evil, 4, 187–88, 208, 234n20; and beauty, 103, 125; human disposition for, 90–97, 121–22; purgation of, 97, 154. See also Satan
exclusion, 11, 55, 197, 223n16; of the condemned man, 17, 51–52, 61, 159, 164, 182, 191; legal exclusion, 51–52
execution: accounts of, 3, 5, 15, 141–42; anticipation of, 29, 32, 208; artistic execution, 125–26; attendance of, 22, 144, 152–53; day of, 32, 35, 152, 155–56, 236n47; disgust in the face of, 3, 136, 142–44, 151–52, 159–64, 167, 169, 172, 186, 189, 213; imminence of, 23, 32, 37–38, 130, 137, 152; invisibility of, 57, 217n27; mock execution, 29; modes of: burning at the stake, 7, 94, decapitation (see decapitation), drawing and quartering, 7, 96, 110, firing squad, 143, 149, 159, 161–62, 216n12, guillotine (see guillotine), hanging, 16, 28, 41, 71, 104, 171–72, 195, lethal injection, 215n5, wheel, 7, 71; obsession with, 33, 41; preparation for, 53; torture of, 55, 61–65, 154, 176, 209, 223n21; wait for, 11, 41, 64, 142, 176–77, 236n9. See also death penalty; scaffold; spectacularity, of execution; voyeurism; witness

executioner, 5, 11, 52, 54, 68–69, 73–74, 90, 92, 94, 104, 122, 150, 188, 226n10, 231n44; praise of, 95–96, 99, 116, 185; sadism of, 71; victim-executioner duo, 71, 113–14, 121, 186, 202, 231n30

fantaisie, 18–19
fantastique, 5, 29, 41
Farcy, Jean-Claude, 8
fascism, 130
fiction, 5, 9–10, 16–17, 22–23, 25, 30, 38, 44, 46, 56, 64–66, 88, 91, 126, 129, 134–37, 143, 145, 147, 151–52, 158, 161, 163–68, 174–80, 184, 186–89, 195, 205–12; defictionalization, 27–31; metafiction, 25, 174, 191–92, 234n22; nonfiction, 133, 160, 167, 234n21; of painless capital punishment, 59
Fifth Republic, 6
Flaubert, Gustave, 44, 218n18, 237n13
Fondane, Benjamin, 94–95
Foucault, Michel, 12, 45–47, 50, 53–55, 61, 65; *Histoire de la sexualité*, 46–47; *L'Ordre du discours*, 61; *Surveiller et punir. Naissance de la prison*, 45–46, 54–55, 61. See also bios
Fourth Republic, 6
Franco, Francisco, 130, 160. See also Spain
French Resistance, 131, 162–63, 235n38. See also Occupation of France; World War II
French Revolution, 4, 8, 18, 62–63, 74, 153, 207, 210, 212; counter-Revolution, 8, 94, 97, 99, 185; and the guillotine, 5, 66, 153, 210; imaginary of, 5; literary evocations of, 5, 10; and penal reform, 7–8, 45, 66; and regicide, 8, 51; Revolutionary tribunals, 8. See also Ancien Régime; monarch; Reign of Terror

Front de Libération Nationale (FLN), 160, 188. See also Algeria; decolonization

Gall, Franz Joseph, 50, 217n22. See also phrenology
Gautier, Théophile, 85–86
Girard, René, 12, 122, 188, 206, 209, 229n54. See also sacrifice, sacrificial crisis; violence, contagion of; violence, essential violence
Goncourt brothers, 67
Gosselin, Charles, 18, 30
Goudall, Louis, 103–4
Goya, Francisco, 110
Grenier, Jean, 160–61
Grimm, Friedrich Melchior, 7
grotesque, 40, 58, 89–90, 108–9, 153, 162, 174, 180, 204
Guillotin, Joseph-Ignace, 6, 59
guillotine, 4, 6–8, 15, 33, 36, 46–48, 51–53, 56–57, 59–61, 70–71, 73–75, 108–9, 129, 155, 172, 185, 205, 207–8, 210–11, 212, 218n10, 228n47: and the Enlightenment, 7, 208; in the French penal code, 6–7, 62, 168; introduction of, 6–7, 58–59, 62; last use of, 6–7, 210; personification of, 48; as Revolutionary icon, 5, 66, 153. See also death penalty; decapitation; execution; French Revolution; Reign of Terror
Guizot, François, 17, 219n3
Guyard, Auguste, 83

Hegel, Georg Wilhelm Friedrich, 78
Henriot, Émile, 29
homo sacer, 51–52, 63–64, 223n16. See also Agamben, Giorgio; bare life; *bios*; criminal; sacrifice
Houssaye, Arsène, 79
Hovasse, Jean-Marc, 88–89
Hugo, Adèle, 66; *Victor Hugo raconté par un témoin de sa vie*, 66, 217n1
Hugo, Victor, 3–13, 15–66, 70, 73–74, 77, 83–97, 100–101, 123,

Index | 259

126–27, 129–130, 133–34, 148, 154, 165–67, 175–80, 183–84, 187, 191, 205–6, 207–13, 231n37, 236n8; on the inviolability of human life, 87, 99–100, 126, 134, 209; on king-condemned man analogy, 50–51; on literary revolution, 22, 43, 66, 84
—WORKS BY: *Bug-Jargal*, 16, 22; *Claude Gueux*, 4, 9–10, 16, 23, 69–70, 83–87, 89, 93, 95, 226n10; *Les Contemplations*, 93–94: "Ce que dit la bouche d'ombre," 93; *Le Dernier Jour d'un condamné*, 6, 9–10, 12, 15–19, 21–66, 84, 123, 126, 129, 133, 148, 154, 165, 166, 175–76, 180, 183–84, 191, 205–6, 207–12, 228n41, 236n8: "Une comédie à propos d'une tragédie," 19, 29, 59, 62, Preface of 1829, 18, 29, Preface of 1832, 18, 19, 27, 46, 50, 57, 65, 133, 166–67, 175, 180, 184, 210, 222n4, 223n22, 224n32; "Écrit sur la première page d'un livre de Joseph de Maistre," 94; *Han d'Islande*, 10, 16, 22, 25, 55–56, 57, 94, 231n44; *Hernani*, 38; *L'Homme qui rit*, 3, 16; *Littérature et philosophie mêlées*, 66; *Les Misérables*, 9–10, 16, 81, 84–86, 88–89, 93–95, 175, 225n49, 228nn36, 39; *Notre-Dame de Paris*, 16, 38; *Préface de Cromwell*, 25, 31; *Quatrevingt-Treize*, 10, 16, 225n49
humaneness, 10–11, 17, 88; inhumanity, 17, 64, 75, 89–90, 153
humanitarianism, 7, 9, 66, 76, 84, 86–87, 91, 94, 96–97, 127; human rights, 12, 87; Universal Declaration of Human Rights, 87. *See also* egalitarianism; liberalism; progressivism; reform; UN
Hus, Jan, 67

imagery, 11, 22, 38–44, 67, 71, 103, 107, 124–25, 131–32, 138, 145, 151, 163, 175, 177, 183, 197, 201–2, 206, 208, 210, 231n29; of *argot*, 40–41; of bloodshed, 108, 113, 126–27; of Hell, 106, 148–49. *See also* metaphor; Rancière, Jacques, sentence-images
imaginary, 100, 236n9; of butchery, 108, 125–26; Christian imaginary, 187; criminal imaginary, 74; of the death penalty, 4–5, 11–13, 67, 104, 127, 189, 199, 205–6, 207–10; of the French Revolution, 5
intersubjectivity, 28, 36–37, 41, 44
intertextuality, 88–89, 114–16, 120, 144–45, 147, 155–56, 164, 201

Janin, Jules, 55, 65, 81–82, 228n41; *L'Âne mort ou la femme guillotinée*, 55, 65, 228n41
July Monarchy (*monarchie de Juillet*), 6
justice, 8, 11, 33, 40, 45, 65–66, 93, 131–33, 137–39; divine justice, 8, 21, 58, 133–34, 231n25; human justice, 9, 21, 58, 66, 148–49, 210; injustice, 4, 84, 139; judicial institutions, 9, 23–24, 35, 49, 51, 53, 133, 135–38, 144, 149, 155, 175, 177–80, 191, 206, 227n22; judicial rhetoric, 177–83, 205–6, 210; lethal justice (*see* death penalty); physical justice, 157–64. *See also* law

Kant, Immanuel, 78, 164
Koestler, Arthur, 133

Laclos, Pierre Choderlos de, 28
Lamartine, Alphonse de, 5
language; *argot* 29, 40–41, 59; articulation of, 31, 40; body language, 32, 63, 190; dismemberment of, 60–62, 176; duplicity of, 33, 35, 40, 148, 167, 210; and ethics, 212; euphemistic language, 148–49, 167; liberation of, 44; performative language, 42,

61; plain language (*langage clair*), 132, 167–74, 205–6, 210; the sign, 35–36; the signified, 36, 40; the signifier, 36, 40, 61–62; and silence, 37, 119, 140, 166–175, 181–84, 190–93, 198, 205, 208–10. *See also* communication; representation; rhetoric
Lavater, Johann Kaspar, 50
law, 6, 10–11, 17, 23, 48–49, 50–53, 56, 58–59, 63, 65, 78, 90, 132–33, 136, 147, 150–52, 157, 162, 206–7, 210–12, 218n18, 227n22, 228n47; humanitarian law, 66, 94; law makers, 7, 137; lawyers, 31–32, 41, 93, 148, 178–80, 182; modern lethal law, 13, 210, 223n25; universal law, 78, 97. *See also* justice
Lefèvre-Deumier, Jules, 18, 22
Lévy, Michel, 79
Leynaud, René, 131
liberalism, 7, 17, 77, 83, 101, 201, 217n23, 219n5. *See also* egalitarianism; humanitarianism; politics; progressivism; reform
Liberation of France, 186–87. *See also* Épuration; Occupation of France; World War II
literature: aestheticist literature, 89–90, 94, 211 (*see also* art for art's sake); autonomy of, 87, 212; and didacticism, 9, 27, 65, 84–86, 93, 95, 100–101, 126, 164, 208–9; humanitarian literature, 84, 87; limits of, 37; literary modernity, 13, 22, 43, 45, 66, 211–12; literary revolution, 22, 43, 66, 84; politically-committed literature (*littérature engagée*), 6, 163, 211; progressive literature, 85–86, 90
Louis XV, 96
Louis XVI, 8, 98–99
Louis, Antoine, 6, 58–59
Louisette. *See* guillotine
Lucas, Charles, 17

Maistre, Joseph de, 10, 74, 94–96, 115–16, 126, 184–86, 231n44; on reversibility, 97–98, 115–16, 121–22; on sacrifice, 12, 95, 97–100, 104, 122, 208–9
—WORKS BY: *Considérations sur la France*, 95; *Éclaircissement sur les sacrifices*, 97, 122; *Essai sur le principe générateur des constitutions politiques*, 95; *Lettres et opuscules inédits*, 95; *Les Soirées de Saint-Pétersbourg*, 95, 115–16, 122, 185. *See also* reactionism
Malassis, Augustin-Jean, 74, 79, 87, 94, 230n23
Marat, Jean-Paul, 18, 74, 186
Martin, Pierre-Louis, 22
Marx, Karl, 184
Mauriac, François, 131
Menander, 115
Meschonnic, Henri, 43, 221nn26, 30, 31
metaphor, 20, 40–43, 58, 62–63, 89, 107, 110, 117, 121, 124, 155, 163, 166–78, 181, 183, 193, 205–6, 210, 233n13; animalizing metaphors, 148–49, 153–54, 162, 177, 233n8; of deafness, 32–35; of incarceration, 23, 41, 64, 137–39; in judicial rhetoric, 179–83, 205–6, 210; military metaphors, 76–77. *See also* imagery; Rancière, Jacques, sentence-images
Michelet, Jules, 5
modernity, 4–6, 78–79, 81, 94, 101, 124, 207, 211; literary modernity, 13, 22, 43, 45, 66, 211–12; modern humanitarian ideals, 88; modern man, 52; modern poet and poetry, 9, 30, 99–100, 125–26, 208; penal modernity, 6, 8, 12–13, 51, 54–55, 57–59, 61–65, 130, 155, 208, 222n1; *querelle des Classiques et des Modernes*, 219n5; violence of, 67, 96, 126–27

monarchy, 6, 8. *See also* Ancien Régime; French Revolution
monstrosity, 85, 89, 94, 110, 148, 202; of the criminal, 46–49, 51, 182; of the guillotine, 61; of the people, 48–49
Montès, Jean-François, 79
Montesquieu, 7, 95
Morellet, Abbé, 7
murder, 3, 52, 90, 110–11, 117, 121, 130–33, 136–37, 142–47, 155, 157–58, 162–64, 169, 176, 181, 184, 186–88, 206, 209, 211; assassination, 96, 145, 160; legal murder, 11, 150, 228n47; mass murder, 10, 110, 124, 130–31, 145, 235n38; murderer, 11, 15, 18, 42, 79, 90, 93, 95, 137, 139, 143, 150, 177, 187–88, 230n16; Sétif massacres, 188. *See also* Camus, Albert, on legitimized murder
myth, 93, 136, 157, 164, 193, 209; Christian mythology, 107, 187–88; founding myth, 151–52; Greek mythology, 106, 195, 205. *See also* Camus, Albert, *Le Mythe de Sisyphe*

Nagy, Imre, 160
narrative, 4, 10, 12, 19, 22, 44, 55–57, 67–68, 75, 78, 84, 113, 134, 136, 151–58, 165, 169, 178, 180, 190–91, 193, 208–10; first-person narrative, 28, 237n13; intradiegetic level, 157, 175; macro-narrative, 144; metanarrative, 150; narrative conventions, 23, 27, 66, 208; narrative discontinuity, 23, 27, 142; narrative ellipsis, 27, 37, 46, 58, 137, 143, 162; narrative inconsistency, 27–31; narrative structure, 23–24, 147, 164, 174, 176; narrator, 136, 138–39, 141, 151, 168, 173–74, 200–205, 235n35; oral narrative, 151. *See also* persona; plot
Naudin, Marie, 176

Nazism, 130, 132, 136, 144, 145, 188, 232n4
Nerval, Gérard de, 195; *Voyage en Orient*, 195
Nietzsche, Friedrich, 156, 161; *Twilight of the Idols*, 161
Nodier, Charles, 18, 22
Nouveau Roman, 29–30

Occupation of France, 132, 136, 144, 188, 198. *See also* Collaborationsim; Épuration; French Resistance; Liberation of France; Pétain, Philippe; World War II
Oehler, Dolf, 78–79, 89, 228n42, 232n45

Pachet, Pierre, 75, 78, 225n1, 231nn35, 37, 40
pacifism, 76
pain, 26, 28, 57, 70, 78, 88, 94, 106, 113–16, 123, 125, 146, 153, 159, 183, 186–87; infliction of, 55, 63, 114; language of, 55; of the Other, 121, 146, 193, 211; painlessness, 7, 58–59, 127, 211; and penal modernity, 12, 61–64, 155. *See also* body; *supplices*; torture; violence
Paris Commune, 6, 16
parricide, 7, 17, 22, 42, 137, 145, 181, 218n18. *See also* crime, capital crime; dismemberment
Pascal, Blaise, 146, 163; *Pensées*, 163
Penal Code, of 1791, 6, 62; of 1810, 7, 17, 222n5
performance, 4, 42, 61, 71, 108–12, 182, 185, 199–205; in the courtroom, 144, 178–80; performative utterance, 24, 166; performer, 180, 199–202, 204. *See also* spectacularity
persona, 11, 76, 89, 116, 125. *See also* narrative
Pétain, Philippe, 160, 233n18. *See also* Collaborationism; Occupation of France

Pétion de Villeneuve, Jérôme, 52
phrenology, 50, 217n22. *See also* Gall, Franz Joseph
Pichois, Claude, 76, 117, 226n17, 229n9
Place de Grève, 25, 36–37, 55, 222n2
Planche, Gustave, 38
plot, 23, 27, 46, 55, 84, 129, 145, 152, 209. *See also* narrative
Poe, Edgar Allan, 75, 79–81, 84, 86, 90, 94, 119, 121–22, 124, 217n24; "The Oval Portrait," 124; "The Philosophy of Composition," 75; "The Poetic Principle," 84, 217n24; "The Sleeper," 199
poetics: abolitionist poetics, 12, 15–66, 209; argumentative poetics, 65, 210–11; of clarity, 132, 167–74, 205–6, 210; definition of, 12; and ethics, 5–6, 12, 113, 174, 207, 210–12; poetic execution, 125–26; poetic language, 22, 39, 43; revolutionary poetics, 43, 45, 66; of sensation, 59–61, 176; of violence, 103–27. *See also* Rancière, Jacques; modernity, modern poet and poetry
politics: modern politics, 131–32, 223n16; political crime, 10, 16, 218n18, 228n42; political discourse, 6, 18, 94, 211; political life (biopolitics), 63–64, 223n16; politically-committed literature (*littérature engagée*), 6, 163, 211; political sovereignty, 201; political status, 64, 208; sociopolitics, 5, 6, 9, 12, 15, 27, 51, 53–54, 77, 89, 122, 126, 129, 206, 211. *See also* liberalism; progressivism; reform
positivism, 91. *See also* Renan, Ernest
Poulmann, Pierre-Joseph, 78–79
prison, 4, 8, 16, 24, 28–29, 37, 43, 50, 56–57, 75, 140, 177, 185; Barberousse prison, 140, 142, 151; Bicêtre prison, 29, 50; mental incarceration, 23, 41, 64; prison cell, 23, 29, 37–39, 42, 46, 53–54, 56–57, 61, 148, 153, 155, 177, 191; prisoner, 37, 54, 57, 111, 137–38, 143, 146, 177; prison worker, 23, 33–36, 43, 54, 221n33
progressivism, 16, 22, 76–78, 84, 87–88, 90–91, 95, 99, 133, 208; and penal reform, 7, 45–46, 56, 59, 65, 75, 232n5; progressive art, 9, 85, 86–87, 101, 126, 184; progressive ideology, 86–87; redefining of, 91–93. *See also* egalitarianism; humanitarianism; liberalism; politics
Proust, Marcel, 139–40, 142
Pucheu, Pierre, 160–61

Rancière, Jacques, 12, 30–31, 38, 42, 207; expressive poetry, 37–44; representative poetry, 30–31, 38; sentence-images, 38, 41–43. *See also* imagery; metaphor; poetics
reactionism, 10, 76, 78, 79, 99, 126, 185, 208. *See also* Maistre, Joseph de
realism, 5, 28, 29, 81–83, 184, 234n20; hyperrealism, 31, 175; political realism, 184; psychological realism, 149, 153–54; subjective realism, 175–76
reform: penal reform, 7, 45, 66, 73–75, 96, 208; reformism, 7, 9, 67, 76–77, 84. *See also* Enlightenment; humanitarianism; liberalism; modernity, penal modernity; politics; progressivism; torture
Reign of Terror, 8, 55–56, 74, 131, 186, 228n47. *See also* French Revolution; guillotine
Renan, Ernest, 91. *See also* positivism
representation: artistic representation, 194–99, 215n4; of the body (*see* body); classical representation, 22–27, 38, 44, 54, 207, 220n21; collective representation, 151; misrepresentation, 181, 195; mythical representation, 195; representability, 11;

representational disorder, 12, 31, 37, 44, 84; of space, 22–23, 27, 58, 112, 115, 117, 122, 200; theatrical representation, 109, 125, 178; of time, 22–23, 27, 37, 46, 139–40, 155, 176, 193, 200; transtextual representation, 144, 164. *See also* language; Rancière, Jacques, on representative poetry
responsibility, 65, 89–90, 125, 133, 146–48; in the administering of the death penalty, 9, 24, 38–39; human responsibility, 8–9; of the individual, 133, 147, 150, 177; irresponsibility, 89–90; literary responsibility, 13, 165–206
retentionism, 58, 72, 74, 75–76, 78. *See also* Baudelaire, Charles, praise of capital punishment; death penalty, legitimation of
reversibility, 97–98, 116, 121–22, 186. *See also* sacrifice
revolution, 53, 76, 80, 82, 92, 131, 172, 202; counter-Revolution, 8, 94, 97, 99, 185; French Revolution (*see* French Revolution); literary revolution, 22, 43, 66, 84; poetic revolution, 43, 45; Revolution of 1830 (July Revolution), 6, 8; Revolution of 1848, 6, 8, 230n14; Russian Revolution, 169
rhetoric, 25, 33, 35, 83, 97, 167, 173, 200, 210, 212, 236n7; judicial rhetoric, 177–83, 205–6, 210; Maistrean rhetoric, 100; manipulation of, 165–66; rhetorician, 16, 132. *See also* communication; language
Ricœur, Paul, 12
ritual, 4, 53, 56, 62, 92, 97–98, 122, 125, 145, 147, 156, 209, 212
Robbe-Grillet, Alain, 29–30
Robespierre, Maximilien de, 4, 74, 186
Romanticism, 5, 9, 11, 18, 25, 74, 219n5

Rousseau, Jean-Jacques, 7, 28, 52–53, 80–81, 83, 227n34; *Confessions*, 80–81, 83, 227n34
Rousset, Jean, 28, 219n3, 220n11

sacrifice, 117, 185, 197, 202, 225n1; in the Ancient world, 12, 97; Christian sacrifice, 98–99; the death penalty as, 12, 68, 97–101, 104, 125–26, 208–9; failure of, 122, 125–26, 188, 197, 202, 209, 212; Maistrean configurations of, 95, 97–101, 115, 121–22, 185, 208–9; praise of, 12, 73–101, 104, 126, 208–9; sacrificial crisis, 122, 126, 188, 209; sacrificial victim, 97, 99, 122; voluntary sacrifice (*sponte sua*), 68–69, 78–79, 83–84, 91, 97–100. *See also* Girard, René; *homo sacer*; Maistre, Joseph de; reversibility; *sponte sua*
Sade, marquis de, 95
Salas, Denis, 164, 188
Sanson, Henri, 79
Sanyal, Debarati, 114, 123, 200, 225n1, 226n7
Sartre, Jean-Paul, 152, 163, 211, 233n18; *Qu'est-ce que la littérature?*, 163
Satan, 71, 100, 106, 183. *See also* evil
scaffold, 22, 37, 55, 71, 89, 91, 94, 142, 152–53, 160, 166, 168, 175, 178, 184, 201, 210, 212, 225n49; journey to, 15, 28, 39, 53, 62, 79; as object of fantasy, 153, 158, 162, 172, 201–2; sanctification of, 131; as site of distinction, 79, 99; spectacle of, 4–5, 73, 143, 158, 228n47; symbolic scaffold, 202; voyeurism around, 38–39, 56–57, 162. *See also* decapitation, execution
Scarry, Elaine, 63
Schinderhannes (Johannes Bückler), 74–75
Second Empire, 76, 237n28
Second Restoration, 8

secularism, 7–9, 125, 134
self-reflexivity; 42, 114, 172, 189, 192, 212
Shakespeare, William, 91
solidarity, 157–58, 189, 192, 197, 206–7, 211; with the condemned, 43–44, 149–50, 160, 163; with the criminal, 11; against death, 133–34; de-solidarization, 164; human solidarity, 89; of the reader, 43–44. *See also* Camus, Albert, on solidarity
Soviet Union, 144. *See also* Stalinism
Spain, 15, 160; Spanish Civil War, 130. *See also* Franco, Francisco
spectacularity, 40, 42, 46, 55–57, 89, 96, 107, 198; of bloodshed, 71, 121–23, 125, 133; of execution, 4, 27, 39, 44–46, 50, 125–26, 133, 149, 151–53, 156, 162, 164–65, 202, 207; and sacrifice, 68; and the scaffold, 4–5, 73, 143, 158, 228n47; spectator, 11, 21, 56–57, 88–89, 144, 155–56, 164, 171, 204–5. *See also* performance; visibility; voyeurism; witness
Spiquel, Agnès, 191
sponte sua, 68–69, 78–79, 83–84, 91, 97–100. *See also* sacrifice
Staël, Germaine de, 23
Stalinism, 130. *See also* Soviet Union
state killing. *See* death penalty
Stendhal, 5, 23, 237n13
suicide, 87, 90, 118, 121, 130, 145, 152, 225n1
supplices, 7, 26, 47, 56, 75, 95, 100, 200, 208. *See also* pain; torture; violence

Tapner, John Charles, 16
Terence, 115–16
Thélot, Jérôme, 95, 225n1, 226n10, 232nn45, 47, 238n32
Third Republic, 6
Toal, Catherine, 121
torture, 22, 26, 71, 99–100, 113, 146, 154, 161, 186–87; under the Ancien Régime, 62, 87; figurative torture, 62–63; and penal reform, 62; reinvention of, 55, 61–65, 208, 223n21; spectacle of, 56; torturer, 63, 71, 111. *See also* body; cruelty; pain; reform; *supplices*; violence
tragedy, 23, 45, 115, 152–53, 178, 205, 238n32; catharsis-free tragedy, 54–55; of the human condition, 130; tragic narrative structure, 24. *See also* Aristotle; Classicism

UN, 132. *See also* humanitarianism
UNESCO, 160

Valéry, Paul, 12, 74–75
Vanney, Philippe, 164
Vidocq, Eugène-François, 18, 220n18
Viggiani, Carl, 160
Vigny, Alfred de, 5, 18
Villier de l'Isle-Adam, Auguste de, 5
violence: anticolonial violence, 188; contagion of, 122–25, 188, 209, 211–12; essential violence, 122–25, 127, 188; gratuitous violence, 145; of human nature, 94, 96–97, 100, 121–22, 187–89, 206; institutional or state violence, 31–32, 132, 177, 199, 207, 212; lethal violence, 6, 116, 125, 175, 177, 186–89, 192, 205, 209–12; organized violence, 188; perpetrator of, 116, 118, 121–22, 212; psychological violence, 55, 61–65, 208, 223n21. *See also* Baudelaire, Charles; body; butchery; cruelty; Girard, René; pain; *supplices*; torture
visibility, 11, 42, 55–57, 64–65, 80, 112, 147, 193, 204; of the condemned man, 11, 34, 46, 52; "instant of invisibility," 57, 217n27. *See also* spectacularity; voyeurism; witness
Voltaire, 7, 95
voyeurism, 17, 24, 38–39, 44, 56–57, 112, 117–18, 162, 191, 212. *See*

also spectacularity; visibility; witness

Warsaw Pact, 160
Watteau, Jean-Antoine, 195; *Pèlerinage à l'île de Cythère*, 195
Weyembergh, Maurice, 145
Wiertz, Antoine, 93
Wilcocks, Robert, 114
witness, 11, 17, 24, 27, 34, 41, 55, 105, 119, 137, 154; body of, 143, 159–63, 196–97; loss of agency of, 162; voice of, 167–71, 181; witnessing, 15, 27, 57, 121, 136, 140, 144, 147, 149, 157–59, 173–74, 189–91, 198, 201, 205, 234n22. *See also* spectactularity; visibility; voyeurism
World War I, 6, 8

World War II, 6, 8, 10, 131, 136, 146, 162, 164, 168, 186, 188. *See also* Collaborationism; Épuration; French Resistance; Liberation of France; Occupation of France
writing: autobiographical writing, 28, 81, 129, 135–36, 141; avatar of the writer, 183, 189–93, 198; blank writing (*écriture blanche*), 9, 236n6; chronicle, 135, 159, 168–69, 173, 205; confessional writing, 81; diaristic writing, 12, 24–25, 28–29, 35, 37, 41, 43–44, 50, 53, 59, 62, 65, 175–76, 178, 183, 210; thematization of, 25–26, 183, 189–93, 206, 213

zoē, 53–54, 63–64, 208. *See also* bare life

FLASHPOINTS

1. *On Pain of Speech: Fantasies of the First Order and the Literary Rant*, Dina Al-Kassim
2. *Moses and Multiculturalism*, Barbara Johnson, with a foreword by Barbara Rietveld
3. *The Cosmic Time of Empire: Modern Britain and World Literature*, Adam Barrows
4. *Poetry in Pieces: César Vallejo and Lyric Modernity*, Michelle Clayton
5. *Disarming Words: Empire and the Seductions of Translation in Egypt*, Shaden M. Tageldin
6. *Wings for Our Courage: Gender, Erudition, and Republican Thought*, Stephanie H. Jed
7. *The Cultural Return*, Susan Hegeman
8. *English Heart, Hindi Heartland: The Political Life of Literature in India*, Rashmi Sadana
9. *The Cylinder: Kinematics of the Nineteenth Century*, Helmut Müller-Sievers
10. *Polymorphous Domesticities: Pets, Bodies, and Desire in Four Modern Writers*, Juliana Schiesari
11. *Flesh and Fish Blood: Postcolonialism, Translation, and the Vernacular*, S. Shankar
12. *The Fear of French Negroes: Transcolonial Collaboration in the Revolutionary Americas*, Sara E. Johnson
13. *Figurative Inquisitions: Conversion, Torture, and Truth in the Luso-Hispanic Atlantic*, Erin Graff Zivin
14. *Cosmopolitan Desires: Global Modernity and World Literature in Latin America*, Mariano Siskind
15. *Fiction Beyond Secularism*, Justin Neuman
16. *Periodizing Jameson: Dialectics, the University, and the Desire for Narrative*, Phillip E. Wegner
17. *The Practical Past*, Hayden White
18. *The Powers of the False: Reading, Writing, Thinking Beyond Truth and Fiction*, Doro Wiese
19. *The Object of the Atlantic: Concrete Aesthetics in Cuba, Brazil, and Spain, 1868–1968*, Rachel Price
20. *Epic and Exile: Novels of the German Popular Front, 1933–1945*, Hunter Bivens
21. *An Innocent Abroad: Lectures in China*, J. Hillis Miller
22. *Form and Instability: East Europe, Literature, Postimperial Difference*, Anita Starosta
23. *Bombay Modern: Arun Kolatkar and Bilingual Literary Culture*, Anjali Nerlekar
24. *Intimate Relations: Social Reform and the Late Nineteenth-Century South Asian Novel*, Krupa Shandilya
25. *Media Laboratories: Late Modernist Authorship in South America*, Sarah Ann Wells

26. *Acoustic Properties: Radio, Narrative, and the New Neighborhood of the Americas*, Tom McEnaney
27. *The New Woman: Literary Modernism, Queer Theory, and the Trans Feminine Allegory*, Emma Heaney
28. *Civilizing War: Imperial Politics and the Poetics of National Rupture*, Nasser Mufti
29. *Late Colonial Sublime: Neo-Epics and the End of Romanticism*, G. S. Sahota
30. *Globalizing Race: Antisemitism and Empire in French and European Culture*, Dorian Bell
31. *Domestications: American Empire, Literary Culture, and the Postcolonial Lens*, Hosam Mohamed Aboul Ela
32. *Behold an Animal: Four Exorbitant Readings*, Thangam Ravindranathan
33. *Capital Letters: Hugo, Baudelaire, Camus, and the Death Penalty*, Ève Morisi

www.ingramcontent.com/pod-product-compliance
Lightning Source LLC
Chambersburg PA
CBHW032030290426
44110CB00012B/740